DATE DUE	

Pioneer: A History of the
Johns Hopkins University,
1874-1889

Daniel C. Gilman

Pioneer: A History of the Johns Hopkins University, 1874-1889

BY HUGH HAWKINS

Amherst College

CORNELL UNIVERSITY PRESS

ITHACA, NEW YORK

First published 1960

This work has been brought to publication with the assistance of a grant from the Ford Foundation.

PRINTED IN THE UNITED STATES OF AMERICA
BY VAIL-BALLOU PRESS, INC.

For Two American Educators

JAMES A. HAWKINS *and* RENA A. HAWKINS

Preface

THE project for investigating the spirit of the early Johns Hopkins University which grew into this book began in the winter of 1952–1953. At that time, both teachers and students felt that the freedom of American universities was threatened, and the search for an earlier "golden age" and traditions justifying the place of universities in American life seemed almost a duty. The treatment of the founding and first academic year that was accepted as a Ph.D. dissertation at Johns Hopkins in 1954 may, therefore, reveal the mood of the time and place in which it was written almost as much as that which it attempts to describe. Military service and teaching allowed a passage of time and the coming of a more confident academic mood before the rewriting of the original study. Although it would be too much to claim that this work is now objective, at least an earlier and later subjectivity have tended to balance each other. Another advantage of the two separated periods of work is that the volume partakes of the insights of both a graduate student and a faculty member. In addition, an account which ended in 1877 now extends to 1889.

I hope that no interested scholar will assume that the early Johns Hopkins has now been "done." The documentary material is rich, and there is much of significance that is not told here. The role which most of the departments played in the development of their disciplines in America and in the creation of new disciplines is only suggested. In striving to avoid filiopietism and promotion, I may have failed to label as "first" or "a triumph in scholarship" what were indeed innovations and triumphs in particular fields. Such judgments come best, however, in interinstitutional studies of particular disciplines. Several of the Hopkins scholars deserve full biographical treatment—Basil L. Gildersleeve, to name only one. By stressing the inner life of the university, I have bypassed much of the story of the university's relations with city, state, and nation and much of its impact on other institutions. There is scant treatment here of buildings, finances, and physical education, though relevant documents abound. A typescript version of this study, longer by one-third, has been deposited in the Lanier Room of the Johns Hopkins University Library. In it, the specialist can find further details on almost every subject treated, notably, however, biographical data on the trustees and on Gilman and studies of the library, the public lectures, and financial aid to students.

My greatest obligation in the writing of this book is to Professor Charles A. Barker of the Johns Hopkins University, who first suggested the possibilities of such a subject and has never ceased encouraging me to develop them. As the original dissertation took shape, Professor C. Vann Woodward, Professor Charles S. Campbell, and the late Professor Sidney Painter offered counsel and encouragement. Two of my fellow students at Johns Hopkins, Professor Benjamin Ring and Professor Tilden Edelstein, read portions of the work and made valuable criticisms. Professor Ring's own interest in Hopkins history was frequently the source of new insights. Two of my present colleagues, Professor Edwin C. Rozwenc and Professor Theodore Baird, have read the entire manuscript, saving me often from imprecision. Professor Frederick Rudolph of Williams College gave unstintingly of his knowledge of the history of American higher education, reading the entire manuscript twice and suggesting major revisions. The responsibility for errors and inadequacies is my own, but there would have been more of both without the aid of these scholars. My thanks go to all of them and to the judges of the Moses Coit Tyler Prize competition for 1959, who gave time and effort in a program which I found a most effective spur to labor.

I thank Cornell University Press for many courtesies. In light of the early history of Cornell-Hopkins co-operation, it is altogether appropriate that the press of one university should publish a history of the other.

Without the work of Miss Frieda C. Thies of the Johns Hopkins University Library in the Gilman Papers this book would have been an impossibility. For those labors, for her clarifying of many matters, and for her continuing friendship and interest in any project I am more grateful than I can say. Other librarians also have put me deep in their debt, including the staffs of the Johns Hopkins University Library, the Maryland Historical Society Library, the Maryland Room of the Enoch Pratt Free Library, the Houghton Library at Harvard, the Amherst College Library, the Smith College Library, and the Division of Manuscripts of the Library of Congress. Mr. J. Louis Kuethe, assistant librarian, Johns Hopkins, and Mr. E. Porter Dickinson, reference librarian, Amherst College, have gone out of their way to aid me.

The best traditions of archivists were fulfilled to my benefit by Mr. Howard B. Gotlieb of the Manuscript Division, Yale University Library; Mr. Kimball C. Elkins of the Harvard University Archives; Mr. Robert W. Hill of the New York Public Library; Professor James W. Patton and Mrs. Carolyn Andrews Wallace of the Southern Historical Collection, Chapel Hill; Mr. Milton Halsey Thomas of the Low Library, Columbia University; Miss Josephine Cole of the Johns Hopkins Alumni Records Office; and Miss Rena Durkan of the Hitchcock Memorial Room, Amherst College.

Miss Lilly Lavarello, secretary of the Department of History, Johns Hopkins, a never-failing friend, has answered special queries in regard to this study. Professor John C. French aided me with his reminiscences and his researches, and Professor C. P. Swanson brought me new light on the biologists. I hope that the many other alumni, former faculty members, their families and friends, and various librarians and academic officials who have answered my questions and my letters will accept a general word of thanks. Their favors large and small give them a claim to special satisfaction in any merit this volume may have.

Two honors students in the class of 1959 at Amherst College, Harvey O. Mierke, Jr., and Fred M. Newmann, who wrote theses in the history of higher education, provided stimulating scholarly comradeship and concrete suggestions during the writing of the second half of this study. Mrs. Evelyn V. Cooley typed the final draft cheerfully and expertly. Mrs. Pamela Gordon and Mr. J. Walter Richard answered calls for aid in proofreading, and Mrs. Britt Guttmann in indexing.

I acknowledge with thanks the permission granted by the Johns

Preface

Hopkins Press to quote from John C. French, *A History of the University Founded by Johns Hopkins,* and from Charles R. Anderson, general editor, *The Centennial Edition of the Works of Sidney Lanier;* by Dodd, Mead & Company to quote from Daniel Coit Gilman, *The Launching of a University and Other Papers: A Sheaf of Remembrances;* by Mr. Thomas W. Dewart to quote from the "Bob Davis Reveals" column of the New York *Sun;* by Mr. Arthur W. Page to quote from Burton J. Hendrick, *The Training of an American: The Earlier Life and Letters of Walter H. Page, 1855–1913;* and by the *American Quarterly* to reprint portions of my article "Three University Presidents Testify," which first appeared in that journal.

H. H.

Plainfield, Massachusetts
July 1960

Contents

Contents

PART THREE

Sharing: In Search of Community

Abbreviations and Special Usages

AFJH   Vertical file, Alumni Records Office, JHU

ARJH   *Annual Report of the President of the Johns Hopkins University*

DAB   *Dictionary of American Biography*

ECM   Minutes of the Executive Committee of the Board of Trustees of the Johns Hopkins University, President's Office, JHU

GP   Daniel Coit Gilman Papers, Lanier Room, JHU Library (all letters to or from Gilman and all Gilman diaries and notebooks are in this collection unless otherwise noted)

JHC   *The Johns Hopkins University Circulars* (the quarto series of 1879–1903):

Volume	Dates	Volume	Dates
I	1879–1882	VI	1886–1887
II	1882–1883	VII	1887–1888
III	1883–1884	VIII	1888–1889
IV	1884–1885	IX	1889–1890
V	1885–1886	X	1890–1891

JHR   *The Johns Hopkins University Register* (a parenthetical year refers to the second year of the term covered)

JHU   The Johns Hopkins University

JHUP   The Johns Hopkins University Papers, Lanier Room, JHU Library

TM   Minutes of the Board of Trustees of the Johns Hopkins University, President's Office, JHU

Abbreviations and Special Usages

All data on degrees and academic posts, unless otherwise noted, are based on W. Norman Brown, comp., *Johns Hopkins Half-Century Directory: A Catalogue of the Trustees, Faculty, Holders of Honorary Degrees, and Students, Graduates and Non-graduates, 1876–1926* (Baltimore, 1926).

All italics in quoted material appear in the original source unless otherwise noted.

Capitalization and punctuation in titles have been somewhat regularized.

Since the institution was chartered as "The Johns Hopkins University," the definite article is sometimes retained in shortened forms of the name ("the Johns Hopkins," "the Hopkins"). In this study it is used only in the full name and is not capitalized.

Part One

❧❧

CREATING: IN SEARCH OF AN IDEA

： CHAPTER I ：

An Educational
Reconnaissance

CHARLES S. PEIRCE once referred to the will of Johns Hopkins as "a certain testament, happily free from all definite ideas." [1] He overstated the matter, but in fact the Baltimore financier, whose orderly and profitable life ended on December 24, 1873, left few instructions or suggestions for the twelve trustees who were to found a university with half of his seven-million-dollar estate.[2] The will directed them to keep the Baltimore and Ohio Railroad Company stock, which constituted the bulk of the estate, to protect the B. & O. from political influence, and to maintain the university without encroaching on the principal. Although Hopkins left his country estate of Clifton to the university, he did not specifically direct its location there. He did, however, leave instructions for a "judicious" number of scholarships for deserving candidates from Maryland, Virginia, and North Carolina.[3]

[1] Draft of a review of *The Physical Papers of Henry Augustus Rowland* for the *Nation*, Charles S. Peirce Papers, Harvard University Archives, Widener Library, Harvard University.

[2] Specifically, to the university he left his 330-acre suburban estate of Clifton, 15,000 shares of B. & O. common stock with a par value of $1,500,000, and other securities estimated at $750,000 (ARJH [1876], 10–11). B. & O. stock was being quoted at almost 100 per cent above par in 1875 (Baltimore *Sun*, March 20, 1875).

[3] *Johns Hopkins University: Charter, Extracts of Will, Officers, and By-Laws* (Baltimore, 1874), 5–6. The only part of the will relevant to the university is re-

3

The Johns Hopkins University

With the largest single bequest that had ever been made to an American institution of higher learning, the trustees had nearly unlimited freedom, considerably more than the trustees of the hospital to which Hopkins left the other half of his fortune.[4] In deciding on the nature of his benefactions, Hopkins may have been influenced by the example and advice of his friend George Peabody, the American-born London banker from whose philanthropies Baltimore had profited in the case of the Peabody Institute, where a scholarly library, musical conservatory, and public lecture program had been developed. It was probably more than coincidence that, shortly after Peabody's return in 1866 to receive the eulogies of grateful Baltimoreans at the institute's dedication, Hopkins directed the incorporation of a university and a hospital bearing his name. The institute and the new university had five trustees in common.[5]

Of the twelve citizens of Baltimore who were given this remarkable opportunity to influence higher education in America, seven were college graduates and three others had attended college.[6] Reverdy Johnson, Jr., son of the former Senator and minister to Great Britain, had even studied in Germany, earning a law degree at Heidelberg. Seven were businessmen—as Hopkins had been—and at least six of them were wealthy.[7] The most successful was John Work Garrett, the nineteenth-century mogul who had made the B. & O. one of the nation's great railroads. A neighbor, colleague, and trusted friend of Hopkins, Garrett

---

printed in John C. French, *A History of the University Founded by Johns Hopkins* (Baltimore, 1946), 463–464.

[4] *Letter of Johns Hopkins to the Trustees of "The Johns Hopkins Hospital"* (Baltimore, 1873). Reprinted in Helen Hopkins Thom, *Johns Hopkins: A Silhouette* (Baltimore and London, 1929), 87–90; in Alan M. Chesney, *The Johns Hopkins Hospital and the Johns Hopkins University School of Medicine: A Chronicle* (Baltimore, 1943–1958), I, *Early Years, 1867–1893*, 13–16.

[5] French, *History of Johns Hopkins*, 4–5; J. Thomas Scharf, *The Chronicles of Baltimore: Being a Complete History of "Baltimore Town" and Baltimore City from the Earliest Period to the Present Time* (Baltimore, 1874), 666; *The Peabody Institute of the City of Baltimore: The Founder's Letters and the Papers Relating to Its Dedication and Its History, Up to 1st January, 1868* (Baltimore, 1868). The Maryland General Assembly passed permissive legislation for the university in January, 1867, and the certificate of incorporation was signed on August 24, 1867.

[6] This analysis is based on various Maryland biographical encyclopedias, obituary notices in the Baltimore press, and data in AFJH.

[7] The seven were John Work Garrett, Galloway Cheston, Francis White, Francis T. King, William Hopkins, Lewis Neill Hopkins, and Thomas Marsh Smith.

gave freely of financial advice to the new university and headed a minority element that wanted it to stay in the path of immediate, practical benefit to the community. The failure of the university to follow his advice here and on the matter of moving to Hopkins' country estate led Garrett in January, 1883, to denounce the board publicly and withdraw from its counsels.[8]

But Garrett was not typical of the board's businessmen. Some of them were among the board's seven Quakers, reflecting Hopkins' own Quaker background.[9] Certain of these men had been active participants in the remarkable educational achievements of the Friends; three were trustees of Haverford and one of Guilford in North Carolina. The one physician on the board, James Carey Thomas, served as Friends minister and executive of the Baltimore Yearly Meeting. Thomas' powerful religious beliefs made him the kind of universal servant whose good deeds defy enumeration, and the promotion of education was one of his chief activities.[10]

Four lawyers, none of whom was a Quaker, joined Thomas in leadership of the board. As chairman of the executive committee, Johnson took on the heaviest burdens when the trustees began their work in 1874. Charles J. M. Gwinn, a less active member of the executive committee, was attorney general of Maryland during the opening years of the university and contributed legal advice and lobbying to ease the relationship of the new institution with the state. Two judges of the Supreme Bench of Baltimore—George Washington Dobbin and George William Brown—brought dedicated service to the university. Dobbin, whose scientific interests led him to maintain a laboratory, had shown his abilities as an educational organizer by reviving the law school of the University of Maryland in 1869 and serving as its dean.[11] Brown was probably the most influential of all the trustees in shaping and

[8] Daniel Coit Gilman, *The Launching of a University and Other Papers: A Sheaf of Remembrances* (New York, 1906), 36; *Address of John W. Garrett, Delivered on the 30th of January, 1883, before the Young Men's Christian Association of Baltimore, on the Occasion of Their Thirtieth Anniversary* (Baltimore, 1883).

[9] I count Cheston here, who attended Quaker meeting regularly, though he never actually became a Friend.

[10] Edith Finch, *Carey Thomas of Bryn Mawr* (New York and London, 1947), *passim;* Anna Braithwaite Thomas, *The Story of Baltimore Yearly Meeting from 1672 to 1938* (Baltimore, [1938]), 97–98, 111.

[11] Binder labeled "Invoice," Dobbin-Brown Papers, Maryland Historical Society; JHC, X, 148–149; "George W. Dobbin," anonymous typescript, biographical file,

maintaining the university, and he was the one member who left a record of his early ideas on the role that the university might play in American education.[12]

As mayor, Brown had played a not ignoble role in quelling the Baltimore Riot of April 19, 1861. Aside from his political and legal career, he participated in many of the educational and cultural organizations of the city and was a visitor of St. John's College, Annapolis. In a speech at Rutgers, his alma mater, Brown in 1851 reported his observations in Europe of a thoroughness and range of studies that America could not hope for without a change in "the popular will." He had no doubt, however, that such a change would come and that republican institutions would provide "the stimulus of freedom . . . essential to the highest achievements of the human mind." [13]

Eighteen years later, in 1869, Brown could speak at St. John's as if his prophecy were on the verge of fulfillment. The new university to be endowed by Baltimore's wealthiest citizen would be able to adopt innovations appropriate to the nation's needs. The new education should have two principal aims, Brown asserted. One of these, to him the more important, was to send into the community "upright, refined, and highly cultivated young men." The other was what became the great differentiating quality of the new university and opened an era in American education: "to bring together a competent corps of professors, some of whom, if possible, should be teachers in the largest sense, that is, should have the ability and the leisure too, to add something by their writings and discoveries to the world's stock of literature and science." As Brown analyzed the situation, America had the best-informed general public in the world, but lacked a high intellectual superstructure. The nation had "erected a temple without a dome, a column without a capital, a

---

Maryland Historical Society; Gilman, *Launching of a University,* 31; Bernard C. Steiner *et al., History of Education in Maryland* (Bureau of Education Circular of Information no. 2; Washington, 1894), 137.

[12] For a detailed account, see Hugh Hawkins, "George William Brown and His Influence on the Johns Hopkins University," *Maryland Historical Magazine,* LII (1957), 173–186.

[13] *The Old World and the New: An Address Delivered by George William Brown before the Philoclean and Peithessophian Societies of Rutgers College, New Brunswick, N.J., at Their Anniversary on the 22d of July, 1851* (New York, 1851), 22–27.

spire without a pinnacle." [14] That Brown was not the only trustee to foresee a special destiny was shown by the elaborate search for ideas which the board undertook in 1874. One Baltimorean who knew its members well described them as "cautious and conservative, going to 'make haste slowly,' " but he found them determined "to place the Concern in the top rank, if money, experience and hard work on their part will do it." [15]

There was room in the top rank, as Brown and other trustees knew. The University of Virginia, which Jefferson had originally envisioned as equaling European universities, had never fulfilled this dream, but had shown surprising resilience after the disintegrations of the war. The classical curriculum was proving inadequate to the needs of an industrially expanding America, and early attempts to circumvent it had led to the beginnings of separate scientific schools at Yale and Harvard in the 1840s and to the opening of the Massachusetts Institute of Technology in 1865.[16] The Morrill Act of 1862, granting public lands to states for the founding of colleges teaching agricultural and scientific subjects, had done little in Maryland except to bolster the weak Agricultural College (opened in 1859) with about $6,000 a year, but elsewhere land-grant colleges were laying stress on long-neglected aspects of higher education. The outstanding example, Cornell University, had opened in 1868 and embodied many of these new ideas, especially equality of vocational, scientific, and literary subjects; nonsectarianism; and coeducation.[17] Harvard had chosen Charles William Eliot as president in 1869, and he had at once set about reforming his alma mater. The Hopkins trustees thought of him mainly in connection with the "new education" (most simply, sciences and modern languages intro-

[14] George William Brown, *The Need of a Higher Standard of Education in the United States: An Address Delivered before the Philokalian and Philomathean Societies of St. John's College* (Baltimore, 1869), 8–15.

[15] James Carey Coale to William Gilman, Nov. 20, 1874, GP.

[16] Richard J. Storr, *The Beginnings of Graduate Education in America* (Chicago, 1953), 9–14; Philip A. Bruce, *History of the University of Virginia, 1819–1919: The Lengthened Shadow of One Man* (New York, 1920–1922), III, 345–385, IV, 1–19; Dirk J. Struik, *Yankee Science in the Making* (Boston, 1948), 337–357.

[17] Steiner, *Education in Maryland*, 324, 326; *Autobiography of Andrew Dickson White* (New York, 1905), I, 294–426; Carl L. Becker, *Cornell University: Founders and the Founding* (Ithaca, 1943), *passim;* Walter P. Rogers, *Andrew D. White and the Modern University* (Ithaca, 1942), *passim.*

duced as equals of the classics) and with the elective system.[18] But Eliot had instituted many other reforms at Harvard by 1874, including higher standards of admission and examination, moderated discipline, earned higher degrees (beginning with two Ph.D.'s and one S.D. in 1873), an "honors" system comparable to the present-day undergraduate major, undergraduate laboratories, "University Lectures" that resembled (at least in effect) later university extension programs, professors' salaries of $4,000 a year, and a doubled teaching staff.[19] The trustees knew that things were stirring in Cambridge, and they were eager to find out more. Yale, by choosing Noah Porter president in 1871, had bound itself once more to the unyielding classical curriculum, so firmly rationalized in the influential "Yale Report of 1828"; meanwhile, the Sheffield Scientific School remained Yale College's despised but inescapable relative. Princeton was slowly slipping out of the clutch of fundamentalist Presbyterianism through the work of James McCosh, the Scotch metaphysician who became president in 1868 and who wanted Princeton to "advance with the times." A partial elective system, a scientific school, and graduate fellowships were among his earliest innovations.[20] Of these colleges and these events, the Hopkins trustees had some degree of knowledge. But none of them was a professional educator, and none of them, in 1874, was near the mainstream of college and university life. These men recognized their limitations. They saw that they had a search before them—a search for a university idea and for a university leader. By the end of 1874 they had found both their standard and their man.

For guidance in the search the trustees turned to men and to books. The books included university histories, accounts of educational reform movements in Britain and America, and reminiscences of scholars.[21] Although there is no proof that many of the trustees read any great number, Thomas wrote his daughter about the time of the purchase of

[18] This is apparent from the questions that they drew up for Eliot to answer (binder labeled "Johns Hopkins University 1874," Lanier Room, JHU Library).

[19] Henry James, *Charles W. Eliot: President of Harvard University, 1869–1909* (Boston and New York, 1930), I, 239–261.

[20] Storr, *Beginnings of Graduate Education*, 29–32; George Wilson Pierson, *Yale: College and University, 1871–1937* (New Haven, 1952–1955), I, *Yale College: An Educational History, 1871–1921*, 57–65; Thomas J. Wertenbaker, *Princeton, 1746–1896* (Princeton, 1946), 313, 293–294, 307–308, 301–302.

[21] See Appendix A.

these books that he was "engrossed and deeply interested in reading up University subjects." [22]

It is not known from how many university presidents the trustees sought information or interviews. McCosh of neighboring Princeton ignored the letter they sent him (in 1875), and the cold shoulder which Noah Porter turned to the new university may have first appeared in connection with some letter of inquiry.[23] Three university presidents responded generously, however, and their names have passed down in the Johns Hopkins tradition as the three great advisers of the trustees. Charles William Eliot, president of Harvard from 1869 to 1909; James Burrill Angell, president of the University of Michigan from 1871 to 1909; and Andrew Dickson White, president of Cornell from 1866 to 1885—these outstanding figures answered the requests of the Hopkins trustees openly and eagerly. All three were deeply interested in rescuing American higher education from what they considered outmoded and trammeling customs.[24] The three were never indifferent to the wealthy new foundation in Baltimore, and though at times envious, they offered it aid without recompense.[25]

These meetings of minds—interviews with Eliot and Angell in June and July, 1874, and correspondence with White—were milestones in educational history.[26] The three presidents have long been heroes of American university development. The trustees, however, were not passive recipients of ideas; their questions were penetrating, and in

[22] Quoted in Finch, *Carey Thomas*, 45.

[23] James McCosh to Gilman, Jan. 24, 1876; Gilman to Porter, May 14, 1881.

[24] Enlightening character sketches of all three are included in Charles Franklin Thwing, *Guides, Philosophers, and Friends: Studies of College Men* (New York, 1927). Although White himself gives the date as 1867 (*Autobiography*, I, 330), he was in fact elected president of Cornell in November, 1866 (information furnished by Neal R. Stamp, Assistant Secretary of the Corporation, Cornell University, from the Minutes of the Trustees).

[25] White to Johnson, May 1, 1874; Angell to Johnson, May 12, 1874; Eliot to Johnson, May 28, 1874; all in "J.H.U. Miscellaneous Letters to Trustees, 1874–1875," Lanier Room (hereinafter cited as "Letters to Trustees").

[26] For a detailed account see Hugh Hawkins, "Three University Presidents Testify," *American Quarterly*, XI (1959), 99–119. See also White to James Carey Thomas, March 13, 1874, AFJH. Typed copies of this letter and of the two interviews are in binder "Johns Hopkins University 1874," Lanier Room. For the Angell interview, I have used the original manuscript in pencil, AFJH. I have also drawn on Angell to Johnson, April 21, 1874, "Letters to Trustees."

9

what was the most important issue of all, their thinking outran that of the experts they were consulting. Scarcely any matter affecting higher education escaped the broad sweep of this survey. Eliot later wrote, "I . . . told them all I knew & a great deal more," and Angell recalled, "I was shut up in a room with these Trustees and a stenographer, and what few ideas I had in those early days were squeezed out of me remorselessly." [27]

The will of Johns Hopkins required that buildings should not be paid for out of capital. The presidents echoed this with their advice. Men were more important than buildings, they said. White and Angell warned against dormitories, and Judge Dobbin also felt that students were better off living in private homes. As to discipline, a problem from which the new university was to prove remarkably free, Eliot recommended only the indirect control of good teaching, good example, and keeping the young men steadily at work. In deference to the views of Johns Hopkins and because of their own beliefs, the trustees were predisposed to nonsectarianism; still, it must have been reassuring to hear from White that it was succeeding at Cornell.

The level of admission was the theme of one of the questions on a list that Johnson handed Eliot. Assuming that students would come from nearby Southern states "at first," Eliot was dubious about their preparation. By the time that Angell arrived a month later and opened his discussion with insinuations that the schools near Baltimore were inferior, Dobbin had had enough. He burst out with a cogent definition of the whole problem faced by the new university and included in it this defense of the lower schools: "We have here very respectable common schools. We have in this city a system of Public Schools not surpassed anywhere. They are very extensively patronized and adequately supported. The teaching is respectable, and is growing better, and we are now about building a City College." The comment showed that sentiment existed among the trustees against being intimidated into founding a weak college. Other descriptions of City College, a public preparatory school which after 1875 included the equivalent of the first year of

---

[27] Eliot to Gilman, May 20, 1875; *Johns Hopkins University Celebration of the Twenty-fifth Anniversary of the Founding of the University and Inauguration of Ira Remsen, LL.D., as President of the University February Twenty-first and Twenty-second, 1902* (Baltimore, [1902]), 133 (hereinafter cited as *Hopkins Twenty-fifth Anniversary*).

college work, support this defense of the readiness of Baltimore youths for higher education.[28]

In granting scholarships and postgraduate fellowships, the board learned, Harvard insisted on need, contrary to the English practice of basing the grant solely on scholastic merit. "I am well persuaded," Eliot told them, "that post-graduate fellowships which give a complete support to the incumbent are of doubtful utility unless rigidly guarded and vigilantly watched." White disagreed, advising the trustees to set up "ten or twenty [fellowships], each one yielding a sum sufficient to maintain a young graduate at the University in a reasonable degree of comfort, while he pursues a more extended course of study under the general direction of the Faculty." Here was a novel system, the lack of which had doomed efforts to develop graduate work in America before the Civil War.[29]

Even as early as these interviews, the problem of coeducation beset the Hopkins trustees, and from the first they differed among themselves. When a member of the board asked for Eliot's opinion, he said that he regarded coeducation as "a thoroughly wrong idea which is rapidly disappearing." Another member wondered, "How are women to get the highest education provided the avenues of education are closed to them?" Eliot said the wise and just solution was separate institutions and cited the success of Vassar and English colleges for women. Angell, whose institution had been coeducational for four years, said that public opinion had forced the admission of women at Michigan, but that their presence had caused no embarrassments. The questions the trustees directed to Angell, however, revealed a mood of decided suspicion. Johnson asked, with obvious distaste, "Do these boys and girls [at Michigan] sit in classes indiscriminately?"

Perhaps nowhere more than in his discussion of professors did Eliot reveal how completely he failed to envision the kind of institution that would open in Baltimore. He suggested that for the first year the university hire only teachers for first-year collegiate work, that the second-year teachers be hired during the first year and so on. White pictured

[28] ARJH (1878), 30; James Chancellor Leonhart, *One Hundred Years of the Baltimore City College* (Baltimore, 1939), 42–43.

[29] Storr, *Beginnings of Graduate Education,* 130–131 and *passim.* White had long pleaded for some such plan at Cornell, but did not succeed in achieving it until 1884 (Rogers, *Andrew D. White,* 198–200).

11

a staff of higher caliber. He advised hiring for terms of five years and suggested that a good collection of books and apparatus could prove more tempting to a scholar than a large salary. A way "to break up provincialism" among the professors, according to White, was to bring in famous scholars as nonresident lecturers. The system had worked well at Cornell, where it prevented "monotony and humdrum sluggishness."

First on the list of questions which the trustees handed Eliot was one inquiring "as to the relative merits and advantages of the Old System and more advanced systems of Education." They realized that the strict classical education was being challenged, and the term "more advanced" implied that they felt the challenging ideas to be better. Eliot referred them to his articles of 1869, "The New Education: Its Organization," in the *Atlantic Monthly*.[30] In these influential articles, Eliot discussed efforts in the United States to organize "a system of education based chiefly upon the pure and applied sciences, the living European languages, and mathematics, instead of upon Greek, Latin, and mathematics." White stressed this matter of modification of the traditional classical curriculum more than anything else. He pointed up the need for technological studies and for social sciences, and he urged that every science course be accompanied by laboratory work. One trustee reported his impression to Angell that Greek was generally losing favor with "the most of people, who think there are so many things more important to be studied."

Second only to the "New Education" in the limelight of the period stood the elective system. It was listed among the four problems that the trustees drew up for Eliot to discuss. He was on record as favoring it, and its all-pervading advance at Harvard lay just ahead. As Eliot presented it to the trustees, such a system was needed since the study of too many worthy subjects within four years led to superficiality. He felt that lack of good preparatory schools near Hopkins would make the elective system inapplicable there. But there was some consolation in not having it: "If as it seems to me probable," he said, "you are unable to undertake an elective system, you would find your organization easier to make, because an elective system involves a great number of teachers." Thus, the great advocate of the elective system (whose other contributions are too often overshadowed by it) did not

[30] XXIII, 203–220, 358–367.

advise that system for the new university; instead, he offered them consolations about not being burdened with it! Michigan, Angell reported, allowed the student to choose the group of studies he would follow, but set down a fixed course after this initial choice. This was also the Cornell system.[31] Such a scheme shortly emerged at Hopkins, though it probably came from the example of Sheffield Scientific School.

Eliot and Angell, but not White, stressed the idea that Hopkins should establish professional schools, which, they implied, would make it a true university. Since the letter of Johns Hopkins to the hospital board said that the university should establish a medical department, one professional school at Hopkins was fairly certain. Questions from the trustees showed that a law school was also being considered.

Neither Eliot nor Angell was so daring as to predict that Hopkins would become America's first great graduate university. It was the trustees themselves who brought up the idea, and in both cases the visiting presidents advised them to limit themselves to less ambitious spheres. Early in Eliot's interview a trustee asked him whether Hopkins "should attempt to give a higher degree of education than has heretofore been done, or whether we should create an institution which should give education to a larger number." Eliot admitted that this was "about the most important matter in education in the United States," but after commenting that the trustees seemed to want to meet the need for an institution of the highest type, he bluntly told them that it was impossible. No educational institution could cut loose from the foundations of its community. The way to establish a higher level of education was by means of the elective system, which gradually expanded the curriculum. In perhaps the worst prediction of educational history, Eliot told the trustees: "The post-graduate course is a matter far off for you. Not until you have organized the whole of the College course, only in the fifth year of the existance [sic] of the college, could that question practically present itself." In Eliot's mind, obviously, graduate work was a continuation of undergraduate work carried on in the same institution.

Angell had scarcely begun his interview when Dobbin interrupted his comments on the low level of students which Hopkins must expect and made a precise and reasoned presentation of the problem facing the board. The principal choice was between "an Institution which shall be

[31] Rogers, *Andrew D. White*, 96–97.

13

devoted to the highest teaching" and one which would "spread its benefits more widely." If the country must have higher institutions like those in Europe, the new university "with a fund perfectly untrammelled" might meet the need. Although Angell said that he supposed the higher course was wiser, "provided at the outset you did not take so high a start as to break your connection with your constituency," he seemed not to comprehend Dobbin's idea fully. He continued to picture Hopkins as a local or regional university without "instruction in the upper ranges." Angell sketched Michigan's own current revival of graduate work, but without suggesting that Hopkins could have such a program.

Implied in White's letter was the idea of graduate study for the new university, and explicitly he presented a plan for making such study succeed by means of fellowships. He did not say that these fellows should engage in original research, though his phrase "under the general direction of the Faculty" suggested that they would not simply take more undergraduate classes. Thus, White had advised the trustees to plan for graduate work before they approached either Eliot or Angell, and he may have stimulated this idea as Dobbin expressed it. But Brown had dreamed of making Hopkins a university in the highest sense as early as 1869.

Although the trustees saw to it that complete records of the two Baltimore interviews were kept, they left almost no mention of their own visits to other universities. They did go to various campuses, especially where new or unusual programs were in effect, and this eagerness to see as well as hear displayed the thoroughness of their search. The university's first president, writing near the end of his life, listed Harvard, Yale, Princeton, Michigan, Cornell, and Virginia as the universities visited. The trip to the University of Virginia probably took place in 1875, as did one to the University of Pennsylvania.[32] Later in the fall of 1874, two trustees were in Europe examining English and Continental institutions.[33]

The search for the man to lead the new university succeeded with remarkable dispatch. Knowing the kind of university that they wanted

[32] Gilman, "Introductory," manuscript of 1906 or 1907, JHUP; George W. Childs to John W. Garrett, Jan. 18, 1875, John Work Garrett Papers, Division of Manuscripts, Library of Congress.

[33] According to James Carey Coale to William Gilman, Nov. 20, 1874, GP, the two had then just returned.

to build, the trustees could measure a man efficiently and promptly; furthermore, the qualities that they sought were almost unique among the available university figures. The first person to suggest Daniel Coit Gilman for the presidency of Johns Hopkins was Eliot. Although the record of his interview in Baltimore does not name any specific candidate and implies that a local person would be desirable, Eliot thought of Gilman for the post as early as July 1, 1874.[34] He may have named Gilman in June, off the record, or he may have done so in September, when the trustees came to Harvard. The trustees traveled on from Harvard to Yale, and there Noah Porter, for all his coldness and refusal to talk about the Sheffield Scientific School where Gilman had taught, repeated Eliot's recommendation. When the trustees called at Cornell on September 30, White, long an intimate friend of Gilman's, did more than submit his name. In the midst of a tour of the campus— on the steps of Sibley Hall, where Gilman had once spoken of the needs of American universities—White made a speech to the trustees praising his friend.[35] Later they received the same response from Angell as from Eliot, Porter, and White: the man they needed was Daniel Coit Gilman.[36]

White's eulogy had included the salient characteristics of the forty-three-year-old educator who headed the University of California. He spoke, for instance, of Gilman's "organizing faculty." This he had first observed a quarter of a century earlier, when Gilman was his admired fellow student at Yale College. Academic duties had not been enough to keep the efficient young Gilman busy. He had earned part of his expenses by private teaching and newspaper work and had helped establish a Sunday school for underprivileged children, including physical as well as religious training. Gilman's "knowledge of educational matters at home and abroad," to which White referred, represented the gleanings from many opportunities, beginning with Gilman's undergraduate experiences at Yale from 1848 to 1852. He had lived in the

[34] Johnson to Eliot, Jan. 25, 1876, Reverdy Johnson, Jr., letter book, Lanier Room; Eliot to Gilman, July 1, 1874.

[35] White to Gilman, Oct. [correctly Sept.] 30, 1874. White told of the trustees' report that Eliot and Porter had also nominated Gilman. See also White to Elizabeth Dwight Woolsey Gilman, May 3, 1909, quoted in Fabian Franklin *et al.*, *The Life of Daniel Coit Gilman* (New York, 1910), 325.

[36] *Hopkins Twenty-fifth Anniversary*, 134. Ira Remsen said that five educational leaders independently recommended Gilman to the trustees, but did not name them (JHU *Circulars* [n.s. 1908, no. 10], 8).

home of an uncle, James Luce Kingsley, professor of Latin and a leading author of the "Yale Report of 1828." [37] From a rigid curriculum of recitations in mathematics, Greek, and Latin, Gilman had found some relief in his last year. To the seniors, President Theodore Dwight Woolsey taught history, political science, and political economy, interposing brief discussions of controversial questions and occasional lectures; Professor Noah Porter taught them mental and moral philosophy without dogmatically labeling any one view as correct.[38] Perhaps more significant in Gilman's educational background was his graduate residence at Yale and Harvard in 1852 and 1853, which had taught him that even great teachers avail an advanced student little where there is no official determination to encourage graduate study.[39] In his first trip to Europe, Gilman's wide-ranging investigations included the school systems, and in the winter of 1854–1855, he attended lectures at the University of Berlin. Although academic friendships seemed to fill more of his time than concentrated study and he rejected advice to live abroad for five years and win a Ph.D., his recognition of the scholarly stature of Berlin brought him ideals that he never forgot.[40]

When White praised Gilman's "catholicity in regard to all departments of knowledge," he made a virtue of what Gilman's friends had once feared as a vitiating weakness. After his return to Yale in 1855, he had entered such an array of activities that some doubted he could "achieve depth and unity of purpose." During his first decade in New Haven, he was propagandizer, lobbyist, and money raiser for the Yale Scientific School (Sheffield after 1861), reforming librarian of Yale College, in practice though not in name superintendent of city schools, organizer of art exhibitions, and (after 1863) professor of physical and political geography at Sheffield. Not even the last of these posts seemed to Gilman a "full-time job." Although he excelled as a teacher, he did not turn to a quiet scholarly career. More typical of his intellectual life were the writing of magazine articles

[37] Franklin, *Life of Gilman*, 8–14; Gilman, "D. C. G.," notebook containing a chronological record of his life, mostly in his own hand; Storr, *Beginnings of Graduate Education*, 29.

[38] White, *Autobiography*, I, 27–29; Timothy Dwight, *Memories of Yale Life and Men, 1845–1899* (New York, 1903), 184–187, 160–161.

[39] Gilman, *Launching of a University*, 8–9.

[40] Franklin, *Life of Gilman*, 22–32; Gilman, "Humboldt, Ritter, and the New Geography," *New Englander*, XVIII (1860), 278.

and membership in "the Club"—a group including the geologist James Dwight Dana and the philologist William Dwight Whitney that met regularly to discuss "science, politics and religion." The vigorous young professor assumed duties as secretary of the new State Board of Education, secretary of the governing board of Sheffield and (in collaboration with George J. Brush, the treasurer) its virtual executive, official visitor to the new land-grant colleges, and leading lobbyist for the extension of the Morrill program.[41] Just as he had encouraged theoretical and applied sciences at Yale, he urged these more practically oriented institutions not to undervalue the study of languages.[42] This sweep of interests, which could have created a dilettante, had been Gilman's school for educational statesmanship. A New England conviction of duty and the seriousness of life had made the difference.

White recognized the desire of the trustees to save Johns Hopkins from religious dogmatism, but he probably supposed too that most of them were personally devout. To put his candidate in the most appealing light, he referred to Gilman's "liberal orthodoxy in religious matters." The hint of inconsistency in the phrase was appropriate for Gilman, who in his California inaugural could assert not only that the university must respect the presence of Roman Catholics, Jews, Confucians, and Protestants by avoiding "denominational zeal," but also that its nonpartisan scholars would teach how Christianity had established "honesty, virtue, and justice" in the world.[43] In the year of his graduation from Yale, he had written a friend of his hatred of "*cant* and all that sort of thing," but this did not prevent his enjoyment of religious discussion with one who believed in "an inner life of faith and joy." [44] In a series of conversations with Noah Porter in 1854, Gilman had shown interest in the ministry as a profession, but declared that if he entered it he would want to stress everyday affairs "instead of dwelling long and regularly upon such points as original sin and the doctrine of election." Five years later, he followed Porter's

---

[41] These activities and many others are traced in Franklin, *Life of Gilman*, chap. ii, written by two daughters of William D. Whitney.

[42] Gilman, "Our National Schools of Science," *North American Review*, CV (1867), 495–520.

[43] Daniel Coit Gilman, *University Problems in the United States* (New York, 1898), 176–178.

[44] Gilman to Charles Loring Brace, Aug. 19, 1852, in Franklin, *Life of Gilman*, 13–14.

lectures on theology and took a license to preach, though he showed no eagerness to use it. If he had been born as much as one hundred years earlier, Gilman would almost certainly have fulfilled his desire "to influence New England minds" [45] by becoming a minister. But in the nineteenth century the new science and the new scholarship—and the new industrialism too—wooed him away. Finding his work in education welcomed and honored, he set his goals in that field, and he then felt it proper to keep "aloof from political and ecclesiastical affairs." [46] Increasingly, he expressed the activist, optimistic, worldly temper of his age. By 1872, he could define the religious spirit as one "which looks 'upward and not downward, forward and not backward, outward and not inward, and which lends a hand.'" [47]

White revealed most about Gilman's recent life when he said that he "would require nothing in the way of absolute power but a great deal of liberty of action." It was precisely the desire for freedom to develop his university ideals in America that took Gilman first to California and then to Johns Hopkins. In 1867, he had expressed his hope that "the present epoch of 're-construction'" would include new educational ideas and opportunities for the "young men bent on progress." [48] His refusal of invitations to the presidencies of the University of Wisconsin in 1867 and of California in 1870 gave evidence that he hoped to do his part in this reconstructing at Yale. His hopes were reinforced by the sense of crisis that swept Yale when late in 1870 President Woolsey announced his intention to retire. Undergraduates held debates on the curriculum; a Young Yale movement among the alumni demanded and received representation on the corporation; certain professors advanced schemes for equalizing departments, building up a graduate school, and raising a huge endowment fund. Agitation reached its height during the first half of 1871. Sentiment for a layman president throve, with Gilman the principal candidate. But conservatism, economy, and suspicion of Sheffield and

[45] Gilman to Maria P. Gilman, April, 1854, quoted in *ibid.*, 28–30; Gilman to Edward W. Gilman, July 10, 1860, in *ibid.*, 36–37.

[46] Gilman, "Introductory," JHUP.

[47] Gilman, *University Problems*, 177. The phrase is based on a motto by Edward Everett Hale.

[48] Gilman to Charles Eliot Norton, Nov. 2, 1867, Charles Eliot Norton Papers, Houghton Library, Harvard University. By permission of the Harvard College Library.

Sheffield men carried the day; Gilman's former professor and confidant, Noah Porter, an eloquent defender of traditional collegiate education, won the post.[49]

It is not surprising, then, that in 1872 Gilman accepted a renewed offer from California, where the youth of the institution and its Western setting promised the "liberty of action" that he required. In his inaugural he asked the state authorities to refrain from "overmuch legislation" and "hasty action"; [50] he made it clear that he had come to lead and would build as advanced an institution as possible. Among the achievements that made his three-year tenure memorable were co-operation with the public school system, absorption of nearby professional schools, increased giving by wealthy Californians, transfer of the university to Berkeley, and a scholarship program which allowed some students to remain for graduate study. But neither Gilman's development of the university nor his skill in human relations could forestall the storm of public abuse that threatened the university. Resentments over its neglect of manual trades and its nonsectarian nature brought early outcries, which were swelled by discontented farmers. The gravest threat of all was editor Henry George's charge of corruption in the building program. With the People's Independent Party, a union of Grangers, workingmen, and dissident Republicans, in control of the legislature, investigation became the order of the day. Although the session at last vindicated the university officials and granted all funds requested, the favorable outcome was never certain until the end, and the affair made the winter of 1873–1874 a nightmare for Gilman.[51] The "confiding support" that he had called for in his inaugural remained to be created, and it was not encouraging to

[49] Franklin, *Life of Gilman*, 98–102; Pierson, *Yale: College and University*, I, 52–57, 61; Gilman, "Proposed Change in the Corporation of Yale College," (New York) *Nation*, XII (May 25, 1871), 355–356; William D. Whitney to Edward E. Salisbury, March 13, 1871, Edward E. Salisbury Papers, Rare Book Room, Yale University Library. Charles W. Eliot to George J. Brush, Feb. 28, 1871, George J. Brush Papers, Manuscript Division, Yale University Library, seems also to refer to Gilman, though he is not named: "I congratulate you on your candidate for the presidency of Yale; your nomination is certainly as hopeful a one as any I have heard of from your side of the house."

[50] Gilman, *University Problems*, 163.

[51] Franklin, *Life of Gilman*, 122–159; Charles A. Barker, *Henry George* (New York, 1955), 219–221; Gilman, *Statement of the Progress and Condition of the University of California: Prepared at the Request of the Regents of the University* (Berkeley, 1875).

hear from one of the regents that "a long period of social war" would find the university continually under attack.[52] Gilman's submission of his resignation in April brought a vote of confidence from the regents and promises of firm backing. Reassured, he spoke of the "smooth prospect for the next two years"; [53] nevertheless, the ascendance of good feeling made it tactically possible for him to withdraw if he chose. The possibility of future struggles of fiercer proportions imbued him with the opinion that he "should listen favorably to any call to work at the East." [54] Thus, his friend White could assume that he was not leading the Hopkins trustees toward an unwilling candidate when he sketched for them Gilman's virtues.

[52] John W. Dwinelle to Gilman, April 1, 1874.

[53] Franklin, *Life of Gilman*, 159–161; Gilman to Andrew D. White, May 12, 1874, quoted in *ibid.*, 162.

[54] Gilman to Louise Gilman Lane, June 2, 1874, quoted in *ibid.*, 163.

: CHAPTER II :

Gilman in Baltimore

and Europe, 1875

RETURNING from their tour of universities with unanimous advice on the most appropriate candidate for the presidency, the trustees directed Reverdy Johnson, Jr., to make an overture to Gilman. His letter stressed the size of the bequest and the fact that it was not bound by "shackles of state, or political influence," or denominational ties, or sectional bias; in short, the institution was "entirely plastic" in the hands of the trustees. Whoever became president would be dealing "with a body of gentlemen, who . . . would not be disposed to throw obstacles, or captious objections" in his way. It was presently agreed that Gilman should come east for an interview. Meanwhile, the board voted a presidential salary of $8,000 a year, or $7,000 with a house.[1]

After an overland journey from California, Gilman reached Baltimore on December 28, 1874. In a formal interview the next day he made it clear that he had no desire to build another college of merely local importance. He felt that the time was ripe for a university national in scope on a plan radically different from any then in opera-

---

[1] TM, Oct. 15, Nov. 24, Dec. 22, 1874; ECM, Dec. 17, 1874; Johnson to Gilman, Oct. 23, Nov. 27, 1874, Johnson letter book; Gilman to Johnson, Nov. 10, 1874, draft in Gilman's hand, AFJH. The first exchange of letters is printed in Franklin, *Life of Gilman*, 184–187.

21

tion in America. According to a report which E. L. Godkin published in the *Nation* after talking with Gilman, he declared that promotion of advanced scholarship and training of graduate students would be his aims in the new university, that he would leave the training of undergraduates to other institutions. Gilman found that the trustees "responded heartily and promptly to this advanced view," and the next day they offered him the presidency. Although he did not give his final acceptance, it was clearly forthcoming.[2]

Johnson soon sent him a letter repeating what Galloway Cheston, president of the trustees, had said to Gilman during his Baltimore visit: because of "the position of our community during the troubles of the war, and its sensitiveness even to this day, in relation to those issues," the board desired "the absence of all sectarian bias, and of political spirit on the part of the President of the University."[3] Following Johnson's suggestion, Gilman enclosed in his formal letter of acceptance a second letter discussing the issues of religion and politics.[4] His statement, probably the most forthright and eloquent that he ever made on the subject of intellectual freedom, might well stand as a Declaration of Rights and Responsibilities for the personnel of the university.

The Institution we are about to organize [he wrote] would not be worthy the name of a University, if it were to be devoted to any other purpose than the discovery and promulgation of the truth; and it would be ignoble in the extreme if the resources which have been given by the Founder without restrictions should be limited to the maintenance of ecclesiastical differences or perverted to the promotion of political strife.

As the spirit of the University should be that of intellectual freedom in the pursuit of truth and of the broadest charity toward those from whom we differ in opinion it is certain that sectarian and partisan preferences should have no control in the selection of teachers, and should not be apparent in their official work.

---

[2] Baltimore *American*, Dec. 29, 30, 1874; Gilman to Louise Gilman Lane, Dec. 31, 1874, in Franklin, *Life of Gilman*, 191; Gilman, *Launching of a University*, 37; Gilman, "Memorabilia Academica," typescript, JHUP; *Nation*, XX (Jan. 28, 1875), 60.

[3] Johnson to Gilman, Jan. 4, 1875, second letter of date, Johnson letter book.

[4] Gilman to Johnson, Jan. 30, 1875, second letter of date, copy in TM, Feb. 11, 1875. A hurried copy in Gilman's hand, AFJH, shows minor mechanical differences.

Gilman in Baltimore and Europe

Permit me to add that in a life devoted chiefly to the advancement of education I have found some of the best cooperators among those from whom I differed on ecclesiastical & political questions; and that I shall find it easy to work in Maryland with all the enlightened advocates and promoters of science and culture. To those who will labor for "The Johns Hopkins University,["] my grateful and cordial appreciation will go forth. We should hope that the Faculty soon to be chosen will be so catholic in spirit; so learned as to what has been discovered and so keen to explore new fields of research; so skillful as teachers; so cooperative as builders; and so comprehensive in the specialties to which they are devoted,—that pupils will flock to their instruction, first from Maryland and the states near to it,—but soon also from the remotest parts of the land. In seeking this result the Board may rely on my most zealous co-operation.

Scarcely had Gilman sent this pronunciamento before he began to learn of obstacles that were not sectional, political, or sectarian, but direct challenges to his educational philosophy. California Grangers, who looked on him as a perverter of the vocational purposes of the Morrill Act, barraged the Hopkins trustees and others with derogatory clippings. Johnson assured Gilman that Maryland had no Grangers, and the Baltimore *Sun* deprecated the attacks. But a series of charges not unrelated to the utilitarian thinking of the Grangers shortly began in the pages of the *Sun*'s rival, the Baltimore *American*. After reprinting the *Nation*'s article announcing that Gilman planned a strictly graduate university, the *American* demanded that an undergraduate division come first. Mr. Hopkins had been interested in "education for the people and not sinecures for the learned." [5]

Although Johnson took this onslaught calmly, he warned Gilman that national stature could not be the university's only goal; it must serve the local community also. He called on Gilman to develop a plan for this "double aspect." Johnson's comments must have given pause to the new president, who had recently told a friend that he hoped to dispense with "the usual college machinery" of classes and commencements. Nor could Gilman have been reassured by a letter from a Baltimore writer branding the city "clannish and provincial" and prophesying that its "commercial spirit, the idea that the horizon of education and the practical are identical, will be apt to give you a

[5] Johnson to Gilman, Feb. 12, 1875, Johnson letter book; Baltimore *American*, Feb. 2, March 6, 1875; Franklin, *Life of Gilman*, 177.

trouble like that which you have had from the 'Grangers' in California." [6]

Shortly before Gilman's arrival in May, the *American* released a final blast, the most searing of all: it had been learned that certain trustees favored the plan described in the *Nation*. This was ominous news, for it showed that they had been "misled and egged on by the 'advice' of shrewd professors, who are chiefly solicitous that their own pampered and established institutions should have no dangerous rival." The whole graduate idea was a plot to keep Hopkins out of competition with other universities. The trustees would offer the youth of Maryland not the "substantial bread of well-grounded education" but the "glittering stone" of "elegant culture." Earlier attempts at graduate education in America had failed, and probably this one would too, losing the fund forever.[7]

Meanwhile, perhaps in hopes of showing the trustees a workable plan for a university of "double aspect," Gilman had written flatteringly of the University of Virginia, where the earned M.A. called for no preliminary B.A. Johnson, however, sent back a disillusioning answer, saying that several trustees had strong objections to the university at Charlottesville. "Don't understand me as partaking of their views," he added. "I only notify of shoals ahead in your navigation." [8] Thus, when Gilman left California for the East, he had a rough chart of the shoals. His California enemies had preceded him with destructive propaganda. The Baltimore press had accused him of warping Mr. Hopkins' intentions and risking the university endowment in a foolish experiment. A portion of the Board of Trustees seemed ready to disavow his plans for advanced training. But in general tone, Johnson's letters had been encouraging, and Gilman had received countless letters from his friends wishing him well in a great pioneering work. Whatever the difficulties, he had to go forward.

On his journey east from San Francisco, Gilman made one important stop. In St. Louis, which the local Hegelians and others had

[6] Johnson to Gilman, March 8, 1875, Johnson letter book; Gilman to Brush, Jan. 30, 1875, Brush Papers, printed in Franklin, *Life of Gilman*, 191–192; Edward Spencer to Gilman, Feb. 23, 1875. However, Spencer had lauded Baltimore as a potential university center in "Should Universities Be Provincial?" *Southern Magazine*, XVI (1875), 71–86.

[7] Baltimore *American*, May 3, 1875.

[8] Johnson to Gilman, April 10, 1875, AFJH.

developed into a center of vigorous new educational ideas, he conferred with M. Dwight Collier, a Yale-educated lawyer interested in university problems; William Torrey Harris, editor of the *Journal of Speculative Philosophy* and superintendent of the St. Louis public schools; and William Greenleaf Eliot, chancellor of Washington University. Gilman gave them hints of his plan to make Johns Hopkins the kind of university that Yale, under the firmly conservative Noah Porter, was failing to become. Deeply impressed with Harris, Gilman later in the month urged him to apply for the superintendency of schools in Baltimore, where he could aid the new university, but Harris declined.[9]

Despite its antagonism, the *American* greeted Gilman's arrival on May 10 courteously, wishfully announcing that popular opposition to a graduate university would probably kill the idea and that Gilman proposed "to inform himself as to the sentiments of the community . . . before committing himself to any plan." Gilman did indeed confer with a great many educational leaders of the city and state. The trustees arranged various social functions for this purpose and took him to visit the Baltimore City College, the State Normal School, Peabody Institute, and the local high schools for girls; by these means came opportunities for Gilman to make graceful speeches telling how Hopkins was to fit in with the local educational structure. According to the *American* he was even collecting statistics on students who left Maryland for college training, with an eye to enrolling them in Johns Hopkins.[10] It is not clear if Gilman disavowed the graduate university idea publicly, but his charm and tact soon dispelled the bugaboo of a radical, wasteful, ultraintellectual university. By the middle of June, the *American* itself had been won over; instead of ranting at the trustees, it began to give sensible warnings against political, sectional, and religious bias. It called on the authorities to make Hopkins "in the highest sense a free University, laying no bounds whatsoever on the thought or investigations of its professors." [11]

[9] Gilman diary of 1875; Collier to Gilman, April 6, 1875, Dec. 26, 1885; Harris to Gilman, May 27, 1875; Gilman to Ralph Waldo Emerson, Jan. 21, 1876.

[10] Gilman diary of 1875, May 10–28; Baltimore *American*, May 12, 13, 18, 20, 1875.

[11] Baltimore *American*, June 15, 1875. "The backing down of the *American* as regards the J.H.U. has amused me very much" (Lewis H. Steiner to Gilman, June 23, 1875).

25

The trustees, whom Gilman reported to be "somewhat conservative but not *set* for or against any particular scheme," [12] decided, the day after his arrival in Baltimore, to begin "the organization and practical operation" of the university in the city itself while proper buildings were being erected at Clifton. Gilman could hardly have been the originator of this idea, but he must have favored it, remembering as he did the misery of university work at Berkeley in isolation from settled homes and businesses. In pursuit of this resolution the trustees purchased, for $75,000, two attached dwellings just north of the new City College building on Howard Street.[13] In this building, considerably remodeled, the university was to begin its work; and despite the original idea that the location was temporary, it was to remain there into the next century.

One immediate problem was the drawing up of a general plan for organizing the university. On this matter too the trustees had waited for Gilman's arrival. During May, he repeatedly conferred with the "Committee on Organization"—Dobbin, Johnson, and Thomas [14]—and at the end of the month the full board approved the committee's "plan of procedure," which served as the constitutional framework of the university during its earliest years.[15]

The plan provided for classes to begin in October, 1876, on the "temporary" Howard Street site, with a reserve accumulating fund set up to provide for future buildings. Classes would be formed gradually, taking the needs of the students into consideration. The eventual matured conclusions of the trustees would be the "principles" of the university, but the methods of carrying these out would depend on faculty action, subject to board approval.

The lineaments of the future faculty were clearly prefigured in the decision to have three categories of teachers: permanent professors giving full-time service to the university, to be "men of acknowledged ability and reputation, distinguished in special departments of study, capable of advancing these departments & also of inciting young men to study & research"; lecturers giving only a limited amount of

[12] Gilman to Charles W. Eliot, May 14, 1875, Charles W. Eliot Papers, Harvard University Archives.

[13] TM, May 11, 17, 1875; Baltimore *American*, May 20, 1875.

[14] Gilman diary of 1875, May 17, 19, 21; TM, May 11, 1875.

[15] TM, May 27, 1875; printed in part in ARJH (1877), 25–29. A draft in Gilman's hand, with "assented to" penciled after each point, is in JHUP.

time—men of marked ability, not necessarily taking up residence in Baltimore, possibly from the staffs of other universities and from foreign countries; and "assistants & adjuncts" holding appointments of from one to five years, to do work "subordinate to & in connection with" the permanent professors, who should be consulted in their selection, and to be "young men of ability & promise from whom the staff of permanent teachers may be in time reinforced." The salaries of assistants would range from $1,000 a year to $3,000; those of professors from $3,000 to $5,000. These figures were significantly higher than those then being paid by American colleges and universities,[16] but Gilman had nevertheless been forced to amend his dream of January, when he had hoped for four professors at $6,000 each and twenty with salaries between $4,000 and $5,000. Then he had predicted $155,000 a year for instruction; [17] now he accepted $60,000 for the first year with a $15,000 increase for each of the next two years.

The executive committee in nominating teachers and the board in electing them were to avoid "political and sectarian influences" and to select men "known and esteemed in different parts of the country." The faculties of law and medicine were postponed. In the philosophical faculty six broadly defined departments were to have priority: ancient languages; modern languages; mathematics (pure and applied); chemistry and physics; "natural science" (geology, mineralogy, botany, and zoology); and an area, reflecting the emergence of the social sciences from "moral philosophy," comprised of philosophy, political economy, history, and international and public law. Initial appropriations were made for books, laboratory apparatus, and scientific collections, to be purchased by the executive committee in consultation with the professors.

The compromise that Johnson had hoped for between local necessity and the ideal of national stature appeared most clearly in the matter of students. Undergraduates—students sixteen years old with the preparation required by the best colleges and scientific schools in the country—would be admitted. They could enter either of two plans of study, a classical course leading to the B.A. or a scientific course leading to the B.Phil. (later changed to the B.A.). Gilman's

[16] According to Gilman, Yale's highest salary was $3,500, and Harvard's $4,000 (Gilman to J. J. Sylvester, Nov. 29, 1875).

[17] Gilman to Brush, Jan. 30, 1875, Brush Papers.

experience at Yale, where the scientific degree of Sheffield, obtainable in three years, was looked down on, appeared in the assertion that the two degrees would be exactly co-ordinate in rank, both requiring four years (later changed to three). No degree would be given without "strict and comprehensive" examinations; there was to be no five-dollar, good-character M.A. at Hopkins. In providing the scholarships directed in the founder's will, further compromise appeared. Some would be awarded publicly on the basis of competitive examinations and some privately according to need. What could have been mere soothing syrup appeared in a promise "to afford the opportunity to residents of Baltimore to pursue certain special lines of study." But the leaders of the university took this pledge seriously and did set up programs which aided particular groups of local citizens. An outstanding example was the Saturday physiology course for teachers, begun in October, 1877.[18]

But compromise never endangered Gilman's central idea for the new university. The plan of procedure promised special encouragement "to college graduates to come and profit by instructions here provided with or without reference to the taking of a degree" and an effort "to extend the benefits of the foundation to distant parts of the land." Those who wanted an advanced degree could not receive it sooner than two years after their bachelor's. There was apparently some doubt about what to call this degree. As the matter turned out, doctorate and master's were united (as often the case in Germany) into one degree, the "Doctor of Philosophy and Master of Arts, Ph.D. and M.A." [19] This part of the plan of procedure, entitled "Special Advanced Instruction," set the course of the university toward a new level of education for America and toward the fulfillment of the hope, shared by Gilman, Brown, and most of the other trustees, for a university of national influence. But one important problem remained: What was to be the "special encouragement" to win graduate students for the new university?

The needs of the university often took Gilman out of Baltimore during the spring of 1875. Among those in Washington with whom he con-

---

[18] ARJH (1878), 33.

[19] JHR (1877), 76. For the use in Germany and the medieval synonymy of *magister* and *doctor,* see Hastings Rashdall, *The Universities of Europe in the Middle Ages,* ed. by F. M. Powicke and A. B. Emden (Oxford, 1936), I, 19–20.

ferred were Joseph Henry, director of the Smithsonian Institution; Spencer F. Baird, his assistant; Theodore N. Gill, a zoologist connected with the Smithsonian and the Columbian (George Washington) University; Ferdinand V. Hayden and James T. Gardner of the Geological Survey (the trustees shortly gave $1,000 to the Survey for a projected collection of specimens from its next Western expedition); Julius E. Hilgard of the Coast and Geodetic Survey; and John Shaw Billings and Joseph J. Woodward of the Surgeon General's office, both of whom were interested in hospital construction. Gilman left Baltimore on May 29 for New Haven for a brief but triumphal homecoming. From May 31 to June 16 he stayed at the United States Military Academy, where he had been appointed to the Board of Visitors.[20]

During these days at West Point, Gilman observed its operations in detail and talked especially to professors who could give him suggestions for the scientific departments at Hopkins. He became well acquainted with Peter S. Michie, professor of physics. When Gilman asked about candidates for the physics department at Hopkins, Michie suggested a promising young instructor at Rensselaer Polytechnic Institute named Henry A. Rowland, who had just published an article in the *Philosophical Magazine*. Thinking of the periodical published by his friends at Yale, Gilman asked why Rowland had not published his article in the *American Journal of Science*. As Gilman related the story, Michie answered:

"Because it was turned down by the American editors . . . and the writer at once forwarded it to Professor Clerk Maxwell, who sent it to the English periodical."

This at once arrested my attention and we telegraphed to Mr. Rowland to come from Troy. . . . He came at once and we walked up and down Kosciusko's Garden, talking over his plans and ours. He told me in detail of his correspondence with Maxwell, and I think he showed me the letters received from him. At any rate, it was obvious that I was in confidential relations with a young man of rare intellectual powers and of uncommon aptitude for experimental science.[21]

---

[20] Joseph Henry to James Joseph Sylvester, Aug. 25, 1875, in George Bruce Halsted, "Sylvester," *Science*, n.s. V (1897), 602; Gilman diary of 1875, May 24–June 16; ECM, May 28, 1875.

[21] Gilman, *Launching of a University*, 15.

In this conversation Gilman learned that Rowland was about twenty-five years old, that his current salary was $1,600, and that he would like a chance to do more advanced and independent experiments. The Yale professors in charge of the *American Journal of Science* had rejected papers by him three times because they thought that he was too young to be publishing such things.[22] Gilman consulted with the executive committee, which authorized a salary of not over $1,600. Rowland came to Baltimore on June 25 and probably was hired on that day.[23]

The recognition of Rowland's promise is often cited as the stellar example of Gilman's ability to see the potential worth of unknown young men. Gilman deserves such credit. But even before the two men met, acclaim in England had begun to break Rowland's isolation. In April he had received a letter from Edward C. Pickering, professor of physics at the Massachusetts Institute of Technology, who had read a "handsome notice" of his papers by Clerk Maxwell. Rowland responded eagerly, telling just how great his isolation had been. He did not remember ever learning anything by word of mouth in the fields of electricity and magnetism. The first galvanic battery, electromagnet, and vacuum tube that he had ever used he had built himself. Since he spent all his money for books, he made every piece of apparatus for his researches. His first experiments in the field of magnetic permeability had been made in a room in his home in 1870–1871, just after his graduation from Rensselaer.

The correspondence throve, and Rowland confided to his new friend that at Rensselaer he received "anything but encouragement" in his wish to devote his life to research. Worst of all, he had no laboratory for his own experiments. He intended to leave as soon as possible and hoped to spend the summer making "a new determination of the Ohm in absolute measure by a new method," but he had no place to do the work. Pickering at once offered him the use of his own laboratory in Cambridge, but Rowland decided to wait "until I am permanently situated somewhere so that I can take a year or so if necessary, and make my determination if possible of equal weight with that of the Brit[ish] Association."

Pickering had already offered to find him a position before the

[22] Gilman notebook of 1875, quoted in Franklin, *Life of Gilman*, 199.
[23] ECM, June 21, 1875; Gilman diary of 1875, June 25.

West Point encounter, but no existing opportunity in 1875 could have been so right for a young man of Rowland's abilities and personality as that at Johns Hopkins. Gilman must have been persuasive, for the young physicist turned down Pickering's offer of aid even before knowing what his rank at Johns Hopkins would be. "I have gone there on faith," he said, "and will do my best to make the institution a success." At any rate, he knew that he would have a year to prepare and perform his planned experiments and would be allowed to do this in Europe. He hoped to spend this time widening his field of competence, perhaps by taking up optics, but he was not sure that he would have time to do this at once, because, he wrote, "I am afraid that the trustees would not like it if I do not get out some papers this year." Already Rowland had sensed the standards of value in the new institution.[24]

Although he found no more Rowlands, Gilman continued his tour of American universities. He called at Cornell, at Swarthmore, and, with Johnson, at the University of Virginia. The visit to Charlottesville was so rapid and cursory that some of the faculty felt slighted, believing that the uniqueness of their institution deserved longer study. Again in the company of Johnson, Gilman set out on June 26 to confer with more of his friends in Northern universities. In New Haven, George Brush, who was now executive head of Sheffield, probably had more of interest to say to the visitors than did the counselor of Gilman's youth, Noah Porter. Gilman and Johnson briefly visited Amherst and Smith, which was to open that fall. They reached Cambridge at the end of June and there conferred with E. L. Godkin; Josiah D. Whitney, professor of geology; and of course the trustees' earliest adviser, President Eliot. With the wisdom of his own country consulted, Gilman was ready to look abroad.[25]

The European mission which Gilman began on July 7, when he sailed from New York in the company of Rowland, was not a unique venture for an American university president. White and Eliot had both conducted preliminary explorations abroad. Even more significant, a thin but steady stream of American students had been returning

[24] Rowland to Pickering, April 19, May 10, 17, June 1, 28, July 4, 1875, Edward C. Pickering Papers, Harvard University Archives.
[25] Gilman diary of 1875, June 17–July 1; Johnson to Gilman, July 19, [1875], AFJH; Brush to Gilman, June 19, 1875.

with ideas from German universities for more than sixty years. There was, nevertheless, a heroic cast to Gilman's travels. He sought ideas and scholars. But he intended also to declare the good news: an American institution now stood ready to adopt essentials of European higher education heretofore neglected. Halting imitation of Europe and hamstrung reform had long been characteristic of American colleges. Now radical innovation in university creating was at hand.

The outstanding value of the journey [26] that took Gilman to Ireland, England, France, Switzerland, Germany, Austria, and Scotland was probably the creation of good will for himself and the new university. Everywhere, as soon as scholars learned of his plans and purposes, they welcomed him enthusiastically. Although his July visits to London and Paris came at a season when there was a dearth of scholars, American students had spread word of his mission by the time that he arrived in Germany, and one Augsburg newspaper was shortly describing it "in a way to set all the young privat-docents in a fever." [27] The acquaintances of his student days in Berlin also helped make his visit there fruitful.

He returned in September to a lavish welcome in Britain, the university reformers receiving him as one of themselves. His talks with William Henry Bateson, master of St. John's, Cambridge, and Benjamin Jowett, master of Balliol, Oxford, proved especially memorable; and he was often to refer to the ideas of Emily Davies and Anne Jemima Clough, heads of the two colleges for women at Cambridge. Although he found fewer innovations in Scotland, even there he heard hopeful predictions about Johns Hopkins from John Tulloch, principal of St. Andrews, who had just returned from America.

The scientists especially seemed to court Gilman, or perhaps he sought them out. In Dublin, Gilman had been pleased at their compliments to Rowland before he separated from his chief to visit Clerk Maxwell. Thomas Huxley and Herbert Spencer were among the scientific elite whom Gilman met in London, where one of his earliest July calls had been on Joseph D. Hooker, director of the botanical gardens at Kew and president of the Royal Society. In Zurich, Dresden,

[26] This account follows the Gilman diary of 1875; letters from Gilman in Franklin, *Life of Gilman*, 198–211; Gilman, *Launching of a University*, 13.

[27] Austin Stickney to Gilman, Oct. 10, 1875.

and Vienna, he gave the polytechnic schools close attention. He chose to stress his interest in the laboratories of chemistry, physics, and physiology, when writing the trustees from Berlin, and carefully informed them that the physics laboratory at the University of Vienna was as large as the building which would house the entire Johns Hopkins.

Part of the function of Gilman's trip was this subtle educating of the trustees by long letters back to Baltimore. He especially tried to encourage them with two examples: the thriving new University of Strassburg, re-established after the German annexation of Alsace, and Owens College, Manchester, like Hopkins a private foundation, which had begun in modest rooms in the center of the city. He took great satisfaction in reporting the complaints of William Thomson (later Lord Kelvin) and other professors at Glasgow about the new Gothic buildings in which they had to work; Gilman and Johnson had already foreseen the disadvantages. Nor did he neglect to forward information on hospitals and medical schools.

The men whom Gilman met in the summer of 1875 aided Johns Hopkins for many years in a variety of capacities. Some lectured there, such as Thomson, Huxley, Tulloch, Arthur Cayley, Cambridge mathematician, and Hermann von Holst, professor of history at Freiburg. So did James Bryce, then a practicing solicitor and professor of law at Oxford, who heard Gilman's plans with enthusiasm and declared that after visiting the United States he had developed a desire "to establish himself there." Many of Gilman's European friends served as later advisers, especially on problems of staffing. Others extended hospitality to Hopkins teachers and students who came to study in Europe. By developing the reputation of the university even before it opened its doors, Gilman influenced European scholars to watch it closely and prepare to applaud its very earliest contributions to learning and to the university idea in America. In the spring of the next year, Lyon Playfair, representative of the University of Edinburgh, cited Hopkins favorably on the floor of Parliament.[28] There was a subtle stimulation and flattery in being visited by a well-informed American asking for advice.

In finding professors, Gilman probably did less well numerically

[28] D. E. Collins to Gilman, April 20, 1876.

than he expected. He made many inquiries and received many suggestions, but the most elaborately recommended prospect was James Joseph Sylvester. Sylvester was an eccentric sixty-one-year-old mathematician who had finished his work at Cambridge with high honors in 1837 but failed to receive his degree because as a Jew he could not subscribe to the Articles of Faith. He had been a professor of mathematics at the University of Virginia during the 1841–1842 term, but left abruptly when the faculty refused to dismiss a student who had insulted him. Although he had wanted to stay in America, he could find no other position; he returned to England to work for an insurance company and study law. Between 1850 and 1854, he and Arthur Cayley collaborated in building up the theory of invariants, and both established solid reputations at that time. In 1855 Sylvester won a post as professor of mathematics at the Royal Military Academy at Woolwich, but he was so erratic and pugnacious that he was eased out in 1870. Lacking an intellectual home, he ceased mathematical investigation and grew painfully restless.[29] When he learned of Gilman's trip and its motive, he wrote to Joseph Henry of the Smithsonian Institution, intimating that he would like a position in the new university.[30] Gilman later explained why a man with so many honors would seek such a post: he was still ruffled by his forced retirement from Woolwich; "he longed not only for a salary, but for the recognition of a university appointment, which for no fault of his own had been denied him in England." [31] Recommendations for Sylvester came to Gilman not only from Henry, but also from Hooker and Benjamin Peirce, professor of mathematics at Harvard, who had tried to find a place for Sylvester in America in 1843. Besides praising the "luminous" Sylvester, Peirce presented a philosophy of university teaching which stressed the role of great scholars in leading the occasional student of genius. "I hope," Peirce concluded, "you will find it in your heart to do for Sylvester—what his own country has failed to do—

---

[29] P. A. MacMahon, "James Joseph Sylvester," *Nature,* LV (1896–1897), 492–494; MacMahon, obituary statement, *Proceedings of the Royal Society of London,* LXIII (1898), ix–xxv; Raymond Clare Archibald, "Unpublished Letters of James Joseph Sylvester and Other New Information concerning His Life and Work," *Osiris,* I (1936), 85–154.

[30] This letter of Aug. 13, 1875, is referred to in Henry to Sylvester, Aug. 25, 1875, in Halsted, "Sylvester," *Science,* n.s. V, 602.

[31] Gilman, *Launching of a University,* 66.

place him where he belongs—and the time will come, when all the world will applaud the wisdom of your selection." [32]

Sylvester and Gilman met several times during Gilman's last busy days in London. The mathematician seemed "willing, perhaps eager" to go to Baltimore, but Gilman "was not so ready to invite him . . . for there were many intimations that he was 'hard to get on with.' " [33] The interviews went pleasantly enough. In fact, Gilman feared that he might have been too pleasant and on October 14 sent Sylvester a highly characteristic memorandum, saying that his friendly remarks had been "personal and not official," but that he would speak highly of him to the trustees and that if he did become a professor at Hopkins he would be given "a large discretion" and would be aided in publication.[34] The next day Sylvester made Gilman a farewell gift of his book *The Laws of Verse or Principles of Versification Exemplified in Metrical Translations: Together with an Annotated Reprint of the Inaugural Presidential Address to the Mathematical and Physical Section of the British Association at Exeter.*[35] This amazing volume is even more variegated than its title implies. If Gilman read it on the ship going home or even glanced at the long chatty footnotes, he learned that he had encountered a powerful mind, undisciplined and childlike, but strangely charming.

Among the American friends with whom Gilman spent time that summer, conquests for Johns Hopkins were also made. The Sanskritist William D. Whitney, whom he met in Geneva, agreed to come as a visiting lecturer, though he would not leave Yale for a permanent chair. Two of the most notable fellows of the first year—Charles R. Lanman and Josiah Royce—traveled with Gilman for a time in Germany, and though they remained uncommitted, their admiration for Gilman and his plans grew during these encounters.[36]

As to ideas, it is difficult to tell just what Gilman did gain. He was an acute observer and an evocative questioner; no doubt he learned a

[32] Henry to Gilman, Aug. 25, 1875; Hooker to Gilman, Sept. 11, 1875; Peirce to Gilman, Sept. 18, 1875.

[33] Gilman to Henry, Nov. 30, 1875; Gilman, "The Early Days of the Johns Hopkins University," *Hullabaloo* (JHU yearbook) for 1899, 11; Gilman, *Launching of a University*, 66.

[34] Preliminary draft, GP.

[35] London, 1870. This inscribed copy is in the JHU Library.

[36] Lanman to Gilman, Aug. 30, 1875; Charles R. Lanman diary, Aug. 22–30, 1875, Charles R. Lanman Papers, Harvard University Archives.

great deal. Certainly in such matters as the requirement of general background training before specialization (stressed by Von Holst and the Berlin scholars), functionalism in buildings (as at Strassburg), well-endowed laboratories, and co-ordinate education for women, he saw outstanding examples or heard intelligent and experienced opinion. In his Hopkins inaugural, he listed among the topics discussed in England the following: the need for universities to elevate preparatory education, train students for modern callings, and improve urban life; the difficulties which excessive collegiate instruction forced on professors; the lack of university recognition of the natural sciences; the burden of ecclesiastical fetters; and the puzzle of how to endow research without establishing sinecures.[37] On the last topic, the ideas of Charles Appleton, founder and editor of the *Academy,* were later described by Gilman as a "very strong" influence on Hopkins; [38] and probably he took a special interest in discussions of the relationship of a university to its environing society, since he had so recently begun to learn the needs and demands of Baltimore.

On October 5, while he was at Oxford, Gilman drew up a "Draft of a plan for organization of Johns Hopkins University," which he described as being written "after many visits & conferences." [39] Although the plan was never formally adopted, it showed how his thinking had developed since the adoption of the "plan of procedure" in May. The powers of the president delineated in this draft indicated that Gilman wanted to clarify his own position. For example, he thought that the president should be eligible for a place on the Board of Trustees and should have the right to appeal any decision of the faculty to the board. Others of his plans for Hopkins here revealed for the first time were annual reports of the president, similar to reports that he had written at Sheffield and the University of California; the office of dean, to be held by a representative of the faculty who would be something of a vice-president and faculty secretary; and an academic council, to aid in governing the university and to consist of the president, the dean, one trustee, one faculty member from the literary division, and one from the scientific. As to students,

[37] Gilman, "The Johns Hopkins University in Its Beginning," *University Problems,* 10. Hereinafter cited as "Hopkins Inaugural."
[38] This comment, made in 1903, applied also to the ideas of Mark Pattison (Gilman, *Launching of a University,* 242).
[39] GP.

Gilman put the minimum age for admission at seventeen, one year above that in the "plan of procedure," and described two standards for admission, one to require Greek, Latin, and mathematics, the other to require Latin, mathematics, either French or German, and one branch of natural science. The most noteworthy thing about this draft plan is how much it resembled the existing American universities and how little it incorporated any French, German, Scotch, or English ideas. Only the awareness of faculty power represents much of a European stamp. Although urged by Johnson to stay longer in Europe if he thought that he could benefit further, Gilman sailed for America on October 16, according to plan.[40] He seems to have been satisfied that no great lessons could be learned by staying abroad longer. Gilman often in later years cited European precedents for activities at Hopkins, but he probably did so more out of a wish to gain respect for his program than out of any real sense of historical obligation. There was no wholesale borrowing. As Gilman later described it, the plan for the new institution was

not to follow exclusively any precedent,—not to attempt to found a German University or a French or an English,—but to derive from all sources such experience and recommendations as might be adapted to this country and lead in course of time to an American University based upon our own educational system, and fitted to meet the wants of our own scholars.[41]

By and large, not very much in the way of European influence can be proved from this trip of Gilman's. It may have done more for him as a vacation than as an education. There were indeed European ideas in the organization of the Johns Hopkins University, but they tended to be the ideas which Gilman and others had already brought to America by the 1850s and instilled in such institutions as Sheffield. The European ideas which Gilman utilized were not raw immigrants: they had dwelt in America for a good many years and had already been subtly Americanized.

[40] Johnson to Gilman, Sept. 4, 1875, AFJH.   [41] ARJH (1878), 8.

: CHAPTER III :

Winning the Faculty,

1875-1876

IF the Johns Hopkins University had opened in the early 1850s, it might have become the home of the Scientific Lazzaroni, a small but vigorous organization of American scientists who desired above all else to be united in one great university. Alexander Bache, super-intendent of the Coast Survey and a leading Lazzarone, stated the case of these "homeless idlers" thus: "For the sake of being together, I know that the leading scientific men of the country, with few ex-ceptions . . . would leave their present homes. . . . There are men enough to make one very brilliant institution by their high qualities and learning." But the efforts of the group to establish a university above the college level in Albany fell through, and the members had to make the best of existing institutions.[1] By the time that Gilman held out the fulfillment of their dream, these men were too old to want to move or too well adjusted where they were; Louis Agassiz, a leader among them, was dead. Soon after Gilman accepted the presidency of Hopkins, a friend wrote him, "You will have your pick of professors all the world over, and I presume the colleges are shaking in their shoes and waiting to see what will happen to them." [2] But it was not so easy as that. There were great and famous scholars in America, but the story

[1] Storr, *Beginnings of Graduate Education,* 68–74.
[2] Frederick J. Kingsbury to Gilman, Feb. 23, 1875.

of Gilman's search for a faculty is largely a story of his failure to bring the men with established reputations to Hopkins. The survivors of the Lazzaroni—men like Benjamin Peirce—wished him well, but they would not pull up roots and join him in Baltimore. Another disappointment was Gilman's failure to attract his former Sheffield colleagues to Baltimore.[3]

If Gilman had become easily tired and discouraged, the weeks of labor and frustration after his return from Europe would have wilted him. From November on, he attended every meeting of trustees and executive committee and wrote countless letters, most of which dealt with the faculty question. He and the leading trustees agreed that the selection of a staff would be "one of the most delicate and difficult tasks" that they would ever face.[4] Johnson had warned Gilman in a letter of July that applications were piling up and would tax his patience and eyesight. What followed Gilman's return was a period of "overtures made to men of mark" and "received from men of no mark," such as the one who offered "to put Geology in its physical *& moral* aspects."[5] By April 1, 1876, the number of applications for teaching positions had mounted to 198. It was a year of depression, and Gilman found "the cry of hard times" widespread among the job hunters.[6]

Believing as ever in forethought and an organized course of action, Gilman drew up for the trustees a brief essay, "On the Selection of Professors."[7] In this paper, he contended first and most strongly that Hopkins must get professors with distinguished reputations, and he quoted Benjamin Peirce's assertion that the greatness of a university depends on its few able scholars. Berlin and Strassburg, Gilman pointed out, demonstrated how institutions can grow famous through the work of gifted individuals.

Gilman foresaw the hindrances to moving American professors. He described the ease with which scholars could be persuaded to change locations in Germany, where there were few personal, ecclesiastical, or geographic ties to particular universities and where a professor's

---

[3] Gilman to Brush, Jan. 30, 1875, Brush Papers.

[4] George William Brown to Gilman, Nov. 8, [1877?]; ARJH (1876), 19.

[5] Johnson to Gilman, July 19, [1875]; Gilman, *Launching of a University*, 14; Gilman to Josiah D. Whitney, April 3, 1876.

[6] ECM, April 1, 1876; Gilman to E. P. Evans, Feb. 11, 1876.

[7] Typescript in JHUP. It is mentioned as being read in ECM, Dec. 4, 1875, and in TM, Dec. 6, 1875.

students would move with him. The situation was different in every regard in America. Although Gilman was not optimistic about transferring any famous American teachers, Hopkins must be on the alert for opportunities which might arise when professors wanted more money, escape from objectionable administrative policies, a chance to specialize, or better laboratory and library facilities.

In the matter of salaries Gilman quoted a letter from Joseph Henry on the importance of paying well and alleged that whereas $10,000 would make men of eminence change universities $5,000, the figure set by the trustees, would not. Hopkins must expect to encounter the kind of tenacious loyalty which had made Whitney, Brush, and William H. Brewer stay on at Yale at salaries of $2,300 when Eliot had offered them $4,000. But Gilman refused to be pessimistic on this account. Instead he made a cheerful adjustment, saying, "Our strength will probably lie among those who have already done enough to show their intellectual qualities but who have not yet attained the more enviable positions in college life." He found cause for optimism in the example of Agassiz, who had been under thirty when he was brought to America, "far enough on to have shown his extraordinary qualities, not so far as to be too old for transplanting." Then too, there was the case of the first faculty of the University of Virginia: Jefferson had found "men of promise rather than of fame." Nor must the distinguished but unmovable scholars be entirely lost to the university. They could become nonresident lecturers, as provided in the "plan of procedure."

Again harking back to his recent European observations, Gilman reported that in English universities the choice was always said to be between a good instructor and a good investigator. Hopkins should try to get both types of men and some men who combined both qualities. But even those whose forte was teaching must be given enough leisure to advance the boundaries of knowledge.

In outlining the desired attributes for Hopkins professors, Gilman listed specialization first. "The day has gone by," he observed, "for *a* professor of science or *a* professor of languages or *a* professor of history. Those gentlemen who are willing to teach anything or take any chair are not those we most require." Teaching power came next, then co-operativeness (a new institution would need men who could value departments other than their own), then an attitude toward

40

religion and politics which "does not prevent wide differences of opinion; but . . . precludes the uncalled-for expression of these differences under circumstances which are likely to impair the usefulness of the University."

The trustees had already reached many of these conclusions. Even before the death of Johns Hopkins, they had received recommendations for university positions.[8] By 1875 they were hardened to appeals, often backed by strong personal pressure, that came by every mail and from every part of the country. Most conspicuous were the efforts of former officers of the Confederate army, who would hear first with joy that the trustees favored Southern men, then with dismay that they were "inclined to New Englandism."[9] There was also pressure to choose local men. Montgomery Blair, Lincoln's Postmaster General and a resident of Maryland, warned against men from far away with big reputations. But the Hopkins trustees loyally embraced Gilman's criterion of original work already performed.[10] As the quest for professors continued, however, it became more and more apparent that young men whose original production was in its earliest stages must meet the need. In December, Gilman saw the answer in "young vigorous men who have won their spurs, and are now ready for a career," expecting that these men would have developed far enough to be given professorships. But by April, 1876, he admitted that the university would "doubtless appoint many 'Associates,' young men of promise, for terms of years; & fill up the professorships slowly."[11]

The mathematics professorship headed the list after Gilman returned to Baltimore and brought word of the eccentric Englishman who seemed willing to come to America, but the filling of the other posts could not wait for the outcome of this case, and the Sylvester negotiation was soon only one of many irons in the fire. As a specialist and proved scholarly investigator, Sylvester perfectly satisfied the criteria set up. But *The Laws of Verse* alone was enough to reveal that he

[8] D. H. Miller to John W. Garrett, May 9, 1873, Garrett Papers.

[9] H. Clay Dallam to William Leroy Broun, Oct. 10, 1874; Charles S. Venable to Broun, Oct. 12, 1874; H. C. Dallam to R. T. Coleman, Oct. 26, 1874; all in William Leroy Broun Papers, Southern Historical Collection, University of North Carolina, Chapel Hill.

[10] Blair to John W. Garrett, Jan. 22, 1876, Garrett Papers; Gilman, *Launching of a University*, 50, 59.

[11] Gilman to James Burrill Angell, Dec. 10, 1875; Gilman to Joseph Henry, April 12, 1876.

41

lacked the power to organize, which was also needed by the new university. He had never demonstrated any ability to inspire advanced students, and though he was free from "ecclesiastical or sectional controversies," his record branded him a frequent controversialist in other matters. Because of the fame he could bring to the newborn university, however, Sylvester was probably not weighed too narrowly in the balance.

The board voted on November 27 to offer Sylvester $5,000 a year plus moving expenses. Since Sylvester had shown "some exaggerated notions" of academic salaries in the United States, Gilman detailed for him the inexpensiveness of life in Baltimore. He reported that Yale's highest salary to a professor was $3,500, and Harvard's $4,000, and that these were unusually high.[12] Sylvester replied by setting three conditions under which he would accept: that the sum be paid in gold, that the university provide him with a residence, and that he be allowed to appropriate student fees. On January 4 Gilman wrote tentatively that the trustees opposed furnishing professors with residences and that the fee system was rare in America, and in medical schools, where it was practiced, it worked a great deal of harm. When the trustees finally agreed to the payment in gold but to neither of the other conditions, Sylvester cabled back: "Untried institution uncertain tenure favorable home prospects stipend crowning career inadequate against risk incurred regret thanks decline." [13] Gilman had foreseen this answer and was already looking over the field of American mathematicians, with his eye especially on Simon Newcomb, the famous astronomer-mathematician who edited the *Nautical Almanac* in Washington.[14]

Gilman's spirits did sink at the loss of Sylvester and several failures in efforts to win American scholars. "We can't have a great University without great teachers; & great teachers won't come to us till we have a great University!" he complained. "What shall we do?" Sylvester was also despondent, and wrote a charming letter thanking Gilman and the trustees for the compliment of considering him, re-

[12] Gilman to Sylvester, Nov. 29, 1875; Gilman to Joseph Henry, Nov. 30, 1875.
[13] Sylvester to Gilman, Dec. 17, 1875, first letter of date; Gilman to Sylvester, Jan. 8, 1876 (cable); Sylvester to Gilman, Jan. 26, 1876 (cable).
[14] Gilman to Brown, Jan. 8, 1876; Gilman to Hubert A. Newton, Jan. 18, 1876; ECM, Jan. 7, 1876.

marking in self-justification that "the course I have taken was not founded on selfish considerations solely and throughout received the approval of Dr Hooker Mr [William] Spottiswoode and Mr Herbert Spencer." [15]

But before this letter reached Baltimore, in fact before it was written, the academic gears had been set turning again by an apparently disinterested third party. Sylvester had shown the entire correspondence to Hooker, president of the Royal Society, who had originally introduced him to Gilman. Hooker sympathized and took it upon himself to give the new university a gentle prodding. He sent Gilman his impression that the offer did not properly recognize Sylvester's "eminence, age, experience, & the fact that his tenure of office could not but be brief." Although fees might properly go to the university, the request for a house or proportionately higher salary did not seem unreasonable. The executive committee gave Hooker's letter careful consideration and decided to offer an additional $1,000 a year. Sylvester accepted these terms with thanks, and on February 18 Gilman was gleefully imparting the news to another candidate for the faculty.[16]

Once the ugly business of money was taken care of, Sylvester loosed all his natural affection and enthusiasm on "our university." Clearly, he had liked Gilman from the first and heard good reports of him. He had been unhappy without a professorship, and this one promised to offer him more freedom for independent mathematical work than any he had held. His appointment made him a frequent conversational topic in English scientific and literary circles. Thus, he could write happily: "I do look forward as you are kind enough to augur to a new course of usefulness in connexion with your and my University to which I already begin to feel the attachment of a favored son."

For his part, Gilman found his university basking in reflected glory. He wrote Sylvester: "It did me good to see the sparkle in the eyes of a mathematical candidate [Thomas Craig] when I told him you were to be here. He knew your writings & could not believe it pos-

[15] Gilman to C. F. B. Bancroft, Feb. 7, 1876; Sylvester to Gilman, Feb. 10, 1876.
[16] Hooker to Gilman, Jan. 31, 1876; Gilman to Hooker, Feb. 15, 1876 (cable); Sylvester to Gilman, Feb. 17, 1876 (cable); Gilman to George M. Lane, Feb. 18, 1876.

sible that it was *the* Sylvester who was to be here next year." This kind of encouragement—unusually warm in such a formal letter writer as Gilman—delighted Sylvester. He wrote exuberant letters, giving ideas and hopes for their coming collaboration. He even took the president into his confidence and told him what a success his poem "Rosalind" had been.[17]

Sylvester came to Baltimore late in May, but his stay was brief. On June 1 he scrawled Gilman a note saying that his most precious box—the one containing his life's work in manuscripts—had been lost in transit and that he must rush to New York to search for it. Sylvester continued northward to pay a visit to Benjamin Peirce, who had been his host repeatedly in 1842 and 1843. Gilman seemed not unhappy to have him gone from Baltimore and in dependable care. Sylvester was still looking out for the interests of his new academic home, especially in the search for an assistant in mathematics. At Cambridge, both Benjamin Peirce and his son James Mills Peirce, who was also a mathematics professor at Harvard, strongly recommended William E. Story, a tutor there. Story's book on higher algebra convinced Sylvester, and he promised to try to meet him. But soon Sylvester was complaining of the heat and his own "depression," two afflictions that dogged him during every American summer. He decided to return to England for a vacation before the opening of the fall term.[18]

It was left to Gilman to follow up the lead on Story, a Harvard graduate and Leipzig Ph.D. of 1875. He found that younger mathematicians could also be difficult. Perhaps with unnecessary condescension, Gilman wrote Story, "If you desire light work and a good place in which to study I think you will find the place of an Associate . . . honorable and advantageous." After consulting with the elder Peirce, Story responded in direct language. He was interested in "original work as a mathematician," he said, not study, and the "high character of the work which seems to be demanded at Baltimore" was more important to him than leisure. Story hoped that in an interview he could explain his plans for a mathematical journal

[17] Sylvester to Gilman, April 22, March 30, 1876; Gilman to Sylvester, March 30, 1876.
[18] Sylvester to Gilman, June 12, July 27, Aug. 14, 1876; Gilman to Sylvester, July 27, 1876.

and a student mathematical society. He had had some hopes for a better offer from Eliot, but when they remained unfulfilled, he accepted the post in Baltimore.[19]

Gilman's first plan in regard to physics and chemistry was to unify them in one department under Wolcott Gibbs. Gibbs, one of the Lazzaroni of the 1850s, was Rumford professor at Harvard, a post which he had won in competition with Eliot in 1863. Eliot had been forced off the Harvard faculty by this event and after his return in 1869 as president had transferred all the work in chemistry to the new college laboratories, out of the hands of Gibbs, whose chair was in the Lawrence Scientific School. This change—which did contribute to efficiency—may not have represented vindictiveness on Eliot's part, but Gibbs felt rather sure that it did.[20] Gilman undoubtedly knew of this discontent. After a three-hour interview, Gilman found that he and Gibbs agreed in general outlook. He pressed his invitation by sending the Harvard professor a description of the many advantages in Baltimore:

I think you will find it [Baltimore] attractive in climate, proximity to Washington, abundance of good society, & moderate scale of domestic expenditure. As for your official duties, I think you will find yourself free for higher work, well supported by adjuncts & assistants, independent of other departments of the Univ[ersity], & from established routine, encouraged to develop a strong school of chemistry & physics.

After expressing some uncertainty, Gibbs on January 18 declined. Of Gilman's many disappointments, this was one of the most keenly felt. Gibbs gave considerable thought to Gilman's problem, stressing his need for young men—"not fossils like myself"—and suggesting that John Trowbridge of Harvard's Lawrence Scientific School be made head of the joint department, with Rowland and Ira Remsen, professor of chemistry and physics at Williams, as his associates.[21]

Rowland had not returned with Gilman, but had gone to Berlin to work in Helmholtz' laboratory. While there he made a discovery of

[19] Gilman to Story, July 13, 1876; Johnson to Gilman, Aug. 4, [1876]; Story to James Mills Peirce, Aug. 1, 1876, Benjamin Peirce Papers, Harvard University Archives. Story quotes the correspondence between himself and Gilman.

[20] Gilman to J. Lawrence Smith, Nov. 29, 1875; James, *Charles W. Eliot*, I, 111–112, 295–297.

[21] Gilman to Gibbs, Dec. 7, 1875, Jan. 4, 15, 25, 1876; Gilman to Brush, Jan. 4, 1876; Gibbs to Gilman, Jan. 18, 1876.

great significance for the theory of electronics by proving that a moving charged conductor would have an effect on a magnet like that of an electric current.[22] Gilman had brought back such excellent reports of Rowland that even before this accomplishment the trustees put a good deal of faith in him. On December 6 they made Rowland "assistant in the Department of Physics," at a salary of $2,000 for the year 1875–1876. He was thus the only faculty member mentioned in the *First Annual Report*. Also in December, the trustees began authorizing Rowland to buy apparatus. His purchases represented a new philosophy of scientific teaching. As Rowland expressed it to Pickering, "They are nearly all for investigation and none of them are for amusing children." [23] An early official description reported the apparatus to be "of the highest order and adapted for exact measurement of physical quantities rather than for the qualitative illustration of the subject." Absolute measurement in electricity and magnetism was the special goal, but good equipment was also provided in the fields of heat and optics.[24]

Gilman had admired Rowland from the first, but he did not originally imagine him in the role of Hopkins' first professor of physics. He made a tentative effort to win the English physicist and astronomer Norman Lockyer, with whom he had conferred in England. Nothing came of this, however, and he began to inquire for suggestions from his friends in America. At Gibbs's suggestion he tried for Trowbridge, but by this time Gilman was convinced of Rowland's stature and planned to make both Trowbridge and Rowland professors of physics. After rousing considerable hope, Trowbridge declined, citing family ties.[25] On April 17 Rowland was officially confirmed as professor of physics, at a salary of $3,000.[26]

A month later Rowland was on his way back to America, having made another visit to Cambridge University, where he again stayed with Maxwell. Shortly before sailing, he had received word of his

[22] Joseph S. Ames, "Henry Augustus Rowland," DAB, XVI, 198.
[23] TM, Dec. 6, 1875; ARJH (1876), 22; ECM, Dec. 4, 1875; Rowland to Pickering, May 17, 1876, Pickering Papers.
[24] JHU *Circulars*, no. 4 (August, 1876), 28.
[25] ECM, Nov. 8, 1875; Gilman to Ogden N. Rood, Jan. 15, 1876; Gilman to Brush, Feb. 4, 1876; Trowbridge to Gilman, March 25, 29, 1876; Gibbs to Gilman, April 30, 1876.
[26] TM, April 3, 17, 1876.

election to the American Academy of Arts and Sciences, which he declared to be a great surprise—"seeing that I hardly considered my scientific life to have yet begun." Return to his homeland was no reason for an extended vacation, Rowland felt. After hurrying to Baltimore to help choose the fellows in physics, he settled at West Point, where he could use the laboratories and the library.[27]

The final choice for a second physicist came from a suggestion made by the new professor of physics. Observing that someone combining the specialties of optics and acoustics would be his ideal colleague, Rowland pointed out Charles Sheldon Hastings as the only physicist that he knew with such a qualification. Overtures were successful, and Hastings, a Sheffield Ph.D. who had studied at Heidelberg, Berlin, and the Sorbonne, accepted a position as associate.[28]

After Gibbs's final refusal, Gilman gave up the idea of a joint department of physics and chemistry. For the post of professor of chemistry another candidate, Ira Remsen, had already volunteered. Remsen, a twenty-nine-year-old New Yorker, whose early career was an echo of Gibbs's, had graduated from the College of Physicians and Surgeons in 1867 and then gone to Germany to study chemistry at Munich and Göttingen, winning his Ph.D. at the latter university in 1870. After a period on the staff at Tübingen, he returned to the United States and became professor of chemistry and physics at Williams. Remsen made the first gesture, writing directly to Gilman on December 12 to ask about prospects. Gibbs, in his letter of declination, made a strong case for Remsen, calling him "a very active hard working chemist doing good work in the way of research." [29] When Brush wrote similarly, saying that Remsen was both an excellent instructor and a good investigator, Gilman was nearly convinced. On March 14 he issued a definite invitation, offering $3,000 and a two- to five-year appointment. Remsen protested that this sum was inadequate, but Gilman, firmly supported in his judgment by Eliot, did not offer to raise the beginning salary. Per-

[27] Rowland to Pickering, May 17, June 1, 1876, Pickering Papers; Rowland to Gilman, July 26, 1876; *Memoirs of the American Academy of Arts and Sciences,* n.s. XI (1888), 54.

[28] Rowland to Gilman, May 17, 1876; Alois F. Kovarick, "Charles Sheldon Hastings," DAB, XXI, 383–384.

[29] W. A. Noyes, "Ira Remsen," DAB, XV, 500–501; Gilman to Remsen, Dec. 20, 1875; Gibbs to Gilman, Jan. 18, 1876.

haps learning that a $500 increase would follow biennially was enough to convince Remsen. At any rate, he came to an agreement and was officially elected on April 17, at the same time as Rowland and on the same terms.[30]

Remsen spent much of the summer of 1876 examining chemical laboratories in America and designing one for his own use in Baltimore. Unperturbed by the many delays, he felt sure that his laboratory would be the best in the country. As in the case of Rowland, Remsen chose his own assistant, Harmon N. Morse, an Amherst graduate and Göttingen Ph.D. of 1875, who had been teaching for one year at Amherst.[31] Hopkins had already made Morse a fellow, but on Remsen's recommendation elevated him to the rank of associate.[32]

Because of the prospective medical school, the department of biology—especially its physiological side—concerned Gilman greatly from the first. Except for Harvard, American colleges barely touched the subject; so Gilman turned at once to his British friends for suggestions. Huxley had suggested Henry Newell Martin to Gilman while he was in England and had given him a copy of the textbook on which they had collaborated. Gilman now asked for further information on the young physiologist, saying, "I cannot hear of any one in this country who is prepared for such a work." [33]

In a letter of March 14, Gilman offered Martin a beginning salary of $2,500 to come to Baltimore "to organize a laboratory & school of biology, on a plan similar to that of Prof. Huxley at So[uth] Kensington," for both students preparing to become physicians and those preparing to become naturalists. Martin declined these terms, but frankly stated the ones which he would accept: $4,000 for two years and $5,000 thereafter, a good laboratory, and the title and authority of professor. Possible insufficiency of laboratory facilities worried him especially. Gilman yielded to all these demands,[34] and Martin joined the growing faculty, sailing for America in the company of Huxley

[30] Brush to Gilman, Jan. 31, 1876; Gilman to Eliot, March 25, 1876; Eliot to Gilman, March 29, 1876; TM.

[31] Remsen to Gilman, June 29, July 28, Aug. 25, 1876; Gilman to Remsen, June 24, 1876; Joseph C. W. Frazer, "Harmon Northrop Morse," DAB, XIII, 243–244.

[32] TM, Sept. 4, 1876; Frederick H. Getman, *The Life of Ira Remsen* (Easton, Pa., 1940), 46–47.

[33] Gilman to Huxley, Dec. 20, 1875; Huxley to Gilman, Feb. 20, 1876.

[34] Martin to Gilman, April 5, 1876; Huxley to Gilman, April 23, 1876; Gilman to Martin, April 25, 1876.

late in July. Gilman met him in New York and found that he was "more youthful in appearance than I supposed," but seemed to show "learning, force & a spirit of work." [35] Martin must have begun mapping out his plans at once, for an August publication of the university contained a prospectus of his laboratory, citing its facilities in physiology as superior to any in the country.[36]

Before electing Martin professor, the trustees had hired Philip R. Uhler as "curator" to help organize the work in biology, while continuing as Peabody Institute librarian. This violation on the "plan of procedure" (which stated that professors would be consulted in choosing "assistants & adjuncts") is directly attributable to Gilman, who had a high regard for Uhler's rather limited capacities and was prone to overvalue collections.[37] The unwisdom of this premature hiring of a man whose basic interest was in collecting local variations appeared in conflicts during the first academic year. Moreover, the value of consulting professors in the selection of subordinates was shown in the case of William Keith Brooks, who filled exactly Martin's request to be backed up by a good morphologist. Brooks, a graduate of Williams, had done advanced work with Louis and Alexander Agassiz at Harvard and won a Ph.D. there in 1875. He had been a lifelong devotee of biology, and, according to Alexander Agassiz, though "not a very cultivated man," he was "good at heart" and had "the making of an excellent original worker." [38]

Gilman's first choice for the chair of Greek was William Watson Goodwin, who had been Eliot professor of Greek literature at Harvard since 1860. Goodwin had given Gilman letters of introduction to English scholars in July, 1875, and at the same time sent a tantalizing description of his attitude toward transferring to Hopkins:

I had a long talk with [Professor Francis J.] Child this morning. He feels very much as I do,—much attached to Harvard, but out of humor with

[35] Martin to Gilman, June 21, 1876; Gilman to Dobbin, Aug. 2, 1876, Dobbin-Brown Papers; Gilman to Johnson, Aug. 8, 1876.

[36] JHU *Circulars*, no. 4 (August, 1876), 6.

[37] ECM, March 13, 1876; TM, April 3, 1876; Gilman to Uhler, April 4, 1876; Gilman to Martin, May 30, 1876.

[38] Martin to Gilman, May 29, 1876; Henry Augustus Pilsbry, "William Keith Brooks," DAB, III, 90–91; [Alexander] Agassiz to Gilman, March 23, 1876, quoted in Abraham Flexner, *Daniel Coit Gilman: Creator of the American Type of University* (New York, 1946), 78.

many little (or great) things here which are taking—or seem to be taking—a wrong turn. . . . I feel strongly rooted here, and naturally love the college; but if the President succeeds in making the Faculty reduce seriously the influence of Greek in the course of preparation for College or in the Freshman year, I shall feel that self-respect requires me to pull down my flag & go somewhere where I can work under more favorable conditions.[39]

Goodwin even asked medical advice on the healthfulness of Baltimore's climate. But at last, underestimating Eliot's tenacity in his epochal battle against required Greek, Goodwin concluded that nobody at Harvard was really attacking his rights or the status of Greek. After talking the matter over again with Child, he wrote Gilman, "I am afraid we have not the courage to pull up all our roots here and transport ourselves into a new soil."

Although disappointed in his first hope, Gilman had good fortune in finding another candidate, Basil L. Gildersleeve, whose appointment Goodwin suggested in his letter of refusal.[40] Besides scholarly ability proved in publications, Gildersleeve had something else to recommend him. He had fought for the Confederacy and bore the mark of his Southern patriotism in a limp from a wound. While sectionalism had been formally ruled out as a basis for choosing professors, Gilman must have realized that in Baltimore a faculty with only Northern scholars would be vulnerable. The rumor was afloat in Baltimore that the South "was to be fairly and numerously represented in the Faculty," in spite of the Northern president.[41] Gildersleeve was born in Charleston, South Carolina, in 1831. He graduated from Princeton in 1849, studied at Berlin and Bonn, and took his Ph.D. in 1853 at Göttingen. In 1856 he became professor of Greek at the University of Virginia, a position he still held in 1875.[42]

Gilman arranged to meet the new candidate in Washington on December 8. Gildersleeve later called this conference, in which the two men talked late into the night on "the high theme of the Univer-

---

[39] Goodwin to Gilman, July 3, 1875.
[40] Goodwin to Gilman, Oct. 27, 1875. George M. Lane, professor of Latin at Harvard; Thomas A. Thacher, professor of Latin at Yale; and William D. Whitney —all vouched for Gildersleeve's capacities, the first two suggesting his name voluntarily (Lane to Gilman, Dec. 6, 1875; Thacher to Gilman, Dec. 13, 1875; Whitney to Gilman, Dec. 12, 1875).
[41] H. C. White to William Leroy Broun, Oct. 25, 1875, Broun Papers.
[42] Francis G. Allinson, "Basil Lanneau Gildersleeve," DAB, VII, 278–282.

sity that was to be," the turning point of his life.[43] He accepted the chair on December 11, telling Gilman, "To such confidence as you have reposed in me my whole nature responds with all its earnestness and I shall enter upon my new duties with heightened interest because my success will be in a measure yours." [44]

Gildersleeve's formal appointment on January 17, 1876,[45] made him the first professor in the university. He had already begun to analyze the problems ahead, writing Gilman:

As I understand my new work, my lowest level is to be the upper tier of my present senior class in which I am doing some real University work. It will take two or three years of earnest effort to get our material up to that point. After that time I should not despair of fair success in the University part of our scheme.[46]

After reading the *First Annual Report* and hearing Gilman's inaugural address on February 22, Gildersleeve testified, "I certainly did not dream that so much enthusiasm was left in me." [47]

Having won a first-rate scholar for the chair of Greek, Gilman felt that he could wait patiently for a Latin professor of equal caliber. There were more applicants for that chair than for any other—twenty by the end of March; even Ralph Waldo Emerson recommended a candidate.[48] George M. Lane, professor of Latin at Harvard, who had suggested Gildersleeve, later wrote Gilman high praise of the Englishman Henry J. Roby, a fellow of St. John's turned cotton manufacturer. At the request of Gilman, Lane sounded Roby, but received a negative reply.[49] Lane was one of the leading figures at Harvard, "a blessed exception" to the usual type of classics professor, a man who stressed the humanistic as much as the grammatical side of his subject. Gilman had taken it for granted that Lane was immovable, but when word reached him that this friendly adviser had dropped hints that he might like to come to Baltimore himself, Gilman promptly sent him an invitation. Lane did not decide at once. He would sorely miss the Harvard

[43] Gilman, "D. C. G."; Gildersleeve in JHU *Circulars* (n.s. 1908, no. 1), 34; Gildersleeve to Gilman, July 13, 1905.
[44] Gildersleeve to Gilman, Dec. 11, 1875, first and second letters of date.
[45] TM.   [46] Gildersleeve to Gilman, Dec. 30, 1875.
[47] Gildersleeve to Gilman, Feb. 28, 1876.
[48] Gilman to Gildersleeve, Jan. 4, March 29, 1876; Gilman to Emerson, Jan. 21, 1876.
[49] Lane to Gilman, Dec. 22, 1875, Jan. 31, 1876.

library, but the presence of Gildersleeve and an income that he could live on made the Hopkins offer tempting.[50] In the end Lane, like the other Harvard men whom Gilman had approached, decided to stay in Cambridge. When the need arose, Eliot could cite enough "university" characteristics at Harvard to hold his scholars. But reform had come none too soon.

Within a few days E. L. Godkin recommended to Gilman the classicist Charles D'Urban Morris.[51] This former fellow of Oriel had attended Lincoln College, Oxford, graduating with high honors in 1849. In 1853 he had come to America, married, and taken up work as head of various boys' schools and finally as professor at the University of the City of New York (later New York University). He had written two textbooks revealing some unusual ideas about the teaching of grammar.[52] Gilman at once reacted favorably to this prospect and asked for further information. Godkin wrote back that Morris was "among the half dozen best Classical Scholars in England or America, and an admirable tutor of College students. He has through a series of unfortunate accidents been wasted on boys." [53] After an interview, Gilman declared Morris "certainly the most fitting candidate who has appeared," but he visualized him in the post of adjunct professor of Greek and Latin, rather than as professor of Latin.[54] Morris at first did not seem to want a post at Hopkins, but Gilman portrayed the work so appealingly that he decided to make the change even though the $3,000 salary involved no financial improvement. Although his position was originally denoted "associate Professor of Greek and Latin," Gilman soon changed the title to "collegiate" professor, making his status scarcely distinguishable from that of professors who would have more advanced students. The choice delighted Gildersleeve, who wrote Gilman, "Morris is full of sap and fervor—he will prove a valuable acquisition." [55]

[50] James, *Charles W. Eliot*, I, 209; Charles Short to Gilman, Jan. 31, 1876; Lane to Gilman, Feb. 15, 1876.

[51] Gilman to Godkin, April 14, 1876.

[52] "The Death of Professor Morris," a brochure; "Charles Durban [sic] Morris," biographical data copied from a memorandum book of Morris'; E. H. C. to editor, clipping from an unidentified New York newspaper; all in GP.

[53] Godkin to Gilman, April 16, 1876.   [54] Gilman to Godkin, April 22, 1876.

[55] Morris to Gilman, June 6, 1876; Gilman to Morris, June 24, 27, 1876; TM, June 5, 1876; Gildersleeve to Gilman, June 10, 1876.

Elsewhere in languages, no noted scholars were won. Gilman angled for Francis J. Child, the leading Anglo-Saxon and Chaucerian expert in the country, who was bound down to reading freshman themes at Harvard. Although he finally declined, Child expressed great gratitude for the invitation because it had improved his status at Harvard.[56] In the field of modern English, nothing came of the excitement Sylvester stirred up over the possibility that Matthew or Thomas Arnold or George Meredith might come from England to Hopkins.[57] Except for visiting lecturers, English was left in oblivion during the first year, and it was long subordinate to German.

The fact that Hopkins opened its doors with an associate in Semitics reflected not the original planning of Gilman but rather his ability to seize unsought opportunities. Thomas Chalmers Murray, a graduate of Williams, wrote offering his services in that department and asking for a fellowship if no teaching post were open. He cogently presented the case for his field of learning, one long limited in America to theological schools and hence deprived of the scholarship needed "for the proper solution of many of our most vital historical and linguistic problems." Lavish recommendations for Murray came from Philip Schaff of Union Theological Seminary.[58] On this basis, Gilman crowded him in, giving him $750 as associate in Semitic languages and $500 as assistant in the library. Murray promptly arrived and—in the hottest part of the Baltimore summer—went to work helping with Gilman's correspondence and arranging the library.[59]

In the modern European languages no professors were appointed. A. Marshall Elliott, a North Carolinian of Quaker ancestry who had attended Haverford and Harvard and then spent eight years in Europe studying languages, at the same time tutoring and writing travel sketches, received an associateship in Romance languages.[60] Hermann C. G. Brandt, a native of Germany and a graduate of Hamilton College, where he had taught since 1874, became associate in German.

Johns Hopkins in its long flirtation with various American and Euro-

[56] Child to Gilman, Dec. 19, 1875; James, *Charles W. Eliot*, II, 15.
[57] Sylvester to Gilman, March 23, April 15, 1876.
[58] Murray to Gilman, March 1, 1876; Gilman to Schaff, April 18, 1876.
[59] Undated memorandum in Gilman's hand, GP; James Carey Thomas to Gilman, Aug. 18, 1876; Gilman to W. D. Whitney, May 29, 1876.
[60] Edward C. Armstrong, "Aaron Marshall Elliott," DAB, VI, 93–94; Elliott to Charles R. Lanman, Sept. 3, Dec. 28, 1875, Lanman Papers; TM, June 5, 1876.

pean philosophers has been well described as a "university in slow search of a philosopher." [61] During this first period of finding faculty members, however, it often appeared that Hopkins would open its doors with a professor in some branch of philosophy. Soon after his return from Europe, Gilman received a letter from William James, then instructor in physiology at Harvard, voluntarily recommending Charles Sanders Peirce for any chair "of Logic & mental science" and saying, "Of late years there has been no intellect in Cambridge of such general power & originality as his, unless one should except the late Chauncey Wright, and *effectively,* Peirce will always rank higher than Wright." Peirce could be to Hopkins, James maintained, what William Stanley Jevons had become to Owens College. [62]

Peirce was ultimately to come to Johns Hopkins, but Gilman, whose ideas on the relevance of religion to education were not far different from those of the old-time college presidents, did not seek him at once. Although he confided to President McCosh that Johns Hopkins "need not regard ecclesiastical relations," [63] he did not intend to ignore religion. There are echoes of his own undergraduate experience as well as forecasts of his community relations policies in his comment to a friend, "As we have no ecclesiastical standing, I feel very desirous to secure a strong & right minded philosopher,—one who can waken & lead forward the students." [64] Perhaps significantly, a Swedish philosopher named Carl Von Bergen, the candidate of the leading Unitarian clergyman of New York, Henry Whitney Bellows, received no encouragement. [65]

Gilman went with his problem to Noah Porter, who was probably still his ideal of a philosophy professor, if not of a university president. Porter recommended George Sylvester Morris, then teaching languages at Michigan, and M. Stuart Phelps, a Yale Ph.D. of 1874; but his highest praise went to Borden P. Bowne, a teacher of modern languages at the University of the City of New York and literary critic for the *Inde-*

[61] Max H. Fisch and Jackson I. Cope, "Peirce at the Johns Hopkins University," *Studies in the Philosophy of Charles Sanders Peirce*, ed. by Philip P. Wiener and Frederic H. Young (Cambridge, Mass., 1952), 280.

[62] James to Gilman, Nov. 25, 1875.

[63] Gilman to James McCosh, Jan. 28, 1876.

[64] Gilman to L. H. Atwater, April 18, 1876.

[65] Gilman to Von Bergen, Dec. 20, 1875.

pendent.[66] The negotiations with Bowne began promisingly and lasted through the first six months of 1876, but he took offense at the idea of a limited appointment.[67] Another candidate was the free-lancing Scotsman Thomas Davidson, whom Gilman thought of for the Latin post, but whose friends described him as a good philosophy teacher.[68] The new president of the University of Wisconsin, John Bascom, who had already had trouble with regents less congenial to higher learning than the trustees of Hopkins, volunteered to come as professor of philosophy, and Gilman arranged an interview in July.[69] But the university opened without anyone to teach philosophy, though among its fellows was a leading American philosopher of the future, Josiah Royce.

The story of the history department began much the same as that of philosophy. Gilman had early planned—as befitted an active member of the American Social Science Association—to found "an institute for the education of publicists, with history, political economy, &c, as leading subjects."[70] For a time it seemed that Francis A. Walker, who had succeeded him at Sheffield, might head such a department, but after the start of the 1876–1877 term, Walker declined.[71] Gilman had put out feelers in regard to John Lothrop Motley, whose diplomatic career had lately ended, and Jeremiah Lewis Diman, professor of history and political economy at Brown, but neither effort succeeded. Meanwhile, he had to fight off the persistent claims for a chair of history made by William Preston Johnston, one of his classmates at Yale, former aide-de-camp to Jefferson Davis, and professor of history and

[66] Gilman to Porter, Nov. 29, 1875; Porter to Gilman, Dec. 13, 1875.

[67] He accepted an appointment at Boston University that fall. See Gilman to Bowne, Jan. 15, 1876; Gilman to William L. Kingsley, April 20, 1876, Kingsley Family Papers, Manuscript Division, Yale University Library; Henry Kalloch Rowe, "Borden Parker Bowne," DAB, II, 522.

[68] Gilman to D. A. Goddard, March 24, [1876], Thomas Davidson Papers, Manuscript Division, Yale University Library; Gilman to Goddard, April 3, 1876; Charles Short to Gilman, Jan. 31, 1876. Still another candidate was J. P. Kennedy Bryan, recommended by McCosh (McCosh to Gilman, Jan. 24, 1876).

[69] Whatever may have transpired in this interview, Bascom was still at Wisconsin the next year and resigned only in 1887. See Merle Curti and Vernon Carstensen, *The University of Wisconsin, 1848–1925: A History* (Madison, 1949), I, 255; Ernest Sutherland Bates, "John Bascom," DAB, II, 33; Bascom to Gilman, May 15, July 7, 1876.

[70] W. D. Whitney to Gilman, March 15, 1875.

[71] ECM, June 5, 1876; Walker to Gilman, [March? 1876], Dec. 11, 1876.

English literature at Washington and Lee.[72] Gilman had arranged, however, to fall back on George Bancroft's secretary, Austin Scott, who was willing to commute from Washington. Scott's teaching experience consisted of two years as instructor at the University of Michigan, but Bancroft sent a very high opinion of him to Gilman, saying that Scott, a Yale graduate and Leipzig Ph.D., had studied history "scientifically and with special devotion to it, as worthy of the employment of a life." [73] Under final arrangements, Scott was to conduct classes—for $700 and his railroad fare—in English history since the Restoration and in sources of American history.[74] In spite of Gilman's elaborate hopes, no other social scientist was hired.

Plans for several departments were dropped before the fall of 1876. If Brush had agreed to come, undoubtedly there would have been a professorship of mineralogy. Persistent rumors that Clarence King of the Geological Survey would come to Hopkins to found a department of geology proved to be inaccurate.[75] William P. Trowbridge, the one Sheffield professor who volunteered to come to Baltimore, would gladly have fulfilled Gilman's plan for an engineering course dealing especially with the requirements of cities, but the department was postponed and the next year Trowbridge went to Columbia.[76] Whitney of Sheffield would have been placed in a chair of Sanskrit and comparative philology if he had followed his original impulse to join Gilman in Baltimore.[77] The suggested plan of one Mrs. Martin of Auburn, New York, to establish an endowed chair of Chinese was declined as premature.[78] The original omission of these professorships fitted the plan to develop the university gradually, but probably neither the trustees nor Gilman realized how long it would be before additions were made to the original staff of professors. It was not until 1883, when Paul Haupt was appointed in Semitic languages, that another professor

[72] Gilman to James Russell Lowell, March 30, 1876; Gilman to Diman, May 16, 1876; Johnston to Gilman, Jan. 7, 1876; R. L. Gibson to Gilman, Jan. 31, 1876; Melvin J. White, "William Preston Johnston," DAB, X, 153–154.

[73] Scott to Gilman, Jan. 19, 1876; Bancroft to Gilman, March 7, 1876.

[74] Scott to Gilman, April 13, June 19, 1876; JHU *Circulars,* no. 1 (June, 1876), 10.

[75] James T. Gardner to Gilman, May 29, 1875; J. D. Whitney to Gilman, April 1, 1876.

[76] Trowbridge to Gilman, Jan. 7, 1875, Feb. 5, 1876, May 14, 1877; Howard Potter to Gilman, Feb. 7, 1876; ECM, March 21, 1876.

[77] W. D. Whitney to Gilman, March 15, 1875.   [78] ECM, Feb. 29, 1876.

joined the staff. There was no professor in any branch of philosophy until 1884, when G. Stanley Hall was appointed in psychology. And it was only in the period 1891–1893, when a great log jam of associate professors finally broke, that professorships were established in history, Sanskrit and comparative philology, Romance languages, Latin, geology, jurisprudence, German, and English.[79]

A symmetry and rightness marked the first group of six who began the adventure of the new university together. During the seven years that they alone held the rank of professor, Gilman forged them into a united intellectual family. Specialists are probably less able than most human beings to survive alone and more in need of community. The specialization and variation within his faculty seemed to Gilman a great advantage. "It is fortunate for us," he concluded, "that although the number of professors is not large, they are men of very different antecedents, and of very different intellectual qualities, so that each in his way strengthens all the others." [80] They were, in fact, so different that each could be considered a symbol of a particular aspect of the university's meaning.

On almost any count Sylvester was the outstanding member of the first faculty. In him was epitomized the good will which the world of accomplished scholarship felt toward the new institution. He stood for the past—wishing the future well—for Europe and its generations of intellectual labor, for the fame of fulfilled genius. Possessed as he was by innumerable eccentricities, he served also to teach the lessons of patience and tolerance to the community and to the university administrators. Sylvester was sixty-two, a great deal older than the rest of the notably young faculty, but of that spirited group he was the most enthusiastic. One would have thought him the youngest of all.[81] He was a leader in the general opposition to rules and restraints. In Britain he had strongly criticized the "frozen formality of our academic institutions," and in a poem written as a young man, he had pleaded:

> Oh! why these narrow rules extol?
> These but restrain from ill,
> True virtue lies in strength of soul
> And energy of will.[82]

[79] Gilman, "The Johns Hopkins University (1874–1894)," in Steiner, *Education in Maryland*, 150.
[80] ARJH (1878), 11.   [81] Gilman, *Launching of a University*, 51.
[82] *Laws of Verse*, 120, 87.

Deeply involved in mathematics as he was, he never let himself become narrowly departmentalized. One of his students later declared that "the infection of his enthusiasm . . . was felt in every department of the University. . . . His aggressive and singular personality seemed to act the part of a ferment which spread itself through the entire body of the University. In its prosperity and progress and fame he took the deepest interest." Gilman testified in 1897 that some of Sylvester's "manifold suggestions" were still in effect.[83] As in everything else, Sylvester's mind was overproductive, turning out mediocre ideas along with the good and in greater quantity than could possibly be adopted. But Gilman, the careful, conscientious selector, was the perfect refining mechanism for this raw material. His fame, his unusual personality, his status as a seasoned warrior in the battle for truth made Sylvester the most conspicuous Hopkins professor of his day and a legend to the generations that followed him.

By the time Gildersleeve died in 1924, having served at Johns Hopkins until 1915, he represented many things to many men. But to an observer of 1876 he would primarily have called to mind the South and the intellectual opportunity that the new university offered it. Out of the poverty into which the war had plunged it, the South could rise to intellectual and spiritual riches, and Gildersleeve as much as any man from his section accomplished this ascent. His personality still holds its fascination as the years pass. What was the source of the strange pessimism that made him expect to fret himself to death long before he was sixty-five? How did this solemn strain combine with his brilliant and sometimes caustic wit? Did he, perhaps, feel himself the last of the dying genus of Hellenists? What kind of somber poetry was in the soul of a man whose everyday letters contained passages like this one?

This respite from my ordinary work has made me already eager to be at something more definite; I realize and realize most painfully that the hey-day of life is over and that I must gather up results with all speed. Perhaps this enormous pressure may result in something commensurate with the generosity on the one part [of the university] and the anxiety on the other [his own],—for now as during my whole life I am haunted by the ghost of failure, which I can only banish by gazing at duty. If the duty were only clearer!

[83] Fabian Franklin, *An Address Commemorative of Professor James Joseph Sylvester* (Baltimore, 1897), 9, 2.

On Gildersleeve's own testimony one thing is certain: without the guidance of Gilman and the nurturing atmosphere of Johns Hopkins, he would never have edited Pindar or founded the *American Journal of Philology*—though he would have done "some honest work." [84]

The young untaught genius of America found its way into the Hopkins faculty in the person of Rowland. In his student days, he would have thrived in a university such as the one he was helping to found, a place for early specialization and freedom from the restraints of group instruction. But he had had no such opportunity, and, as Gilman said of him, he was "one of those rare scholars who owe but little, if anything, to a mortal teacher." According to Gilman, Rowland said of the humble building in which the university was to begin operations, "All I want . . . is the back kitchen and a solid pier built up from the ground." The university gave him what he wanted, as it consistently did; and though "his requests were not always so restrained," justification came in his achievements. According to the analysis of one of his pupils, "In Rowland were combined to a marked degree the scientist's grasp of fundamental principles, the engineer's understanding of practical mechanics, mathematical aptitude, and manual dexterity." He was "erratic and moody but supercharged with new ideas." In an age "when the scientific lecture-rooms in America gloried in demonstrations of 'the wonders' of nature—'the bright light, the loud noise, and the bad smell,'" Rowland introduced instruments of precision—the best available, no matter what the cost; and when what he needed was not available, he built it himself. [85] The same characteristic that made him want the precise instead of the spectacular made him scorn scientists who posed as prophets of truth but cared most for fame and material gain. After Rowland's death at the age of fifty-two in 1901, John Trowbridge, who never failed in his praise of Gilman, Rowland, and their university and who perhaps regretted his refusal to join the staff in 1876, wrote to Gilman, "You gave him a great opportunity—one which he could not have had anywhere, I believe, in the world at the time he was in the greatest flower—and he was the man to seize it." [86]

Remsen, in contrast with Rowland, was a young American with

[84] Gildersleeve to Gilman, July 16, 1881, June 9, 1880, July 13, 1905.

[85] Ames, "Rowland," DAB, XVI, 198; G. Stanley Hall, *Life and Confessions of a Psychologist* (New York and London, 1923), 237; Gilman, *Launching of a University*, 70–71.

[86] Trowbridge to Gilman, Oct. 12, 1901.

enough money to go to Germany for advanced training, and he exemplified the German aspects of Johns Hopkins even more aptly than Gildersleeve, because he was from 1870 to 1872 a lecturer and laboratory assistant at Tübingen and thus actually on the staff of a German university. He experienced the frustration of the young scientists who, eager to continue their German-inspired researches, returned to America to find the colleges organized for an entirely different type of work. When he applied for a small room for a private laboratory at Williams, the president told him, "You will please keep in mind that this is a college and not a technical school." Although he was given a room for research after his first year, it was entirely inadequate, and only his own driving impulse toward experimentation kept him from surrendering and falling back on his unusual talent as a lecturer to beginners. Of the ideas which he and Morse put into effect at Hopkins, Remsen said, "They were not original, but they had never been tried in this country." This awareness of the German ideals that he was importing and a strong sense of the status and dignity of professors point up Remsen's claim to being the most German-oriented of the first Hopkins staff, despite the fact that Gilman, Gildersleeve, Rowland, and several of the associates and fellows had also done work at the German universities or laboratories. Remsen was outstanding also for his teaching ability; clarity, logic, and charm marked his lectures. He had none of the eccentricities which breed anecdotes or legends; in fact, he was the polished gentleman, and it reveals much of the man that no one in his laboratory dared work in shirt sleeves.[87]

The second Hopkins professor to come from England was Martin. Although inconspicuous in his own person, the field that he represented suffered intense public opposition because of the supposed antireligious implications of Darwinism and the horror aroused by vivisection. In the face of outcries against Martin's work on both these counts, the university stood firm. As Gilman wrote in 1905, "It is now hard to believe what prejudices then prevailed in respect to 'biology.' The science was dreaded as if it were to overthrow, or at least to undermine, religious belief."[88] Thus it was largely the theories and methods of

[87] Getman, *Life of Remsen*, 32, 42–43, 47, 67, 51–52, 68; William Albert Noyes and James Flack Norris, "Biographical Memoir of Ira Remsen, 1846–1927," *National Academy of Sciences Biographical Memoirs*, XIV (1931), 216–217.
[88] Gilman, *Launching of a University*, 52.

Darwin, Foster, and Huxley and through them a new way of looking at life that gave Martin his importance.[89] He was pre-eminent in the innovation of experimental procedures in physiology in this country and in his own researches developed new techniques for studying the isolated mammalian heart. Although he was a firm believer in the study of physiology for its own sake without consideration of its use in medicine —as a pure rather than a practical science [90]—his appointment still suggests the early awareness at the university of its potential role in medical education. Martin became in 1883 the first professor of the medical faculty, and his ideals of the primacy of science over practical application, of the study of healthy organisms before the study of those diseased, were among the ideals of the Hopkins medical school and important contributions to American medical education.

A friend commented of Charles D. Morris in 1876: "He is singularly transparent simple & modest, with a certain wholesome robust uprightness & manliness of nature. . . . He is a thorough gentleman—not the least of a prig, but lives habitually by a high standard, & could not possibly tolerate anything mean or tricky or vicious." [91] Besides these qualities, Morris had a strong religious inclination, and he liked to work with young men; his students were devoted to him.[92] His early death, in 1886, and the coincidence that a more famous Morris [93] was simultaneously connected with Johns Hopkins have robbed him of much attention from later generations. Nevertheless, at the time that Johns Hopkins opened, he signified an important aspect of its work. Whereas the other professors represented the innovations in graduate education, Morris represented the classical college, having his origins in the English colleges which were the forerunners of the American. In a statement which reveals more than he intended, Gilman said of Morris, "For some reason or other, the times seemed to be against him, and the number of students who elected his courses was never very large." [94] It is not hard to discover this reason: the university of which Morris was a part stood

[89] William H. Howell, in JHU *Circulars* (n.s. 1908, no. 5), 55.
[90] Russell H. Chittenden, "Henry Newell Martin," DAB, XII, 337–338.
[91] Merritt Trimble to Francis King, April 29, 1876, GP.
[92] Albert Shaw, "Recollections of President Gilman," typescript, GP; James P. Wright to Gilman, March 30, 1878.
[93] George Sylvester Morris, lecturer in the history of philosophy. The marble bust of Charles D'Urban Morris in the JHU Library is often identified as George Sylvester Morris.
[94] Gilman, *Launching of a University*, 52–53.

in basic antagonism to the type of collegiate training which he valued. The Hopkins idea was radical, stressing science and research and individual brilliance. Morris stood for the old foundations in classical learning, for the ideas of the "Yale Report of 1828." That few students who came to Hopkins studied with Morris is not surprising—Hopkins was designed only secondarily for those seeking collegiate training in the classics. Morris' presence at Hopkins showed that Gilman in fact believed to a considerable extent in the traditional college and in firm grounding to precede specialization. But Gilman's belief that Morris' work was a failure highlights the whole anticollegiate revolution centering in Hopkins, a revolution in which the kindly schoolmaster seemed out of place.

With these six men filling the professorships, the Johns Hopkins University began its academic career in the fall of 1876. Each man brought many contributions. But most conspicuously, Sylvester came with world renown, Gildersleeve with the sympathy and respect of the South, Rowland with youthful genius yet to be cultivated, Remsen with the ideals of the German universities, Martin with a publicly offensive science and the courage to withstand calumny and obscurantism, and Morris with the heritage of the old-time classical college. Uniting them all, evoking the best in them, granting simultaneous freedom and encouragement, asking only that they do their best work in their own way, stood Gilman, the leader in the great adventure.

: CHAPTER IV :

Birth and Trauma

GILMAN'S address at his inauguration on February 22, 1876, repeated the important declaration made in the *First Annual Report* of the month before. The university authorities would, he stated, proceed gradually and carefully, keeping regulations tentative, as befitted the liveliness of educational discussions in Europe and America.[1] The university, Gilman later recalled, "began without formulas and rules, without decrees of the faculty or the trustees, without regulations, and yet with that which was more binding than any code, the unanimous recognition of certain clear and definite principles."[2] The Hopkins plan of operation must therefore be sought in events and practices. Although officially 1876–1877 was "to be regarded simply as a preliminary or tentative year,"[3] many procedures that came to typify Hopkins emerged during this first term. On the other hand, several important general principles appeared in earlier public statements.

The most important principle lay, of course, in the meaning ascribed to "university." Gilman and other educators had long been trying to teach the public that "university" should mean something different from "college." As Johns Hopkins grew over the years, Gilman's mind pene-

---

[1] ARJH (1876), 15; "Hopkins Inaugural," 12. Gilman's address also appears in *Addresses at the Inauguration of Daniel C. Gilman as President of the Johns Hopkins University, Baltimore, February 22, 1876* (Baltimore, 1876), 17–64, with minor typographical differences. Page citations in notes for the inaugural address refer to *University Problems.*

[2] Gilman, "The Johns Hopkins University," *Cosmopolitan,* XI (1891), 463.

[3] JHR (1877), 61.

trated ever more deeply into the potentialities of the university idea, but the rather inexact definition given in his Hopkins inaugural was his best up to that time. "The University," he said, "is a place for the advanced and special education of youth who have been prepared for its freedom by the discipline of a lower school." Although the forms and methods of universities might vary, Gilman felt that three functions must always belong to them: investigation, teaching, and bestowal of honors. But the only one of these functions that he labeled an obligation was teaching. As he made clear in the *First Annual Report*, "the chief work of the University" was "the instruction of youth." He reiterated this primacy of the teaching function over the research function when he differentiated the university from the learned society: "In the universities teaching is essential, research important; in academies of science research is indispensable, tuition rarely thought of." [4] When Charles S. Peirce defined "university" for the *Century Dictionary*, he implied that it had nothing to do with instruction; and though his statements were not always so strong as his assertion that "the chief obstacle to the advance of science among students of science in the modern era has been that they were teachers," he did insist on the subordination of the university's teaching function to its research function.[5] Possibly his contact with the actual practices at Johns Hopkins, which he often praised, influenced Peirce in this idea, but it was clearly not the definition that Gilman adhered to when the university opened. To Gilman, the outstanding factor making a university was that (albeit in an advanced and special way) it taught.

Yet to informed and objective observers, the most important principle of the Johns Hopkins leaders in 1876 must have been their belief that research was desirable for the sake of both its power to add to knowledge and its effectiveness as a method of graduate training. What brought their institution immediately to the forefront in American education was their determination that the long-ignored investigative function of the university be given new stress. A casual listener, however, might have sat through Gilman's inaugural and missed this point altogether; his words tended to conceal the radically new position to be given research. For example, Gilman asked, "Of what grade will [the

[4] "Hopkins Inaugural," 13–14; ARJH (1876), 19.
[5] Max H. Fisch, "General Introduction: The Classic Period in American Philosophy," in Fisch, ed., *Classic American Philosophers* (New York, 1951), 30–31.

students] be?" and answered by saying, "Mature enough to be profited by university education." [6] Coming after his vague definition of "university," this was not very enlightening. The research side of the university could have been forecast, however, by any close observer of Gilman's procedure in selecting a faculty. In the *First Annual Report,* his reference to the professors revealed his intention to have Hopkins advance knowledge as well as educate youth:

It is their *researches* in the library and the laboratory; their utterances in the class room and in private; their example as students and *investigators,* and as champions of the truth; their *publications* through the journals and the scientific treatises which will make the University in Baltimore an attraction to the best students, and serviceable to the intellectual growth of the land.

He specifically cited Rowland's published discoveries as "an indication of the work which the trustees are ready to encourage." [7] In 1876, Gilman felt sure that scholarly investigation made better teachers and teaching made better investigators,[8] and partly because of his faith that the two main functions of a university strongly complemented each other, his public statements, especially the inaugural, did not indicate how revolutionary for America was this conscious fostering of research. Undoubtedly, Gilman was enthusiastically in favor of research, but publicly at least, he chose to defend it less for itself than for its enhancing of the teaching function.[9]

In 1871 Gilman had forecast a university for graduate study only, "to which young men will resort for the highest sort of scholastic training, and to which they should be refused admission, unless they have previously been well trained for a considerable period in the institutions of the next lower or collegiate grade." [10] At that time he had thought that the country needed at least one strictly graduate university, and

[6] P. 30.   [7] ARJH (1876), 21–22. Italics added.

[8] "Hopkins Inaugural," 19.

[9] As the years passed, however, Gilman lost some of his faith in the interrelationship between productive investigation and good teaching (Gilman, *Launching of a University,* 244).

[10] "On the Growth of American Colleges and Their Present Tendency to the Study of Science: A Paper by Daniel C. Gilman, One of the Professors in the Sheffield Scientific School of Yale College," 114. This expansion of the "Sibley College Address," from an unidentified printed source, is bound in "Various Speeches and Articles," I, GP.

the plan for such an institution seems to have been strong in his mind in January, 1875. By the time of his inaugural, however, his thinking involved a more complex university, offering varied opportunities to teachers, students, and the public. Hopkins would have a collegiate section. It would function as an examining and degree-granting agency for others besides its students, it would offer special training and cultural development to various groups within the community, and it would disseminate knowledge through publications.[11] Partly because of public pressures, Hopkins was made to fit a definition which was broadly inclusive. That Gilman was not as single-eyed in his interest in graduate education and research as tradition pictures him, that he bent with the wind of public opinion, that he placed the effect of higher studies on the student over their contribution to the advancement of knowledge, should not lessen his stature. Much of his importance and most of his success came because his aims were plural, his method pragmatic, and his values centered in the living individual.

Although a university must furnish a retreat where scholars can feel the reality of past and future, it must live also in the present. No university is an island. It must relate itself to the surrounding community and to its fellow institutions, if for nothing more than to assure its survival.

The Johns Hopkins University was bound to the outside world, for example, by its financial dependence on the B. & O. Railroad, in whose securities the founder had placed so much faith. By the fall of 1878 the Howard Street property alone had cost over $220,000, more than one year's income, and a reserve accumulating fund to provide for eventual building at Clifton drained about 50 per cent of all income. The amount reserved was at first $100,000 a year.[12] This high figure is explained in part by the fact that the reserve fund was not solely to provide buildings. Certain board members suspected that B. & O. stock might not have the stability attributed to it by the founder. At a surprisingly early date, the potential danger was recognized. In May, 1874, Francis White and Francis King of the finance committee reported that they agreed with the stipulation in the will that the B. & O. stock should not be sold, yet they could not fail to see "from the instability of all things, that temporary suspension of Dividends from Balto & Ohio R. R. Stock

[11] "Hopkins Inaugural," 34–35.
[12] TM, Nov. 4, 1878, April 2, 1877; "Hopkins Inaugural," 5.

might follow upon War, or the occurrence of other National Calamity, and that prudence will require provision to be made for such possible event." It is significant that Garrett, president of the B. & O. and chairman of the finance committee of the university, had not yet attended any of its meetings when this report was drawn up.[13]

Gilman explained to the public in his inaugural the financial necessity for moderation and did his best to dispel the exuberant imaginings of the community, especially those involving "dreams of monumental structures and splendid piles and munificent salaries." Hopkins did not seem so fantastically wealthy on the basis of its actual income, which Gilman estimated as a little more than half the income of Harvard. Vague utterances and overgenerous expectations forced him to speak frankly: "Till the original benefaction is supplemented by other gifts, or the growth of Baltimore increases the value of our present investments, we must be contented with good work in a limited field." [14] "Good work in a limited field" was of necessity the motto of Johns Hopkins throughout Gilman's administration and into the twentieth century.

Financial dangers seemed distant and unlikely at the time of Gilman's inaugural, but the threat to the university from anti-intellectualism and provincialism was very much in the president's mind. His experiences in California had perhaps made him more wary in this regard than was actually necessary. On the assumption that the known would be less feared or distrusted than the unknown, Gilman from the first advocated wide publicity for the university's affairs, feeling that "although this is a private corporation, it is founded for public purposes,—and there is no surer safeguard for the wise administration of its affairs in all the years to come than a knowledge that it will be scrutinized by enlightened men." [15] In going to the public, as in his inaugural, Gilman made an emphatic case for the potential usefulness of the kind of knowledge that the university fostered. He did not present a narrowly utilitarian defense—he carefully maintained that remote utility was as worthy of support as immediate advantage; but it was nevertheless the social contribution of his university that he put forth as its justification. He stressed the likelihood that Hopkins would provide departments of learning which were then being neglected to the detriment of the country. Among these he numbered training in medicine, "the princi-

[13] TM, May 4, 1877.   [14] "Hopkins Inaugural," 4–6.   [15] ARJH (1876), 8.

ples of good government," engineering for municipal needs, subjects affecting national surveys, architecture, and those fields in which professors were needed "for the highest academic posts." Gilman hoped, as he had at California, that a higher caliber of political leader would emerge from the university:

There is a call for men who have been trained by other agencies than the caucus for the discussion of public affairs; men who know what the experience of the world has been in the development of institutions, and are prepared by intellectual and moral discipline to advance the public interests, irrespective of party, and indifferent to the attainment of official stations. To this end our plans converge.

The missionary impulse, bred so intimately into Gilman's life, illuminated his defense of the university: it would aid students from the desolated South; it would set an example for "backward" nations where efforts to found universities were currently being led by Americans. Some years later Gilman entitled an address "The Utility of Universities." The idea was not new to him then; it permeated his inaugural. The establishment of universities stood for many things, he asserted, first among them, however, "a reaching out for a better state of society than now exists." Even the freedom which he demanded for the university he justified by its need to adjust to a rapidly changing world.[16]

Another potential pitfall for the university was the publicly felt antagonism between science and religion, most specifically between evolutionism and natural theology. The battles of sectarianism had scarred many of the older American colleges.[17] Against these dangers, the new university had carefully bulwarked itself, declaring a sort of benevolent neutralism (in the interests of which Gilman refrained from joining any local congregation, leaving his membership in the Yale College church[18]). Gilman hoped that a similar wide sympathy would offer protection against the warfare between science and religion. He announced as one of the postulates of university education: "Religion has nothing to fear from science, and science need not be afraid of re-

[16] "Hopkins Inaugural," 18, 20–26, 30, 12, 35.
[17] For a general account, see Richard Hofstadter and Walter P. Metzger, *The Development of Academic Freedom in the United States* (New York, 1955), chaps. iv–vii.
[18] Gilman to F. B. Dexter, Nov. 10, 1877, "Miscellaneous Letters by and about Daniel C. Gilman," Rare Book Room, Yale University Library.

ligion. Religion claims to interpret the word of God, and science to reveal the laws of God. The interpreters may blunder, but truths are immutable, eternal, and never in conflict." [19] As at California, he instituted a voluntary daily chapel. It was Gilman himself rather than one of the devout Quaker trustees who suggested this idea.[20] He conducted the brief religious service personally for many years, and his past activities indicate that this program was motivated by a profound interest in the students' religious life. It was, however, also a very apt device to soothe a community where godlessness was constantly attributed to the university.[21] This charge came alive even before instruction began. True to the new age, it was not a sectarian controversy, but a quarrel between orthodox Christianity and the theory of evolution. The religionists chose the ground.

Gilman had invited Thomas Huxley, with whom he had conferred in England and whose collaborator Martin he had appointed to his faculty, to give a course of public lectures at Johns Hopkins. Huxley, who was to be in America only during August and September, could not accept, but he did agree to give an "opening address." [22] By inviting the most famous publicist of Darwin's ideas, Gilman gained for the university some of the publicity attached to a tour which made news throughout the country. But among those reading the accounts of Huxley's every step were some who had not forgotten his offenses. This was, after all, the man who had humbled Bishop Wilberforce in the famous monkey-grandfather exchange.[23] To many of the orthodox he embodied atheism and materialism, and they were on the alert.

The affair in Baltimore promised to be a great success. The trustees were enthusiastic, and the public overwhelmed them with requests for tickets. But with his usual prescience about public reactions, Gilman asked two of the trustees if they did not think that there should be a prayer. They felt it inappropriate; [24] so Huxley spoke in the jammed Academy of Music on September 12, 1876, without priestly ceremonies. The speech, consisting in large part of "good advice" on medical educa-

[19] "Hopkins Inaugural," 18.   [20] Thomas to Gilman, Aug. 2, 1876.

[21] William Peters Reeves, "The Hopkins in '84," typescript, JHUP.

[22] Gilman to Huxley, June 8, 1876. For an account of Huxley's trip to America, see Leonard Huxley, *Life and Letters of Thomas Henry Huxley* (New York, 1901), I, 493–502.

[23] Huxley, *Life of Huxley*, I, 192–204.

[24] Johnson to Gilman, Aug. 20, 1876; Gilman, *Launching of a University*, 22.

tion, must surely have bored part of the audience, but others found it inspiring. A West Virginia physician determined, on hearing the address, that his four-year-old son must attend Johns Hopkins.[25] Although catching no such note of inspiration, the Baltimore newspapers praised the address.[26] But one of Huxley's passages did offer grounds for rational attack by orthodox Christians:

So sure as it is that men live not by bread, but by ideas, so sure is it that the future of the world lies in the hands of those who are able to carry the interpretation of nature a step further than their predecessors; so certain is it that the highest function of a university is to seek out those men, cherish them, and give their ability to serve their kind full play.

The stress on the "interpretation of nature" carried through the entire address, and in defining liberal education, Huxley spoke of the equal importance of "the two great sides of human activity—art and science." [27] A Baltimore citizen wrote a local editor in criticism of this aspect of the speech: "He says not a word about the science of *morals*, and of course he takes no account of revealed *religion*." [28] But this objection was a mere fluttering of wings: the attack came not simply against Huxley's narrowness.

A Presbyterian weekly, the New York *Observer*, launched the major assault. Its reporter impartially summarized Huxley's speech and praised his oratorical style. But the closing paragraphs of the article loosed the barrage:

The lecturer took his seat amidst "full handed thunders." A momentary pause followed, which was terminated by President Gilman, who pronounced the exercises closed. As they had been *opened*, so they were *concluded*, without *prayer or benediction*.

The writer implied that perhaps this "honor which was done Evolutionism" by neglecting Christian duty might represent truckling to Huxley. In fact, he hoped that it was nothing worse, observing:

Honor here was refused to the Almighty. The gentlemen at the head of the University were well aware of this. But if the neglect was due to the un-

[25] Accordingly, Newton Diehl Baker, who was to become Wilson's Secretary of War, entered the university twelve years later (Elting E. Morison, "Newton Diehl Baker," DAB, XXII, 17).

[26] Baltimore *American, Sun*, Sept. 13, 1876.

[27] Thomas Huxley, "Address on University Education," *American Addresses, with a Lecture on the Study of Biology* (London, 1886), 119–120, 102.

[28] P. H. to editor, Baltimore *American*, Sept. 15, 1876.

christian or materialistic sentiments of the authorities, then we can only say, God help them, and keep students away from the precincts of the young institution.[29]

A great outcry followed this article, and one of the fellows predicted that his friends would now blame any objectionable religious views that he might hold on his connection with the university.[30]

But Hopkins was not without defenders. John Leyburn, a local Presbyterian minister and a trustee of Princeton, wrote both the *Observer* and another offended journal, the *Presbyterian,* assuring readers "that there was prayer at the inauguration & a full & very evangelical one & that there was no more reason for prayer before Huxley's than before any other College or Lyceum lecture." [31] One letter printed in the *Observer* suggested that inviting Huxley to speak merely supported Gilman's statement in his inaugural that religion had nothing to fear from science. Another letter announced that half the professors and fellows were sons of Presbyterians and recalled the "known energy and Christian courtesy of Mr. Gilman." [32] At length came a *détente.* A New York minister replied to a Baltimore colleague's protestation of the university's innocence:

It was bad enough to invite Huxley. It were better to have asked God to be present. It would have been absurd to ask them both.

I am sorry Gilman began with Huxley. But it is possible yet to redeem the University from the stain of such a beginning. No one will be more ready than I to herald a better sign.[33]

But the sixteen public lectures on "The Theories of Biology" which Brooks gave early in 1877, with concentration on the ideas of Darwin, must have seemed only another evil omen.[34]

Gilman already knew from his own experiences at California and Andrew D. White's troubles in New York the power of the religious issue. Long before Huxley's address he had shown great eagerness to avoid offending religious sensibilities. This attitude at times brought

[29] S. S., "Johns Hopkins University and Prof. Huxley," New York *Observer,* Sept. 21, 1876.

[30] Walter Hines Page to Sarah Jasper, Oct. 15, 1876, quoted in Burton J. Hendrick, *The Training of an American: The Earlier Life and Letters of Walter H. Page, 1855–1913* (Boston and New York, 1928), 71.

[31] Leyburn to Gilman, Oct. 2, 1876.   [32] New York *Observer,* Oct. 5, 19, 1876.

[33] Quoted in Gilman, *Launching of a University,* 22–23. Italics apparently added by Gilman are deleted.

[34] JHC, I, 109.

him close to compromising his professed standards of freedom. Among the episodes in which he seemed to truckle to clerical opinion was one notable case in 1885 involving Herbert B. Adams' choice of textbooks.[35] On another occasion, when the biology students purchased a bust of their hero Darwin, Gilman encouraged them to put the busts of other scientists alongside it, making it less conspicuous.[36]

Seldom has advice been so superfluously given as when Richard T. Ely, associate in political economy, wrote Gilman that "the favor of religious newspapers is a help to the work of any university, while their disfavor may become a very serious injury." [37] Nothing pleased Gilman more than to let the press know of addresses by famous clerics at the opening of the Hopkins term, such as those of Arthur Penrhyn Stanley in 1878 and Frederic William Farrar in 1885, dean and archdeacon respectively of Westminster.[38] In the fall of 1879, Gilman himself gave a series of Sunday evening talks on great scientists, no doubt showing the compatibility of their intellectual achievements and religious faith.[39] In his *Annual Reports,* in his speeches, in writings for religious periodicals, he made a specific plea for Johns Hopkins as nonsectarian, but not irreligious, and a broader plea for learning as congenial to religion. Although not many undergraduates chose the Hopkins pretheological course, ministers often came as special students in history or languages; thus, in 1886, the university could announce that thirty-eight of its "former students" were clergymen.[40] Gilman could, furthermore, point to contributions of his faculty to the understanding of scriptural languages. But beyond the religious applications of any subject, he insisted that study itself was "on the whole, favorable to the growth of spiritual life, to the development of uprightness, unselfishness and faith, or, in other words, it is opposed to epicureanism and materialism." In the religious press, he pleaded for the discussion of "great themes in a manly spirit, rather than petty differences in a narrow way." [41] He was educating the public, and his touch was ever deft.

It was also Gilman the community relations expert who instituted at

---

[35] See pp. 175–176 below.
[36] William H. Howell, "Daniel Coit Gilman," typescript, GP.
[37] Ely to Gilman, Aug. 2, 1882.
[38] ARJH (1879), 37; JHC, V, 28; Gilman, *Launching of a University,* 75–78.
[39] Lanman diary, Oct. 26, Nov. 23, Dec. 7, 1879.
[40] JHC, V, 79; ARJH (1880), 8.
[41] JHC, IV, 47; *The Congregationalist,* Oct. 12, 1881, copy in GP.

the very beginning of the first academic year a program of public lectures. The announced purpose was to show the public "the methods and principles on which we rely." [42] During the first year, at least ten lecturers gave approximately twenty lectures each in Hopkins Hall, an auditorium which had been built onto the back of the Howard Street building. "The afternoon lectures have proved a hit," Gilman wrote President White, "—those of [James Russell] Lowell & [Francis J.] Child being so especially. They 'captured' the town, & people talked of the Chaucer & Dante revival, much as they do of Moody & Sankey!" But William D. Whitney, who lectured on philology, was unhappy with the ostentation of the program, calling it "too much like 'starring it in the provinces'—an occupation which I cannot possibly relish." [43]

Three of the lecture series of the first year were later published in book form. Besides teaching a small group in constitutional law, Thomas M. Cooley, judge of the Michigan Supreme Court and professor of law at the University of Michigan, lectured on torts, and the resulting book was long the authority on the subject.[44] Simon Newcomb published his lectures as *Popular Astronomy*, and Francis A. Walker's lectures on money were published in 1878. Other lecturers were J. E. Hilgard of the Coast Survey, who spoke on geodetic surveys, and John W. Mallet, professor of chemistry at the University of Virginia, who discussed waste chemical products.[45] To show the public that the university had not forgotten its obligation to medical training, John Shaw Billings was scheduled to lecture on the history of medicine, but this course was delayed until the second year.[46]

As the university touched the citizens of Baltimore through public lectures, so it reached out to its fellow universities through scholarly periodicals. For the idea of university-sponsored publications, Gilman gave primary credit to his trip to Europe and especially to his observations in Germany. There were, however, in the United States such publications as the *Smithsonian Contributions to Knowledge* and the *American Journal of Science*, which proved the usefulness of scholarly

[42] ARJH (1878), 28.
[43] Gilman to White, April 29, 1877; Whitney to Gilman, May 9, 1877.
[44] George M. Sharp to Simeon E. Baldwin, May 9, 1877, Baldwin Family Papers, Manuscript Division, Yale University Library; A. C. McLaughlin, "Thomas McIntyre Cooley," DAB, IV, 393.
[45] ARJH (1878), 43.
[46] ARJH (1877), 10–11; Chesney, *Johns Hopkins Hospital*, I, 46.

periodicals; furthermore, the printed proceedings of various societies pointed out a need by their painful inadequacy.[47] Johns Hopkins was the cradle of the scholarly journal in America, and the year 1878 is usually associated with its first venture. But as a matter of fact, the beginnings of this new contribution to the intellectual life of the country trace back to the fall of 1876, when the first moves toward organizing the *American Journal of Mathematics* were made.

This journal has a dual importance: as the first publication in America to deserve classification with the leading European mathematical journals and as the prototype of the multitude of American scholarly periodicals now in existence. As in all such ventures, a number of people interacted to bring forth the new creation, and Gilman cited the influence of Sylvester, who had since 1855 edited the British *Quarterly Journal of Pure and Applied Mathematics,* and of Rowland, Newcomb, and Story.[48] Gilman held a dinner for various American mathematicians on November 3, 1876, in honor of Sylvester, and quite probably saw to it that the idea of a journal "emerged." Sylvester reported later that Gilman had badgered him to found the journal almost from the moment of his arrival.[49]

As a result of the November 3 meeting, on November 8, 1876, scarcely a month after classes had begun, a crudely duplicated letter went out from Baltimore, proposing the establishment of "the American Journal of Pure and Applied Mathematics." Past efforts in this direction, it said, had suffered from the lack of two things—contributors and funds. The first could be remedied only by the efforts of American mathematicians, but the Hopkins trustees might provide financial support. The letter cited as an example for the trustees the action of "the enlightened government of Prussia" in promising to make up deficits for *Crelle's Journal of Pure and Applied Mathematics.*[50] Gilman reported to the trustees more than forty letters in response, all but one favoring the new journal. Almost all who wrote promised to subscribe,[51] and many

[47] Gilman, *Launching of a University,* 116.
[48] Gilman, manuscript draft of a report to the trustees [spring, 1877], GP.
[49] Benjamin Peirce to Gilman, Oct. 30, 1876; "Remarks of Prof. Sylvester, at the Farewell Reception Tendered to Him by the Johns Hopkins University, Dec. 20, 1883 (Reported by Arthur S. Hathaway)," typescript, GP.
[50] Sylvester's draft and several duplicated copies are in GP. It was signed by Sylvester, Rowland, Newcomb, and Story.
[51] See note 48 above.

74

sent suggestions—such as not to set standards so erudite as to frighten off American readers. In a detailed letter, Joseph Henry suggested that the new journal should be an instrument for education as well as for publication of advanced researches.[52] His advice was not taken.

All the good will in the world could not solve the business problems of starting a new journal. Gilman failed to find a publisher to assume the actual ownership, despite the promise of subsidization from the trustees. It was suggested that Gilman himself take over the financial control, but he demurred.[53] On Gilman's advice, the trustees then turned over the business aspects of the project entirely to Sylvester, promising limited aid. But financial responsibilities, Sylvester insisted, would disturb his mind and handicap him in fulfilling his scientific duties.[54] As the matter was finally settled, the associate or assistant editor handled the business affairs of the journal, and the trustees gave a $500 subsidy per volume, about one-fifth the total cost.[55] The journal was published "under the auspices" of the university, but the trustees specifically limited their part of the risk.[56]

It was January, 1878, before the first issue of the journal reached the press;[57] by that time, *Notes from the Chemical Laboratory*, precursor of the *American Chemical Journal*, had already come into existence. This venture seemed necessary because of the refusal of the *American Journal of Science* to print the reports of Remsen's laboratory in its already-crowded pages and the irregular publication of the *American Chemist*. On May 7, 1877, Remsen wrote Gilman (probably having been asked to put in writing an earlier request) that since four men in his laboratory were doing original research it was desirable to publish announcements of accomplished and proposed work:

1st. That we may be recognized as soon as possible as belonging to the working Chemists of the country; 2nd. That the results of our labors may be insured to us or, in other words, to establish our priority.

[52] William G. Peck to Newcomb, Jan. 22, 1877; W. H. Pettee to Story, Dec. 18, 1876; Henry to Sylvester, Newcomb, Rowland, and Story, Dec. 12, 1876; all in GP.
[53] See note 48 above. [54] Sylvester to Gilman, May 9, 1877.
[55] The first four volumes cost $9,654.83 (Craig, "Financial Report of the American Journal of Mathematics," Nov. 8, 1882, GP).
[56] *American Journal of Mathematics*, I (1878), title page, iv.
[57] Sylvester to Newcomb, Jan. 14, 1878, Simon Newcomb Papers, Division of Manuscripts, Library of Congress.

In Germany, France and England there are journals intended for such preliminary publications, and articles sent to them are sure to appear promptly.

Gilman's keen interest in the plan and the trustees' willingness to cooperate brought authorization on the day that Remsen submitted his formal request. The first three numbers of the *Notes* were brought out that month.[58]

According to Gilman's inaugural, Hopkins sought "a generous affiliation with all other institutions, avoiding interferences, and engaging in no rivalry." [59] The most important of these affiliations was with Harvard. Eliot early extended invitations to Gilman and the trustees to come to Harvard as his guests and make whatever observations they cared to, and in March, 1876, Gilman and King (and probably Francis White) visited Harvard to study the techniques used by its treasurer.[60] Gilman attributed to Eliot "a strong influence upon my personal character," [61] and it would be hard to overemphasize the fact that he asked Eliot, and not Porter or Brush, to give an address at his inauguration. Gilman made the request, he said, not only because of Eliot's inspiring ideas of future university development but also because "historically, it would be a grand thing to have the oldest College in the land greet the youngest,—especially as the counsels of the Senior were sought so early & have been followed in so many important measures, by the junior." [62] The idea of the *Annual Report* had its most direct source in the example of Eliot's reports at Harvard; Gilman copied by hand long sections of Eliot's report for 1874–1875.[63] He never concealed from Eliot his efforts to win Harvard faculty members and wrote him somewhat guiltily, "I shall be sorry if without gain to our work, we make trouble in yours; but what can we do, when we receive information that this or that desirable person would like to come here[?]" If the men approached would not tell Eliot the situation, Gilman assured him, he would, re-

---

[58] Gilman, *Launching of a University*, 116; Remsen to Gilman, May 7, 1877, with marginal note by Gilman; ARJH (1878), 49.

[59] P. 35.

[60] Gilman to Eliot, Jan. 15, March 15, 1876; Nette Silsbee to Gilman, March 6, 1876.

[61] Gilman to Eliot, Dec. 1, 1876, Eliot Papers.

[62] Gilman to Eliot, Jan. 25, 1876.

[63] Gilman to Eliot, Jan. 18, 1876; ARJH (1876), 8; Gilman notebook, "1876± Notes Chiefly on Universities."

vealing what was written "word for word." Eliot sent a congenial answer, commenting that he would "have thought it very odd if there had been no men here whom you cared to try for." Later Eliot let Child and Lowell miss classwork in order to lecture at Hopkins.[64]

Although Hopkins failed to lure any of the leading Harvard figures away, the entry of a new university with large salaries into the field did hamper Harvard's attempt to enlarge its faculty. But it was not long before Hopkins was preparing professors for Harvard, starting with Lanman, who became professor of Sanskrit there in 1880. Another way that Hopkins aided Harvard was in teaching the importance of advanced training and research. Grants for scholarly investigation seemed to be more easily obtained from Eliot after the Baltimore experiment began.[65] Eliot's statement at the Hopkins twenty-fifth anniversary celebration has been often quoted: "I want to testify that the graduate school of Harvard University, started feebly in 1870 and 1871, did not thrive, until the example of Johns Hopkins forced our Faculty to put their strength into the development of our instruction for graduates." [66] But the letters of the 1870s and 1880s prove the influence of Hopkins even more clearly. Charles Eliot Norton, John Trowbridge, and Benjamin Peirce were especially forthright in their statements that Hopkins was a great stimulus to their university in Cambridge. Peirce, according to his son, considered Hopkins "as a great advance in the university system of this country, and as the only American institution where the promotion of science is the supreme object, and the trick of pedagogy is reckoned as of no value." [67]

There were, of course, moments of acrimony in the generally friendly competition between the two universities. Certain Harvard men complained about the importation of Lanman from Hopkins rather than the elevation of one of their number.[68] When Gildersleeve was in England seeking professors for Hopkins, he reported to Gilman disturbing signs of the aggressive competition for scholars which Hopkins had aroused in Harvard. "I wish the other colleges all prosperity," he wrote,

[64] Gilman to Eliot, March 15, 1876; Eliot to Gilman, March 23, 1876, quoted in James, *Charles W. Eliot,* II, 13; Eliot to Gilman, March 1, 1877.
[65] James, *Charles W. Eliot,* II, 14, 19–20.
[66] *Hopkins Twenty-fifth Anniversary,* 105.
[67] Norton to Gilman, Feb. 14, 1881; Trowbridge to Gilman, Dec. 10, 1879; James Mills Peirce to Gilman, April 21, 1882.
[68] William E. Story to Gilman, July 26, 1880.

"but I am not Christian enough to rejoice at being thwarted. You take a different view, I know, and I rejoice that we have a philosophic mind at the helm." [69] Generally Gilman's "philosophic" attitude prevailed. As for Eliot—"our early counsellor and our constant friend," as Gilman called him [70]—he never showed any deviation from the view that he once expressed to Gilman: "There is no doubt that good work done in one university helps all other growing universities. You help us therefore." [71]

The university was born. It had suffered the first shocks of a harsh environment and survived. It had begun to adapt itself as any living thing must. It had reached out to others for communication and help as any human thing must. And it welcomed life with a readiness, an impatience, to be off on the missions which the age had given it.

[69] Gildersleeve to Gilman, June 30, 1880.
[70] *Launching of a University*, 129.
[71] Eliot to Gilman, March 9, 1880, in James, *Charles W. Eliot*, II, 30.

: CHAPTER V :

Fellowships and Fellowship

A FAMILYLIKE unity bound the members of the early Hopkins together. Partly this sprang from a mutual sense of the novelty of the institution, partly from felt common aims. As Gilman wrote in 1891 and as had been even truer before that time, "Here are masters and pupils, not two bodies, but one body, a union for the purpose of acquiring and advancing knowledge." [1] Another factor linking professors and students was the lack of any real break between them—the fellows were a vital bridge.

The fellowship system probably did more than any other program to establish the success of Johns Hopkins as an institution dedicated to the advancement of knowledge. Gilman's definition of a university entailed the highest scholarly work, the trustees favored it, and productive scholars held the professorships. But these alone would probably have failed—as earlier brave attempts had failed—if some system of financial support for advanced students had not been worked out. Earlier experience had convinced many American educational leaders that without financial aid to students no graduate school could flourish.[2] It would therefore be fruitless to assign credit for the fellowship idea to any one man or university. The inspiration came ultimately from the English fellowship system, and Gilman's preservation of quotations on the subject from Mark Pattison and John Henry Newman showed that he recognized this ancestry.[3] But modifications in the English system were

[1] "Hopkins," *Cosmopolitan*, XI, 466.
[2] Storr, *Beginnings of Graduate Education*, 130–131.
[3] Collection of unbound quotations labeled by Gilman "Value of Fellowships—Opinions from Harvard Yale Princeton etc," JHUP.

obviously required. The religious and life-tenure aspects of the Oxford and Cambridge plans were thoroughly inapplicable, and as Eliot had pointed out to the trustees, fellowships could become meaningless when no fruits were demanded from year to year. White of Cornell had pressed for the establishment of annual fellowships very much of the sort finally adopted, and Gilman himself had fostered a somewhat similar program during his last year at California. Before 1876, the few American colleges and universities offering fellowships gave them only to their own graduates, and sometimes, as in the cases of the Parker and Kirkland fellowships at Harvard, the grants encouraged study abroad.[4] In contrast, the idea at Hopkins was to furnish graduate training in America to students from all parts of the country; Hopkins could not give its fellowships to its own alumni because it had none. Nowhere in America in 1876 was there any program offering stipends so consistently large or so numerous as those at Johns Hopkins; and that institution may justly claim credit for the first large-scale fulfillment of the fellowship idea in America.[5]

The special means of attracting advanced students, forecast in the "plan of procedure" of May, 1875, appeared in detail early in 1876 in the *First Annual Report*. Ten fellowships of $500 each were offered to "young men from any place," who exhibited a decided proclivity toward a special line of study in one of these fields: philology, literature, history, ethics and metaphysics, political science, mathematics, engineering, physics, chemistry, and natural history. Law, medicine, and theology were not acceptable fields, for the trustees were fostering a new profession, "the pursuit of literature or science." Occasional services —aid as examiners or even as teachers—might be required, but fellows were not to teach elsewhere. They must give evidence of progress each year by "the preparation of a thesis, the completion of a research, the delivery of a lecture or by some other method." [6] Letters to applicants emphasized specialization: degree of attainment rather than breadth of interest was what counted, and examples of completed work were

---

[4] Wertenbaker, *Princeton*, 301–302; Yale College catalogue (1875–1876), 57–58; Harvard University catalogue (1875–1876), 151–153. One of the original fellows at Hopkins at first refused to accept his fellowship because it was for study in the United States (Samuel F. Clark[e] to Gilman, June 10, 1876).

[5] [Charles F. Thwing], "College Fellowships," *Scribner's Monthly*, XVI (1878), 660–662.

[6] TM, Jan. 3, 1876; ARJH (1876), 23, 32, (1877), 13; JHR (1877), 81–82.

requested. The authorities from the first expected to renew fellowships, possibly two or three times.[7]

The response to the program seemed to surprise everyone. When the competition closed in June, the total of those applying had reached 152, of whom 107 fulfilled the requirements for eligibility. Those eligible represented forty-six different colleges, and applications had come from Trinity College, Dublin; Göttingen; and Heidelberg. In the face of so many desirable candidates, the trustees increased the number of fellowships from ten to twenty.[8]

The young men who sacrificed other considerations to come to Hopkins as fellows had foreseen accurately the type of reception awaiting them. In June, Gilman asked one of the successful candidates to send the names of books which he felt would be important for his studies and promised to try to get them for the library.[9] This gesture typified the attitude of Hopkins toward its fellows: they were not to be passive recipients, but rather builders of the new institution along with the faculty and trustees. The fellows responded in the same vein from the beginning. One of them, William White Jacques, aptly referred to his "triple duties of student, fellow and instructor," specifying that he had been "studying German, reading up for a research and guiding students in the elements of phys[ical] manip[ulation]." [10] David MacGregor Means presented a course on the "Eastern Question." Ernest G. Sihler gave three lectures on "Attic Life and Society" and a regular course to two undergraduates on *The Acharnians* of Aristophanes. Besides a course on Schopenhauer, Josiah Royce gave five public lectures on the "Return to Kant." [11] The second year it became even more common for fellows to teach.

The breadth of origin of the first fellows proved that Johns Hopkins was at its very opening an institution of national influence. The chance for advanced study under recognized scholars brought a response from

[7] Gilman to H. J. Rice, March 25, 1876; Gilman to S. E. Morgan, May 4, 1876; Gilman to W. F. Tillett, April 13, 1876.

[8] Gilman to Joseph LeConte, April 27, 1876; JHU *Circulars*, no. 3 (June, 1876), 2–3; TM, May 9, 1876.

[9] Gilman to D. MacGregor Means, June 21, 1876.

[10] W. W. Jacques to Edward C. Pickering, Nov. 7, 1876, Pickering Papers.

[11] ARJH (1878), 13; Ernest G. Sihler, *From Maumee to Thames and Tiber: The Life-Story of an American Classical Scholar* (New York, 1930), 103; Lanman diary, March 13, 22, 1877. For courses by Craig and Lanman see Appendix B.

all sections of the country. The twenty-one who actually entered upon their fellowships during the first year [12] represented thirteen colleges. Three were graduates of Yale (one a Sheffield Ph.B.); two each of Amherst, Lafayette, the University of Virginia, Princeton, and Cornell; and one each of Iowa College (later Grinnell), Columbia (a Ph.B. from the School of Mines), Massachusetts Institute of Technology, Randolph-Macon, the University of California, Harvard, and Concordia Gymnasium in Fort Wayne, Indiana. In addition, two had Ph.D.'s: Charles R. Lanman from Leipzig and Herbert Baxter Adams from Heidelberg. One fellow, Samuel F. Clarke, had no degree at all, but had worked as a zoologist with the United States Fish Commission.[13] As to fields of interest, the first twenty-one were divided as follows: five in philology; three each in mathematics and chemistry; two each in political science, natural history, and engineering; and one each in history, physics, literature, and ethics and metaphysics.[14] Gilman showed no compunction about granting fellowships in political science, engineering, and philosophy—fields in which he had no faculty members. This probably represented a combination of factors: hope for early expansion of the faculty, faith in the ability of advanced students to do independent work, and assurance of help from visiting lecturers. Of these twenty-one all but four were fellows a second year. One left to become a professor, one was advanced to associate, one went to study in Germany, and the other at least planned to study in Germany.[15]

The high caliber of fellows during the first year and later was indicative of careful selection by Gilman and the faculty. But in plain fact there was no such opportunity for free graduate education anywhere else in the country; thus, most young college graduates seriously intending to become professional scholars gravitated toward Hopkins —especially if they could not afford to go to Europe or had returned from Europe and failed to find teaching positions. With no American graduate school seriously competing, it was easy to win bright young men during Hopkins' opening years. Furthermore, it must be a debit against Gilman's fame as a selector of young men that in the competition for fellowships John Bates Clark, who was to become one of the

[12] ARJH (1877), 14–15. Brooks and Morse had been advanced to associateships before the beginning of the first term, and Porter Poinier had died.
[13] ARJH (1877), 14–15.   [14] JHR (1877), 64–66.
[15] ARJH (1878), 46–47; TM, May 7, 1877.

country's greatest economists, lost out to distinctly inferior scholars.[16]

The first twenty-one fellows at Johns Hopkins were nevertheless a more remarkable group of college graduates than had ever before gathered for study anywhere in America. Two became professors at Johns Hopkins: the mathematician Thomas Craig and the historian Herbert Baxter Adams (who, being still in Germany when he applied, was the least known of the candidates and at first suspected of being a sham).[17] Two became professors at Harvard: Charles Lanman and Josiah Royce. In both these cases it was Johns Hopkins that approached the candidate. Gilman had humbly asked Royce to come if he could find nothing better and promised Lanman early advancement to an associateship.[18] Two other fellows who became professors ranked as national leaders in their fields: Henry Carter Adams, professor of political economy and finance at Michigan, 1887–1921, and Edward Hart, professor of chemistry at Lafayette, 1882–1924. Others with academic careers and their most noteworthy positions were Ernest G. Sihler, professor of Latin at New York University, 1892–1923; John H. Wheeler, professor of Greek at the University of Virginia, 1882–1887 (he died in 1887); George Bruce Halsted, professor of mathematics at the University of Texas, 1884–1903; Daniel W. Hering, professor of physics at New York University, 1885–1916; Joshua W. Gore, professor of natural philosophy at the University of North Carolina, 1882–1908; D. MacGregor Means, professor of economics at Middlebury, 1877–1880; and Samuel F. Clarke, professor of natural history at Williams, 1881–1916. Lyman Beecher Hall, who succeeded to a fellowship in February, 1877, upon Means's resignation,[19] was professor of chemistry at Haverford, 1880–1917.

Two had their principal careers in law: Means and Frederick B. Van Vorst. E. Darwin Preston worked for the Coast Survey, and Malvern W. Iles as a chemist for mining companies. A. Duncan Savage, a paleographer, served at the Metropolitan Museum of Art. After employment with both the Maryland and United States Fish Commissions, Henry J. Rice taught at Brooklyn High School; he died in 1885.[20] William W. Jacques invented much of the apparatus involved in long-

[16] Gilman to Clark, Sept. 1, 1876; TM, Sept. 4, 1876.
[17] Gilman to Adams, May 3, 1876; Gilman to E. L. Godkin, July 7, 1876.
[18] Gilman to Royce, March 20, 1876; Gilman to Lanman, May 2, June 29, 1876.
[19] ECM, Jan. 23, 1877.   [20] French, *History of Johns Hopkins,* 43–44.

distance telephoning and various submarine-detection devices for the British Admiralty.[21] Walter Hines Page, later editor of the *Atlantic Monthly* and the *World's Work* and ambassador to Great Britain under Wilson, was the only one of the first fellows to achieve fame outside the ranks of scholarship.

Nearly the youngest of the fellows, Page had never, before coming to Hopkins, been north of Ashland, Virginia, where he attended Randolph-Macon. His letters home show considerable prejudice against Yankees and surprise when one of them—Jacques—turned out to be a "gentleman." Gildersleeve's successor at the University of Virginia, Thomas Price, had recommended his student Page highly,[22] and Gildersleeve was eager for him to win a fellowship. Having already selected Wheeler from the North and Sihler from the West, Gildersleeve felt that to have also a fellow from the South would give his work "quite a national air."

Gildersleeve had some doubts, however, about the scholarly bent of the young North Carolinian, and these proved well founded.[23] Although Page recognized Gildersleeve as a great teacher and felt himself growing under his guidance,[24] he was from the first unhappy with the Germanism of the Baltimore university, which seemed to him "at least unnatural" in a Southern city. He described Lanman as a horrible example:

He lives in a back third-story room of a desolate old house. His apartment is uncomfortably bare of all comfort-giving things; but one end of the room is stocked with the most desirable collection of the Greek, Latin, German, French, Sanskrit, and Arabic classics. Not an English book (with two or three unimportant exceptions) there! He can make dictionaries but can no more appreciate the soul beauties of literature than a piano manufacturer can appreciate Wagner. He is a native of Connecticut; and Connecticut, I suppose, is capable of producing any unholy phenomenon.[25]

Page chafed under the abstruse philological assignments, such as tracing the peculiarities of a certain Greek adverb from Homer to the

[21] *Who Was Who in America . . . 1897–1942* (Chicago, 1942), 626.
[22] Hendrick, *Training of an American,* 91, 67.
[23] Gildersleeve to Gilman, June 7, 10, July 20, 24, Aug. 7, 1876.
[24] Hendrick, *Training of an American,* 106, quoting Page.
[25] Page to Sarah Jasper, Oct. 15, 1876, quoted in Hendrick, *Training of an American,* 75–76.

Byzantine writers.[26] He expressed an attitude which every graduate student feels occasionally, but his intensity showed more than ordinary dissatisfaction: "In dead earnest, I have a strong mind at times to throw up all my scholarly plans, and go to work, go among men, I mean—go into politics, for example. Active work is worth tenfold more than book speculation." [27] A summer in Germany, where he went with his Yankee friend Jacques on money saved from his fellowship, did not convert him to the great traditions of classical scholarship. He gave up his fellowship and left Johns Hopkins without waiting to complete the 1877–1878 term.[28]

A more typical fellow was Thomas Craig, an example of those who planned from the first to devote their lives to scholarly investigation. Craig was the son of a Scotch mining engineer who had emigrated to Pennsylvania, where Thomas was born in 1855. He obtained the degree of Civil Engineer from Lafayette College in 1875 and then spent a year teaching.[29] His strong ambition led him to write to Benjamin Peirce in August, 1875, asking how he could best pursue a career in pure mathematics. The kindly Harvard professor agreed to guide him, saying, "It is my greatest delight to foster high mathematical ability in America, so that you need have no fear that you will cause me unpleasant trouble by your application to me." Peirce advised him that *"true original work"* was what really counted.[30]

Learning from an article in the New York *Tribune* of the Hopkins fellowship program, Craig wrote Gilman of his relation with Peirce and with Professor P. G. Tait of the University of Edinburgh, who had approved the course of study that he was undertaking in quaternions. He reported his reading in detail. Gilman wrote back directly, assuring him, "If you have been as thorough as you have been comprehensive you are clearly one of the young men whom we desire to reach." Gilman then let him in on the secret that Sylvester was to lead the mathematics department. Within a week, Craig came to Baltimore for

[26] Burton J. Hendrick, *The Life and Letters of Walter H. Page* (Garden City and New York, 1922), I, 26–27.

[27] Page to Sarah Jasper, Nov. 30, 1876, quoted in Hendrick, *Training of an American*, 77.

[28] Hendrick, *Training of an American*, 90–91, 106.

[29] David Eugene Smith, "Thomas Craig," DAB, IV, 496. His daughter, Miss Ethel Craig, has verified the date of his birth as December 20, 1855.

[30] Benjamin Peirce to Craig, Aug. 18, Sept. 18, Oct. 10, 1875, GP.

an interview.[31] Gilman practically guaranteed him a fellowship and sent him to Washington to meet Newcomb.

Newcomb treated the aspiring mathematician with kindness and gave him a job for the summer which would allow him time to study. He wrote Gilman that if Craig "is really a 'sample,' you will start your university full-fledged indeed." Gilman kept in touch with Craig by mail, lending him money and urging him not to injure his health by overstudy.[32] He learned how hard Craig was working from Newcomb, who said that the young man went "through the most difficult works of the great mathematicians, Abel for instance, as if they were dime novels" and understood them all.[33] For his part, Craig was in bliss. He wrote Gilman that "to study under Prof. Sylvester and Prof. Newcomb and the other splendid men, is more fortune than I ever dared look for." [34] During his first year as a fellow, when he was still only twenty years old, Craig took it upon himself to aid the less-advanced students. Although there were many changes in his status, he never stopped teaching at Hopkins until his death in 1901. He succeeded Sylvester and Newcomb as editor of the *American Journal of Mathematics*.[35]

In the same way that Page represents the nonscholarly fellow somewhat out of place and Craig the youth of ability needing exactly the support and opportunity which Hopkins offered, Charles R. Lanman may be considered a third type of fellow—too advanced for student status, but preferring a fellowship with uncertain responsibilities at Johns Hopkins to the known evils of elementary college teaching. Like Gilman, Lanman was born in Norwich, attended Norwich Free Academy, and went to Yale, where he graduated in 1871. Like Gilman he stayed to do graduate work. He began as a student of chemistry in Sheffield Scientific School (while Gilman was still on its faculty), but left the physical sciences after finding inspiration in the teaching of James Hadley in Greek and William D. Whitney in Sanskrit. In two years he won a Ph.D. and set off for Germany. Three years at the Universities of Tübingen, Leipzig, and Berlin followed, years of "hard work with inspired and inspiring teachers." [36] Before he left, he had

[31] Craig to Gilman, March 23, 1876; Gilman to Craig, March 24, [1876]; Gilman to Sylvester, March 30, 1876.

[32] Craig to Gilman, April 1, 1876; Newcomb to Gilman, April 3, 1876; Gilman to Craig, April 29, May 3, June 9, 1876.

[33] Newcomb to Gilman, June 23, 1876.   [34] Craig to Gilman, April 1, 1876.

[35] Craig, untitled undated memorandum, AFJH.

[36] Untitled autobiographical sketch of 1925, Lanman Papers.

established enough of a reputation to publish a scholarly review in the *Jenaer Literaturzeitung* and to win encouragement to stay in Germany as *Privatdocent.*[37]

Lanman had no thought of becoming an expatriate, but he was concerned about what use he could make of his talents and training once he was home. His record at Yale guaranteed him a tutorship there. At the same time, Gilman, who had traveled with him in Europe, wanted him as a fellow at Johns Hopkins. Lanman's dilemma typified the problems and temptations of young men determined to be professional scholars in the America of the 1870s. He felt that his choice lay between exhausting teaching of elementary branches at a good salary, which would dissipate the advantages of his European training, and the Hopkins fellowship, which offered "a little too much to die upon, and not enough to live upon." To his family, who wondered why he was not satisfied to come home and be a "teacher," he explained:

As for what I mean by "original investigation";—I mean to do what I can for the cause of science in general, and in particular for the cause in my own country, so that it will be more respected abroad,—and at home by those who would otherwise come abroad,—and, further, by doing my best in some higher institution of learning to elevate the standard of the lower ones, and so to be of some use to *society.*

Sure though he was that he wanted to dedicate himself to "investigation," Lanman did not find the decision easy.

As I was despairingly thinking [he wrote home] what I had better decide upon as to the Baltimore question, I rec[eive]d a card from [Bernadotte] Perrin (he graduated Ph. Dr. at the same time I did) and going to the hotel found him just arrived. . . . He . . . told me about the *tutorships* at Yale. . . . I should very likely have to teach Algebra or some thing else that I don't know enough about, to put in your eye, and that 16 hours a week to immense classes. The result would be plainly, just ruinous to my prospects.

Yet even after making the decision in favor of Hopkins, Lanman declared himself "not particularly anxious to go to Baltimore at all"—not a surprising attitude in light of the income and status that would

---

[37] Lanman to Abby Lanman, Dec. 26, 1876, *ibid.* The review of Hermann Grassmann's *Wörterbuch zum Rigveda* is in the issue of December, 1875, pp. 915–917, copy in *ibid.*

follow his five years of postgraduate study. But he would not be a tutor at Yale "under any circumstances." [38]

Perhaps to show his ability and guarantee promotion, but more probably because he was bursting with his subject, Lanman determined from the first that he would conduct classes in Sanskrit at the new university. Gilman approved his plan, but was dubious about the number of partakers to be found.[39] Early in October, Lanman approached members of the university who might want to study with him. On October 19 he delivered his first lecture to a class of five, three of whom were also fellows. Attendance proved unstable, but usually Lanman could muster two or three, Royce being among the faithful. Undaunted, on March 1 he launched a second class of two students into the glories of beginning Sanskrit.[40]

The young philologist also participated in the university's efforts to interest the city of Baltimore in its work. He wrote a letter to a local newspaper on the importance of Sanskrit, lauding Whitney's forthcoming lectures and suggesting his own course as preparation.[41] He was probably the first fellow to give a public lecture, his topic being "the place and bearings of historical linguistic studies in the University, with especial reference to the Ancient Indian Literature." [42] Later in the year he spoke on "The Excavations at Olympia," illustrating his talk with slides.[43]

Nor was Lanman deprived of his fulfillment as an investigator. With stern self-discipline he set himself to work on what was to become his first important published research. His diary recorded his perseverance in the often tedious labor. Finally came the joyful entry of October 11, 1877: *"Finished collecting the materials* for a treatment of the noun-declensions of the Rig veda from Grassmann's Dictionary. I began Dec. *4th* 1876, and since then have spent *104* working days or parts of days on it, I believe." The work was published by the American Oriental Society.[44]

In recompense for attendance at his classes by some who were per-

[38] Lanman to Abby Lanman, May 21, 28, June 18, 1876, Lanman Papers.
[39] Gilman to Lanman, Sept. 1, 1876, *ibid.*   [40] Lanman diary.
[41] Baltimore *Evening Bulletin,* Oct. 19, 1876; Lanman diary, Nov. 18, 19, 1876.
[42] Printed broadside, Lanman Papers; Lanman diary, Nov. 23, 1876.
[43] Lanman diary, Feb. 16–19, 1877.
[44] "A Statistical Account of Noun-Inflection in the Veda," *Journal of the American Oriental Society,* X (1871–1878), 325–601.

haps not utterly imbued with a desire to learn Sanskrit, Lanman contributed his presence when other fellows taught, notably in Royce's
small class on Schopenhauer.[45] Royce echoed something of the spirit
of this class in a letter to Lanman more than a year later:

I fear that in this mass of inflections you are forgetting the truly and sub-
stantially Uninflected of which divine philosophy treateth. In other words
you are forgetting to *think.* You were once trained to *think* in a certain class
of young students of Schopenhauer, who sat at the feet of a venerable
and penurious instructor. I fear you are forgetting. Spend some two hours
a day now in *thinking.* Stand on your head, if you would be saved, or stand
in any other philosophical position, and *think* of das reine Sein, of die
vierfache Wurzel, and of

> Yours Ever
> J. Royce.[46]

There was a suggestion of fallen aristocrats' supporting themselves by
taking in each other's laundry in the reciprocal patronage of the
scholars at Hopkins during 1876–1877. But these aristocrats were simply
waiting to rise, and it was very fine laundry.

Although the fellows organized themselves to the extent of electing
Lanman president,[47] the organization which has lived in the traditions
of Johns Hopkins was neither so formal nor so inclusive. It sprang from
the background in German university life of certain fellows and associates. Many of these men had already met each other as they moved
from one European university to another; they found comfort in recalling together the splendors left behind. What could follow more
naturally than a loosely organized *Kneipe* to bring back memories and
introduce less fortunate friends to German student customs? What
seems to have been the first *Kneipe* took place on December 6, 1876,
and included five fellows (Royce, Means, Hering, H. B. Adams, and
Lanman) and two associates (Brandt and Hastings). Lanman recorded
of it: "Pleasant eve. We spoke German & drank a glass of beer." From
then on Lanman's diary mentioned the weekly gathering of the "German Club." Sihler years later spoke of the meetings as "our very simple
and frugal symposia. . . . Here, over a pint of beer, with some cheese

---

[45] Lanman diary, December, 1876, January, 1877.
[46] Royce to Lanman, June 11, 1878, Lanman Papers.
[47] Lanman diary, Jan. 19, 1877.

and crackers and some tobacco, we discussed many kinds of questions and problems." [48]

On May 9 Gilman told Lanman of his appointment as associate at a salary of $1,250. Recording the momentous interview in his diary, Lanman wrote excitedly: "The appointment was voted *Monday*. He said I had *earned* it." [49] He had indeed. In fact, he had earned a professorship. But that was to come three years later and from a university president further north.

The fifty-four original graduate students—counting both fellows and nonfellows—specialized in the following subjects: nineteen in biology, nine in chemistry, two in physics, six in mathematics, twelve in language, two in political science, one in history, one in philosophy, and two in engineering.[50] The concept of the graduate work in which these students engaged was officially expressed in these words, after the trial period of the first year:

Advanced and graduate students will find that the University professors are not absorbed in the details of college routine, but are free to give personal counsel and instruction to those who seek it. . . .

The instruction is carried on by such methods (varying of course with individual scholars, and with the different departments of work) as will encourage the student to become an independent and original investigator, while he is growing more and more familiar with the work now in progress elsewhere, and with the results that have been obtained by other scholars in the same field.[51]

The definiteness of purpose in this statement, lacking in earlier announcements, implied a healthy contact with experience.

During the 1876–1877 term, the graduate students at Hopkins, and to a lesser extent the twelve matriculated candidates for the A.B., faced a crazy-quilt curriculum.[52] Courses began and ended more or less when the teacher pleased. Some were taught by visiting lecturers, some by students. The professor of one course would sit among the students in another. But these characteristics represented more than the disorganization of an opening year. They were relatively permanent results of the freedom given each department to design its own pattern of work and

---

[48] *Ibid.*, esp. Dec. 6, 13, 1876, Jan. 10, 17, May 18, 1877; Sihler, *From Maumee to Thames*, 100.

[49] Lanman diary, May 9, 1877.   [50] JHR (1877), 64–68.

[51] JHR (1878), 16.   [52] JHR (1877), 71–75. See Appendix B.

of the absence of fixed requirements for students. On the whole, this casualness regarding classes stimulated a healthy independence, though a student without any personal plan of development could become extremely confused.

The climate of Johns Hopkins was, by design, a climate of freedom. Whatever the spiritual unity of the old sectarian college, it had neither in activity nor in expression any such liberty as was from the first the keynote at Hopkins. At the fifth Commemoration Day, Gilman could announce with pride that no one had complained about any limitations on freedom of action: the founder had not fettered the trustees, or the trustees the instructors, or the instructors the students.[53] The trustees responded in one case of outside pressure in 1876 by resolving that "the Board does not interfere with the scholastic arrangement of the University." Gilman, earlier the same year, had written one giver of gratuitous advice: "In any case, I should be sorry to see fetters put upon a professor in any department of science,—as to what he should or should not hold. Our plans look toward the freedom of 'the University' and not to the restrictions of 'the College.' "[54] Indeed, Gilman announced in his inaugural that the freedom within the university was for both faculty and students. The teachers should be free to choose their own methods of instruction and the students their own courses. But this was a freedom "based on laws," and it could be granted only by first exacting something from its recipients. The students must have the maturity which supposedly came from the discipline and "pursuit of fundamental knowledge" in the colleges, and the teachers must renounce "all other preferment" and unselfishly devote themselves to "the discovery and advancement of truth and righteousness."[55]

At the first Commemoration Day, February 22, 1877, after the university had made a solid beginning in proving itself to the community and the other universities of the land, two professors testified to the realization within its walls of the freedom that Gilman had declared to be his object. Gildersleeve spoke first:

In full sympathy with the proposed motto of our institution—"The truth shall make you free"—I insist on the utmost latitude of the expression of opinion. I have no ambition—if I had the ability—to be the founder of a

[53] Untitled notes for address of Feb. 22, 1881, GP.
[54] TM, Nov. 6, 1876; Gilman to John Miller, Jan. 5, 1876.
[55] "Hopkins Inaugural," 33.

school, no desire to impose my views on any set of younger men, to urge the advocacy of this or that principle, or the carrying out of prescribed lines of thought. . . . Honest work, earnest work, clean work, this must be required of all university students. . . . Beyond this there must be freedom.[56]

Sylvester congratulated the students on the freedom which they deservedly had, and also the professors

on the free scope that is given to each to carry out in the manner that may seem to him most likely to be conducive to a useful result, the combined objects which this University has been founded to promote, under its twofold aspect as a teaching body and as a corporation for the advancement and propagation of science and learning.[57]

With men of such views to guide it, Johns Hopkins remained a university without an elaborate design. Instead, it was dedicated to the proposition that men can make their own designs and that the freer they are the better will they discipline themselves. It was a university that refused to make its future a slave to any method, routine, or pattern that had gone before.

In this atmosphere of freedom there grew up a spirit which was rare, perhaps even unique, in the history of American education. The universal enthusiasm, the intimacy and unity, the sense of intellectual adventure were developed to a degree that any university of today might envy. Josiah Royce, though qualifying his praise with recollections of premature and hasty "original work" and certain difficulties in overcoming sensitiveness and establishing "the true freedom of enlightened controversy," recalled the beginnings of the university as

a dawn wherein "'twas bliss to be alive." Freedom and wise counsel one enjoyed together. The air was full of rumors of noteworthy work done by the older men of the place, and of hopes that one might find a way to get a little working-power one's self. . . . One longed to be a doer of the word, and not a hearer only, a creator of his own infinitesimal fraction of a product, bound in God's name to produce it when the time came.[58]

In the rooms of the old building on Howard Street, where the stoves were deficient in poor weather and "pieces of wall paper would swing

[56] Baltimore *Evening Bulletin,* Feb. 23, 1877.

[57] H. F. Baker, ed., *The Collected Mathematical Papers of James Joseph Sylvester* (Cambridge, Eng., 1904–1912), III, 73–75.

[58] Josiah Royce, "Present Ideals of American University Life," *Scribner's Magazine,* X (1891), 383–384.

gently in the air," [59] students and professors came eagerly together to build "scientifically" the kingdom of truth. Gildersleeve, always a qualifier of things praised and admired, recalled that "there was not much comfort in the hallbedroom studies and kitchen laboratories. There was not much peace in the to-and-fro of drawing up programmes and holding consultations and going to lectures in order to encourage our colleagues, but it was a glorious time for all that." [60]

A reporter who had interviewed many of the men at Hopkins declared that under its method students were "permitted and directed how to grow, not molded, and hammered, and chiseled into form." [61] The effect of this regimen on the students was praised by Sylvester in his Commemoration Day address. When he heard of students "only hoping to be enabled to keep body and soul together" in order to go on studying, of "classes diligently attending lectures on the most abstruse branches of scholarship and science, remote from all the avenues which lead to fortune or public recognition," and of "the absence of all manifestations of disorder or levity," he felt that it was the students who made Johns Hopkins worthy of the name university. It was not numbers that counted, he assured his auditors, but the "spirit which actuates and the work that is done." [62] The frivolities of college life were spurned by young men who felt that "the eyes of all the world are on us here." [63]

The door that opened in Baltimore in 1876 opened into more than the dowdy rooms of the made-over dwelling houses. It signified for those who were to enter through it—trustees, president, teachers, students—new opportunities and new duties, but duties full of joy because they were freely assumed. For the universities and colleges of the world it meant a new comrade, and for those of America a new leader. For the community that was Baltimore and the community that was the whole world it promised such help as can come when human minds set themselves to solving problems. It was a door that opened into endless opening doors.

[59] George Dobbin Penniman, "The Beginnings of Hopkins Athletics," *Johns Hopkins Alumni Magazine*, XXVII (1938–1939), 101–102.
[60] JHU *Circulars* (n.s. 1911, no. 1), 8.
[61] [Sophie B. Herrick], "The Johns Hopkins University," *Scribner's Monthly*, XIX (1879–1880), 203.
[62] Baker, ed., *Collected Papers of Sylvester*, III, 73–74, 77.
[63] Page to Sarah Jasper, Nov. 30, 1876, quoted in Hendrick, *Training of an American*, 77.

Part Two

BUILDING: IN SEARCH OF SCHOLARS

: CHAPTER VI :

Emerging Patterns

NOT until the torrid Baltimore summer had receded, not until the very end of September or the first of October, when autumn fogs blurred the mornings, would the academic year begin at the Johns Hopkins University. The opening ceremony, more informal than the Huxley program of 1876, often presented a visiting speaker who could give members of the young institution a word of praise and a sense of participation in a wider community. There would be an opening reception, at times in Gilman's home, with intellectual overtones, such as a talk by some faculty member on his summer accomplishments. Then work began.

No sharp division of the year into semesters existed.[1] Undergraduate courses lasted the full term, and the formal university-directed examinations came only in the spring. The central point of the year was Commemoration Day, February 22, the anniversary of Gilman's inauguration. The day gave an opportunity for stocktaking and for reasserting goals. Often Gilman would ask a faculty member to speak, thus forcing such taciturn figures as Rowland into self-revelation and unexpected eloquence. In addition, there might be a guest speaker— the president of some other university or a public official. At a time of crisis, Gilman himself might give the principal address. In any case, he would offer a short speech, the "Annual Apology for the Existence of the J.H.U.," as a member of the university labeled it.[2] Naked of traditions of its own, the institution needed such self-consciousness.

[1] Thomas R. Ball to Captain Howell, Dec. 14, 1888, GP.
[2] Minton Warren to Charles R. Lanman, March 8, 1886 [1885], Lanman Papers;

The Johns Hopkins University

The year ended without fanfare. No horde of alumni came to recapture their youth. The first degrees were given in 1878, but diplomas were not used until 1886, and a student felt no compunction about leaving before the "conferring of degrees," a brief ceremony, not graced with the name "commencement." [3] June would see many members of the university off for Europe. A few might continue their scholarly labors in the Baltimore heat. The only summer program was the Chesapeake Zoological Laboratory, and it was out of sight on the coast.

Such were the punctuations of the year. Within this framework of ceremonies, other patterns developed. Chief of the pattern makers was Gilman, who in shaping the university shaped the outlines of his own office.

"College presidents all over the country are getting more absolute, as well as more specially fitted for their work," J. Franklin Jameson, an unhappy Hopkins graduate student, wrote in his diary in 1881.[4] Strange if it had been otherwise. In a society growing ever more complex, specialization was appearing in all institutions, including the educational. And power, of course, was an absolute requisite for the reshaping of higher education. Even the University of Virginia overcame its Jeffersonian scruples and chose a president in 1904, yielding to the uniquely American tendency for university power to inhere in one specialized leader, a symbol to the world.[5] A president who refused to make his office an instrument of power, such as Noah Porter at Yale, stunted valuable impulses in his institution. Eliot and White are traditionally linked with Gilman as the three great new-style university presidents. But they are merely representatives. Angell at Michigan, Folwell at Minnesota, Barnard at Columbia, and others, though achieving less, showed many of the same characteristics during the 1870s and 1880s.[6]

---

similarly, John Franklin Jameson diary, Feb. 23, 1885, Jameson Papers, Division of Manuscripts, Library of Congress.

[3] JHC, VI, 124; *I Remember: The Autobiography of Abraham Flexner* (New York, 1940), 63.

[4] Jameson diary, May 20, 1881.

[5] For an official statement of the duties of the Hopkins president, see JHR (1885), 21. For an analysis of the uniqueness of the office, see Harold J. Laski, *The American Democracy: A Commentary and an Interpretation* (New York, 1948), 348.

[6] For descriptions stressing the new-style university presidents of this period, see George P. Schmidt, *The Liberal Arts College: A Chapter in American Cultural*

A good university president, old-time or new, contributed his whole spirit and energy to his task. Whatever Gilman's flaws, this he surely did. "His one thought," wrote a fellow, "is the Johns Hopkins University for its glory and perfection."[7] To attain its glory, he must be an ambassador; for its perfection, he must be a builder. The conflicts that Gilman faced tended to be precisely those in which to seek the glory of the university in the eyes of the world was to inhibit its perfection internally. In some cases, one or the other must suffer. The charge was made that he put the fame of the institution above justice to its members.[8] But those who belittled Gilman's courting of the world were willing to accept the resulting favors of the world. For example, the graduate student who could scorn Gilman's " 'politic' character" could happily think, when planning a project that required the co-operation of the federal government, "Gilman would help get all needed opportunities."[9]

New-style president though he was, Gilman had time for students, especially during the opening years. Such actions as giving a room in his home to an arriving student till he could find lodgings and lending money to students and graduates bespeak a generosity beyond the requirements of his position.[10] When undergraduates registered in the early years, he gave them a personal welcome. He set nine to ten every morning as a time when he could be seen on minor matters.[11] At the request of a professor he once talked with a student for twenty minutes "seriously—& gave him clearly to understand that this was a place for workers only." But elementary discipline he refused to administer, writing to one instructor of undergraduates that only he himself could control reported classroom disturbances and that "any

History (New Brunswick, N.J., 1957), 168–180; Ernest Earnest, *Academic Procession: An Informal History of the American College, 1636 to 1953* (Indianapolis and New York, 1953), 133–168; Hamilton W. Mabie, "The American College President," *Outlook*, XLVIII (1893), 338–341.

[7] A. Duncan Savage to Thomas Davidson, Jan. 13, 1879 [1880], Davidson Papers.

[8] Minton Warren to Charles R. Lanman, May 2, 1881, Lanman Papers.

[9] Jameson diary, March 24, 1881, April 30, 1883.

[10] Gilman to W. J. Berry, Nov. 8, 1877; Gilman to Thomas Craig, April 29, 1876; Edward L. White to Gilman, Feb. 6, 1892; Lanman diary, June 20, 1879; Gilman, *Launching of a University*, 16.

[11] C. W. R. Crum and Lawrence H. Baker, "Picturesque Personalities of Johns Hopkins," *JH Alumni Magazine*, XV (1926–1927), 144; Howell, "Daniel Coit Gilman," GP; JHC, I, 14.

interference of outside authority" would merely increase the problem. Gilman did not believe in intellectual coddling of students. He wrote a mother whose son was being readmitted on probation that "if he does not devote himself with energy to his studies, his connection with the University shall be terminated without any words." [12] Graduate students Gilman encouraged by inviting them to give public lectures and readings, discussing their fields with them, urging vigorous action when job opportunities appeared, and saving them from despair if they failed to win a position.[13] For intellectual stimulation he did not simply relegate them to seminars, association meetings, and public lectures; he would invite five or six to his home to hear a visitor from abroad "converse" on a topic of the day.[14]

The assembling of a gifted faculty was a pre-eminent mark of Gilman's greatness as a university president. Perhaps the most generally made observation about his character is that he could distinguish promise in young men, often when they themselves were not fully aware of it. But his ability to foresee promise was no greater than his ability to nurture it, and both are signified by his wife's comment that he discovered people to themselves. His "mild but fatal insistence" overcame much of the human inertia that keeps scholars from accomplishing great things, yet he also knew when to warn against overwork, treating his faculty members "as a lover of horseflesh does a valuable horse." [15] His unusually broad (though not consistently deep) intellectual interests allowed him to talk intelligently and genuinely about almost every man's field. In contrasting Gilman's attitude with that of a later president, one professor reported that whenever he took any of his work to Gilman he "was pleased and interested. We had a long discussion and I went away from his office with a warm feeling that he appreciated and valued my work." [16] Nor did Gilman wait to be

[12] Gilman notebook, "J.H.U. Conclusion Book," Nov. 8, 1879; Gilman to George H. Emmott, Jan. 9, 1889; Gilman to ——, Dec. 29, 1886.

[13] Herbert Weir Smyth to his mother, Feb. 13, 1886; Smyth to his father, April 20, 1888; both in Herbert Weir Smyth Papers, Harvard University Archives; Jameson diary, April 28, 1882.

[14] Jameson diary, Nov. 22, 23, 1880. The visitor, James Hack Tuke from England, spoke on the Irish land question.

[15] Elizabeth Dwight Woolsey Gilman, quoted in Franklin, *Life of Gilman*, 430; Basil L. Gildersleeve, in JHU *Circulars* (n.s. 1908, no. 10), 36–37; Paul Haupt, quoted in an unidentified newspaper, Feb. 28, 1926, biographical file, Maryland Historical Society.

[16] Maurice Bloomfield, quoted in Howell, "Daniel Coit Gilman," GP.

called on. He would drop in informally on a faculty member, showing the proper degree of interest in whatever project was under way. Such simple thoughtfulness as putting a clipping that praised a teacher's work on the bulletin board or reading to the trustees a letter of praise from a foreign scholar bred a satisfaction that was at the same time a stimulus to "eager, unforced work." [17]

Of course every president-faculty encounter was not pleasant. Reproving a faculty member for an overlong public lecture might hurt his sensibilities. Letting a young teacher go could lead several faculty members to cast Gilman in the role of villain.[18] In one case obligation to the public, in the other to long-range departmental development, carried an importance in Gilman's mind which the offended members of his staff did not comprehend. There was little chance to forget that the institution was made up of human beings. Some of his difficulties gave Gilman insights which he expressed in the pages of the *Nation*. He saw the university president as representative of the faculty to the trustees and of the trustees to the faculty. In this combination of "two distinct offices" the president might find himself serving divergent interests, "for example, the need of expansion and the need of economy." "Here," Gilman said, "is a fruitful source of misunderstandings, all the more serious because neither party, the faculty nor the trustees, completely knows both sides of the question." That trustees as well as faculty might fall short in understanding was shown in the private comment of one board member: "Mr Gilman's theory is to run the University in the interest of its paid employees, and as far as I can see almost exclusively for that." [19]

In spite of obstacles Gilman strove to be peace preserver and harmonizer. "He was no lover of controversy," Charles M. Andrews said of him. "He saw in it only a grievous intellectual waste." [20] One of the best ways that Gilman knew of avoiding disputes was to refuse

[17] C. W. Whitmore, "An Interview with Dr. Welch," typescript, GP; Richard T. Ely, *Ground under Our Feet: An Autobiography* (New York, 1938), 101–102; Minton Warren to Charles R. Lanman, June 2, 1881, Lanman Papers.

[18] Gilman to Sidney Lanier, Nov. 17, 1879; Minton Warren to Charles R. Lanman, May 2, 1881, Lanman Papers.

[19] [Gilman], "College Controversy," *Nation*, XXXIX (July 17, 1884), 50; "Another Word on College Controversies," *ibid.* (July 24, 1884), 69; Lewis N. Hopkins to John W. Garrett, July 6, 1882, Garrett Papers.

[20] "Daniel Coit Gilman, LL.D.," *Proceedings of the American Philosophical Society*, XLVIII (1909), lxix.

to commit himself to any course of action until it had been approved by all those with any degree of authority in the matter. Although he was always friendly with reporters, "it was impossible for them to extract from him what he was unwilling to tell." [21] His own letters were usually dry and to the point, concealing his real feelings under a mask of courteous and stereotyped phraseology. It can be doubted that he ever broke a confidence.

Not only in dealing with organizations and the public at large, where he resembled the present-day public relations expert,[22] but also in the more intimate side of his life, Gilman showed remarkable skill at keeping people happy. Such faculties as memory for names and faces and agility in finding the kind and winning conversational comment made him an accomplished social tactician. One friend felt that "urbanity" best summed up these traits.[23] His abilities here often eased friction inside the university. But a nickname has seeped through the barrier of accolade to reveal that Gilman did not universally charm. To some of the less respectful students at Hopkins, he was known as "Oily Dan." [24] Jameson, who often dipped the pen for his diary in vinegar, called Gilman's speeches "extremely neat and disagreeably affable"; one commencement address, he reported, was "full of the usual taffy, flattered the Baltimoreans and lugged in religion to please them." [25]

It became apparent in the age of the American university that the newly specialized and powerful president, if he were to build and preserve a community of scholars, must himself renounce achievement as a scholar. Eliot early accepted the predicament, writing in 1875: "What people call administrators are second-hand humbugs who are the mechanics of colleges, learned societies and governments. Their work is necessary but humble. They are not intellectual producers—any more than statesmen are." [26] Gilman reached the same conclusion, perhaps more slowly. At the University of California, he had taught

[21] Baltimore *News*, Oct. 14, 1908.
[22] Paul Haupt called him "one of the first men in the country to recognize the value of publicity." See note 15 above.
[23] Harmon N. Morse, quoted in Baltimore *Sun*, Oct. 14, 1908; Thwing, *Guides, Philosophers, and Friends*, 64.
[24] Interview with Professor John B. Whitehead, July 6, 1953.
[25] Jameson diary, Sept. 26, June 8, 1882.
[26] Eliot to George Brush, Jan. 13, 1875, Brush Papers.

economics, geography, and history. At Hopkins he never offered a full course, but in the early years he attempted special participation in the work of the history department, scheduling in 1888 twelve lectures on "The Scope and Principles of Social Science." He was first president of the Historical and Political Science Association, formed in 1877. In the early eighties he read papers there and at the Maryland Historical Society.[27] Even as administrative duties crowded in upon him, he still fancied himself a geographer. Although he had taught geography, his knowledge remained elementary, a fact which became all the clearer in an institution dedicated to *expertise*.[28] Gilman's handicaps in scholarship appear plainly in his *James Monroe*, published in the American Statesmen series in 1883. Admitting the limitations of his research, he forecast "a more elaborate portrait" from another hand.[29] He may have been helped in seeing the book's inadequacies by Jameson, who assisted in its preparation. The sharp-eyed young scholar found forty-two errors in the thirty-eight pages of Chapter III.[30] As the years passed, Gilman's attempts at scholarship became fewer, whereas he increasingly welcomed new administrative tasks. In 1890 he recorded a quotation from Michael Foster, of which he must have realized the truth: "Administrative activity & original inquiry cannot well live side by side." [31] Gildersleeve was sure that Gilman "was too much a student not to regret that in his busy life he had not found time to set his seal on some supreme achievement in letters or science." [32] Yet perhaps this unfulfilled desire gave him his dedication to encouraging others. There is nothing to indicate more than prosaic scholarly abilities in Gilman; on the other hand, as Nicholas Murray Butler observed, he had "a natural fondness for administrative detail and for problems of classification and organization." [33] He chose the road which for him led higher.

With frequent social gatherings, both large and small, Gilman unified the internal Hopkins community and, insofar as these affairs brought scholars and outsiders together, smoothed relations with the

---

[27] JHC, VII, 103; III, 46; II, 38.　　[28] Jameson diary, Nov. 23, 1880.

[29] Gilman, *James Monroe in His Relations to the Public Service during Half a Century, 1776 to 1826* (Boston), 3.

[30] Jameson diary, Oct. 7, 8, 24, Nov. 14, Dec. 13, 1882.

[31] Gilman notebook, "Notes from Books, 1890."

[32] JHU *Circulars* (n.s. 1908, no. 10), 37.

[33] "President Gilman's Administration at the Johns Hopkins University," *American Monthly Review of Reviews*, XXIII (1901), 50.

surrounding world. His status as a widower somewhat handicapped him in this function. In 1877, however, he married Elizabeth Dwight Woolsey, a niece of President Woolsey of Yale. The second Mrs. Gilman met the approval even of Jameson, not one to relax his critical standards; he called her a charming hostess, and though she appeared not to be at all learned, he found her "very bright." [34]

In the opening years of the university, president and trustees were collaborators. Gilman's consultations with such trustees as Brown, Dobbin, and Thomas went far beyond mere necessary form. Even though he attended all board meetings, Gilman felt a certain awkwardness in the relationship, which became keener when the university passed through a vale of troubles in the late eighties. He could look at the examples of his friend White, who was a trustee ex officio at Cornell, and of the presidents of Harvard and Yale, who were by law members of their corporations. At last he sent a letter to the board asking in the interests of the future welfare of the institution that the president be an ex officio member. The board agreed unanimously. [35]

The need for this institutionalization of Gilman's relationship with the board was accentuated by the deaths within a period of slightly over a year of three of the trustees with whom he had been most intimate. The loss of Brown in 1890 and of Dobbin and King in 1891 removed some of the closeness between president and trustees and some of the serene wisdom and sense of continuity of the board. Only four of the trustees who had chosen Gilman president remained.

Early changes in membership had not lessened the tolerant, forward-looking character of the board. Charles Morton Stewart, the first choice unguided by the founder, was an auspicious addition. Elected on January 7, 1878, when he was forty-nine, he added to the youthful character of the board. A Baltimore banker and shipowner who had received part of his education in Switzerland and had traveled widely, he was to send five sons to the university and to serve as the board's third president from 1891 until his death in 1900. [36]

The election of two other new trustees further interlocked the boards of the hospital and the university. Joseph P. Elliott, a merchant, chosen

[34] Franklin, *Life of Gilman,* 404; Jameson diary, April 13, 1883, Oct. 13, 1882.
[35] Gilman to trustees, Dec. 4, 1891; C. Morton Stewart to Gilman, March 10, 1892.
[36] ARJH (1878), 41, (1900), 3; Gilman, *Launching of a University,* 31; French, *History of Johns Hopkins,* 357.

on February 7, 1881, after Johnson's resignation, and Alan Penniman Smith, elected the same year on November 7, were both members of the hospital board. Smith held an M.D. from the University of Maryland and had taught in its medical school from 1867 to 1874. Elected the same day as Smith was J. Hall Pleasants, a merchant, whose later contribution as chairman of the building committee won praise from Gilman and the faculty.[37] The vacancies filled by Smith and Pleasants resulted from the deaths of William Hopkins and Galloway Cheston. Dobbin succeeded Cheston as president of the board.

The one other vacancy and replacement during the 1880s resulted from the death of John Work Garrett. This was the most complex co-option problem the board faced. After much worry and a delay of twenty-six months, they chose Garrett's son Robert, who had followed him as president of the B. & O.[38] Thus they abided by the wish of the founder that the institution remain closely linked with the railroad.

The election of the younger Garrett followed one unhappy episode and preceded another, but on the whole the board continued harmonious. Certainly some members remained as interested in the university and its personnel as they had been when the whole endeavor was still an experiment. The elder Garrett offered impressive hospitality at his country home, Montebello, when famous guests came to the university. Less formally, Johnson would invite some of the bachelor faculty members out for "a breath of country air" at Evesham. Dobbin took special interest in the work of Brooks and the Chesapeake Zoological Laboratory, and Brown attended meetings of the Historical and Political Science Association and gave papers there.[39] The trustees felt their responsibility to keep abreast of intellectual currents in the country and arranged a special visit to "the Scientific and Literary establishments of Washington." Gilman could have been describing the course of the Hopkins trustees when he set forth the precept, "Trustees should not, except in great emergencies, or in cases of serious controversy, interfere with or overrule the action of the

[37] Gilman, *Launching of a University*, 36; JHC, III, 87.
[38] TM, Dec. 6, 1886.
[39] Gilman, *Launching of a University*, 35; Johnson to Lanman, June 5, Oct. 18, [1879], Lanman Papers; Gilman to Dobbin, July 31, 1885, Dobbin-Brown Papers; JHC, I, 17, III, 46, X, 7.

faculty." But the trustees' record was better than one of mere restraint; they were eager to encourage, as with their special vote of commendation to president and faculty in 1887 for the results of "earnest labors." [40] In recompense for the burdens of their office, the trustees could share some of the same adventure as the youngest candidate for matriculation.

The university continued to welcome visiting lecturers who could supplement the courses of the faculty.[41] But the visits of famous scholars were never again quite so gala as they had been the first year. Child came from Harvard a second year and spoke on English ballads. He wrote to a Cambridge friend that though the pressure for tickets had been great his lectures were designed "as for a university class," and his hearers were probably disappointed. Child's choice of the academic high road was vindicated by a decision of the executive committee in that spring to frame future lecture series "more towards the University side as distinguished fom popular courses." [42] In later years, a standing announcement in the *Circulars* affirmed that "these lectures are not intended for popular entertainment" and that preference went to teachers from other institutions or those professionally interested in the topic. No amount of stress on the academic side of the lectures, however, could dampen the interest of Baltimore society. Literary lectures were especially popular; those of Hiram Corson of Cornell in 1884, for which attendance averaged three hundred, were moved to a large room in the Peabody Institute.[43] Even in the earliest lectures, the university presented nothing it need blush for, Child's lectures on Chaucer representing the not very extreme limit of compromise with popular tastes. If Gilman felt any qualms about the fanfare surrounding famous visitors, he had consolation from Eliot, who wrote him in 1880: "Dignified silence, a mere list of lectures, are not for you just yet. . . . We are compelled by the rawness of the country to proclaim in set terms the advantages which we offer." [44]

[40] TM, Oct. 6, 1879; "Another Word," *Nation*, XXXIX, 69; TM, Feb. 7, 1887.

[41] Some of these lectures were not open to the public, even though they were listed as "Hopkins Hall Lectures," for example, those in 1884 of John Shaw Billings on municipal hygiene and of James Bryce on Roman legal history (JHC, III, 16).

[42] Francis J. Child to Grace Norton, [Feb. 3, 1878], Norton Family Papers, Houghton Library (by permission of the Harvard College Library); ECM, April 25, 1878.

[43] JHC, III, 16, 50.   [44] Eliot to Gilman, April 6, 1880.

For ten years the university vigorously pursued the policy of lecture series by celebrated visitors, including many Europeans. Among them were William F. Allen of the University of Wisconsin, who lectured on "History of the Fourteenth Century"; Edward A. Freeman of Oxford University, on "Historical Geography of South-eastern Europe"; Samuel P. Langley of the Allegheny Observatory, on "Sun and Radiant Energy"; John Trowbridge of Harvard, on "Philosophy of Physics"; Alexander Melville Bell of Washington, D.C., on "Phonetics and English Pronunciation"; William Thomson of Glasgow University on "Molecular Dynamics"; J. Willard Gibbs of Yale, on "Theoretical Mechanics"; and Arthur Cayley of Cambridge University, on "Abelian and Theta Functions." [45] But in 1886, by which time the university possessed local good will, a secure reputation in the educational world, and an expanded faculty, the executive committee reassessed the need and declared against any "long courses of public lectures, by persons from a distance." [46] There was no end to single lectures by outsiders, however, and the Hopkins Hall series continued, given usually by faculty members. At the end of the 1880s, the first of the endowed lectureships, the Turnbull Memorial Lectureship in Poetry, began a happy and surviving adaptation of the program.[47]

The first issues of *Notes from the Chemical Laboratory* in 1877 and of the *American Journal of Mathematics* in 1878 were the advance guard of an army of scholarly journals and monograph series that was to spring from the Baltimore experiment. The same considerations of prestige and priority and lack of openings for scholarly reports applied to all the disciplines. Of the major departments at the opening of the university, only physics did not breed a periodical.

The resistance of the trustees to assuming actual ownership of the journals continued. They preferred to grant a large subscription, letting the library use the copies for exchanges.[48] But in spite of limited or nonexistent financial support from the trustees, approximately one scholarly periodical a year emerged from the Hopkins matrix. In 1879, Remsen enlarged the *Notes* into the *American Chemical Journal*. The same year Martin with the assistance of Brooks began publish-

[45] Steiner, *Education in Maryland,* 152; ARJH (1882), 61–63, (1885), 11–15.
[46] ECM, Dec. 18, 1886.　　　[47] Gilman to James Russell Lowell, May 10, 1889.
[48] TM, Dec. 6, 1880; ECM, Jan. 30, 1879. The one early exception came in 1882, when the university assumed ownership of the mathematical journal (TM, Dec. 2, 1882).

ing *Studies from the Biological Laboratory,* which unlike Remsen's journal remained strictly limited to reports of Hopkins researches.

Although it was the editorial gifts of Gildersleeve that guaranteed the success of the *American Journal of Philology* after it began in 1880, he pointed out that only Gilman's insistence had overcome his aversion to editorial work.[49] Gildersleeve's formal proposal for such a journal was accepted by the trustees in June, 1879, and they voted a limited subsidy.[50] A review in the *Nation* of the *Journal's* first ten years declared: "No other university had funds for such a use. No other scholar was better fitted for the work. . . . With the best of German scholarship, Prof. Gildersleeve is never heavy nor dull." [51] Most readers turned at once to the editor's regular department, "Brief Mention," "there to find a rare combination of scholarship with ebullience, wit with authority." [52]

Although the year 1881 saw no new publication, ambitious dreams continued. Herbert Baxter Adams, busy at making good, proposed a plan to Gilman in the summer of 1882 for an English-American historical journal to be partly financed by Hopkins. "The thing," he wrote, "would be a scientific tentacle reaching over England and drawing life to our little Baltimore centre from the best intellectual resources of the old world." [53] It was another plan of Adams' which, in 1882, succeeded: *The Johns Hopkins University Studies in Historical and Political Science.* Although larger in scope, its purpose resembled that of the *Studies* edited by Martin—to guarantee for the researchers at the university the consummation of the printed page.

[49] JHU *Circulars* (n.s. 1908, no. 10), 36–37. For a statement of the need for such a journal, made in Gildersleeve's presidential address to the American Philological Association in 1878, see Basil Lanneau Gildersleeve, *Essays and Studies: Educational and Literary* (Baltimore, 1890), 98.

[50] TM, June 12, 1879.

[51] [Thomas D. Seymour], "The American Journal of Philology," *Nation,* LI (July 10, 1890), 33–35, reprinted in JHC, X, 38.

[52] Frank Luther Mott, *A History of American Magazines, 1865–1885* (Cambridge, Mass., 1938), 536–537. See also Charles W. E. Miller, ed., *Selections from the Brief Mention of Basil Lanneau Gildersleeve* (Baltimore, 1930).

[53] Adams to Gilman, July 3, 1882, in W. Stull Holt, ed., *Historical Scholarship in the United States, 1876–1901: As Revealed in the Correspondence of Herbert B. Adams* (*JHU Studies in Historical and Political Science,* LVI, no. 4; Baltimore, 1938), 56. Austin Scott, associate in history, had written Gilman on October 27, 1878: "I am greatly taken with the idea of putting out a Volume under the auspices of the Hist. Dept. of the Univ." This abortive plan may also have originated with Adams, whom Scott expected to include in the volume.

At first the monographs were so brief as to be scarcely discernible from articles, but they gradually became longer. *Notes Supplementary to the Studies,* begun in 1889, presented during its two-year existence brief papers and addresses.[54] Monographs of greater length appeared as extra volumes, beginning in 1886. Adams felt that he need not fear the effects of the *Political Science Quarterly,* begun in 1886 at Columbia, for his concept was essentially different and revolutionary—"the development of the monograph-idea into a series of books." [55] Even one of the harshest critics of the *Studies,* Harold Laski, admitted its significance as "a landmark in the academic history of the United States." [56]

During the heyday of archaeology at Hopkins, in 1885, the *American Journal of Archaeology* was born. Edited by Arthur L. Frothingham, Jr., a fellow by courtesy, it was never subsidized by the Hopkins trustees, and when Frothingham left in 1886 for a professorship at Princeton, the journal went with him.[57]

Another new journal not financially supported by the university was *Modern Language Notes.* A. Marshall Elliott, associate professor of Romance languages, initiated the project in 1886 with the co-operation of other young teachers at Hopkins whose work did not often fit into the classically oriented *American Journal of Philology.* Not until 1903 was its business management assumed by the Johns Hopkins Press.[58]

In the earliest issues of his new periodical, the *American Journal of Psychology,* the university's professor of psychology and pedagogics, G. Stanley Hall, expressed his versatile interests. Although the stated purpose of the journal was to bring together "the psychological work of a scientific, as distinct from a speculative character," Hall included articles in religious philosophy, logic, and anthropology.[59] The first number in 1887 was well received. Hall longed for controversy, however, and reported himself "sick of the [pallid], mostly goody things" written about it and "longing to have some one attack it." [60] Every article in the first number was by a Hopkins student, former student, or faculty member, but the journal was never an official publication of the university (Hall paid deficits from his own savings). For a year

[54] JHC, VIII, 49.   [55] Adams to Gilman, July 17, 1886.
[56] Laski, *American Democracy,* 374–377.   [57] JHC, IV, 124.
[58] JHC, V, 47; French, *History of Johns Hopkins,* 55.
[59] JHC, VI, 130; Hall, *Life and Confessions,* 227–228.
[60] Hall to Thomas Davidson, Dec. 6, 1887, Davidson Papers.

after Hall's resignation in 1888, a period he spent in Europe, the Hopkins Publication Agency controlled the journal; it was then shifted to Clark University.[61]

The support given by Johns Hopkins to two other journals demonstrated its ties to European scholarship. From 1881 to 1884, after a suggestion from Martin and with the urging of Thomas, the trustees began paying a $250 yearly subsidy to the *Journal of Physiology,* edited by Michael Foster of Cambridge University with Martin as one of the associate editors.[62] Later in the eighties the trustees helped finance *Beiträge zur Assyriologie und vergleichenden semitischen Sprachwissenschaft.* The title, usually shortened to *Contributions to Assyriology, etc.* in statements of the publication agent, was properly Germanic for a journal edited by Friedrich Delitzsch of the University of Leipzig and the German-born, German-trained Paul Haupt of Hopkins. The plan of the serial, announced in 1887, was to print issues only as appropriate material accumulated. The first number appeared two years later, with half its contents written by Haupt.[63]

Of the three periodicals that reflected the total work of the university, the *Register* was the catalogue, and the *Annual Report* was not much different from the presidential reports at Harvard and Columbia. The *Circulars,* however, was peculiarly a product of the Hopkins environment. An octavo *Circulars* had been issued during the first academic year, announcing plans and programs. As the university became more stable, the *Circulars* appeared less often. The annual *Register* seemed to be replacing it. But much was happening worthy of communication to the world, and Gilman was not one to leave the university's light under a bushel. In December, 1879, the first number of a new, quarto *Circulars* appeared, modeled in part on the *University Reporter* of Cambridge, England. Gilman called the *Circulars* "photographs of the horse in motion," and indeed events in the university were probably recorded more minutely than those of any other American educational institution of the day.[64] There were lists of

[61] ARJH (1889), 74.
[62] James Carey Thomas to Gilman, Aug. 9, 1880; ECM, Dec. 28, 1881; TM, April 7, 1884.
[63] JHC, VII, 19, X, 39; ARJH (1890), 70.
[64] TM, Dec. 1, 1879; JHC, I, [iii]; Gilman to Thomas Davidson, Jan. 21, 1884, Davidson Papers.

faculty, students, courses, and the students in each course and lists of periodicals in the library, publications by members of the university, and papers read before university societies. But far more than lists was included. Important speeches were printed in full. Often an entire issue would be devoted to a particular topic—the work in mathematics or biology, the university's collegiate program. At the end of each year detailed course descriptions were given for the year's work concluded and the year's work ahead. The greatest amount of type went to the "Notes and Communications" section, usually papers or summaries of papers presented before the societies and seminars or awaiting publication in more formal journals. Although sometimes minutiae and initial plans for research that would have been better left in the notes of the creator gained the printed page, some of the brief articles were of great scholarly merit. Peirce's "Introductory Lecture on the Study of Logic," [65] for example, which has been at least twice reprinted, would have been lost but for the *Circulars*. The *Circulars* served most importantly to give a sense of the whole. Members of the university could see their individual efforts as part of a larger framework, and outsiders saw proof of a community of scholars.

Although Gilman had general oversight of the *Circulars*, and much of his character is expressed in it, its detail and accuracy were the work of Nicholas Murray. Nicholas was the older brother of the university's first teacher of Semitic languages, Thomas C. Murray, and like him a graduate of Williams. The two lived together in Baltimore, though Nicholas at first had no official connection with the university. After the sudden death of the promising Thomas in 1878, the executive committee agreed to give Nicholas temporary employment; he stayed at Hopkins for thirty years.[66]

The newly reborn *Circulars* became his responsibility. This initial supervision of one publication was enlarged to include the business and printing problems of other journals, then of the monograph series, facsimile editions of Biblical manuscripts, and Rowland's maps of the solar spectrum. During the 1880s the term "Publication Agency of the Johns Hopkins University" came into use; an early statement specifically denied that a university press had been founded. It was

[65] JHC, II, 11.   [66] J. S. Jones to Gilman, April 2, 1879; ECM, April 12, 1879.

never founded, in fact; it evolved. In 1891 the name "The Johns Hopkins Press" was at last used.[67] The press had an international influence by that time. In spite of its achievements, one student pointed out that it had "the ugliest binding of the age" and was "governed by a primitive law of the Medes and Persians regarding the maintenance of the octavo form." [68] But whatever its failures in beauty, the university publication agency through unspectacular adaptation to needs had brought into American scholarship a new institution of lasting value.

Gilman himself had later second thoughts about the flood of scholarly journals that followed the early publications at Johns Hopkins. In 1902, when thirty institutions were engaged in publishing ventures, he feared that the engulfed scholar could scarcely fish out the significant memoirs.[69] There had been a legitimate call for the first journals. Edward L. Youmans, editor of the *Popular Science Monthly,* had urged Hopkins in 1877 to "hurry up their proposed *Mathematical Journal*" to spare the popular journals from the more recondite discussions.[70] Journals were needed that would take articles on their merits, rather than judging by the author's age, as the *American Journal of Science* had done in the case of Rowland. Specialization was a mark of the era, and the good that was in it—exactness, division of labor, pushing to frontiers of knowledge and across them —marked the specialized journals. Yet the price had to be paid in pages that were sterile, involuted, supercilious, and narrow. Nor can the effect on the scholar's style of life be counted all to the good. Publication became so pressing a demand that young men rushed into it when they had nothing worth saying. The diary of Jameson reveals his disgust with Adams for forcing monographs out of his colleagues without setting stern tests of quality. Too often it seemed to interested observers that a man's bibliography had been the determining factor in his selection or promotion; the publication of personal bibliographies in the *Circulars* stimulated such a belief. The resulting standard of "success" weakened devotion to teaching and to sound learning. Hopkins itself was fortunate in the presence of men

[67] ARJH (1880), 6; French, *History of Johns Hopkins,* 219–227.
[68] Walter B. Scaife to Gilman, March 9, 1893.
[69] *Launching of a University,* 136.
[70] *Popular Science Monthly,* X (1876–1877), 612.

who escaped these pitfalls. Gildersleeve brought humanity into the most abstruse philological researches, and Rowland, hearing a membership recommendation for the National Academy of Sciences on grounds that the candidate had published six hundred papers, leaped to his feet and declared, "Mr President I oppose any man who has printed six hundred papers." [71]

The tendency toward association evidenced in the Middle Ages found one of its most lasting fulfillments in the university. The associational yearnings in the age of equalitarianism, long observed in America, demanded more than the institutional framework of the university; they created in addition a host of interuniversity and intra-university organizations. The students who formed the pre-Civil War literary and debating societies, once in command of the educational process, transmuted their earlier impulses into something more formal and scholarly, but often no less alive to the currents of contemporary life. Rarely was intra-university associationalism so consciously nurtured by an administration, or nurtured to so serious an academic purpose, as at Johns Hopkins.

The same fostering interest in intellectual expression and interchange that led Gilman to encourage scholarly journals turned his mind to the possibilities of scholarly associations within his university. The first year, when the community was still small and inchoate, the trustees, faculty, and advanced students met monthly in a social gathering, for which Gilman arranged semipopular lectures on "the excavations at Olympia, by an eye witness; the Bayreuth festival, by an auditor; the U.S. Fish Commission, by a collaborator; the Biological Laboratory, by the Biologists; the Peabody Institute, by the Provost, etc." The healthy intellectual appetites assembled in Baltimore did not require such pabulum a second year, and Gilman knew it. At his direction, the members of the university divided into more specialized societies. One of these, the Philological Association, was organized before the end of the first term, on May 31, 1877.[72] Although described as "an organical portion of the University work," its meetings were to be open to the public. Its object was "not only the furtherance of original research, but also the maintenance of intercommunication amongst the representatives of the different branches of this im-

[71] John Trowbridge to Gilman, Oct. 12, 1901.
[72] ARJH (1878), 20.

portant discipline." [73] The next fall, the Philological Association and two others, a "General Scientific Association" and a "Historical Association," began to hold monthly meetings. A fourth association in the initial list, the "Mathematical Conference," was less clearly set apart from the curriculum, being often listed as Sylvester's seminary; not until 1882 was it regularly called the "Mathematical Society." [74] After Sylvester's departure, the society continued under the leadership of Simon Newcomb, though according to Gilman, mathematical activity was "more obvious in three seminaries, each guided by a different instructor, and each devoted to a different line of inquiry." [75] But it was well that the society continued, for precisely as seminaries became more specialized, the communicating function of the societies became more valuable.

What one historian of the university says of the Philological Association applies largely to the other two:

It was not a club, spontaneously formed with elaborate democratic machinery. It was a university function formally approved in advance by the authorities. Dr. Gildersleeve was the only president the association ever had until his retirement in 1915; and in his farewell remarks he explained that thirty-eight years before, Mr. Gilman had asked him to organize a philosophical association and preside over its deliberations and he had merely obeyed orders.[76]

Similarly, the electing of officers in the Scientific and Historical Associations at first merely ratified the institutional hierarchy—Sylvester and Gilman being the first presidents respectively. But the lack of spontaneous democratic creation did not mean that the groups were frozen into a preconceived form. Although the initial pattern comprised presentation of one major and one minor paper, followed by discussion, other functions developed: memorials when a field lost a leader (such as Rowland's remarks on the death of Maxwell), panels (such as the discussion of the Blair Bill by Woodrow Wilson, Burr Ramage, Albert Shaw, and Davis Dewey), a critique and defense of a thesis (Charles H. Haskins, critic; Philip W. Ayres, author of the thesis).[77]

During the 1879–1880 term, two new societies appeared. At Martin's

[73] Lanman diary, May 31, 1877; [Ernest G. Sihler], in Baltimore *Evening Bulletin*, Oct. 9, 1877.
[74] ARJH (1878), 20, (1879), 51; JHC, I, 34, II, 38.   [75] ARJH (1886), 26–27.
[76] French, *History of Johns Hopkins*, 46.   [77] JHC, I, 16; III, 137; VII, 90.

suggestion, members of the university organized a "Naturalists' Field Club." From the first the group included local citizens, and "Baltimore" was prefixed to the name. The chairman continued to be a Hopkins faculty member, and collections were preserved at the university. Saturday excursions during the spring and fall and monthly papers and discussions were the initial program. In time the organization subdivided into three sections—geological, zoological, and botanical, but monthly meetings of the whole group continued.[78]

The second new society of 1879–1880, the Metaphysical Club, reflected the arrival of Charles S. Peirce as resident lecturer. Peirce probably consciously chose the same name that had designated a group of friends who had met in Cambridge in the 1860s, famous as the seedbed of American pragmatism. Just as the title there was half-ironic, so it seemed to be at Hopkins.[79] Metaphysical topics were far less common than epistemological ones. David Stewart's paper, "The Ethics of Belief," dealt with "the moral grounds of a belief in the supernatural, and pointed out the dishonesty of treating as positive fact, dogmas which are matters of doubt or dispute." Of papers by Peirce himself, "Questions concerning Certain Faculties Claimed for Man" denied the existence of intuition and declared that all thought was in signs.[80] The departure of Peirce in 1884 and the promotion of G. Stanley Hall to professor changed the tenor of the club and then destroyed it.[81]

Once the establishment of societies was initiated, creation of others was easy. Finding the meetings of the Philological Association too formal and too classical in orientation to serve their purposes, a group formed a Modern Language Club in 1881, and during 1884 an Archaeological Society was greatly in vogue.[82]

In membership, function, even identity, the associations overlapped the seminaries. In history the confusion was so great that the same meeting could be referred to on one page of the *Circulars* as of the seminary and on another page as of the association.[83] This merger

---

[78] ARJH (1880), 21, (1886), 26; JHC, I, 121, III, 106.

[79] Peirce, quoted in Philip P. Wiener, *Evolution and the Founders of Pragmatism* (Cambridge, Mass., 1949), 19.

[80] JHC, I, 34, 18.   [81] JHC, IV, 28; ARJH (1885), 59, (1886), 27.

[82] Minton Warren to Lanman, Feb. 9, 1881, Lanman Papers; JHC, IV, 18, 40; ARJH (1886), 27.

[83] JHC, III, 128, 137.

raises the question: were the associations worth while in an institution where the seminar method was widespread? [84]

Even aside from the fact that the natural sciences did not often rely on seminars, there were important justifications for the associations. For one thing, they established interdepartmental communication. The associations that brought together the natural scientists or literary scholars or those in history and the social sciences were of a breadth that prevented extreme compartmentalization without greatly lowering the common denominator. Especially was this true of the Scientific Association, where a typical meeting included papers from three departments.[85] Nor did those who prepared papers that would be meaningful to nonexperts find the effort stultifying. The idea for one of Sylvester's most remarkable memoirs came to him after a day's fretting about how he could communicate to a group including nonmathematicians.[86] But the most obstructive barriers are those that separate natural scientists, humanists, and social scientists, and the associations would not have sufficed had they been the only source of interdepartmental rapport. Yet each association was open to all members of the university. The Metaphysical Club, notably, included representatives of a variety of departments. At one of its meetings in 1883, Gildersleeve read a paper on "Rhythm in the Classic Languages" and Remsen on "Wundt's Logic of Chemistry." [87] Papers at the Historical Association were similarly diverse, especially before the formation of the Metaphysical Club. In 1878, Royce, fellow in literature, gave a paper on Spinoza's *Tractatus Theologico-Politicus;* and Lanman, associate in Sanskrit, gave one on the lake dwellers of Switzerland. In 1884, J. Rendel Harris, lecturer on New Testament Greek, read "The Development of the Passover Scandal" before the group.[88] Naturally, a scholar did not disclose his most recondite researches when he crossed to another group, but before his own society—though he might have to adopt some revealing device of analogy—he could present very nearly the most specialized

[84] For analysis óf the Hopkins seminars, see pp. 224–232 below.
[85] JHC, I, 33.
[86] "On an Application of the New Atomic Theory to the Graphical Representation of the Invariants and Covariants of Binary Quantics,—with Three Appendices," in Baker, ed., *Collected Papers of Sylvester*, III, 148–206.
[87] JHC, II, 156.
[88] Lanman diary, March 1, Oct. 11, 1878; JHC, III, 96.

of his work. To an extent, specialists of today can only envy scholars of a past era who could present advanced research to colleagues from several departments and be understood; yet such latter-day organizations at Johns Hopkins as the History of Ideas Club and the Colloquium on the Philosophy of Science have done much to keep open lines of communication between disciplines.

Another value that the associations offered which the seminaries could not was the lowering of barriers between faculty and students. The seminary, whatever it may in time have become, was initially and essentially a teaching device. The association, on the other hand, was designed as a free assembly of scholars, though attendance was probably almost mandatory at the Historical and the Philological. It was the mood that mattered. In the associations, both graduate students and faculty members presented their researches; even advanced undergraduates at times did so.[89] The master-pupil demarcation of the classroom and seminar was a proper function of the university, but the societies symbolized a livelier comradeship of searching.

Nor was it unimportant to provide a forum for visitors with topics too specialized to justify a hearing by the full university. Such outsiders would have corrupted the purpose of a seminar; in the associations they found an atmosphere scholarly enough to be appreciative, yet with a certain conviviality, honoring their presence. Meetings were sometimes followed by receptions or *Kneipen* (the musical aftermath of a *Kneipe* in honor of Von Holst attracted the attention of police).[90] Through the Historical and Political Science Association, in keeping with the ambitions of H. B. Adams, passed a parade of scholarly and not-so-scholarly visitors, full advantage being taken of the proximity of Washington. Justin Winsor, Harvard's librarian, spoke on early American cartography; Edward Channing, instructor at Harvard, on "Town and County Government"; and Senator Henry L. Dawes of Massachusetts on the Indian question.[91] In the other associations outsiders read papers less frequently, but there were such examples as John Sundberg, fresh from experience among the Bengals, presenting

[89] JHC, I, 48.
[90] JHC, I, 17; Clayton Colman Hall, "Early Memories of the University," *JH Alumni Magazine*, I (1912–1913), 305–306.
[91] JHC, I, 17; III, 70; VI, 55.

a paper on "Customs and Language of the Santals" at the Philological; Emil Bessels, naturalist on the *Polaris* expedition of 1871–1873, on the history of Arctic explorations at the Scientific; William Woolsey Johnson, professor at the Naval Academy, "On Integration in Series" at the Mathematical; Lester Frank Ward, already known for his *Dynamic Sociology*, on "Mind as a Social Factor" at the Metaphysical; and John Wesley Powell, director of the Geological Survey, on "The Archaeology of the Aboriginal Races of the United States" at the Archaeological.[92] Hopkins partook of the vigor of the larger American intellectual community through such specialized papers by outsiders just as it did through the elaborate public lecture series.

A probably unintended but extremely valuable contribution of the associations, which the seminars could not have made so well, was the chance, even the invitation, to give papers on subjects not in the curriculum. Of the departments later added at Hopkins, many—certainly political science, economics, philosophy, education, geology, and botany—appeared first in the guise of papers before the associations, papers by students who pursued their interests beyond the bounds of the university's departments, by faculty members who were expanding and specializing the older disciplines, and by visitors who were dramatizing new areas of learning that still had little formal academic recognition. The emergence of a new subject in a curriculum has traditionally been a slow process; at Hopkins it was often initiated and hastened by the associations.

Many of the functions of the associations were partially filled by other aspects of the institution. They were somewhat forced in creation, and their democratic trimmings were of little significance. But they were not an excrescence of university life—they were part of the living pattern.

The appropriation in December, 1876, of an additional $400 in order that the library might remain open from 9 A.M. to 10 P.M. must have brought forcibly to Gilman's mind the difference between Hopkins and the Yale of the 1860s, where he had begged in vain for money even to heat the library.[93] But the trustees did not intend to make the library a principal expenditure. By 1889, they had, in fact,

[92] JHC, I, 18, 33; VII, 80; III, 138, 70.
[93] TM, Dec. 4, 1876. For a detailed history of the library, including the problems of departmental division, see French, *History of Johns Hopkins*, 206–213.

spent only $71,000 for books, depending in large part on the Peabody Institute Library.[94] The Peabody in 1876 contained only about 60,000 volumes, but under the guidance of Johnson, who was chairman of its library committee, they had been selected to form a truly scholarly library. Professors and fellows alike made frequent use of the Peabody, and when the summer heat arrived, its high-ceilinged rooms were the only "place of refuge" for a dedicated scholar. In 1881, Gilman declared that use of this library had saved Hopkins $200,000.[95] Yet the situation was not a permanently satisfactory one, and even in the early years there were frictions, as when C. S. Peirce complained of "the jailer of the Peabody library."[96] Although the Mercantile, Maryland Historical, and Baltimore Bar Libraries also proved useful and a Baltimore union catalogue was printed, there remained inconvenience and uncertainty; this Gilman must have known, since he once wrote, "There is no such thing as a strong university apart from a great library."[97] Even if one granted the Peabody to be of highest quality and assumed that Gilman's past experience as a librarian made every purchase by Hopkins careful and valuable, the number of accessions was surprisingly small. Although one thousand serials by 1889 represented a remarkable collection from many countries, scarcely surpassed in German universities, the number of bound volumes was less than one-tenth of the 360,000 volumes which Harvard claimed in that year.[98]

Nor was the supervision of the Hopkins library as professional or consistent as would have been best. In April, 1876, Thomas Murray

[94] Thomas R. Ball to Charles Graham Dunlop, Jan. 16, 1889, GP; Johnson to "Read," May 17, 1876, Johnson letter book.

[95] Gilman, "Hopkins Inaugural," 8; "Use of the Library of the Peabody Institute by Members of the Johns Hopkins University," manuscript report prepared by a Peabody official, apparently for 1876–1877, GP; Albert S. Cook to Lanman, May 27, 1880, Lanman Papers; Gilman, untitled notes for address of Feb. 22, 1881, GP.

[96] Peirce to Gilman, Nov. 15, 1883; Nathaniel H. Morison to Gilman, Feb. 25, 1886; Lanman diary, March 5, 1880.

[97] Jameson diary, Nov. 8, 1880, Feb. 15, 17, 1882; Herrick, "Hopkins," *Scribner's Monthly*, XIX, 206; ARJH (1878), 32.

[98] Arthur W. Tyler to Gilman, Sept. 24, 1878; JHC, IV, 108; ARJH (1889), 47; [Herbert B. Adams] to editor, May 14, 1878, *Amherst Student*, May 18, 1878; Harvard University catalogue (1889–1890), 340. For the distress which the limitations of early library policy caused faculty members of a later generation, see Kemp Malone, "Some Observations on Gilman's Hopkins," *JH Alumni Magazine*, XIX (1930–1931), 306–307.

took charge of setting up the library. His major interest was in his post as associate in Semitic languages, however, and early in the first term a new librarian, Arthur W. Tyler, came from the Astor Library. Tyler stayed only until November, 1878. A resolution by the trustees aimed at discouraging "loud talking and conversation" in the library indicated that his successor, A. Duncan Savage, fellow in Greek, guided the library with a loose hand during his year's tenure.[99] The librarian who followed Savage, William Hand Browne, held the post until 1891, during a period when he was also associate in English.

Like many other aspects of Hopkins life, the library reflected the growing mutual support among American universities. The very first year, Lanman was able to borrow copies of the *Archaeologische Zeitung* by mail from the Cornell library, and Gilman reported co-operation whenever such loans from other libraries were sought. In time Hopkins was able to reciprocate.[100] As Gilman said, it was not enough for books to be "collected and stored away for the generations to come." He had known of "libraries where a book off the shelves was regarded as a book out of place, where the librarians were indeed the keepers of the books, where every inquiry for a rare or costly volume was received by the officer in charge . . . as if his private cashbook had been called for." Gilman was well aware that use, after all, was what counted.[101] Whatever its handicaps in quantity and personnel, that was the dedication of the Johns Hopkins library.[102]

The fellowship system, which had brought such a remarkable group of young men to Johns Hopkins in 1876, remained a major strand in the university's pattern—"the key to our position," Trustee Brown called it.[103] The earliest significant revision of the fellowship policy came in 1885 with a limitation of tenure to one year "except for unusual considerations." Further undercutting came in 1888 after financial reverses. The trustees voted that fellows should no longer be exempt from tuition, thus effectively lowering the stipend from $500

[99] ARJH (1877), 33; Tyler to Gilman, Oct. 17, 1876, Sept. 20, 1878; TM, Dec. 2, 1878, Feb. 3, 1879.

[100] Lanman diary, Feb. 3, 1877; ARJH (1880), 25; Browne to Lanman, Feb. 26, 1881, Lanman Papers.

[101] ARJH (1878), 32; *University Problems*, 253.

[102] For the relationship of the growth of universities to the growth of their libraries, see Arthur E. Bestor, Jr., "The Transformation of American Scholarship, 1875–1917," *Library Quarterly*, XXIII (1953), 164–179.

[103] Brown to Gilman, Aug. 11, 1881.

to $400.[104] That these changes deprived the university of promising graduates can hardly be doubted, especially since the system had by the mid-eighties been widely imitated. If there was no sudden drop in quality, this was largely because other policies brought men to Hopkins more cheaply, with the fellowship as a goal to be sought while in residence. The *Annual Report* of 1880 revealed this tendency: "It is obvious from the nature of the case that Graduate Students residing in Baltimore must have better opportunities than others of making known their powers to the appointing board." [105]

Learning that the full $500 fellowship was not necessary to attract a good graduate student, the trustees were soon to institute initial scholarships of much lower value. In 1879, the president and professors had themselves contributed $500 for two graduate scholarships, both of which went to members of the class of 1879 at Hopkins. The trustees then set up an annual program of ten $250 scholarships plus free tuition, beginning in the 1880–1881 term. These scholarships were given at mid-term to graduate students of merit.[106] Ideally, from the point of view of the administration, a graduate came to Hopkins at his own expense with ambitions and hopes, winning a scholarship by his efforts one year and a fellowship the next. This plan produced a good many more gifted and hard-working students per dollar expended.

In 1887, $10,000 was given to found a fellowship in biology in memory of Adam T. Bruce, a former Hopkins fellow who had died shortly after being appointed instructor. This grant added to the series of progressive goals, for only former Hopkins fellows were eligible.[107] It also forecast the future salvation of the fellowship program by private donors.

The title "Fellow by Courtesy" was an extremely useful one, giving honor but no money; and as time passed, the university grew more and more able to give the former, less and less the latter. Hopkins was a way station between German training and American teaching positions, and very often the fellowship by courtesy represented a formal welcome. Some with this status remained only part of a year, some for several years, some entered vigorously into the activities of the

---

[104] JHR (1885), 64, 61; (1888), 112.   [105] ARJH (1885), 16; (1880), 52.
[106] TM, June 12, 1879; JHR (1884), 35–36; Jameson diary, Jan. 17, 1881.
[107] TM, May 2, 1887; JHR (1889), 113.

place, and it was not unknown for a fellow by courtesy to join the paid teaching staff.

In scholarship and fellowship policies, the decade of the eighties ended with more openings offered to graduates than at its beginning, but with none so generous as the original $500 fellowships with free tuition. As to undergraduates, six of the grants were more generous than the mere tuition exemption which the trustees had offered in 1880, but there were only fifteen undergraduate scholarships, all designed for Marylanders. The early purpose of the grants to attract good students to a new university, although not altogether absent, had largely yielded to the purpose of stimulating good work among students already enrolled and keeping them at Hopkins with gradually increasing rewards. No special consideration was given to the needy student; all decisions were based on merit. The daring prominence of the fellowship policy was gone, partly because financial difficulties had lessened its benefits, partly because it was no longer unique. By 1889 the pioneering work of Hopkins in student stipends had ended.[108]

From 1878 to 1889, Johns Hopkins awarded 151 Ph.D.'s. During the same period Harvard granted 43 Ph.D.'s and 12 S.D.'s. Yale granted 101 Ph.D.'s from the time that it introduced the degree in America in 1861 to 1889.[109] Thus, numerical pre-eminence alone would attach particular interest to the Hopkins Ph.D., which was granted for the first time on June 13, 1878. The four recipients were Henry C. Adams in political economy, Thomas Craig in mathematics, Josiah Royce in the history of philosophy, and Ernest Sihler in Greek history and literature, each of whom became professor of his specialty in a leading American university. In either the written or oral examinations for each candidate, the university had utilized a scholar not on the Hopkins staff. The four had been expected to display a reading knowledge of Latin, French, and German and to prove that they were acquainted with the "methods of modern scientific research." (This was interpreted as meaning that they must have pursued at least one

[108] The further development of fellowship and scholarship policies can be traced in Thomas R. Ball, "Student Aid in the Johns Hopkins University," *JH Alumni Magazine*, IV (1915–1916), 196–203.

[109] Edward G. Bourne, "The Early History of the Degree of Doctor of Philosophy in the United States," *Educational Review*, X (1895), 81–84; catalogues of Harvard and Yale.

branch of natural science. This was not a requirement in later years.)
The thesis requirement was the only one which seems lenient by later
standards. Although the thesis must show the candidate's "mastery of
his subject, his powers of independent thought as well as of careful
research, and his ability to express, in a clear and systematic order,
and in appropriate language, the results of his study," it was submitted to just one reader and required the candidate's labor only "for
the greater part of an academic year." [110]

As Gildersleeve observed in a speech at the bestowal of degrees,
the university itself was on trial:

We can only say that we have not done this lightly. We have tried them for
two years of unresting activity; we have examined them over and over in
class-room and in *seminarium;* we have repeatedly put them to the test of
original work. Mindful of what the word *doctor* means, we have given them
opportunity to show their power of expression as lecturers, their didactic
faculty as teachers.

But none of the tests Gildersleeve listed carried the impact of his
statement that the institution granted these men its degree "not only
for the knowledge acquired but for the spirit manifested—that spirit
'which counts nothing done while aught remains to be done.' " Their
acceptance of congratulation, he told them, was "a pledge of higher
achievement." [111]

The regulations that appeared in *Registers* of the 1870s were never
quite so grueling as those for this first group of Ph.D.'s. But revisions
which gradually added difficulties began in 1881, when the required
period between bachelor's and doctor's was lengthened from two to
three years. In October, 1883, the Academic Council created a group
including president, professors, and associate professors, eventually
known as the Board of University Studies, to control "the instruction
and examination of graduate students." [112] This board added ever
more specific regulations. In 1884, for the first time, two subordinate
subjects rather than one were required. In 1885, details as to the
format of the thesis were outlined, the typewriter recommended, and
one copy required for deposit in the library. In 1887, the ability to

---

[110] ARJH (1878), 37–39.
[111] *Johns Hopkins University, Baltimore: First Bestowal of Degrees,* printed
broadside, copy in Josiah Royce Papers, vol. XCVI, Harvard University Archives.
[112] JHR (1881), 30; French, *History of Johns Hopkins,* 341; TM, Dec. 5, 1887.

translate French and German at sight (probably an unwritten requirement earlier) was specified. An official adviser for each candidate was to be appointed, and two referees were to read the thesis. Printing of the thesis, or a sizable portion thereof, and presentation of 150 copies to the university also became requirements.[113]

If precision of standards made a degree meaningful, then the Hopkins Ph.D. of 1889 excelled that of 1878; but if infection with the spirit of learning was the test, then probably all the new regulations never produced so deserving a class as the four Ph.D.'s of 1878.

That the doctorate was precious in Gilman's sight is shown by his refusal to be lured into wholesale granting of honorary degrees. "Universities should bestow their honors sparingly," he had said in his inaugural. In 1902, at the twenty-fifth anniversary celebration, the university granted ten honorary M.A.'s (to former graduate students who had not taken degrees) and twenty-four LL.D.'s, but until that time it had awarded only two honorary degrees.[114] Rowland's Ph.D. in 1880 recognized his original contributions to physics and his need to stand in judgment over candidates for the degree. More traditional motives led to the other exception. On February 12, 1881, President Rutherford B. Hayes, then in his lame-duck period, came to visit the university. Not till he was already on the grounds, apparently, did the idea strike Gilman that he should be granted a degree. With probably the greatest speed and least red-tape in educational history, a quorum of trustees was rounded up, the degree voted, an assembly of students called, and an LL.D. presented to the guest.[115]

As life went by at Hopkins, a day must have seemed only a day and a year only a year. Growth is difficult to observe when one is part of it. But Gilman's efforts on Commemoration Day and in his *Annual Report*, the ever-increasing number of faces, and the ever-mounting statistics must have shown participants that this was no longer the Hopkins of 1876. The change lay not only in numbers, but in the very patterns of the university life. In spite of the words of Lanier's ode, "So quick she bloomed, she seemed to bloom at birth," [116] Hopkins undeniably matured with the years. Yet it is amazing how much that still merits applause was present in the first year and

[113] JHR (1884), 30; (1885), 59–60; (1887), 75–77.
[114] "Hopkins Inaugural," 19; *Hopkins Twenty-fifth Anniversary*, 96–103.
[115] TM, Feb. 12, 1881; JHC, I, 134.   [116] JHC, I, 39.

how much that seems to a later generation injurious sprang from the pressure of events—especially financial need.

Praiseworthy patterns—the president's specialized roles as unifier and ambassador, the trustees' roles as friends and counselors as well as final authority and financial guardians, publication as stimulus, preserver, and external contact, and associations as paths of internal communication—all began in the first year. Certain later decisions are of more questionable merit: the curtailment of visiting lecturers, the lessening of fellowship and scholarship stipends, the limitation of the library in size. With enough money, all these practices could have been improved. The bureaucratizing of the degree-winning process was perhaps necessary to accommodate the greater number of candidates, but it made the experience more impersonal.

These were the minor lights and shadings. The major patterns involved the three essentials of the most rustic classroom—teachers, students, and ideas. It is by the record of these that a university must be judged.

: CHAPTER VII :

A New Profession

GILMAN once pictured for the public a faculty that "no love of ease, no dread of labor, no fear of consequences, no desire for wealth" could divert from their pursuit of learning.[1] His own faculty, however, deemed significant the mundane matters of rank, tenure, and salary. Whether consciously or not, these men were building a new profession in America, that of university professor. Their story cannot be told as a monastical striving for truth isolated from considerations of income and prestige.

As to rank, the simplicity of the first year gradually yielded to a proliferation of titles, and of meanings for the same title. The position of professor stayed relatively stable. The original six remained the nucleus of the faculty without change till 1883, and there were never more than nine professors during the 1880s.[2]

The original title of associate covered a broad swath of relationships. For example, Philip R. Uhler held the rank from 1876 till his death in 1913, without salary and without teaching a course, largely as a courtesy to one who was librarian and later provost of the Peabody Institute. Yet until 1883 it was also the title of William E. Story, who arrived with a Ph.D. and teaching experience and kept a full schedule of classes. In the late 1870s, some wanted to add the title of assistant professor as a stage above that of associate. Lanman at first believed this to be his title when his salary as associate was

[1] JHC, IV, 47.
[2] The analysis of ranks is based on JHR unless otherwise noted.

increased in 1878. H. B. Adams, after a year as associate, asked if he might not take that title. But no such change was made, and as other positions were added, the associates came to be regarded as equivalent to assistant professors elsewhere. Not until 1945, however, did the title actually become "assistant professor." [3]

The addition of the rank of assistant in 1879 gave a certain status to the associates. The next year the title "instructor" was also used, but assistants and instructors were classified together, and there seems to have been no meaningful distinction between them. The number in this lowest faculty category varied during the 1880s from six to fifteen.

By 1883, many of the associates had served the university for seven years without a change in rank. Rather than make them professors, however, the trustees created the new position of associate professor, and eight associates were at once advanced.[4] By the 1888–1889 term, the faculty included sixteen associate professors.

Examiners not on the faculty received fees during the second year,[5] and by the third year seven examiners were listed with the members of the academic staff. Although the practice of using outside examiners continued throughout the 1880s, in the 1882–1883 term the university publicly named only the two who actually conducted classes in the university (William Hand Browne and Charles Frederick Raddatz). From 1884 to 1886 only Raddatz held this rank, and he was counted with the associates in computing faculty totals for the *Register*. The title then disappeared.

The most confused title was that of lecturer. Not until the 1883–1884 term did the *Register* begin to specify those giving only short courses, and even then resident and nonresident lecturers were not discriminated. But from 1886, only one lecturer was listed as a member of the staff: John Shaw Billings, librarian of the Surgeon General's office, adviser in the organization of the hospital and medical school.

In the spring of 1887, the executive committee requested a study of the possibility of instituting at Hopkins the *Privatdocent* system of the German universities. The result seems to have been the appointment that fall of five "readers," but not under the *Privatdocent*

---

[3] Lanman diary, June 5, 14, 1878; H. B. Adams to Lanman, Sept. 1, 1878, Lanman Papers; Gilman to H. B. Adams, June 20, 1879; French, *History of Johns Hopkins*, 347.
[4] TM, June 4, 1883. [5] TM, June 7, 1878.

system of payment by student fees. In its first year, this new rank included both Edward Cowles, who gave only two lectures in psychology, and Herbert Weir Smyth, who taught three courses in Greek throughout the year.[6] The next year it seemed that the chief use of this rank would be to encourage young men of promise who had their doctorates and could not fit into the ever-less-flexible fellowship system. It was as a reader that Woodrow Wilson returned to lecture at Hopkins. Although the readership never matured into a new way of aiding young scholars, it did strengthen course offerings without costly additions to the resident staff. By 1890 those of this rank were indistinguishable from visiting lecturers.

The early Hopkins had no system of guaranteed tenure. The professors who came with established reputations were appointed indefinitely, but the trustees formally reserved "the right to remove from office any president or professor in active service, who may, in their opinion, be unworthy of his position by reason of character, conduct, or inefficiency." As one professor pointed out, legally speaking tenure was "merely on suffrance." [7] A younger professor would be appointed for a term of years, usually three.[8] Similarly, associates were appointed for limited terms, often of only one year. This insecurity occasioned dissatisfaction among the associates, and one of them, Charles S. Hastings, went to Gilman with the complaints. Soon afterward, the trustees passed a resolution that associates would hold office "during the pleasure of the board," a phrase which they said implied six months' notice.[9] Within a year, however, an associate learned as late as May that he was "not rehired" for the next term.[10] Later in the decade, an appointment as associate professor was said by the trustees to be a contract for a minimum of six months' notice before termination by either party. Ever careful to protect itself from faculty claims, the board voted when it created the rank of associate professor that "continuance in the office of Associate Professor for any period" would not entitle a faculty member to promotion to professor.[11] Important work in behalf of faculty tenure was to take

[6] ECM, May 21, 1887; JHC, VII, 3, 54.

[7] TM, June 15, 1881; Sylvester to Gilman, Oct. 24, 1884.

[8] Gilman, draft answer to letter of Karl J. Trübner to Thomas R. Ball, May 4, 1892.

[9] Gilman to Hastings, Jan. 30, 1880; TM, May 3, 1880.

[10] See p. 166 below.   [11] TM, June 4, 1888, June 4, 1883.

place at Hopkins in 1915, when its professors took the lead in the formation of the American Association of University Professors, but in the 1880s the staff had no guarantee of tenure except assurance by Gilman, accurate to be sure, that the trustees had "never been inclined to changes in the personnel of the university." [12]

In an era of low costs and no income tax, Sylvester's $6,000 a year, the highest of the early salaries, was far from miserly. Nor was the $5,000 that other professors attained a poor salary, even though Gildersleeve complained that it was hard to keep up appearances. (He warned, in fact, against hiring wealthy professors, who might set an even higher standard of life.) [13] Gilman at first had doubts about paying men of the same rank different salaries. Assured by Brush that this was proper, inasmuch as it was done in Germany, he used the practice with skill, giving Remsen and Rowland the same title as Sylvester at a salary half as large.[14] The difference between the highest and lowest salaries was remarkable. With a new Ph.D., Jameson as instructor in history earned $600 a year, one-tenth of Sylvester's salary and only one-fifth more than the fellows. Associates initially earned as little as $1,250, though after four years those with the longest tenure received raises to $2,250. When the rank of associate professor was created in 1883, its maximum salary was set at $3,000, "to be reached by successive advancements." [15] Some young men of promise received nothing but their titles. Henry H. Donaldson, for example, served one year as instructor in histology of the nervous system without pay.[16] No sabbaticals are on record at Hopkins during the 1870s or 1880s, though Harvard had such a program; however, one associate professor was granted a year's leave with half pay because of a severe illness.[17]

Gilman has been almost universally praised for believing in "men not bricks." [18] But the statistics indicate that the university could have

[12] Hofstadter and Metzger, *Development of Academic Freedom*, 476–477; Gilman to Herbert E. Greene, June 8, 1893.

[13] Gildersleeve to Gilman, July 27, 1882.

[14] George Brush to Gilman, Jan. 9, 1876.

[15] Jameson diary, June 6, 1882; Lanman diary, June 4, 1877; ECM, April 10, 1880; TM, June 4, 1883.

[16] Gilman memorandum, [August, 1888]; other examples from interview with Professor Whitehead.

[17] ECM, June 9, 1888.

[18] E.g., Ely, *Ground under Our Feet*, 100; Flexner, *I Remember*, 49.

afforded more generous salary and leave policies before its drastic losses of the late 1880s. Professor Kemp Malone has acutely observed that the Howard Street land and buildings cost nearly one million dollars and that the percentage of receipts spent on salaries was 36 in 1880–1881 and 47 in 1885–1886, compared with approximately 70 in 1929–1930.[19] Of course a new university has obligations that an established one does not. It cannot, for instance, rely on alumni aid in emergencies. Nor could the trustees of Hopkins forget their obligation to plan for a medical school. Nevertheless, the record of faculty building includes some penny-wise decisions that seem today unduly costly to the intellectual life of the institution and the development of professional standards.

The youth of the early Hopkins faculty made it easy to ignore the question of a pension system. Sylvester, the only member conceivably near an age for retirement, indicated that nothing was further from his mind. Yet it was the university's effort to win more scholars from Europe, where university teaching was a profession with well-established perquisites, that forced it to consider pension programs. In 1879, Hermann von Holst gave the lack of pensions at Hopkins as an important reason for refusing its professorship of history and remaining in Germany. Trustee Thomas in Europe in the spring of 1881 found that lack of pensions handicapped the university in its efforts to win the Scotch philosopher Robert Flint.[20] Apparently with Flint and other European scholars in mind, the trustees in June, 1881, voted that the president and professors could retire or be retired at sixty-five with one-third of their regular salary during the year before retirement (this might be raised to one-half, but not more). The trustees might still require some services of the pensioners. This step, they said, was to "affirm their purpose to make the position of a professor in this University permanently attractive to those who are called to it."[21] The program never went into effect. In 1885, the matter was raised again by another Scotch professor, Matthew Hay, whom the trustees had elected professor of pharmacology and

---

[19] Malone, "Gilman's Hopkins," *JH Alumni Magazine*, XIX, 308, 305. By 1882 the total spent for land, ground rent capitalized, and buildings was $324,729.39 (Francis White to John W. Garrett, April 24, 1882, Garrett Papers).

[20] Von Holst to Gilman, Aug. 12, 1879; Thomas to Gilman, June 7, 1881.

[21] TM, June 15, 1881.

therapeutics, to take office in 1887. In answer to Hay's query, the executive committee said that the pension program was under consideration.[22] That summer they paid Clayton Colman Hall, a graduate student, to make an analysis of various pension systems; his report was the basis of a discussion in November, but no decision was reached.[23] In the meeting of June, 1886, aided no doubt by the recent drop of the B. & O. semiannual dividend, the sentiment for economy triumphed with the passing of Gwinn's resolution for complete repeal of the pension system.[24] This decision permanently weakened the attractiveness of the institution to scholars and ended another pioneering program.

With considerable insight, Gilman publicly described needed reforms in the emerging profession of university professor, even though he did not always win them for his own institution. In 1879 he advocated before the American Social Science Association the enhancing of such a career, especially by "the certainty of official tenure, and the expectation of a pension." He could cite from his own failures the appeal of these aspects of the profession in Europe. He also emphasized the importance of salary, insisting that potboilers, lyceum lecturing, and worry about grocer's bills represented "force withdrawn from higher labors." [25]

For a time it seemed that Johns Hopkins might make even more dramatic advances in the professionalization of university teaching. Encouraged by the 10 per cent annual dividend record which B. & O. common stock had maintained since 1872, the trustees had included an elaborate outline for a financially satisfied and widely inclusive faculty in their plan of procedure of 1875.[26] But future vicissitudes of those dividends set unwanted boundaries to their program. A dip during the years 1877–1880 hampered expansion. A confident period followed with dividends at 10 per cent from 1881 to 1885, but the

[22] ECM, March 2, 1885.   [23] ECM, June 18, Sept. 28, Nov. 28, 1885.

[24] TM, June 14, 1886. This decision may have been the unknown factor that brought Hay's resignation in August, 1886. Cf. Chesney, *Johns Hopkins Hospital*, I, 88.

[25] "American Education, 1869–1879: Annual Address of the President, D. C. Gilman, LL.D., Delivered in Saratoga (Wednesday Evening, September 10, 1879)," *Journal of Social Science*, X (1879), 15; Gilman, "The Idea of the University," *North American Review*, CXXXIII (1881), 364–365.

[26] See p. 27 above.

decline that began in 1886 reached an absolute bottom from 1888 to 1890 with no dividend either in cash or in stock.[27]

The trustees never aimed at the total curricular variety that was the goal of Cornell and rejected suggestions for courses in music and military science.[28] On the other hand, it had never been their intention to have only five departments headed by professors, and in the fall of the second academic year, the executive committee set up a sub-committee to report on enlarging the staff. The three branches of learning where development was felt to be most necessary at that time were philosophy, history, and modern language.[29] But no better solution was immediately found than the continuation of part-time lecturers. On December 2, 1878, however, a report of the executive committee to the full board charted a major enlargement of the faculty.[30] Calling the university's principles sound and all existing departments worthy, the report listed eight fields requiring additional instruction. These were history (including jurisprudence, political history, political economy, and social science), philosophy (including logic, psychology, ethics, and the "history of opinions"), English language and literature, applied mathematics (including mechanics and astronomy), Latin, botany, physical geography, and drawing and vocal culture for undergraduates. All these needs could not be filled at once, it was noted, but $14,500 was on hand to make a start. Apparently in the interests of saving money for permanent staff members, it was suggested that expenditure for visiting lecturers be cut from $4,000 to $1,500. For two of the most conspicuous lacks—English and Latin—associates were found by the beginning of the 1879–1880 term; elsewhere part-time lectureships were the most that was provided. But a path was now marked.

Since three of their original six professors had been Europeans, it was not surprising that the trustees again looked across the Atlantic. The search was intensified in the spring of 1880 by sending Gilder-

[27] The percentage of annual dividends was as follows: 1872–1876, 10; 1877, 8; 1878, 8 (stock); 1879, 4 (stock) and 4; 1880, 9; 1881–1885, 10; 1886, 8; 1887, 4; 1888–1890, 0 (*Moody's Transportation Manual* [New York, 1957], 568).

[28] White, *Autobiography*, I, 300; ECM, Oct. 31, 1883, Jan. 31, 1885.

[29] ECM, Nov. 2, 1877; Gilman to George S. Morris, Dec. 11, 1877.

[30] "Report from the Exec. Committee to the Board of Trustees, Dec. 2, 1878," manuscript copy, JHUP.

sleeve abroad. His reports were disconcerting, telling of "the difficulty, indeed the impossibility of moving anybody from these older seats of learning." From the vantage point of London, the Greek professor reflected unhappily on the imbalance of the university.[31]

The summer having yielded no notable additions, the trustees felt compelled to take radical measures. In their meeting of November 1, 1880, they resolved to add to the staff "before the beginning of the next academic year, several (eight or more) teachers, of whom three or more shall be of the grade of Professor, and the others of the grade of Associate." This time they listed ten fields in which teachers were needed: Sanskrit and comparative philology, Semitic language, ethics and psychology, political economy, jurisprudence and public law, literature, mechanics, astronomy, botany, and geology. With a tone of urgency, the board recommended that $20,000 be spent for the new faculty members and appointed Cheston, Brown, Thomas, and Gilman as a committee to search by letter or travel and to consult the Hopkins professors for suggestions. On the following Commemoration Day, Gilman admitted that the staff was too small, but confided the good news of the decision to expand.[32]

Although Thomas and King went to Europe in the spring of 1881 and searched assiduously, though Sylvester continued to make daring proposals (one of which did bring his friend Arthur Cayley for an extended period of lectures the next term), no new professors were found for the fall of 1881.[33] A Hopkins Ph.D. returned to become associate in Sanskrit, and one associate in English who had studied in Germany was exchanged for another with a Leipzig Ph.D. An American with a Ph.D. from Heidelberg was made assistant in political economy. Only a tiny fraction of the charted course had been traversed, and not nearly $20,000 was spent. But it was not from lack of trying.

The impetus which could have enlarged the faculty of philosophy at the opening of the 1880s failed. This was the greater misfortune because the trustees were never again to feel so confident about the financial capacities of the university. Before any diminution of the

[31] Gildersleeve to Gilman, May 17, June 9, 1880.
[32] Gilman, untitled notes for address of Feb. 22, 1881, GP.
[33] Dobbin to Gilman, July 25, 1881.

B. & O. dividend occurred, as early as 1884, they were pulling in sail.[34] The drive to open the medical school and the need to provide buildings for the sciences seem to have been the chief causes. When Gilman went to Europe in 1883, he found a professor of Semitics, but it was a pathologist that the trustees particularly instructed him to seek out.[35] Never again in sweeping strokes would the board list the departments that it would like to create. By the end of the decade the president of the crippled university in a public statement limited his aspirations to two fields where the lack of professors was most keenly felt—philosophy and English.[36] Nor would the trustees soon again launch experiments to make the American academic profession the equal of the European.

[34] On May 5, 1884, the trustees began to plan special savings for building purposes. On May 28, 1884, the executive committee decided "to give an intimation to members of the Academic Staff not to expect an increase of salary."
[35] TM, May 7, 1883.   [36] JHC, VIII, 14.

: CHAPTER VIII :

Mathematics and
Natural Sciences

SUCH was the "assured renown" which Sylvester continued to bring to the mathematics department that Gilman and the whole university honored him and gave special understanding to his eccentricities. His public reading of his poems, his early spring departures for Europe, and his pre-emption of most of the mathematical columns in the *Circulars* could not diminish his stature. Sylvester spoke of his connection with the university as "a new lease of mathematical life" and felt that he had "every reason in the world to think well of America and Americans."[1] For three years Story was the only other teacher of mathematics on the faculty, but in 1879 two more were added with the rank of assistant—Craig, one of the first class of Ph.D.'s, and Fabian Franklin, a fellow who was to win his Ph.D. in 1880. The next year Craig was advanced to associate "in applied mathematics," a phrase which remained part of his title in 1883 when both he and Story became associate professors. Meanwhile, Craig had refused an invitation from Harvard.[2] Franklin, made associate in 1882, displayed skill and sympathy in the teaching of undergraduates, which was his chief responsibility.[3]

[1] Sylvester to Mrs. Benjamin Peirce, March 25, 1880, Benjamin Peirce Papers.
[2] Craig to Charles W. Eliot, April 28, 1881, Eliot Papers.
[3] Interview with Mr. Edward Duffy, March 6, 1953; Frederic C. Howe, *The Confessions of a Reformer* (New York, 1925), 30.

The Johns Hopkins University

The most significant change in the mathematics department, indeed an end to its golden era, came in 1883, when Sylvester resigned to become Savilian Professor of Geometry at Oxford. The institution retained some of the luster of its most famous mathematician, however, by naming him professor emeritus.[4] At an elaborate farewell assembly in Hopkins Hall on December 20, 1883, Gilman cited Sylvester's dual achievement in making Baltimore "the stronghold of mathematics in America" and presenting "an ideal standard of university life."[5] In his hour-long speech of farewell, Sylvester said that his successor at this "Normal School of the United States" would have the responsibility for molding the mathematical education of the American people—"an influence far greater than any influence I can exercise in any chair that I know of in either of our great Universities in Great Britain."[6] Although he retained the friendliest relations with his former Hopkins colleagues, Sylvester never returned to America.

The search for Sylvester's successor was a major test. The result would forecast whether or not the university could continue to attract first-rank scholars without regard to nationality. Sylvester cooperated fully in the search. During the summer of 1883 in England, he had discussed the problem of a successor with Gilman and suggested that the worthiest prospect was Felix Klein of the University of Leipzig, a mathematician in his thirties. Gilman was skeptical, having dealt with German professors before. He declared that they tended to fish for prestige-giving invitations which they had already determined not to accept. Nevertheless, Klein was offered a professorship at $5,000 a year, shortly before Sylvester's departure.[7] In his farewell speech, Sylvester described his expected successor like a John the Baptist describing the coming Messiah. But the Messiah did not choose to come, and the second choice of the trustees, Sylvester's English friend Arthur Cayley, would not move either.[8]

Finally elected was the man who had been second choice in 1876—Simon Newcomb, head of the Naval Observatory in Washington and editor of the *Nautical Almanac*. Although he once referred to him-

[4] TM, Oct. 1, 1883.
[5] Unidentified Baltimore newspaper, Dec. 21, 1883, AFJH.
[6] Sylvester, "Remarks at Farewell Reception," GP; JHC, III, 31.
[7] Sylvester to Gilman, Sept. 15, 1883; TM, Dec. 11, 1883.
[8] TM, Feb. 4, 1884; Gilman to Sylvester, Feb. 7, 1884.

self as merely "a good computer who has hit upon some fertile ideas," [9] Newcomb was the most famous living American mathematician in 1884. He had long been connected with Johns Hopkins as visiting lecturer, examiner, and associate editor of the *American Journal of Mathematics*.[10] In many ways the choice of this "big, lusty, joyous man" [11] of forty-nine seemed a logical and auspicious one.

But there were less happy aspects. For one thing, Newcomb was not a full-time replacement for Sylvester. He received a salary of $2,500 with the understanding that he would "devote half his time to the service of the University," and it was easily foreseeable that the center of his activity would remain elsewhere.[12] He was not a gifted teacher; [13] his title was "Professor of Mathematics and Astronomy," and most of his courses were in the latter field. After 1888, ill-health limited his work at the university even further.[14] His forays into the field of economics included public assaults on his colleague Richard T. Ely.[15] Through no fault of Newcomb's, the university had lost the potential éclat of installing another famous European.

The university could for the first time, however, offer advanced work in astronomy. This had been one of the goals set in 1880, and in 1882 the executive committee had begun plans for an observatory. A small observatory was included as part of the new physics building, completed in 1887. In that year, also, Newcomb began to list his courses separately from the mathematics department.[16] No one earned a Ph.D. in astronomy, however, until 1891.

Another gain was the better organization of the mathematics department. The course offerings became systematized and carefully graded. Story instituted an introductory course for graduate students, which surveyed the whole field. The monthly "seminary" became

[9] Newcomb to Arthur Cayley, Jan. 26, 1874, Newcomb Papers.

[10] TM, June 7, 1878; JHC, IV, 26. Two years earlier he had written Gilman that he considered his failure to lecture at Hopkins one of his sins of omission, but that his interest in the university remained strong (letter of Sept. 29, 1882).

[11] Howe, *Confessions*, 30.

[12] TM, Oct. 6, 1884; J. E. Walker to Newcomb, Oct. 16, 1884, Newcomb Papers.

[13] Crum and Baker, "Picturesque Personalities," *JH Alumni Magazine*, XV, 153; W. P. Holcomb to Albert Shaw, Feb. 26, 1887, Albert Shaw Papers, Manuscript Division, New York Public Library.

[14] Thomas Craig to Gilman, June 23, 1888; Ira Remsen to Gilman, May 19, 1890; Newcomb to Gilman, Sept. 10, 1890.

[15] See pp. 179–186 below.

[16] TM, Nov. 1, 1880; ECM, April 10, 1882; JHC, VI, 92.

the mathematical society, and three seminaries were established to hold meetings weekly, as in other departments: Newcomb's on astronomy; Story's on geometry and quaternions; and Craig's on theory of functions and differential equations.[17] But the inspiration of an ecstatic creator and living link with the mathematical past had departed with the stocky, absent-minded Victorian gentleman who was so poor an organizer.

In mathematics Johns Hopkins contributed to the two universities whose rising stars dimmed its own. Oskar Bolza, a protégé of Klein, who had just passed a winter in the English universities, spent a year as reader at Johns Hopkins—the ideal starting point, according to Klein, for Bolza's plan to develop a mathematical career in America.[18] From there he joined the original faculties of Clark in 1889 and Chicago in 1892. Story also moved to Clark when it opened, as professor of mathematics.

In contrast with the lessened achievement in mathematics after Sylvester's departure, the physics department and Henry A. Rowland moved from triumph to triumph. Rowland like Sylvester had a personality that yielded little to the demands of community harmony. The executive committee had to request formally that he give general lectures in physics; he spent money without authorization, felt his fox hunting more important than an "ordinary" meeting of the Academic Council, and could only fidget at a reception in his honor.[19] But his work in determining the mechanical equivalent of heat and his inventions in spectroscopy won fame throughout the scientific world, and the government made him its representative at various international electrical congresses.

The presence of Charles S. Hastings as an associate probably helped direct Rowland's interest to problems of light.[20] Hastings himself developed a theory of the sun's corona which he tested as a member of the expedition to the Caroline Islands in 1883 to view a solar

---

[17] Florian Cajori, *The Teaching and History of Mathematics in the United States* (Bureau of Education Circular of Information no. 3; Washington, 1890), 275–277.

[18] Klein to Newcomb, April 4, 1888; Bolza to Newcomb, Sept. 26, 1889; both in Newcomb Papers.

[19] ECM, June 7, 1878, Feb. 28, 1883; Rowland to Gilman, March 12, 1884; Crum and Baker, "Picturesque Personalities," *JH Alumni Magazine*, XV, 150.

[20] Thomas C. Mendenhall, "Henry A. Rowland: Commemorative Address," in *The Physical Papers of Henry Augustus Rowland* (Baltimore, 1902), 7.

eclipse. Having perhaps felt overshadowed by the firmly self-confident Rowland, Hastings returned from this expedition brimming with ambitions and new problems to attack.[21] He was promoted that year to associate professor, but in 1884 he left to take a professorship at his alma mater, Sheffield Scientific School. Meanwhile, Hopkins had sent to Harvard in 1881 Edwin H. Hall, whose discoveries in electromagnetism had won him a Ph.D. and a post as assistant in 1880.

Early in 1878, Charles S. Peirce, not then a member of the university, had advised Gilman that Rowland, of whom he had "a very high opinion," was not a good administrator or organizer. Hopkins needed two professors of physics, he urged, and Rowland should not be the department head.[22] Rowland himself suggested that an effort be made to win the "rarely excellent" J. Willard Gibbs of Yale for a chair of mechanics.[23] Gibbs came for a series of lectures on rational mechanics during January and February, 1880, and shortly afterward was offered a professorship with a two-year appointment at $3,000 a year. Gilman promised him much discretion "in the suggestion of courses & modes of instruction." He was to have his own laboratory and any books that he required. At first favorably inclined, Gibbs found the breaking of his ties at Yale more difficult than he expected, and there he remained.[24] Sylvester hoped that the university would not take no for an answer. He wrote Gilman that "no inducements held out to [Gibbs] could be too high," that at $5,000 a year he would be "dirt cheap." [25] But in this period of greatest financial sanguineness among the trustees, no higher offer was made. Rowland was to remain the only professor in the department, though many young men with bright futures came and went.

Harry Fielding Reid was assistant from 1882 to 1884, when he left for study abroad; he was to return permanently to the Hopkins staff in 1896. Arthur L. Kimball, a Ph.D. of 1884, remained as associate and was promoted to associate professor in 1888. Charles A. Perkins, Henry Crew, Gustav A. Liebig, and Joseph S. Ames all held assistantships in the late 1880s. In 1886, Louis Duncan, a graduate of the Naval Acad-

---

[21] Hastings to Gilman, June 12, 1883; JHC, II, 152–153.
[22] Peirce to Gilman, Jan. 13, 1878.   [23] Rowland to Gilman, May 8, 1879.
[24] Gibbs to Gilman, March 30, April 29, 1880; Gilman to Gibbs, April 8, 1880; all in Josiah Willard Gibbs Scientific Correspondence, Rare Book Room, Yale University Library.
[25] Sylvester to Gilman, June 10, 1880.

emy and a Hopkins Ph.D., was appointed associate in electricity; his courses, treated as a section of the physics department, were described as "electrical engineering." In 1887 the university announced a two-year course in applied electricity, leading to the Certificate of Proficiency in Applied Electricity.[26] Thus the remarkable blending of imaginative theorist and practical inventor in Henry Rowland came to be reflected in the department he founded.

Stability characterized the chemistry department, reflecting the conservative natures of Remsen and Morse. Both remained at Hopkins until their retirements in the next century. Morse became associate professor in 1883, a rank achieved by no one else in the department during the eighties. Out of the half-dozen assistants, only Edward Renouf won promotion to associate (1886). Renouf was attuned to the German orientation of the department; a Ph.D. from Freiburg, he had been assistant in chemistry at the University of Munich for five years before coming to Hopkins in 1885. Students found his methods in qualitative analysis "distractingly new and searching." [27] He too remained until well into the next century.

Biology had its utilitarian fulfillment in the medical school, and by the end of the eighties the physics department had developed a program in electrical engineering. In chemistry, however, Remsen stood firm against "practicalism." As long as he taught, he refused all offers of consultantships from private industry.[28] When one of his students suggested to him that private industries might support the financially beleaguered university by paying for laboratories and cited German examples, Remsen responded that he could think of no worse fate for the university than such an invasion.[29] Others have regretted Remsen's negative attitude toward the chemical industry as a failure to follow a worthy German precedent.[30]

In spite of Remsen's professed attitude, a highly important industrial application of chemistry emerged from his laboratory. It came in the

[26] JHC, VIII, 85; VI, 76.

[27] Charles Skeele Palmer, "The Old Johns Hopkins and the New Opportunity," *JH Alumni Magazine*, XI (1922–1923), 93–94.

[28] W. A. Noyes, "Ira Remsen," DAB, XV, 502.

[29] Letter from Judge Morris A. Soper, March 13, 1953; interview with Judge Morris A. Soper and Judge Jacob M. Moses, April 3, 1953. The student was Alfred R. L. Dohme.

[30] E. T. Allen, "Impressions of Ira Remsen," *JH Alumni Magazine*, XVI (1927–1928), 222–223.

course of the long-range program of the department which sought "the determination of the law governing the conduct of a large class of substitution products towards oxidizing agents." [31] Among the various investigations that Remsen had mapped out was one involving the oxidation of derivatives of toluene, a hydrocarbon which comes from coal tar. Part of this research, in 1879, was being carried out by a fellow in chemistry, Constantine Fahlberg, a German with a Leipzig Ph.D. Some of the resulting compound sputtered onto Fahlberg's fingers. He stuck them into his mouth and tasted an intense sweetness. The tale as told in the chemistry department is that Fahlberg caught the first train to Washington to patent the substance. Although the discovery was published in February, 1880, with Remsen and Fahlberg as joint authors, it was Fahlberg who made the fortune with the industrial development of the new sweetening, under the name "saccharin." In spite of the ill will that developed between Remsen and his student as to who deserved the credit, the university stressed the event as a utilitarian justification for its nonutilitarian methods.[32]

During Gilman's absence in 1889–1890, Remsen became acting president. On the whole, he found the duties light and enjoyable, although he told Gilman in June, 1890, that he was ready to yield the helm "without a sigh, save one of relief." [33] Soon afterward President William Rainey Harper beckoned to Remsen from the wealthy new university in Chicago. Fear swept Johns Hopkins. If this luminary departed, the university might appear moribund before the world. To everyone's relief, Remsen decided to stay. The price that the university had paid, younger faculty members believed, was an understanding that Remsen would succeed Gilman as president.[34] If Remsen asked for the presidency, recalling only the pleasant side of his single year's tenure, he was often to be reminded of the cares that he had felt by June. The administrative duties on which Gilman throve were a bane to Remsen, who retained his chairmanship of the chemistry department and con-

---

[31] JHC, III, 36.

[32] Interview with Judge Soper and Judge Moses; Getman, *Life of Remsen,* 61–62; JHC, VI, 81.

[33] Remsen to Gilman, Dec. 17, 1889, June 2, 1890.

[34] Interview with Judge Soper and Judge Moses. Thomas Wakefield Goodspeed, *The Story of the University of Chicago, 1890–1925* (Chicago, 1925), 86, implies that a promise of the presidency kept Remsen at Hopkins after Harper made "every effort" to secure him.

tinued his researches. "What!" he once exclaimed to a caller at the presidential office. "Are you bringing me more work to do?" [35]

It was under the auspices of the chemists that Hopkins developed the department of mineralogy and geology envisioned by the trustees in their plans of 1880. During the 1881–1882 term Morse initiated a course in mineralogy. Remsen pointed out that this was extra work carried on without compensation and that the university's mineralogical collection burdened the department in the absence of an instructor in the field.[36] The answer shortly came in the person of young George Huntington Williams, an Amherst graduate fresh from taking his Ph.D. at Heidelberg and eager to show America the importance of the microscope as a geological instrument. As a fellow by courtesy, he directed the work in mineralogy during the second half of the 1882–1883 term. Beginning as a narrow specialist in microscopic petrography, he grew as his department grew.[37] His skill as a teacher and the competing alternative of government employment aided him in gaining quick recognition at Hopkins. In 1883 he was appointed associate in mineralogy at a salary of $1,000 a year, and two years later he advanced to associate professor. He continued to teach within the chemistry department until 1885, when mineralogy and geology received separate status as a one-man department.[38]

Williams won a colleague in 1887 when William Bullock Clark, also an Amherst graduate with a German Ph.D., came to Hopkins as instructor in paleontology. When Williams died in 1894, it was the presence of Clark that saved the department with its courses unique in America.

Because of its significance as forerunner of the medical school, the biology department continued to receive particular scrutiny from the trustees. In some unspecified way (possibly by his inadequacies as a

[35] Interview with Professor Whitehead.

[36] ARJH (1882), 26; Remsen to Gilman, Oct. 10, 1882.

[37] W. S. Bayley, "Hopkins' Contributions to Geology during the Past Fifty Years," *JH Alumni Magazine*, XV (1926–1927), 130, 133; Gilman diary, "1882–1887 to California & Alaska," Feb. 16, March 11, 1883; JHC, II, 124; Henry M. Hurd, remarks in *George Huntington Williams: The Minutes of a Commemorative Meeting Held in the Johns Hopkins University, October 14, 1894* (Baltimore, 1894), 12.

[38] George P. Merrill, "George Huntington Williams," DAB, XX, 263; TM, May 7, 1883; Jameson diary, May 19, 1884; JHC, IV, 92; JHR (1886), 80.

lecturer),[39] Martin's work of the first two years left the executive committee dissatisfied, and in 1878 they offered him a renewal of three years at a continuation of his $4,000 salary. Martin promptly wrote back that this was a breach of the original agreement (a charge which the correspondence of 1875 bears out) and offered his resignation. Faced with an ultimatum, the committee seemed ready to overlook "results . . . not so great or so definite as they had hoped" and to lay stress on "so much that is excellent & promising." Martin soon obtained fulfillment of the original agreement—a salary of $5,000.[40] To save $1,000 a year, the trustees had risked losing a professor whose work in the university's laboratories brought world recognition in the 1880s.

In respect to the practice of vivisection, however, Martin received full support from the university authorities. In his inaugural address in 1876 he had spoken bluntly: "Physiology is concerned with the phenomena going on in living things, and vital processes cannot be observed in dead bodies; and from what I have said you will have gathered that I intend to employ vivisections in teaching." He would use no painful vivisection for demonstrations, he said, but research was a different matter. He stated his principle thus:

In any case where the furtherance of physiological knowledge is at stake— where the progress of that science is concerned, on which all medicine is based, so far as it is not a mere empiricism—I cannot doubt that we have a right to inflict suffering upon the lower animals, always provided that it be reduced to the minimum possible, and that none but competent persons be allowed to undertake such experiments.[41]

Seven years later, at the opening of the new biology laboratory, Martin recalled this statement of principle. He could proudly announce that there had been "no hole-and-corner secrecy about the matter," that no part of the laboratories had been closed to any Hopkins student, and yet in those years he had heard not a "murmur of objection." But in 1885 came the "energetic" distribution of an issue of an English journal,

[39] C. P. Swanson, "A History of Biology at the Johns Hopkins University," *Bios*, XXII (1951), 232.

[40] ECM, April 25, May 2, 16, 1878; Martin to Gilman, April 29, 1878; Gilman to Martin, May 2, 1878.

[41] Henry Newell Martin, "The Study and Teaching of Biology," *Popular Science Monthly*, X (1876–1877), 306.

the *Zoophilist,* attacking Martin's "brutal" experiments on dogs' hearts. Martin published an answering pamphlet, explaining his procedures and inviting any Baltimorean to visit his laboratory.[42]

In his 1876 address, Huxley had cited physiology and morphology as the two most important sciences for premedical study.[43] In keeping with this observation, Martin's work as physiologist was appropriately supplemented by the morphology courses of Brooks. In imitation of Louis Agassiz, Brooks began a new phase of work for the department in 1878, when the trustees appropriated $500 for a summer school of biological research on Chesapeake Bay.[44] After a small beginning that year the school, known as the Chesapeake Zoological Laboratory, with Brooks as director, continued its work from various stations along the bay, at Beaufort, North Carolina, and in the Bahamas, receiving occasional aid from the federal government. It attracted both Hopkins students and others, its enrollment reaching a high of sixteen in 1883. That year arrived one of its most notable students, the Englishman William Bateson, who performed his investigation of *Balanoglossus* while enrolled in the summer laboratory; later he credited Brooks with redirecting his thought by introducing him to the "new idea" that "there was a special physiology of heredity capable of independent study." [45]

Brooks, an adept with tobacco juice, avoided the social life which grew up around the university, but he was not without influence on its relations with the outside world. His discoveries in the propagation of the oyster, which helped restore a waning industry of the region, were the most immediate demonstration during the early years of the "practical" benefits of institutions of higher learning. Gilman did not allow this work, understandable in dollars and cents, to go unpublicized. Within the intellectual community of the university, a community undergirded by Darwinian thought, Brooks, who was an observer and philosopher rather than an experimenter, stood closest to the field of

[42] JHC, III, 89, 87; Martin, *A Correction of Certain Statements Published in the "Zoophilist," Also a Castigation and an Appeal* (Baltimore, 1885).

[43] Huxley, *American Addresses,* 119.

[44] Herrick, "Hopkins," *Scribner's Monthly,* XIX, 207; TM, May 6, 1878.

[45] JHC, III, 91–93; ARJH (1887), 61–65; Bateson, "Evolutionary Faith and Modern Doubts," in Beatrice Bateson, *William Bateson, F.R.S., Naturalist: His Essays & Addresses together with a Short Account of His Life* (Cambridge, Eng., 1928), 389–390.

Darwin's original biological theories and presented them most directly in his teaching. Of these theories, he was both interpreter and amender.[46]

Among the temporary members of the department, two were appointed associates in the early eighties while Brooks was still at that rank (he became associate professor of morphology in 1883). Henry Sewall, one of the university's original graduate students and a Ph.D. of 1879, was associate from 1880 to 1882 and later held professorships in medical schools in Colorado. William Thompson Sedgwick, a Sheffield graduate with a Hopkins Ph.D. in physiology, left an associateship in 1883 to become professor of biology at the Massachusetts Institute of Technology. Martin bemoaned the loss of Sedgwick with his "neat and orderly systematic ways" in the very year when the new biology laboratory opened.[47] Three young men were added to the staff that year, however, among them Henry Herbert Donaldson, whose association with Johns Hopkins continued until 1888. He then followed the famous route to Clark and to Chicago. In 1884, William Henry Howell, who had done both his undergraduate and graduate work at Hopkins, became assistant in biology. Then after three years as associate, he became associate professor of animal physiology in 1888. He was later a distinguished member of the medical school.[48]

A need which the trustees repeatedly cited was botany. Garrett was particularly eager for a botanist, one who could develop the grounds at Clifton.[49] In a venture not unlike that involving Willard Gibbs, the university invited William G. Farlow to give a series of lectures and then offered him a "professorship" of botany, which would have required him to spend five months a year in Baltimore. Farlow declined. It was more than coincidence that in the year of this offer, 1879, Farlow was promoted from adjunct professor to professor at Harvard.[50] The university continued through the decade without a botanist. Such little

---

[46] ARJH (1882), 34; JHC, III, 14, X, 58–59; Herrick, "Hopkins," *Scribner's Monthly*, XIX, 207; Swanson, "Biology at Hopkins," *Bios*, XXII, 236–239.

[47] Martin to Gilman, July 11, 1883.

[48] Data on Howell taken from JHR. The *Half-Century Directory* is in his case inaccurate.

[49] Memorandum from Gilman to trustees, [1877?], GP.

[50] ARJH (1879), 29; ECM, Feb. 20, April 5, 1879; A. Hunter Dupree, *Asa Gray, 1810–1888* (Cambridge, Mass., 1959), 404.

teaching as was done in the field came from graduate students or instructors whose major interests lay elsewhere.[51]

The desire for courses in botany yielded to the trustees' greater interest in preparing for the medical school and their belief that they could not afford both. Although the medical school did not open till 1893, it was never far from the minds of president and trustees. The board had purchased a site for the school in May, 1876, near the land which had been left for the hospital.[52] Also in 1876, the executive committee agreed to pay for the collecting of pathological specimens from the Bay View Asylum; and shortly after Gilman's inaugural, the university accepted an endowment for a medical professorship from Henry Willis Baxley, a Baltimore physician.[53]

These early activities proved premature. Gilman agreed with Billings in 1878 that it was a pity to have the school postponed, but pointed out that lack of money left no choice. He promised, however, that the university would continue to stress its premedical course.[54] In Britain, too, observers held high expectations for the new school. Huxley had made it the major theme of his Hopkins address in 1876, and in 1879 Henry Acland, regius professor of medicine, had given a public lecture at Oxford on the probable effect of the related hospital and university in Baltimore on American medical education.[55] The belief grew that the hospital would be opened on October 1, 1885. Although this prediction proved in error by nearly four years, it encouraged the university trustees to begin selecting a faculty of medicine.[56] In 1883 they decided that a professor of pathology should be the initial appointment.

Knowing the superiority of European medical scholarship, Gilman

---

[51] E.g., Adam T. Bruce (TM, June 14, 1886). The subject was taught briefly during the 1880–1881 term by a fellow whose major interest was botany—A. F. Wilhelm Schimper, holder of a Ph.D. from Strassburg (Swanson, "Biology at Hopkins," *Bios,* XXII, 248).

[52] TM, Dec. 6, 1875, May 9, 1876. The cost was $33,800.

[53] ECM, March 21, 1876. The Baxley chair was not filled until 1901, when the fund was assigned to a professorship of pathology already held by William H. Welch (French, *History of Johns Hopkins,* 378–379). A plan to establish the chair in 1888 came to nothing (TM, June 4, 1888).

[54] Gilman to Billings, April 1, 1878. The next year a survey of British physicians and scientists was made to obtain advice on the premedical course (TM, May 5, 1879; ARJH [1879], 33).

[55] London *Times,* Dec. 2, 1879, cited in JHC, I, 19.

[56] Chesney, *Johns Hopkins Hospital,* I, 73.

again looked abroad. He crossed the Atlantic himself in the summer of 1883, provided by Martin with the names and descriptions of leading European professors in the field. One of those whom he consulted, Edwin Klebs of Zurich, intimated that he himself would like to go to America, especially because of his desire to study yellow fever. At the mention of Hopkins, he doffed his hat and shook hands with a heart-warming "Bravo!" [57] But it was not a European whom Gilman found most highly recommended. Julius Cohnheim in Europe and Billings in America pointed out a professor at the Bellevue Hospital Medical College in New York—William Henry Welch.[58] As a matter of fact, the young pathologist had had his eye on the university in Baltimore since 1876, when he was pursuing advanced study in Germany.[59] The offer was made to Welch in March, 1884. Certain of his friends and colleagues in New York told him that it would be folly to bury himself in a provincial city like Baltimore. They suspected the unhealthy influence of "German ideas" when he seemed inclined to accept. But Gilman knew the type of man with whom he was dealing, and he knew how to make his offer attractive. The "quieter, more academic" atmosphere, the set salary rather than income from student fees and practice, the chance for original work in a laboratory of his own design with assistants, the offer of an initial year abroad—all these appealed to the brilliant and ambitious pathologist. At thirty-three he was young enough to move. Before the month was out he had become the eighth professor appointed at Johns Hopkins and the first with an appointment strictly in the medical school. The university's announcement of Welch's appointment indicated two standards of the philosophical faculty that were to carry over into the medical: ability in independent investigation and skill in teaching.[60] The careful selectivity of the earliest appointments was again apparent.

After a year of profitable study in Europe, Welch settled in Baltimore. During the 1885–1886 term he began investigations first in three rooms in the biological laboratory, later in a two-story pathology labora-

---

[57] Martin to Gilman, [1883], July 11, 1883; Gilman notebook, "Europe, 1883."
[58] ECM, Feb. 27, 1884; Flexner, *I Remember*, 63; Billings to Gilman, March 1, 1884, JHUP.
[59] Simon Flexner and James Thomas Flexner, *William Henry Welch and the Heroic Age of American Medicine* (New York, 1941), 102.
[60] *Ibid.*, 130–134; JHC, III, 95.

tory on the hospital grounds, which he called "certainly a great contrast to my so-called laboratory in New York." [61] Welch had the aid of William Thomas Councilman, who had pursued studies intermittently at Hopkins since 1878, when he had received his M.D. from the University of Maryland. Councilman was given the rank of associate and promoted to associate professor in 1888; he left to become professor of pathology and anatomy at Harvard in 1892.

Although no formal classes were organized the first year, Welch gave a series of nine lectures to physicians and advanced biological students on "Micro-organisms in Disease," the first comprehensive lectures in bacteriology ever given in America. In the 1886–1887 term, systematic instruction began with seventeen physicians enrolled, and Welch declared that he and Councilman gave all the work that would be found in a department of pathology in a German university.[62] Also in 1886, the department received the final accolade, the right to name a fellow. The first fellow chosen, Franklin Paine Mall, an M.D. of the University of Michigan, became assistant in 1888 and the next year struck out on the Clark-Chicago hegira. Unlike others, he returned to Johns Hopkins. In 1893, as professor of anatomy, he joined the newly opened medical school.[63]

Less happy was the effort to win a second professor for the medical faculty. Although in 1884 Matthew Hay of the University of Aberdeen accepted a professorship of pharmacology and therapeutics, with the understanding that he would take office in 1887, he resigned at the beginning of the 1886–1887 term.[64] In spite of this reverse, the executive committee in December, 1886, received the first "Minutes of the Medical Faculty," and the "nucleus of the medical faculty" was publicly declared to be in existence. Included were Gilman, Welch, Martin, Remsen, Billings, as "lecturer upon hygiene," and Councilman.[65] At the beginning of the 1888–1889 term William Osler, Canadian born and Canadian trained, was called from the University of Pennsyl-

[61] Welch to Gilman, Aug. 4, 1885; Flexner and Flexner, *Welch*, 151–152; JHC, VI, 64.

[62] JHC, V, 32, 54, VI, 64; Flexner and Flexner, *Welch*, 152.

[63] See Florence R. Sabin, *Franklin Paine Mall: The Story of a Mind* (Baltimore, 1934).

[64] Chesney, *Johns Hopkins Hospital*, I, 86–88; TM, Oct. 6, 1884, Oct. 4, 1886; ECM, Nov. 29, Dec. 1, 1884, June 5, 1886.

[65] ECM, Dec. 4, 1886; JHC, VI, 64.

vania to become professor of theory and practice of medicine. He had at first no teaching duties and received his total salary as physician in chief of the hospital.[66] The ground was ready for the change, signalized by the opening of the hospital in May, 1889, that was to shift the pioneering effort and the attention of the public from the faculty of philosophy to the medical school.

[66] JHC, VIII, 7; ECM, Oct. 1, 1888.

: CHAPTER IX :

Languages

LONG before 1889, murmurings against the university's stress on biology and the other natural sciences had forced Gilman to disavow any intended imbalance. In the *Annual Report* of 1878, he published Remsen's Commemoration Day speech of that year, in which the chemist declared that he would be "sorry if the day ever comes when it can be said that here science is fostered and other subjects neglected, or the other subjects are specially fostered and the sciences neglected." Gilman himself reported the next year that Hopkins had given equal emphasis to literary and scientific subjects "so far as I can judge," and in his Commemoration Day speech of 1881 he offered further refutation of recurring accusation that natural sciences were favored.[1] The charge had come from within the university itself. Gildersleeve, citing the need to attract "new forces," had written Gilman in 1880: "It is true that our strength is almost wholly on the scientific side." The fact was that the university suffered from overcompensation for the past neglect of the sciences by American higher education. In the abstract, Gilman wanted balance, and he fully agreed with a correspondent in 1882 "that the higher work in the department of language and literature is not inferior in kind to any other."[2] Yet the appointments of 1875 and 1876 had set a course from which deviation proved difficult. Partly

[1] ARJH (1878), 19, (1879), 5–6; Gilman, untitled notes for address of Feb. 22, 1881, GP.
[2] Gildersleeve to Gilman, June 9, 1880; Gilman to C. S. Smith, April 25, 1882.

through concrete choices, partly through bad fortune, the university failed to bestow as much of its wealth and honor on languages as on mathematics and natural sciences.

The Greek department alone among the languages had full stature at Hopkins from the beginning, and it was regarded by some as a dying study. Gildersleeve met such challenges with predictions of the survival of his discipline and declarations of its right to survive. "To disentwine the warp of the classics from the woof of our life," he said, "is simply impossible." [3] In light of Gildersleeve's long career at Johns Hopkins, the first dozen years seem only an intriguing prologue. He felt the promise of his work in Baltimore and was not tempted to accept the offered directorship of the new American School of Classical Studies in Athens. During his thirty-nine years as professor at Hopkins, most of his co-workers in classics died or departed, but Gildersleeve's presence and his continuing achievement guaranteed constant growth in his department, and his authority touched all the work in letters and language at the university.[4]

Gildersleeve had counted escape from the drudgery of elementary instruction as one of the greatest advantages of his professorship at Hopkins.[5] It was the good fortune of the institution, especially its undergraduates, that his colleague Charles D. Morris delighted in such instruction. He brought to it a skill that won for him in the middle of the twentieth century inclusion in Professor Gilbert Highet's discussion of great teachers. Although he produced no monuments to compare with Gildersleeve's, he joined the drive toward investigation with occasional scholarly articles.[6] His death on February 7, 1886, just before the university was to celebrate its tenth anniversary, brought a two-month postponement. The loss of this "model of unselfishness" [7] did more to knit tight the university community than any planned ceremony could have done.

Morris had not taught the undergraduate classics courses single-handed. From 1876 to 1881 he had the collaboration of John M. Cross, who until 1880 was also registrar. Cross, after some personal difficulties with Gildersleeve, resigned in 1881 and became headmaster of a

[3] JHC, V, 105–106. [4] JHC, III, 13; Gilman, *Launching of a University*, 54.
[5] Gildersleeve to Gilman, Feb. 29, 1876.
[6] Gilbert Highet, *The Art of Teaching* (Vintage ed.; New York, 1954), 216; JHC, V, 96, 99.
[7] Jameson diary, Feb. 7, 1886.

preparatory school.[8] He was succeeded for one year by a graduate student in Greek, George Frederick Nicolassen. In 1882 Edward Henry Spieker, who had enrolled at Hopkins on a scholarship in 1877 and received both his A.B. and Ph.D. there, became assistant in Greek and Latin. Promoted to associate in 1886 and associate professor in 1888, Spieker was to remain at Hopkins until his death in 1918, at which time he held the title "collegiate professor," earlier that of Morris. Morris' immediate successor was John Henry Wright, but he remained only one year. It was Spieker, Morris' student, who came closest to carrying on his pastoral tradition in the teaching of classics.

During the heyday of archaeology in Baltimore, it seemed that the Hopkins classicists might be permanently joined by a follower of that discipline. Alfred Emerson, an enthusiast with a Munich Ph.D., and Arthur Lincoln Frothingham, Jr., with a Ph.D. from Leipzig, were both resident at the university from 1882 to 1886, variously as fellow, instructor, and fellow by courtesy. Both had important archaeological careers ahead of them, Frothingham at Princeton and Emerson at Cornell and in Athens. Failing to attach either of them permanently, Johns Hopkins saw archaeology drop out of vogue by the end of the eighties.

New Testament Greek was taught by Cross, beginning in 1879. After his departure, Gilman made a sustained effort to win some gifted scholar in this field. Probably the religious significance of the subject and the role that it could play in winning public approval kept it at the forefront of the president's mind. His two great frustrations in this department have significance beyond mere modification of faculty structure.

It was apparently for other than academic reasons that James Rendel Harris, an Englishman recently graduated from Cambridge University, moved in 1882 to Baltimore, where he at once became active in Friends meeting. Once on the scene, however, his lively interest in New Testament criticism drew the attention of certain trustees.[9] His initial appointment in 1882 was in the tentative category of lecturer. In his first year he showed his versatility by instructing physics courses during

[8] French, *History of Johns Hopkins,* 350; James C. Mackenzie to Gilman, Dec. 11, 1882.
[9] A. B. Thomas, *Baltimore Yearly Meeting,* 111–112; James Carey Thomas to Gilman, July 25, 1882; Thomas Chase to Gilman, Nov. 5, 1882.

Hastings' absence on a scientific expedition. A year later, his responsibilities were broadened to include the required undergraduate course in philosophy. Harris' discoveries of New Testament documents and his theories were widely discussed and praised, Gilman noted with pleasure.[10] Trustee Thomas admired his enthusiasm, his wide correspondence with New Testament scholars, and his sleuthing in Near Eastern monasteries for ancient documents.[11] Harris' *New Testament Autographs,* published in 1882, a facsimile edition with criticism, forecast other such contributions to come. All in all, he seemed one of the most promising members of the faculty. He was promoted to associate professor of New Testament Greek and paleography in 1884, and a field dear to Gilman's heart seemed securely provided for.

Harris was strongly given to analysis and criticism of the university scene and had a Quaker penchant for the "good cause." The breaking up of the library by departments drew his disapprobation, as did a dance held after the opening of the new gymnasium in 1883. He warned Gilman that at Clare College, Cambridge, such amusements had caused much trouble, taking the students' time and arousing antagonisms against professors who disapproved and students who did not attend.[12] His tendency toward outspoken criticism led him in 1885 to publish an attack on vivisection. Since the *Zoophilist* "exposure" of Martin's investigations with dogs was being circulated at the time, the attack reflected on the Hopkins biology department. Strongly disapproving, the executive committee had Gilman write Harris that his public comments were ill-advised. To Harris, the reprimand seemed a limitation on his freedom to speak his convictions, and he wrote accordingly to the executive committee. Gilman relayed their response: "The Committee are not disposed, as you are well aware, to exercise any control over the ordinary exercise of opinion among the members of the university; but if the expressions of opinion involve attacks upon the work of the university openly or covertly, they will require notice." [13] In the exchanges that followed, Harris held firm to his principles and was not moved by Gilman's contemporaneous public statement that those who opposed the study of biology would be looked upon in the future as

---

[10] ECM, March 8, 1883; TM, June 4, 1883; Gilman diary, "1882–1887 to California & Alaska," Jan. 25, 1883.

[11] Thomas to Gilman, July 10, 1884. [12] Harris to Gilman, Dec. 25, 1883.

[13] ECM, Feb. 18, March 2, 1885; Gilman to Harris, Feb. 19, March 3, 1885.

obscurantists. He declined reappointment if it meant limitation on his freedom of speech. Although Gilman thus lost his New Testament scholar, he seems never to have doubted where his responsibility lay.[14]

The disagreement left no heritage of bitterness. In his *Annual Report,* Gilman observed that Harris "had done much to awaken an interest in the studies to which he was devoted, but in matters which pertain to another department of the University he was not in accord with the policy here pursued and consequently gave up his chair." [15] Although conciliatory, this statement ignored the issue of freedom of expression. Harris next taught at Haverford and then at Cambridge University. Yet he allowed the Johns Hopkins publication agency in 1887 to bring out his edition of the *Teaching of the Apostles* with photographic plates from the long unavailable Bryennios manuscript, a venture begun during his Hopkins tenure.[16] And in the 1894–1895 and 1909–1910 terms he returned to Hopkins to give lectures.

The very fall after his departure, Harris wrote that he was "sincerely grateful" to Gilman "for putting so much better a man into the harness." [17] He referred to the appointment of Caspar René Gregory, who was indeed a man of rich achievement. An American who won a Leipzig Ph.D. in 1876, he had remained in Europe, carrying on the work of his mentor, L. F. K. von Tischendorf, after the latter's death. His thoroughness and accuracy gained him praise in Germany and anonymous financial assistance from various American scholars, led by former President Woolsey of Yale and Professor Ezra Abbott of the Harvard Divinity School.[18] In 1884 he became *Privatdocent* at Leipzig, a distinction "almost if not quite unprecedented among Americans." Succeeding to Harris' title of associate professor in 1885, Gregory visited Hopkins briefly, but was allowed a year's delay in taking up his duties in order to continue his researches abroad. He had hinted in his letter of acceptance that Baltimore might prove "too far from MSS." Perhaps

[14] JHC, IV, 48; ECM, March 25, April 16, 1885; TM, May 4, 1885; Philadelphia *Press,* May 6, 1885, clipping in JHUP; Sylvester to Gilman, Aug. 24, 1885. I have not discovered Harris' "communication to one of the newspapers." It was apparently an attack on the work of Pasteur, not of Martin.

[15] ARJH (1885), 23.

[16] French, *History of Johns Hopkins,* 222–223; JHC, VII, 20; TM, June 14, 1887.

[17] Harris to Gilman, Oct. 31, 1885.

[18] Abbott to Woolsey, Nov. 5, 19, 1878, Jan. 20, Feb. 1, 1884; Timothy Dwight to Woolsey, Jan. 28, 1884; all in Timothy Dwight Woolsey Papers, Manuscript Division, Yale University Library.

for this reason he was still absent in the fall of 1886.[19] He made some request, perhaps for additional delay or the right to spend part of each term abroad, which the trustees did not grant; instead, they released him altogether. If Gregory had foreseen a career for himself in Germany, he was correct. By 1891, he was professor at Leipzig, and in 1917 he died fighting for his adopted country.[20] The lesson for Johns Hopkins seemed to be the unhappy one that even in the case of an American scholar its opportunities could not offset the attractions of a German university. Gilman's ambitions for the field of New Testament criticism were swamped by financial difficulties, and from 1887 a fellow by courtesy, William Muss Arnolt, taught the subject, quite possibly without pay.

Hopkins did not appoint a Latinist with a reputation equal to Gildersleeve's; rather it followed the alternative policy of hiring the young man of promise, in this case Minton Warren. A graduate of Tufts, Warren had pursued advanced studies at Yale in 1871–1872, taught in a high school, and then departed for study at the German universities in 1876. Warren had become acquainted with Charles Lanman during his year at Yale and often wrote from Germany to his friend, who was doing so well at Johns Hopkins. In these letters Warren prescribed radical reform for American education, including the exorcising of "the 'pork & beans' idea." He pictured himself participating in the movement at some preparatory school, but he had no intention of neglecting scholarship even there. His letters reflect an attitude similar to Gilman's a quarter-century earlier: a desire "to exert direct influence on men" and a resolve not to let scholarship cut him off from the world.[21] Meanwhile, Lanman neglected no opportunity to suggest his friend to Gildersleeve for the unfilled position of Latinist. There was talk of a fellowship for the 1878–1879 term, but by spending a third year abroad Warren completed work for his Ph.D. at Strassburg and received an appointment at Hopkins as associate. Like Lanman, he declined a Yale tutorship at a higher salary.[22]

At first Warren taught mostly undergraduates, Cross dropping Latin

[19] JHC, V, 33, VI, 1; Gregory to Gilman, Nov. 16, 1885.

[20] ECM, Feb. 7, 1887; Gilman to Gregory, Feb. 8, 1887; James H. Ropes, "Caspar René Gregory," DAB, VII, 601–602.

[21] Warren to Lanman, Jan. 20, 1878, Lanman Papers.

[22] Lanman diary, Dec. 23, 1877, March 22, 1878; Warren to Lanman, Jan. 20, May 28, [1878], Lanman Papers.

for New Testament Greek. By 1881, however, he had his own seminary, and in the 1883–1884 term, his first as associate professor, he introduced pioneer courses in paleography and epigraphy. He was an admirable teacher, critical and stimulating with his graduate students, patient and gentle with undergraduates, fulfilling both his heritage of German training and his early interest in the teaching of younger men.[23] Warren was less than contented at Hopkins. In 1887 possibilities of moving to either Columbia or Clark appealed to him,[24] but it was not until 1899 that he left to become professor at Harvard.

Few events of the early years reverberated as widely as the departure in 1880 of Charles R. Lanman, associate in Sanskrit, to a professorship at Harvard. There was the satisfaction of knowing that President Eliot regarded Hopkins as a source of personnel for his program of expansion. A chair in the country's oldest university was a goal whose seriousness the Hopkins fellows covered by jesting about it, but after Lanman received Eliot's offer, another former fellow soberly described it as "your Goethe's call to Weimar." [25] Although Gilman took the matter calmly, seeing perhaps a prestige gain for his university, some of the professors were less serene at the departure of so gifted a young man.[26]

Before the offer came, Lanman had agreed to a reappointment as associate at $2,000, his only tenure the pleasure of the board (six months' notice). The position at Harvard was a permanent professorship at $3,000 with $500 increases the second and third years plus a year's leave at half pay once every seven years. The Hopkins authorities offered to equal these conditions, and had Lanman stayed he might have brought the sabbatical system to the university.[27]

Lanman sought the counsel of William D. Whitney, who answered that though Gilman was probably a better man to work under than Eliot he had given him less than his deserts at Hopkins. In the letter informing Gilman of his decision to move, Lanman observed that the

[23] JHC, I, 155, III, 112; George Lincoln Hendrickson, "Minton Warren," DAB, XIX, 485; Flexner, *I Remember*, 52–54.

[24] Warren to Lanman, May 8, 1887, Lanman Papers.

[25] Lanman to Gilman, Sept. 2, 1880; Ernest G. Sihler to Lanman, June 1, 1880; both in Lanman Papers.

[26] Albert S. Cook to Lanman, May 27, 1880; Gilman to Lanman, May 29, 1880; both in Lanman Papers; Sylvester to Gilman, June 10, 1880.

[27] Gilman to Lanman, May 5, 22, 1880; Lanman to Gilman, May 10, 1880 (copy); all in Lanman Papers; Lanman diary, May 20, 1880.

Peabody library did not serve Hopkins as a *"living, teaching power,"* something that the Harvard library did for its university. But he assured Gilman that he had decided only after receiving from Eliot "assurance that with the position is coupled that academic freedom for independent scientific work which is enjoyed by the Baltimore professors." [28]

Brief though Lanman's career at Johns Hopkins was, he had not failed to produce a successor. After one year's residence (following a year of study at Yale with Whitney), Maurice Bloomfield had won a Hopkins Ph.D. in 1879. He studied during the next two years at Berlin and Leipzig and in 1881 inherited Lanman's title of associate in Sanskrit. Austrian by birth, Bloomfield had immigrated at the age of four. He attended the old University of Chicago and Furman University in South Carolina. His selection for the Hopkins faculty was praised by Whitney, who predicted that he would "bring credit to American scholarship" and urged Gilman not to "load him with work that will take away his leisure for investigation." [29] Like Lanman, Bloomfield taught both Sanskrit and comparative philology. He published a lively case for these subjects in the *Circulars,* claiming that comparative philology "lights up the past of our race, when all other records have given out." [30] His faith carried with it a personal dedication that led to unremitting investigation.

Bloomfield was often unhappy at Hopkins, finding it less than the haven for the creative scholar it purported to be. He found his teaching responsibilities "very exacting" and declared that his isolation could hardly be greater if he held "a chair in the University of Kamchatka." Although he had been one of the original group advanced to associate professor in 1883, he was still earning less than $3,000 a year by 1888, and Hopkins finances then looked most unpromising. Like many others at the university, Bloomfield yearned for a chair at Clark, which was dreamed of as the new academic Elysium.[31] He was destined, however, to become a grand old man of Johns Hopkins, remaining until 1926.

Early in 1879 death removed the university's first associate in Se-

[28] Whitney to Lanman, April 11, May 11, 1880; Lanman to Gilman, May 22, 1880 (draft); all in Lanman Papers.

[29] A. V. Williams Jackson, "Maurice Bloomfield," DAB, II, 386–387; Whitney to Gilman, Oct. 27, 1881.

[30] JHC, IV, 119–120.

[31] Bloomfield to Lanman, Dec. 8, 1886, July 16, 1888, Lanman Papers.

mitics, Thomas Chalmers Murray, whose ability had been hailed by Whitney. Gilman's interest in the field continued, possibly as in the case of New Testament Greek because of its religious significance. After 1879, Hebrew was taught by Cross and then by Bloomfield, though it was the principal interest of neither.[32]

Semitics was among the subjects for which the trustees set aside money in the fall of 1880, and they were willing to give its representative the rank of professor. The search led inevitably to Europe, for in America there was only limited teaching of Semitics in theological schools. The success of this search brought to the university Paul Haupt, the only German-born, German-trained scholar that the university was able to attach permanently. Haupt's youth was a factor in his willingness to move. He had won his Ph.D. at Leipzig before his nineteenth birthday and was not yet twenty-five when he arrived at Hopkins in 1883. He had been *Privatdocent* at Göttingen since 1880, and his publications record allowed Gildersleeve to support him strongly before the trustees. In 1883 they voted him a three-year appointment as professor of Semitics at a salary of $2,000—the first professorship created since 1876.[33]

During his trip to Europe in the summer of 1883, Gilman conferred with his new faculty member and disabused him of rumors floating through the German universities that Sylvester had killed a man and that Hopkins had lost money in Confederate bonds. After Haupt described the pension system of the German universities and observed diffidently that his Hopkins salary was very low, Gilman promised to ask the trustees to increase it and to give him a moving allowance. The salary was increased to $3,000 after his arrival in the fall.[34]

Shortly before leaving Germany, Haupt was commissioned professor of Assyriology at Göttingen. To fulfill the duties of this second professorship, the trustees repeatedly let him depart early in May; but in 1888 they cited financial reverses and denied him such permission. The next year, Haupt ended his connection with Göttingen.[35]

---

[32] William D. Whitney to Lanman, July 25, 1876, Lanman Papers; ARJH (1879), 34, (1882), 41.

[33] ECM, Jan. 13, 1883; TM, March 5, May 7, 1883; George A. Barton, "Paul Haupt," DAB, VIII, 401–402.

[34] Gilman notebook, "Europe, 1883," Aug. 11, 1883; TM, Oct. 1, 1883.

[35] Barton, "Haupt," DAB, VIII, 401; ECM, Jan. 11, 1886; Gilman to Haupt, April 30, 1888.

On his arrival Haupt did not find himself wanting students; one, Carl F. Lehmann, had followed him from Göttingen. Gilman declared that Haupt at once attracted "a company of well-trained and enthusiastic students, more numerous than we had reason to expect." But in some of the lesser Semitic languages, his students were ready only for beginning work. Abstruse though it was, Haupt's field brought him into contact with the general public and the government. In 1887 he initiated the novel procedure of stopping all his classes during the month of January and presenting an intensive course in Assyriology. Clergymen and teachers from other institutions came to Hopkins for this work in a language little known in America.[36] For his proposed Mesopotamian expedition in the fall of 1888 Haupt asked Newcomb to help him raise funds from government officials, but the plan collapsed when the trustees decided that the university's financial condition did not allow the absence of one of its professors.[37]

The young Haupt was an impressive figure. Students dubbed him the "oiled and curled Assyrian bull," and Albert Shaw later recalled him as "huge, glowing, a teacher as well as scholar, and you envied men who studied Ethiopian dialects." Prodigy though he seemed to his students, he proved a difficult colleague. Rendel Harris reported from Germany in 1884 that Haupt was involved in an "absurd" lawsuit there. Bloomfield found him "more and more impossible" as the years went by and regarded some of his public battles as "literary rowdyism." [38] He won an enviable reputation in Assyriology and Semitic philology, but a scholarly evaluator of his work has concluded that, especially in Biblical criticism, Haupt's fertile imagination too often used the possible for the probable.[39] He died in 1926, still in active service at the university.

In 1887 Haupt's load was lightened by the appointment as instructor of Cyrus Adler, who had just received at Hopkins the first Ph.D. given in America in Semitics. Adler was to remain on the faculty until 1893, but work at the Smithsonian Institution took an increasing amount of his

---

[36] Cyrus Adler, quoted in Abraham A. Neuman, *Cyrus Adler: A Biographical Sketch* (New York, 1942), 22; ARJH (1884), 8; JHC, III, 112, V, 125, VI, 71, 104–105.

[37] Haupt to Simon Newcomb, April 15, 1888, Newcomb Papers; ECM, April 30, 1888.

[38] Shaw, "Recollections," GP; Neuman, *Adler*, 21; Harris to Gilman, Sept. 10, 1884; Bloomfield to Lanman, Oct. 24, 1889, April 17, 1888, Lanman Papers.

[39] Barton, "Haupt," DAB, VIII, 402.

time. He became librarian there in 1892; later he was president of
Dropsie College and of the Jewish Theological Seminary. He had com-
muted to New York to teach at the latter institution during his years
on the Hopkins faculty.[40]

Although modern languages were granted a position of greater respect in the undergraduate course than was typical in American colleges, the Johns Hopkins trustees seemed loath to include them among
the major graduate departments. Léonce Rabillon, whose qualifications
included French birth and a dilettantist interest in the *Chanson de
Roland,* used his native tongue in the public lecture series and was the
university's first teacher of undergraduate French. At the time of his
death in 1886, the trustees were planning to end his lectureship. They
had never regarded him as a scholar around whom a department could
be built.[41]

The years were to prove that A. Marshall Elliott was such a scholar.
In fact, most Romance-language scholarship in America traces to the
department that he erected at Hopkins. But the authorities of the university gave him recognition only slowly, and he himself originally regarded Romance languages as an interest secondary to Sanskrit and
comparative philology.[42] During his first two years as associate, Elliott
taught Italian, Spanish, and Persian.[43] In 1878, he began to add courses
in French—first in Old French and Provençal, later in modern French.
The executive committee rather casually asked him to assume these
additional responsibilities, and when Gilman's thoughts turned to a
chair of Romance philology in 1878, he seemed not to envision Elliott
in it.[44] But Elliott made the most of every encouragement. When asked
to teach courses in French, he responded by promising "to thoroughly
organize the Department of Romance Languages." He asked for assurance that the department would not be ignored in future plans and
that he would have the same privileges in buying books and other
"apparatus for scientific investigation" as the other language depart-

[40] Abraham A. Neuman, "Cyrus Adler," DAB, XXII, 5–7; Cyrus Adler, *I Have
Considered the Days* (Philadelphia, 1941), 64, 66.
[41] Henry Wadsworth Longfellow to Gilman, Oct. 6, 1879; TM, June 14, 1886;
JHC, VI, 36.
[42] Edward C. Armstrong, "Aaron Marshall Elliott," DAB, VI, 93–94; French,
History of Johns Hopkins, 432; Edward C. Armstrong, "A. Marshall Elliott: A
Retrospect" (*Elliott Monographs in the Romance Languages and Literatures, no.
15;* Princeton and Paris, 1923), 5–6.
[43] JHR (1878), 12. See Appendix B.
[44] ECM, April 26, 1879; Austin Stickney to Gilman, Feb. 16, 1878.

ments. During the 1879–1880 term he joined with the associates in German and English in a formal communication to the executive committee urging further development of instruction in modern languages. The committee reported itself favorably inclined to "suggestions made in respect to books and assistance." One of the results was the appointment of Philippe B. Marcou as assistant in 1880. Marcou's presence allowed Elliott to teach more advanced courses, but his interests were not truly prospering. On a European trip in 1880, Gildersleeve asked about Elliott's reputation in Munich, where he had studied, and declared his junior colleague "as much a riddle to me now as he was four years ago." [45] The executive committee cited the university's need for a professor of modern languages in 1882, but uncertainty about Elliott's abilities and his severe illness during the 1882–1883 term prevented the trustees from adding him to the original list of associate professors in 1883. A year later, after he had played a leading role in the founding of the Modern Language Association of America in December, 1883, and had been elected its secretary, he was promoted. Gilman thereupon sent him a somewhat patronizing letter, saying that the uncertainty about him had been "largely dissipated" and hoping for "better things" from his department.[46]

The better things were indeed forthcoming. Elliott had already instituted seminary work.[47] Tended by a man serenely willing to sacrifice his own scholarship for the development of his students, this seminary became a seedbed of Romance scholars for American universities. Two younger men joined Elliott in the department. Henry A. Todd, appointed instructor in 1883, advanced to associate after winning his Ph.D. under Elliott in 1885. He departed for the newly opened Stanford in 1891, but soon after began his long tenure at Columbia. In 1886, Frederick Morris Warren, returning to Hopkins from studies at the Sorbonne, accepted an instructorship in French, and in 1887 took his Ph.D. He too left the university in 1891 and was to have a notable career at Yale.

The work in German was marred by an uncertainty similar to that in Romance languages; but whereas Elliott had produced two students worthy of the Ph.D. in 1881, no Ph.D. was given in German until 1887.

[45] Elliott to Gilman, May 4, 1878; ECM, Jan. 2, 29, 1880; Gildersleeve to Gilman, Aug. 8, 1880.
[46] ECM, Sept. 19, 1882; ARJH (1882), 42–43; Armstrong, "Elliott," *Elliott Monographs*, no. 15, p. 10; Gilman to Elliott, May 21, 1884.
[47] ARJH (1882), 42.

Hermann C. G. Brandt, the original associate in German, taught courses in Gothic, Old High German, and Middle High German to very small classes, but was mainly concerned with undergraduates. His advanced linguistic training was limited to a single year at Göttingen, though C. D. Morris judged him "capable and energetic." Gildersleeve declared him a man who "dared to think for himself," but regretted his getting "into the text-book line, which is always dangerous for a University teacher." The senior professor feared that this venture and Brandt's decision in 1882 to return to the faculty of Hamilton might mark the end of a creative career.[48] With Brandt's departure Gildersleeve proposed that the university seek "a strong Modern Languages man and let him set that whole department straight, the hardest by the way to get straight in the whole scheme." [49] But no heroic measures followed. As far as German was concerned, Henry Wood, associate in English since 1881, and James Wilson Bright, the university's first Ph.D. in English (1882), did stopgap teaching, aided by Charles F. Raddatz, professor of German at Baltimore City College, who took the title of examiner at Hopkins from 1882 to 1886.

The interest of Henry Wood was to prove the salvation of the German department. A Haverford A.B. of 1869, he won a Ph.D. at Leipzig in 1879. He had a great fondness for the land of his advanced studies and an "exaggerated scorn of every product of scholarship not German." [50] During 1883–1884 his work was once again altogether in English (stressing Anglo-Saxon, Old Saxon, and general English philology); in 1884 he requested a permanent change to the German department.[51] The trustees not only granted his request, but also promoted him to associate professor of German in 1885. The first Ph.D. (1887) in German, Marion Dexter Learned, remained on the faculty as instructor, associate, and associate professor until he accepted a professorship at the University of Pennsylvania in 1895. The tenure of several other instructors was much briefer.

The high ambitions for the English department which had led the

---

[48] JHU *Circulars* (n.s. 1926, no. 8), 31, 33; Morris to Gilman, July 31, 1882; Gildersleeve to Gilman, July 27, 1882. Brandt remained at Hamilton until his death in 1920. His publications were, in fact, principally textbooks, and his useful career fell short of scholarly eminence (*Who's Who in America*, XI [1920–1921], 335).

[49] Gildersleeve to Gilman, July 5, 1882.   [50] Jameson diary, June 1, 1883.

[51] JHC, III, 113, 131.

Hopkins authorities to invite Child of Harvard to a professorship in 1875 continued for a decade and a half. For the first three years there was no English department. Gilman regarded this as a major weakness, but part of the delay came from his own elevated standards. In 1878, he described his goal as "the man who has both literary & philological aptitude—a future Child or [Thomas R.] Lounsbury." [52]

The man first thought of was the English philologist, Henry Sweet, already renowned for his work in phonetics and his *Anglo-Saxon Reader,* but without an academic position. Meeting this scholar was a major purpose of Gildersleeve's trip to Europe in 1880. The interview raised Gildersleeve's opinion of Sweet, but he nevertheless reported him "not magnetic" and also inexperienced in teaching. Apparently the Englishman found Johns Hopkins less than magnetic, too, for the invitation sent him in 1881 to come as professor at $5,000 was declined.[53] The next two efforts to win a professor of English stressed literary merit over philological scholarship. In 1882, Richard Watson Gilder, editor of the *Century,* recommended the innovation of hiring a novelist who had never been to college—William Dean Howells, former editor of the *Atlantic Monthly.* Although Gilder made the recommendation rather tentatively, Gilman picked it up and asked for further guidance. Gilder, whose magazine published most of Howells' writings, replied that his novels did not bring Howells enough to live on and that Baltimore should hold the attraction of giving him insight into the Southern character for use in his writing.[54] After some talk of inviting Howells as lecturer, Gilman and the trustees decided to plunge all the way. In November, they offered him a three-year appointment as professor at $5,000. Gilman was honest enough to declare that free though the atmosphere at Hopkins was, a writer might find it confining; but he praised the students and hoped that Howells would come to "awaken among them as much love of literature as there is of science." [55] Howells refused an immediate acceptance, and a year later the offer was repeated. But Howells' friend James Russell Lowell advised him against

[52] Gilman to Thomas R. Lounsbury, May 2, 1878, Thomas R. Lounsbury Papers, Rare Book Room, Yale University Library.
[53] Gildersleeve to Gilman, June 25, 1880; Gilman to Henry Sweet, April 27, 1881; George W. Brown to Gilman, July 2, 1881.
[54] Gilder to Gilman, July 6, Sept. 7, 1882.
[55] ECM, Sept. 25, 1882; George W. Brown to Gilman, Sept. 28, 1882; Gilman to Howells, Nov. 14, 1882.

accepting, and in the fall of 1883 he sent a final negative, saying that "he desired to make his work as a writer his chief vocation." [56]

During the summer of 1883, Gilman had gone after even rarer game. Armed with a letter of introduction from Hiram Corson, professor of Anglo-Saxon at Cornell, he had interviewed Robert Browning in London and invited him to come as a lecturer.[57] But Corson's prediction that Browning could not be captured proved correct. Another Englishman, less of a poet than Browning but more of a scholar, Edmund W. Gosse, was under consideration at the same time. He was a good friend of both Browning and Howells, and Gilman probably heard him recommended by them. His election as Clark Lecturer at Cambridge University must have heightened his attractiveness. When the Lowell Institute brought Gosse to America in December, 1884, he repeated his lectures at Hopkins. He was offered a professorship of English literature, but though he regarded Baltimore as the most attractive American city he had visited, he declined to move there.[58]

In the fall of 1888, Gilman had to admit that, in the field of English, Hopkins to its shame lacked a professor. But he insisted that it was not from lack of trying. Although there were many philologians, he said, Hopkins wanted a Matthew Arnold or a James Russell Lowell. By sending invitations to an "impressive list" of men of literary genius, the university had learned that they usually preferred "the freedom of their own libraries to the fetters of a professorship." [59]

But the record was not blank, for one man of literary genius had taught at Johns Hopkins, and it was death, not lack of recognition, that ended his connection with the university. Sidney Lanier had been one of many residents of Baltimore who had dreamed of a chair at Johns Hopkins before it had opened; his idea had been a professorship of music and poetry.[60] His appointment as lecturer in English literature

----

[56] ECM, April 10, 1883; James Russell Lowell to Charles W. Eliot, Dec. 7, 1886, Eliot Papers; TM, Nov. 5, 1883.

[57] Hiram Corson to Gilman, June 9, 1883; Browning to Gilman, July 2, 1883.

[58] Gosse to Gilman, July 2, 1883; ARJH (1885), 15; George W. Brown to Gilman, Jan. 11, 1885; Evan Charteris, *The Life and Letters of Sir Edmund Gosse* (New York and London, 1931), 159, 173. In his account of Gosse, *Dictionary of National Biography* (1922–1930), 354, Charteris states that Gosse was invited to a professorship at Harvard. This I believe is a confusion with Hopkins, since the biography mentions an offer from Hopkins but not from Harvard.

[59] JHC, VIII, 14.

[60] Charles R. Anderson, gen. ed., *The Centennial Edition of the Works of Sidney Lanier* (Baltimore, 1945), I, *Poems and Poem Outlines,* ed. by Anderson, lv.

in 1879 led to two series of public lectures: on English verse and on the English novel. He also offered informal courses on Chaucer and Shakespeare, seeking to awaken interest in their writings "solely as works of art." [61]

Lanier made it his business to keep reminding Gilman of the role that literature could play in "counteracting that very lamentable narrowness of range which seems peculiarly incident to the absorbed specialist in modern physical science and modern linguistics." He sent the president detailed course outlines for both undergraduates and advanced students, and Gilman's continuing determination to add a literary figure to his staff may well have been stronger because of insights that Lanier gave him.[62] Had Lanier himself survived, students of his life assert, "he might have been a pioneer in the introduction of literature, studied as such, in the graduate schools of America." [63]

Lanier's "Ode to The Johns Hopkins University," [64] read on Commemoration Day, 1880, is not one of the works on which his reputation as a poet rests. Nevertheless, to the new and unsung university his words rang sweet:

> How tall among her sisters, and how fair,—
> How grave beyond her youth, yet debonair
> As dawn, 'mid wrinkled *Matres* of old lands
> Our youngest *Alma Mater* modest stands!
>
> .   .   .   .   .
>
> And many peoples call from shore to shore,
> *The world has bloomed again, at Baltimore!*

The raw new institution needed a mythology, and in 1881 the death of this gentle hero at the age of thirty-nine provided a beginning. A special payment to his widow and family, a memorial plaque, and in 1887 the unveiling of a bust in Hopkins Hall, all testified to the university's continuing interest in the poet after his death. A memorial Lanier meeting on his birthday, February 3, 1888, presented not only the poetry of Lanier, but poems by his friends and former students. In his history of the university, Gilman devoted more pages and emotion to

[61] ARJH (1880), 20, (1881), 15; JHC, I, 18.
[62] Lanier to Gilman, July 13, Dec. 17, 1879, in Anderson, ed., *Sidney Lanier*, X, *Letters, 1878–1881*, ed. by Anderson and Aubrey H. Starke, 129–132, 159–163.
[63] Anderson, ed., *Sidney Lanier*, VII, *Letters, 1857–1868*, ed. by Anderson and Starke, xlviii.
[64] JHC, I, 38–39.

the "always cheerful, always gallant, always trustful" Lanier than to many faculty members whose contributions were greater.[65]

The university's first associateship in English went in 1879 to one of those philologians whom Gilman declared "numerous, especially among the younger men who have grown up under German influences." [66] The appointee, Albert S. Cook, had graduated from Rutgers in 1872 and studied for two years in German universities without taking a degree. Cook began at once, like a proper German-trained philologian, to stress Anglo-Saxon, touching nothing later than Shakespeare.[67] But he was a popular teacher, attracting graduates as well as undergraduates; and Jameson, one of the former, found him both learned and likable.[68] When Gilman and the trustees decided against his reappointment in May, 1881, apparently because they expected Sweet to accept a professorship, the university shook with recriminations and ill will. While Cook rushed away to Cambridge to counsel with his friend Lanman, the other language teachers agreed among themselves that there had been an injustice. H. B. Adams wrote to Gilman in alarm, and students drew up a petition to the trustees, which Gilman convinced them to withdraw only with his suavest maneuverings.[69] When Sweet's refusal arrived, the rumor spread that Cook might stay, but Gilman was either too far committed to withdraw gracefully or else he had other reasons for wanting Cook's departure.[70] Cook went to Europe, studied, ironically, with Sweet in London for a time, and took his Ph.D. at Jena in 1882. The breach between Gilman and Cook was not a permanent one, and in 1882 Gilman played a key role in winning Cook's appointment as professor at the University of California.[71]

Since the hope for a professor of English in 1881 proved a false dawn, Cook was replaced as associate by Henry Wood, who turned his attention entirely to German in 1884. William Hand Browne, the university's

---

[65] TM, Oct. 3, 1881; Gilman diary, "1882–1887 to California & Alaska," March 19, 1883; JHC, VI, 72; Gilman, *Launching of a University*, 94–97.

[66] JHC, VIII, 14.   [67] ARJH (1880), 48; (1881), 15.

[68] Jameson diary, Feb. 2, 1881; Minton Warren to Charles R. Lanman, Jan. 24, 1881, Lanman Papers.

[69] Minton Warren to Lanman, May 2, 1881, Lanman Papers; H. B. Adams to Gilman, May 11, 1881 (copy); Jameson diary, May 7–17, 1881.

[70] Jameson diary, May 10, 1881. Some insight into Gilman's views at the time comes from his letter to B. G. Wilder, April 4, 1881: "*Stability* is of prime importance in a college; but what can be done if an unsatisfactory appointment has been made?"

[71] Minton Warren to Lanman, July 10, 1881 (post card), June 4, 1882; Cook to Lanman, Aug. 30, 1882; all in Lanman Papers.

librarian, began teaching English literature and composition to under-graduates in 1882 with the title of examiner and in 1884 advanced to associate. Although he had been coeditor of the *Southern Review* and the *New Eclectic Magazine,* his only formal university training had been work for an M.D. at the University of Maryland. He had been a commission merchant in Baltimore before the Civil War and was over fifty when, at Hopkins, he began the first teaching of his life.[72] He varied the general tendency of his department in that he opposed "swamping literature in philology," and he taught with the belief that "it is thoughts of great men, and not the laws of Teutonic vowel-change, that move and mould the world." [73] Far from being the accomplished literary man for whom Gilman continued to search, Browne neverthe-less achieved enough success as a teacher to become professor of English literature in 1893.

Throughout these departmental vicissitudes the young man with whom the future fame of the study of English at Johns Hopkins rested, James W. Bright, remained an inconspicuous participant. A Pennsyl-vanian by birth, Bright had graduated from Lafayette in 1877, inspired by the path-breaking teaching of Francis A. March in English and comparative philology. He came to Hopkins in 1879 and the next year won a fellowship. He studied under both Cook and Wood and in 1882 received his Ph.D., the only one given by Hopkins in English until a student of Bright himself earned one in 1887. He remained at Hopkins as assistant in German during 1882–1883 and then went to Germany for a year of further study. Without a job, he gravitated back to Hop-kins, taking the title of fellow by courtesy for the 1884–1885 term. During January and February he substituted for Hiram Corson at Cornell. Wood had just shifted his interests to German and cut his teaching in English to one hour a week of *Beowulf;* the only other ad-vanced courses in English were offered by two graduate students. Thus, Bright's lectures in Anglo-Saxon grammar from March through May, 1885, were welcomed, and he was appointed instructor for the next term. In the fall he instituted a "Teutonic Seminary," changing the name the next year to "The English Seminary." [74] The official reports of work

[72] John Martin Vincent, "William Hand Browne," DAB, III, 170–171; French, *History of Johns Hopkins,* 207–209.

[73] Browne to Gilman, [January?], [1892?].

[74] JHC, IV, 6, 72; C. B. Wright to Albert Shaw, Nov. 22, 1884, Shaw Papers; David Moore Robinson, "James Wilson Bright," DAB, III, 45; JHC, III, 110, IV, 98, V, 126; ARJH (1885), 50.

for 1886–1887 and 1887–1888 listed Wood as in charge of the English seminary, though Bright clearly directed most of its work.[75] By 1887, Bright had two students ready to receive Ph.D.'s, the first of the fifty-five he was to train before his retirement in 1925.[76]

Yet it was Bright's own tenacity that kept him at Hopkins while Gilman's eyes were straying to Europe. In June, 1888, when Bright, not hearing of his next year's prospects, grew restive and requested an interview, Gilman wrote him that he doubted whether his appointment would be renewed: "If your interview has reference only to your work of next year, I should prefer not to enter upon the discussion of that subject." [77] Probably at Bright's request, Wood interceded, admitting that Bright was difficult, but praising his teaching. Perhaps there was a disappointment in regard to some other scholar during the summer. At any rate, Bright wrote a strong letter in August insisting on promotion to associate with a salary of $1,200 and detailing his plans for strengthening the graduate work in English. His wish was granted at the fall meeting of the trustees, with the proviso that no re-engagement was implied. He did, however, regain full control of the English seminary.[78]

Bright's future career proves the power of him who can endure. In three years he was promoted to associate professor (1891) and two years later to professor (1893). Perhaps the caliber of Bright's scholarly achievement does not justify a charge that Gilman refused to see the "Acres of Diamonds" on his own campus, but surely here was a sturdy scholar with the pioneering spirit of the institution, who would have been lost to it save for his own self-confidence and determination.

[75] JHC, VI, 13, 69, 105–106; VII, 5, 56. Because Bright was an instructor till 1888, it was probably regarded as unseemly for him to head a seminary.

[76] Kemp Malone, "Historical Sketch of the English Department of the Johns Hopkins University," *JH Alumni Magazine*, XV (1926–1927), 124. For an appreciation of Bright's work, see *ibid.*, 123.

[77] Gilman to Bright, June 6, 1888.

[78] Gilman to Bright, June 9, 1888 (draft); Wood to Gilman, June 11, 1888; Bright to Gilman, Aug. 6, 1888, two letters of date; TM, Oct. 1, 1888; JHC, VIII, 5.

: CHAPTER X :

History and Political Economy

"YOUR own ultimate success may depend on getting History, Political Economy and Metaphysics well taught there," wrote Henry Adams to Gilman early in the second academic year of the Johns Hopkins University.[1] There was nothing magical about these three disciplines, yet they did stand apart from others in the inadequacy of their representation in the university's opening year and in the interest and potential opposition that their idea systems might arouse in the nonacademic community. In one of these fields, the presence of an ambitious and tenacious fellow guaranteed "ultimate success." In another, the university harbored a young scholar whose unorthodox writings invited criticism from both academic and nonacademic circles. And from a triangular struggle for control in the third emerged a victor whose aspirations shortly carried him away from Johns Hopkins, leaving his department a ruin.

A year after the university opened, in November, 1877, the trustees authorized Gilman to inquire of Henry Adams, who had that spring resigned his assistant professorship in history at Harvard and moved to Washington, if he would come to the history department at Hopkins. Adams showed some willingness to serve as part-time adjunct, but wanted to keep his residence in Washington. He declined "to become again a Professor on any terms." Although the trustees had a high opinion of Adams, their desire for a full-time resident professor pre-

[1] Henry Adams to Gilman, Dec. 1, 1877.

vented their adding him to the staff. Sympathizing with this aim, Adams sent recommendations for others, including John Fiske; Lewis Henry Morgan, whose *Ancient Society* had just appeared; and Senator Lucius Q. C. Lamar of Mississippi. Lamar's recent antisilver stand had gone against the wishes of the Mississippi legislature, and his resignation appeared likely. Gilman's interest was aroused, but nothing came of the suggestion.[2]

The most famous historian for whom Hopkins angled was Hermann von Holst, who combined the attractions of being a German professor and having an interest in the American past. He had counseled Gilman during his European trip of 1875, and when he visited America in 1878, he expressed a strong desire to see Gilman and the university that he had created. Seizing the opportunity, Gilman persuaded the visitor to give a series of public lectures. These ten lectures on the German Empire were a great success, despite Von Holst's forebodings. In fact, the university wanted much more, and in February, Gilman began asking him if he would accept a professorship. At a special meeting in July, 1879, the trustees agreed to offer Von Holst the professorship of history at $5,000. Believing the appointment accepted, Sylvester exulted that the reputation of Johns Hopkins in Germany was now assured and that other leading scholars would follow Von Holst to Baltimore.[3]

Von Holst had indeed seemed close to accepting, but at the last he cited his moral obligation to the government, his life tenure, and the pension for his widow as factors keeping him from Baltimore, even though he realized that he could serve "science" better there. The tone of his refusal led the trustees to think that their chances might improve in a year, and in 1880 the offer was renewed, though without success. Relations with the German scholar continued cordial. Two trustees traveling in Europe in 1881 called on him, and in October, 1883, he gave another series of public lectures at Hopkins.[4] Von Holst was only in his thirties during these negotiations, and they proved not to be his last

[2] ECM, Nov. 27, 1877; Gilman to Henry Adams, Nov. 8, 28, 1877; Henry Adams to Gilman, Dec. 1, 1877, Feb. 14, March 5, 1878. Some of these letters appear in W. Stull Holt, "Henry Adams and the Johns Hopkins University," *New England Quarterly*, XI (1938), 632–638.

[3] Von Holst to Gilman, Sept. 12, 17, Oct. 5, 1878; Gilman to Von Holst, Feb. 26, 1879; ECM, May 26, 1879; TM, July 7, 1879; Sylvester to Gilman, July 30, 1879.

[4] Von Holst to Gilman, Aug. 12, 1879; Cheston to Gilman, Sept. 10, 1879, Aug. 6, 1880; TM, June 7, 1880; James Carey Thomas to Gilman, Aug. 22, 1881; JHC, III, 16, 43.

opportunity to come to America. In 1892, the University of Chicago made him the first chairman of its history department.

One sign of Von Holst's continued interest in Johns Hopkins was his correspondence with Gilman, in which he wished the university success in making Thomas M. Cooley one of its staff. Cooley, one of the original visiting lecturers, had returned briefly during the second and third terms. In the 1878–1879 term he conducted in addition to his lectures six meetings of what was called the "Seminary of English Constitutional Law." The authorities had from the beginning implied that they might call him from the University of Michigan law school.[5] The formal offer of a professorship of jurisprudence at a salary of $5,000 came as part of the 1880 drive to expand the faculty. Since Hopkins had no law school, his teaching was to be in history and political economy, but in these fields he was promised a wide opportunity to advance the "idea of good government." After three months' consideration, however, Cooley declined, and another opportunity for "acknowledged eminence" was lost. The next summer, after visiting Cambridge University, Trustee Thomas ventured the opinion that Johns Hopkins could win any of the history corps there from John Robert Seeley "on down—if thought desirable." [6] But none of the Englishmen was invited.

While Gilman and the trustees sought to bring fame to the history department from without, young, little-known scholars within were dedicating themselves to its development. Austin Scott, the first associate in history, continued to live in Washington and work with Bancroft, commuting to Baltimore once a week. During the 1879–1880 term, his weekly visits covered a period of only two months. Scott preferred his teaching in Baltimore to his work with Bancroft, however, and in 1880 and again in 1881 he requested advancement to full-time service, offering to drop his other obligations. In 1881, he ended his work with Bancroft and bid for advancement with a course of Hopkins Hall lectures on the development of the American Constitution.[7] But he was not reappointed in 1882. In 1883 he went to Rutgers, where he later became president.

[5] Von Holst to Gilman, May 11, 1881; ARJH (1879), 56; Gilman to Cooley, Nov. 8, 1877.

[6] Gilman to Cooley, Nov. 16, 1880; Cooley to Gilman, Feb. 15, 1881; Thomas to Gilman, June 14, 1881.

[7] JHR (1880), 24; Scott to Gilman, March 7, 1880, May 2, Sept. 24, 1881.

The reason for Scott's failure at Hopkins was probably not so much any inadequacy in his work as the presence of another young historian of unlimited ambition and great adroitness. One of the original fellows, Herbert Baxter Adams had won his Ph.D. at Heidelberg before arriving at Hopkins and regarded himself from the beginning as more teacher than student. He was one of the fellows who organized voluntary classes among the students. When only one volunteered for American constitutional history during the 1877–1878 term, Adams gave him a peripatetic course with walks in Baltimore parks. In the spring of 1878, during his second year as fellow, Adams was invited to give lectures at Smith College. He continued to teach at Smith each spring, though refusing a professorship there.[8]

Scott expressed his pleasure at Adams' appointment as associate in 1878, hoping for "an impetus . . . to the study of History such as it shall not lose in many a year." But in the same letter he took pains to make sure that his own associateship would be renewed. During his first year as associate, Adams, even though he continued his work at Smith, taught three courses to Scott's one and gave ten public lectures on "Beginnings of Church and State." By the end of the year he was asking to change his title from associate to assistant professor. Gilman felt obliged to caution him that the university was "still looking for a man of the years & standing of Prof Holst" and that such an appointment might not redound to his benefit. "But," Gilman concluded, "—it may not be made." [9] Adams was willing to take the gamble. The vigor of his activity and the continued refusal of Von Holst led to just such a letter as he might have prayed for from Trustee Brown to Gilman: "The Fates seem to forbid our securing Von Holst. I am sorry, but he is not indispensable. Adams is developing remarkably well and for the present at least supplies our needs." Another threat to Adams was the trustees' continued interest in J. Lewis Diman, professor at Brown. Diman gave twenty lectures in 1879 on the Thirty Years' War and agreed to lecture again in 1881. Gilman reminded Adams that the trustees wanted Diman for a professorship and that this might slow

[8] John Martin Vincent, "Herbert B. Adams: A Biographical Sketch," in *Herbert B. Adams: Tributes of Friends* (*JHU Studies in Historical and Political Science,* extra vol. XXIII; Baltimore, 1902), 15.

[9] Scott to Gilman, June 13, 1878; JHR (1879), 20; Gilman to H. B. Adams, June 20, 1879.

Adams' advancement.[10] But Diman's death in 1881 prevented even his second visit as lecturer.

By May, 1881, having failed to win Von Holst, Cooley, or Diman, the trustees asked Adams to end his spring trips to Smith and offered him a two-year appointment as associate with a salary of $2,250. Adams did not accept at once. He observed that the salary offered was $500 less than he could earn as a full-time teacher at Smith. "I am getting rather tired of following an uncertain path," he wrote; but he shaded the tone of his letter by saying that he did not consider himself worthy of being a professor of history and that he sometimes felt that he "would rather be a door-keeper in the house of Science than to dwell in a Woman's college." [11]

Although Adams apparently failed to get his increase, he agreed to shift all his energies to Johns Hopkins. His energies were prodigious. He took full control of the historical seminary and initiated plans for the famous monograph series. He was the star of the account of historical work in the 1882 *Annual Report,* which described Scott as part of the past. Gilman gave up his thoughts of importing an older man. "In our H. B. Adams," he wrote President White, "we have a capital teacher —who will I think hold this place." [12] The favorable mention which Edward A. Freeman had included in an article describing his trip to America had certainly not harmed Adams in Gilman's eyes. Early in 1883, according to departmental rumor, Adams was "about ready to 'pry' for a professorship." [13] What he got was one of the newly created associate professorships at $2,750 a year. His salary was higher than certain others of the new rank, partly because an invitation to become professor at the University of Pennsylvania had strengthened his hand. In 1885, Adams, without consulting the Hopkins authorities, refused a professorship at Michigan, which Cooley then accepted. A year later Adams reasoned as follows in an elaborate plea to the trustees for expansion of the department and his own promotion: "Inasmuch as Judge Cooley was once called to the position which I now crave in Baltimore,

---

[10] Brown to Gilman, Aug. 4, 1880; ARJH (1879), 29; JHC, I, 99; Gilman to Adams, April 29, 1880, in Holt, ed., *Historical Scholarship,* 39.

[11] Gilman to Adams, May 5, 1881; Adams to Gilman, May 11, 1881.

[12] Gilman to Adams, May [17?], 1881; ARJH (1882), 44–46; Gilman to A. D. White, Sept. 24, 1882.

[13] Vincent, in *Adams Tributes,* 16; Jameson diary, Jan. 6, 1883.

that is, headship of a department of Historical and Political Science, it seems to me that the logic of the present situation is somewhat in my favor." The question, he said, was less a matter of money than "a point of personal honor and of just recognition." The promotion did not come. Adams, his good humor undampened, wrote to Gilman, "I feel constrained either *to resign or be resigned.* Either horn of the dilemma is equally uncomfortable." [14] He chose the latter, remaining with un-diminished loyalty at Hopkins, winning his promotion to professor in 1891. That same year he rejected, after much pondering, an invitation to join the University of Chicago as professor and dean of the graduate school.[15]

Freeman once called Adams the most energetic man that he knew in two hemispheres.[16] Energy and enthusiasm were the traits most often cited in the memorials after Adams' death in 1901. His junior colleague Jameson recorded the reverse side of this virtue: "Adams is full of projects for wider and wider work; but the fault is, that meanwhile he doesn't pay attention to details, nor care enough to do well the original, fundamental work of instruction. As he gains reputation in the world at large, he loses it among his students." Yet Adams was a rare teacher. His students cited his comradeliness, which made him like "an older and wiser fellow student," and his ability to inspire them to work.[17] Although a second-year graduate student could write in his diary that an Adams lecture "didn't give much," an entry in the diary of an equally able student, Albert Shaw, soon after his arrival at Hopkins in January, 1882, showed a different reaction: "At 12, heard Dr. H. B. Adams on 'Institutional History.' His lecture was of intense interest. It was on the 'Constable,' which ministerial officer of the New England town he traced back to the ancient Saxon titheing-man [sic]. . . . Evolution of policeman—etc."

When he moved his seminary to the former biology laboratory, the greatest cause of Adams' delight was the prospect that the new quarters

[14] Adams to Gilman and executive committee, May 29, 1886, in Holt, ed., *Histori-cal Scholarship*, 85–87; Adams to Gilman, July 17, 1886.

[15] Adams to Albert Shaw, May 2, 1891, Shaw Papers.

[16] Gilman diary, "1882–1887 to California & Alaska," [April 21, 1883]. Gilman saw the comment in a letter to Professor Allen Clapp Thomas of Haverford.

[17] Jameson diary, Jan. 12, 1883; Howe, *Confessions*, 30; A. S. Eisenstadt, *Charles McLean Andrews: A Study in American Historical Writing* (*Columbia Studies in the Social Sciences*, no. 588; New York, 1956), 9; interview with Judge Soper and Judge Moses.

would " 'quicken' the young men." [18] His own technique of quickening appeared in the diary of a first-year graduate student:

My paper, which was rather too long and I thought dry, seemed to me to fall rather flat. . . . So I was very pleasantly surprised when Adams commended me quite highly, saying I had made an interesting paper out of a dry subject, and he liked both my arrangement and the style of phraseology. His praise seemed very hearty . . . and I went home feeling quite encouraged, and felt as if my work had after all amounted to something.[19]

Even today the stridency of some of Adams' promotional activity pierces the swathes of time; his former student Woodrow Wilson chose an apt encomium when he called him "a great Captain of Industry." [20] But as he promoted himself, Adams promoted also the good of his university and of the historical profession in America.

The quality of the man was tested when he faced a clearly identifiable violation of academic freedom. The challenge came when William Paret, the new Episcopal bishop of Maryland, informed Gilman of his displeasure at a textbook assigned by Adams in a required undergraduate course. The bishop declared of the book, Edward Clodd's *The Childhood of Religions:* "It is unjust, unfair toward the Bible & the Christian Religion; asserts things with regard to them w[hi]ch it does not prove, and presents in subtle form, very taking with the immature minds of Undergraduates, a strong un-Christian influence." The letter closed with a request for the withdrawal of the book and an implied threat: "I feel the Matter the More, because I had been earnestly Commending the University, & urging some young men to go there." Gilman answered at once, thanking the bishop and declaring that though he had never read the book himself he would at once investigate. Queried by Gilman, Adams sent word that Clodd was "a very good little book which I have used at Smith College and the Johns

---

[18] Jameson diary, Oct. 12, 1881; Albert Shaw diary, Jan. 11, 1882, Shaw Papers; Adams to Lanman, Nov. 9, 1883, Lanman Papers.

[19] Jameson diary, March 18, 1881.

[20] Quoted in Richard T. Ely, "A Sketch of the Life and Services of Herbert Baxter Adams," in *Adams Tributes,* 46. During his student days, Wilson had called Adams "a disciple of Machiavelli, as he himself declares" (Wilson to R. Heath Dabney, Feb. 17, 1884, quoted in Ray Stannard Baker, *Woodrow Wilson: Life and Letters* (Garden City, N.Y., 1927–1939), I, *Youth, 1856–1890,* 178.

Hopkins for the purpose of giving some idea of the kinship of Indo-European religious ideas." Still not having read the book (he was on summer vacation), Gilman informed Adams that it had offended "a gent[leman] of high education & standing" and admonished him, "I have no doubt [that] on reflection if not spontaneously you will agree with me. Whether the work in question is censurable and/or objectionable I do not know; but it certainly appears so to one whose views are entitled to respect." [21] Adams did agree. Like Gilman, he valued the good opinion of men of high standing. The administrator in him bowed to the same pressures that forced conciliations from Gilman. His surrender was perhaps eased by Gilman's careful distinction between the maturity of graduate students and the immaturity of undergraduates, who must be shielded. The report of the course for the following year still listed the second text, Keary's *Dawn of History*, but Clodd had disappeared.[22]

Beginning in 1882, Adams had the assistance of J. Franklin Jameson, another Amherst graduate, whom he had urged to come to Hopkins in 1880 and who had been the first to win a Hopkins Ph.D. in history.[23] Jameson's diary contains many sour reflections on Adams, but perhaps because Jameson's irritations found such an outlet, the two could work together without friction. When most objective, Jameson admitted the mutuality of their support, realizing that he was "too cautious and conservative" and "too intent upon an ideal excellence" not to need the counterweight of Adams' breadth and suggestiveness. Adams' warmer personality passed an easier judgment on Jameson, and he wrote to Gilman that he was "really an able, scholarly, conscientious, manly fellow." [24] Jameson's abilities had been recognized by a promotion to associate in 1883, after one year as instructor. In 1887 he had hopes of becoming Adams' successor should his chief accept a professorship offered by Western Reserve. Adams did not leave, and in 1888 Jameson became professor at Brown. But the achievements which made him one

[21] William Paret to Gilman, Aug. 20, 1885; Gilman to Paret, Aug. 20, 1885 (draft); Adams to Gilman, Aug. 24, 1885; Gilman to Adams, Aug. 26, 1885 (draft).

[22] JHC, IV, 105; V, 133.

[23] Elizabeth Donnan and Leo F. Stock, eds., *An Historian's World: Selections from the Correspondence of John Franklin Jameson* (*Memoirs of the American Philosophical Society*, XLII; Philadelphia, 1956), 1–2.

[24] Jameson diary, Jan. 19, 1883; Adams to Gilman, July 7, 1885.

who "had no predecessor and would have no successor" in the historical profession came outside the universities in scholarly foundations in the nation's capital.[25]

Although Johns Hopkins gave a Ph.D. in political economy in 1878, no classes in that subject were offered by a staff member until early in 1879. Henry Carter Adams, the recipient of the degree, left for study in Germany in 1878 with the financial assistance of Trustee White. In letters to Gilman he described his new-found faith that political economy had "power to benefit mankind," and wondered if Johns Hopkins might hire him to teach it. He was careful to inform Gilman that he was not a socialist, although aware of socialism's value in pointing out "the injurious workings of free competition." Included were a sketch of an ideal program for an economics department and some details of his philosophy of teaching.[26] Through his acquaintance with Andrew D. White, then minister to Berlin on leave as president of Cornell, Adams received an appointment as lecturer at Cornell for the 1879–1880 term. He was also invited to return to Hopkins with the new title of assistant for two months in the spring of 1880. But the honor of being the first staff member to teach political economy at Hopkins went to the ever-ready Herbert B. Adams, who had offered an introductory course for two months in the second half of the 1878–1879 term and repeated it early in 1880, before Henry C. Adams came to give his course on money and banking and public lectures on national debts.[27] "Dr. Henry" told Gilman that he would prefer a position at Johns Hopkins to any other in the country, but though Gilman invited him back for a half-year's teaching in the fall of 1880, he felt that he was not "just adapted to our wants, as a permanent instructor."[28] What H. C. Adams lacked is not clear. At any rate, he taught no more at Johns Hopkins after 1880, supporting himself with half-year lectureships at Cornell and the University of Michigan.

The scholar who won the place at Hopkins which H. C. Adams desired, Richard T. Ely, was, like Adams, to be remembered as a leader in the attack on laissez faire and the movement toward historical

[25] Jameson diary, June 3, 1887; Donnan and Stock, eds., *Historian's World*, 17.
[26] H. C. Adams to Francis White, Aug. 15, 1878, GP; H. C. Adams to Gilman, Dec. 15, 1878, Jan. 7, 1878 [1879].
[27] JHR (1879), 20, (1880), 4, 24; JHC, I, 30.
[28] H. C. Adams to Gilman, June 28, 1879; Gilman to A. D. White, March 4, 1880; TM, May 3, 1880; JHR (1881), 61.

economics.[29] A graduate of Columbia College in the year that Hopkins opened, Ely had followed the well-beaten track to Germany, taken his Ph.D. at Heidelberg in 1879, and returned inspired but unemployed to the United States. While in Berlin, however, he had formed a friendship with Andrew D. White and done research for him, and with White's support he won a modest position at Johns Hopkins in the fall of 1881.[30] The trustees felt that political economy did not deserve a major appointment, that it was an appropriate department for some young scholar, and Brown wrote Gilman that Ely was "one who ought to be tried." Originally appointed instructor for a half-year at $600, Ely won an extension to the full year and an additional $500. He was promoted to associate for his second year, and for his third year the trustees, citing his ability and his large number of students, advanced his salary to $1,750.[31]

To one of his first students Ely appeared "an insignificant-looking, homely little man" with a less engaging manner than his predecessor H. C. Adams. Ely, who made "a great parade of authorities," seemed so "steeped in German prejudices" that he failed to see any good in English economists, especially the Manchesterians.[32] But though little older than his students, he had a remarkable power, akin to that of H. B. Adams, to stimulate them and set them to work. Partly he did this by his own example of labor, the 1880s being one of the most productive periods of his life. Partly he did it by his reformist zeal. In the pages of the *Circulars,* he denounced the policy of laissez faire as "foreign to the spirit of true progress," and he published vigorous articles in the Baltimore *Sun* on problems of government and economics.[33] Before the decade was out, he had aided tax commissions in drawing up reform programs for both Baltimore and Maryland.[34]

[29] For a survey of Ely's thought during his Hopkins years, see Joseph Dorfman, *The Economic Mind in American Civilization* (New York, 1946–1959), III, 161–164.

[30] Ely, *Ground under Our Feet,* 63; A. D. White to Ely, Sept. 20, 1881, GP.

[31] George W. Brown to Gilman, Aug. 11, 1881; TM, Oct. 3, 1881, Oct. 1, 1883; ECM, March 4, 1882.

[32] Jameson diary, Oct. 7, 14, 18, 1881, May 2, Nov. 17, 1882.

[33] Albert Shaw to Nicholas Murray Butler, Sept. 27, 1937, Shaw Papers; bibliography in Ely, *Ground under Our Feet,* 309–310; JHC, II, 27; Ely, *Problems of To-Day: A Discussion of Protective Tariffs, Taxation, and Monopolies* (New York, 1888).

[34] JHC, VII, 41–42; Ely, *Ground under Our Feet,* 172–173.

Ely had visited the paternalistic city of Pullman in 1884 and described it in an article in *Harper's Monthly*. Although he considered himself "the only one who has given an honest, impartial description of Pullman," he wrote in a private letter on the subject: "It makes me indignant to see a thoroughly selfish man, who is attempting to enslave labor, pose as a philanthropist." His indignation against abuse of economic power did not abate, and as the end of the turbulent year 1886 drew near, he wrote a former student: "We will be slaves in *twenty years* if we do not resist the aggressions of vast corporations." In a university that was financially dependent on the profits of a large railroad corporation, he read in the spring of 1886 a paper entitled "The Reform of Railway Abuses." [35] The pressure that Ely feared was not that of the B. & O., however, but of "the *Nation* crowd."

It was at Wisconsin in 1894 that Ely became the center of a historic academic-freedom case.[36] But he came close, or so he and his friends feared, to martyrdom at Johns Hopkins in 1886. In that year of the Haymarket Riot, he came under heavy attack from E. L. Godkin in the pages of the New York *Evening Post* and the *Nation*. Ely began to regard these attacks as a danger to his position at Hopkins, especially inasmuch as one of his colleagues there, Simon Newcomb, was a leading antagonist.

Newcomb had published two books and many articles on political economy before coming to Hopkins and had given a brief lecture series on the subject at Harvard in 1879–1880. He was a follower of Stanley Jevons in the movement to introduce mathematics and the concept of marginal utility into economics, and he has been hailed as a pioneer in developing the "equation of exchange." But his extreme adherence to laissez faire limited his work as a creative theorist.[37] With this economic background, Newcomb felt justified in launching an attack on Ely's ideas in the spring of 1884, before he had formally been elected to the professorship of mathematics which he assumed that fall. What had aroused him was Ely's monograph *The Past and the Present of Political Economy*.[38] Ely contrasted the "modern" or "historical" or "statistical" school which he represented with the "orthodox English or

[35] Ely to Albert Shaw, Jan. 10, 1885, Nov. 1, 1886, Shaw Papers; JHC, V, 96.
[36] Hofstadter and Metzger, *Development of Academic Freedom*, 425–432.
[37] W. W. Campbell, "Simon Newcomb," *Memoirs of the National Academy of Sciences*, XVII (Washington, 1924), 14; Dorfman, *Economic Mind*, III, 83–87.
[38] *JHU Studies in Historical and Political Science*, II, no. 3 (Baltimore, 1884).

classical" school, of which he considered Newcomb a member. Although like Newcomb he admired Jevons, he specifically discounted the "Mathematical School," with which some connected the English economist. Ely was surely guilty of narrowness of vision in his belief that "the works which have advocated the application of mathematics to economics form no essential part of the development of economic literature." He pictured himself and other young Americans as "clearly abandoning the dry bones of orthodox English political economy for the live methods of the German school," a change which he hailed as "a return to the grand principle of common sense and Christian precept." [39]

In a letter to Gilman, Newcomb called Ely's pamphlet the first work he had seen "in which the disciples of the new school clearly laid down the difference between their view of the subject and that of the old school." This, he announced, had stirred him up, and he hoped to present a lecture answering it. He pressed Gilman for a consultation on the Hopkins economics department and later sent him a paper, "The Two Schools of Political Economy," whose bearing on Ely was clear from Newcomb's accompanying comment: "It looks a little incongruous to see so sweeping and wholesale [an] attack upon the introduction of any rational or scientific method in economics come from a university whose other specialties have tended in the opposite direction." He paralleled Ely's view of traditional economics to "the general objections of the public against the value of theoretical science." [40]

Newcomb made good use of the structure of the university to air his views, and he did so with what was remembered as irritating assertiveness. Before the Scientific Association in February, 1885, Newcomb read a paper, "On the Possibility of Applying Mathematics to Political Economy"; two days later one of Ely's students, Charles H. Levermore, led a discussion at the Historical and Political Science Association of "Newcomb on Mathematical Economy." [41] But the reasonable next step of a face-to-face debate between Newcomb and Ely did not follow. Ely had the advantages of teaching the economics courses and of being in full-time residence; still, he was of lower rank and he was worried.

[39] *Ibid.*, 20, 23, 43, 45, 56, 60n, 64.
[40] Newcomb to Gilman, May 3, 14, June 1, 4, 1884. The paper was later published in the *Princeton Review*, n.s. XIV (1884), 291–301.
[41] Albert Shaw, "Recollections," GP; JHC, IV, 66.

Concerning his successful efforts of 1885 to create an American Economic Association (which Newcomb later claimed Ely had intended as "a sort of church, requiring for admission to its full communion a renunciation of ancient errors, and an adhesion to the supposed new creed" [42]), Ely wrote that his major aim was to organize the young economists opposed to extreme individualism in order to combat "the Sumner, Newcomb crowd." William Graham Sumner had "nagged [Francis A.] Walker until he got him out of Yale," Ely believed, and he feared that Newcomb would do the same to him at Hopkins. The influence of these conservative economists Ely called "in every way pernicious." He conceived of them as arrogantly persecuting "all who do not accept their dogmas." [43]

The gulf between the two men widened when each published a major book. Newcomb's *Principles of Political Economy* appeared in 1885; Ely's *The Labor Movement in America*, in 1886. The very titles indicated the difference in approach. Newcomb claimed to present economics "in a scientific form as an established body of principles." He felt that the most unsatisfactory feature "from a scientific standpoint" of the teaching then going on in economics was "the presentation of too many opposing views and arguments." [44]

Ely's assault on Newcomb's volume took place through his former student Albert Shaw, who recalled, "I reviewed it with the irreverent scorn of a confirmed Elyite, and called it an essay in logic that undertook to treat the law of supply and demand as the analogy in social science of the law of gravitation in physics." As a matter of fact, Shaw granted that the book had merits and that Newcomb attempted to state disputed questions fairly, but he declared that in matters of social organization, Newcomb's astronomical bias was vitiating.[45] The review was far milder than the one Ely had urged Shaw to write. The teacher had sent a detailed letter pointing out what parts of the work especially called for exposure. According to Ely's reading, Newcomb recommended starvation as one method of philanthropy and his statement that "men cannot promote their own economic interests except through

[42] Newcomb, review of Ely's *An Introduction to Political Economy* and *Outlines of Economics*, in *Journal of Political Economy*, III (1894–1895), 106.
[43] Ely to Albert Shaw, May 7, 1885, Shaw Papers.
[44] Newcomb, *Principles*, iii.
[45] Shaw, "Recollections," GP; Shaw, "Recent Economic Works," *Dial*, VI (1885), 210–213.

promoting those of their fellow-men" meant that "Jay Gould must be one of the greatest benefactors of his time." Ely assured Shaw that Newcomb was "an ignoramus as regards the investigations of scholars during the past generation." Something evangelical imbued Ely's admonitions: ethics, he said, must not be divorced from economics, and "right-thinking Christian men" must speak out clearly.[46]

Before Ely's book appeared in 1886, the two Hopkins teachers had a chance to clarify their disagreements, not within the walls of their institution, but in a series of articles in *Science*.[47] Newcomb contended that his approach to the subject was no less ethical than Ely's, which he accused of confusing facts and values. Ely, though observing that it would require a large book to expose Newcomb's errors, stated his broadest objection: Newcomb failed "to distinguish between mathematical sciences and those which are more descriptive in their nature, and have to do with growing, changing bodies." The interchange ended with what appeared to be a peace bid by Newcomb. He called his article "Can Economists Agree upon the Basis of Their Teaching?" His answer was yes, and he drew a parallel with physics, where both experimentalists and those stressing mathematical deduction contributed without antagonism or accusations of ignorance. In economics, he felt, the tendency to divide into "schools" represented one of the worst failings of the medieval philosophers. As a common aim, he recommended "the improvement of society." He called for a "judicious combination" of deduction from general principles and historical and statistical analysis: "What is really urgent is that [the student] shall know how to study facts effectively, and be able to understand principles rationally."

If as soon as this article appeared Gilman had brought the disputants together, he might have transmuted their disagreements into fruitful stimulation. But the optimal moment came in the summer. By fall the country was alarmed and divided over the "labor question," and when Ely's book, sympathetic with labor, appeared, Newcomb took advantage of the anonymity of the columns of the *Nation* for a scathing review. Far from seeking common ground this time, Newcomb loosed his attack on the man as well as his ideas. The review opened by citing

[46] Ely to Shaw, Nov. 19, 1885, Shaw Papers. Ely cited Newcomb, *Principles*, 532–533, 535.

[47] *Science*, VII (1886), 529–533, 538–542; VIII (1886), 3–6, 25–26.

Ely's position as "the leading professor of his subject in the Johns Hopkins University" and, after accusing him of bias, obscurantism, and intellectual confusion, concluded with another direct reference to his academic position: "We have devoted so much space to this production less on account of its importance than of the position and reputation of the author. . . . Dr. Ely seems to us to be seriously out of place in a university chair." [48]

Little wonder that Ely and his students feared Gilman might yield to such pressures. Besides the attacks from the *Nation*, there was the foreboding case of Henry Carter Adams, who was in trouble at Cornell because of statements on the rights of labor akin to those of Ely, and he was in fact dismissed.[49] In commenting on H. C. Adams' danger, Ely observed:

It is not yet safe for a man to investigate and discuss freely social phenomena as he can the phenomena of external nature. I think in the opinion of most people a political economist is a man whose duty it is not to ascertain truth but to advocate certain things well pleasing to powerful private interests.

It was a crisis—Ely had no doubt of that. But H. B. Adams proved "a true friend," helping to keep his hopes up,[50] and his former students rallied. Albert Shaw wrote a favorable review of the book in the *Dial*, calling it "conservative in the truest sense of that word." In the same review article, Shaw attacked a briefer book by Newcomb, *A Plain Man's Talk on the Labor Question*, with criticisms suggested to him by Ely. He linked Newcomb with Sumner and compared his economic ideas with those of a Biblical fundamentalist and shallow empiricist who was sure on grounds of authority and observation that the sun revolved around the earth.[51] Reassured by Shaw's review and a more influential

[48] [Simon Newcomb], review of Ely's *Labor Question*, in *Nation*, XLIII (Oct. 7, 1886), 293–294. It is conceivable that Godkin may have added the more extreme passages. But Newcomb never informed Ely if part of the review was inserted by another hand, for in 1938 Ely still regarded him as the sole author (Ely, *Ground under Our Feet*, 184).

[49] Marvin B. Rosenberry, "Henry Carter Adams," in *Michigan and the Cleveland Era: Sketches of University of Michigan Staff Members and Alumni Who Served the Cleveland Administrations, 1885–89, 1893–97*, ed. by Earl D. Babst and Lewis G. Vander Velde (Ann Arbor, 1948), 27–30.

[50] Ely to Shaw, Oct. 3, 18, 1886, Shaw Papers.

[51] Albert Shaw, "Seven Books for Citizens," *Dial*, VII (1886), 149–152; Ely to Shaw, Oct. 18, 19, 1886, Shaw Papers.

one by Lyman Abbott in the *Christian Union,* Ely concluded that though Gilman had been "becoming shaky under pressure from the *Nation* crowd" the danger was past.[52]

After Ely regarded the crisis as ended, another former student, Edward W. Bemis, who was to have a stormy academic career of his own, launched a program to plant favorable notices of Ely's work in the press. He felt that "Pres. Gilman's desire to be popular is so great that he will be influenced by such articles." It was perhaps in response to urgings by Bemis that Washington Gladden, a leader of the social gospel who had just published *Applied Christianity,* wrote to Gilman in praise of Ely, stressing clerical approval: "I think no man in the country is more widely known or more cordially liked by the clergy than Professor Ely. It is greatly to the honor of Johns Hopkins that she has given him the chance to do this work." [53]

What was going through Gilman's mind during these days remains hypothetical. But certain facts deserve notice. Ely felt himself out of danger before the strongest part of the movement in his support developed. The chairman of the executive committee had stated precisely in reference to attacks in the *Nation* that Ely's approach to economics deserved to be tried. Ely himself had taken the precaution to preface his book with a moderating statement: "I do not think it incumbent upon me to say on every page, that I am so far from sympathizing with schemes for destruction, that I regard them as damnable. I regard this as a most conservative work." Similarly, in an article early in 1887, he presented his stand as an impartial one, writing, "It is only necessary to restrain a comparatively few hot-headed and vicious capitalists and a comparatively few hot-headed and vicious laborers, to insure a peaceful evolution of industrial society." Both statements were reprinted in the university's *Circulars.*[54] Another factor in the situation was that Godkin, although abusing Ely in the pages of his publications, refrained from using his friendship with Gilman as a channel of attack.[55] It would seem, then, that Ely was in less danger than he and

[52] Ely to Shaw, Nov. 18, Dec. 1, 1886, Shaw Papers.

[53] Bemis to Shaw, Dec. 6, 1886, *ibid.;* Washington Gladden to Gilman, Dec. 25, 1886.

[54] George W. Brown to Gilman, Aug. 12, [1884?]; JHC, VI, 56, 82.

[55] This is proved by E. L. Godkin to Gilman, Feb. 17, 1892, written when Ely did leave Hopkins: "At the risk of not meeting with a sympathetic response, I am going to congratulate you on the departure of Ely for other fields. I think he

Bemis thought. In fact, at the end of the 1886–1887 term he was promoted to associate professor. Whatever his suspicions of 1886, Ely could say of Gilman in 1938, "He held firm to his belief that academic freedom must prevail." [56]

As for the Ely-Newcomb conflict, after 1886 it abated. Probably as a gesture of good will, Ely included one of Newcomb's books among several "references" in his elementary course for the 1886–1887 term. Gilman gave Newcomb an outlet for his economic interests in the 1887–1888 term through lectures to undergraduates on American business and financial institutions.[57] Newcomb found that Ely had grounded his students in "those principles of economic theory" which Newcomb regarded as "essential to a comprehension of the subject on its scientific side." Perhaps most significantly, the astronomer began to feel the penalties of living in an age of specialization. After his review of Ely's book in 1886, he published nothing relating to economics for nearly four years.[58] When he reviewed two of Ely's books in 1894, he did not repeat the extravagant language of 1886.[59] In the same year, Newcomb admitted to Charles Peirce, "My experience leads me to believe that people have very little confidence in my views on subjects outside of mathematics and astronomy." [60]

There were probably personal failings in the inability of Newcomb and Ely to co-operate for the advancement of political economy, but it was an institutional failure also. Gilman's mechanisms did not succeed in bringing these two men together and helping each to see the good that was in the other. This was a major loss for American economics. In the 1880s, Newcomb was the American closest to the "mathematical" or "marginal utility" school in Europe, and Ely the closest to the historical. Had these new veins of economic thought come

---

has been for years a discredit to you and mischievous to the community in spite of his extraordinary industry, or rather because of it. Professors of Political Economy preaching their own philanthropic gospel as 'Science,' are among the most dangerous characters of our time, and Ely was one of them. I have been itching to say this for years, but feared to do so. Now I shall feel easier."

[56] Ely, *Ground under Our Feet*, 102.   [57] JHC, VI, 113; VII, 74.

[58] Simon Newcomb, *Reminiscences of an Astronomer* (Boston, 1903), 408, 406; Raymond Clare Archibald, "Simon Newcomb, 1835–1909: Bibliography of His Life and Work," *Memoirs of the National Academy of Sciences*, XVII (Washington, 1924), 60.

[59] See note 42 above.

[60] Newcomb to C. S. Peirce, Jan. 3, 1894, Newcomb Papers.

fruitfully together at Hopkins, the university might have given American scholarship an economic renaissance. The failure is all the more poignant because by 1903 Newcomb could speak warmly of Ely, and by 1906 Ely could write to Newcomb expressing a wish to get together to talk over old times. In his *Reminiscences,* Newcomb claimed that at Hopkins "each professor was a factor in the department of another in a helpful and not an antagonistic way, and all held counsel on subjects where the knowledge of all was helpful to each." The irony with which the Newcomb-Ely breach touches this generalization bespeaks intellectual tragedy.[61]

It was by Ely's own choice that he left Johns Hopkins in 1892 for the University of Wisconsin. He was angered that the trustees would not release him from undergraduate teaching, give him a separate department, or advance him to the same rank as H. B. Adams. None of his complaints involved academic freedom. His life at Hopkins he recalled as "golden years; . . . the fullest and happiest of my life," and in 1901 he wanted to be invited back to fill H. B. Adams' place.[62] His autobiography he dedicated to Gilman, declaring that he owed him "an inestimable debt of gratitude."

[61] Dorfman, *Economic Mind,* III, 82–83; Newcomb, *Reminiscences,* 406–408; Ely to Newcomb, Feb. 7, 1906, Newcomb Papers.

[62] Ely, *Ground under Our Feet,* 175, 165; Gilman to Ely, Jan. 4, June 7, 1892; Ely to Albert Shaw, Aug. 27, 1901, Shaw Papers.

: CHAPTER XI :

Philosophy

PERHAPS in no area of learning did the Johns Hopkins University more consistently choose teachers of intellectual stature than in philosophy, and in no other area did its program collapse so abruptly. In studies of this department, historians of philosophy have told its story as a tragedy for American learning. What happened in philosophy at Johns Hopkins has, in fact, been presented as the key to unlock the mind of an era and expose its flaws. The drama requires careful reconstruction of the framework of appointments and promotions within which it was played.

Johns Hopkins conducted its first year without a faculty member who taught philosophy, unless C. D. Morris' course in Aristotle's *Ethics* or Cross's in Plato's *Apology* be counted. But one of its fellows, Josiah Royce, taught a voluntary class in Schopenhauer and gave public lectures on "German Literature." During the second term, a beginning was made with visiting lecturers. One of these was William James, then assistant professor of physiology at Harvard, who gave ten lectures on "The Senses and the Brain and Their Relation to Thought." [1] James was recommended to Gilman by Charles S. Peirce, who had called him the only man fit to lecture on psychology, a subject just emerging from "empty talk & metaphysical nonsense" and entering "the scientific stage." For a time James declared himself a candidate for a professorship at Johns Hopkins, but family ties and encourage-

[1] Lanman diary, Dec., 1876, Jan., 1877; ARJH (1878), 13; JHR (1878), 12.

ment from Eliot as to his future at Harvard led him to withdraw, even though he had "more sympathy in many respects" with Hopkins than with Harvard. Gilman then asked him to come as visiting lecturer for the next three years, to spend two or three months a year lecturing on psychology—or logic, if he preferred.[2] Although James would not accept a lectureship, in 1881 he again bid for a professorship at Hopkins. He bluntly declared that the principal reason for his change of mind was pecuniary need and offered as minimum conditions: "A 4 or 5 years appointment; the first year to be spent in preparation in Europe on a salary of $2000; the salary of the other years to be $5000 per annum." After negotiations in Baltimore, Gilman explained to James that the trustees felt their first appointment in philosophy should not be in psychology and that a European scholar was under consideration.[3]

The European in question was the Scotsman Robert Flint, professor of divinity at Edinburgh since 1876 and former professor of moral philosophy at St. Andrews. He had attracted the trustees' attention during his Stone Lectures on "Agnosticism" at Princeton Theological Seminary in the fall of 1880. At that time they had unsuccessfully invited him to lecture also at Johns Hopkins.[4] The unflattering theory that Gilman and the trustees wanted Flint chiefly because his Christian orthodoxy would help redeem the university from the damaging publicity of the Huxley episode[5] finds strong support in the fact that the New York *Observer*, the Presbyterian newspaper which had scored the Huxley address, praised Flint during his American visit as "a young, hopeful, progressive theologian," with an "aspiring and reverent spirit."[6] The trustees made a similar estimation and decided that Flint was the man to establish their philosophy department. They agreed to cable Flint on the day that they declined James's offer.

Gilman wrote Flint shortly thereafter telling him that Thomas and King would call on him when they reached Europe and begging him

[2] C. S. Peirce to Gilman, Sept. 13, 1877; Gilman to James, Sept. 21, 1878, Jan. 20, 1879; James to Gilman, Jan. 18, 1879.

[3] James to Gilman, April 3, 1881. Much of the correspondence involved is published in Jackson I. Cope, "William James's Correspondence with Daniel Coit Gilman, 1877–1881," *Journal of the History of Ideas*, XII (1951), 609–627.

[4] ECM, Sept. 28, 1880.

[5] Fisch and Cope, "Peirce at Hopkins," in *Studies of Peirce*, ed. by Wiener and Young, 285.

[6] Quoted in Donald Macmillan, *The Life of Robert Flint, D.D., LL.D.* (London, New York, Toronto, 1914), 338.

to withhold his answer till he talked with them.[7] In June the two trustees found him undecided, hesitant about deserting home and church ties, Edinburgh's six-month annual vacation, and its pension system. Thomas predicted his refusal and added pessimistically: "It is however quite certain that he is about the only man that we know of on this side [of] the water—who would be able fully to meet our wishes for a Professor of Moral Philosophy.—We must I fear at present be content with smaller men & a less organized department." [8] The only other possibility seemed to be James Ward, fellow of Trinity College, Cambridge, and lecturer in philosophy. The visiting trustee who interviewed him described the need for an orthodox Christian in the Hopkins chair of philosophy, especially after the Huxley affair.[9] Thomas wrote Gilman that though Ward was "a man of power" he was "not firm in the Christian position we would like." The two trustees returned without a philosopher, and later efforts to bring Flint to America as a visiting lecturer in conjunction with Andover Theological Seminary came to nothing.[10]

The failure of 1881 seemed to demonstrate the impossibility of applying to philosophy the pattern of bringing from Europe an established scholar. The longer search for a professor of philosophy went on inside the university among three Americans brought there with the amorphous title of lecturer. Of the three aspirants, the first to arrive was George Sylvester Morris. He preceded James as visiting lecturer in the 1877–1878 term, giving twenty lectures on the

---

[7] ECM, April 16, 1881; Gilman to Flint, April 27, 1881.

[8] Henry Van Dyke to Gilman, May 7, 1881; J. C. Thomas to Gilman, June 7, 14, 1881.

[9] This interview is so frequently cited as an indication of religious illiberality at Hopkins that the only known account deserves quotation in full. It appears in a letter from James Ward to James Mark Baldwin, Sept. 15, 1903: "I do not know if I ever told you that I was once interviewed and cross-examined by a wealthy Quaker gentleman—his name I think was Thomas—over twenty years ago when they were starting a chair of philosophy. He told me frankly that I was not orthodox enough—and then went back and appointed Stanley Hall! 'At Baltimore,' he said, 'we are a church-going people'; and he had awful stories of the consternation that Huxley—or perhaps it was Tyndall—had produced by a special course of lectures." The letter appears in full in James Mark Baldwin, *Between Two Wars, 1861–1921: Being Memories, Opinions, and Letters Received* (Boston, 1926), I, 118–119.

[10] Thomas to Gilman, June 14, 1881; Egbert C. Smith to Gilman, Nov. 11, 1881, Jan. 14, 1885.

history of philosophy. Having found his studies at Union Theological Seminary disappointing, Morris had worked in the German universities from 1866 to 1868, but had not elected to take a Ph.D. His translation of Überweg's *History of Philosophy* and his own articles brought him a reputation in his chosen field, even though he had been miscast as professor of modern languages and literature at the University of Michigan since 1870. Noah Porter had recommended him to Gilman for a philosophy chair in 1875. Unlike James, Morris was to continue his connection with Johns Hopkins for seven more terms, though, as his biographer has pointed out, in that time he spent less than eighteen months there.[11]

To the original invitation to come as a visiting lecturer, Morris at once assented. But he did not want the lectures to be a mere lyceum series; he hoped for guided study, organized problems, and "a fixed and constant nucleus" of students. Gilman assured him that Hopkins had "a very intellectual company of young men" who read, thought, and talked much on philosophical questions and also read *Nineteenth Century* and *Mind.* He especially cited Royce as "a man of mark and influence," who read Schopenhauer, Hartmann, and Lotze. As the matter turned out, Royce guided a class preparatory to Morris' lectures, a service performed by Allan Marquand the next year. Although he showed his delight in at last teaching philosophy, Morris may have been perturbed by Gilman's mention that among the philosophical young men were some "very well informed upon the physiological side of Psychology" and by his warning that lectures devoted to ancient philosophy would have few hearers.[12]

In January, 1879, Morris returned, giving ten public lectures in historical and practical ethics. The trustees were in the midst of a plan for faculty expansion, in which philosophy played a large part. Although they did not offer Morris a professorship, they proposed a "lectureship" with three years' tenure, a salary of $1,500 a year, and a three-month annual residence in Baltimore. In accepting, Morris declared that he would turn all his "thought and labor" to doing well at Hopkins, making special sacrifices to get time for study and reflec-

[11] JHR (1878), 13; Porter to Gilman, Dec. 13, 1875; Robert Mark Wenley, *The Life and Work of George Sylvester Morris: A Chapter in the History of American Thought in the Nineteenth Century* (New York, 1917), 142.

[12] Gilman to G. S. Morris, Nov. 29, Dec. 7 [10], 11, 1877, Oct. 4, 1878; G. S. Morris to Gilman, Dec. 7, 10, 11, 1877.

tion so that he might reach "the plane contemplated by your admirable University ideal." The fact that he saw demagoguery striking "deadly blows" at the University of Michigan strengthened his dedication to the institution in Baltimore.[13]

A few months after appointing Morris lecturer in the history of philosophy, the trustees reached an agreement with Charles Peirce that he should come to Hopkins as lecturer in logic. Peirce, like Morris, had been under consideration since 1875, William James having given him a strong recommendation. Peirce had participated in the abortive program of University Lectures at Harvard and had been employed by the Coast Survey since 1859.[14] Early in 1878, Peirce paid a visit to Hopkins and submitted an elaborate critique of the program in physics. Believing that his father, the famous Harvard mathematician, had recommended him for a chair in physics, he expressed confidence that he could aid the work in that department. He felt, however, that in logic lay his greatest strength: "In logic, I am the exponent of a particular tendency, that of physical science. I make the pretension to be the most thoroughgoing and fundamental representative of that element who has yet appeared." [15] Gilman rightly saw the high caliber of Peirce's report and predicted a "great career" for him. He broached the possibility that Peirce might continue his Coast Survey work and come to Hopkins to teach logic part time. In March, Peirce wrote that he had given much consideration to Gilman's tentative proposal, because he knew if he accepted a professorship of logic his "whole energy and being would be absorbed in that occupation." The teaching of logic seemed to him of surpassing importance, and, he wrote, "With these sentiments, whether my work in the University were contracted for as half-service or not, it could not possibly *be* half-service." But foreseeing that his work with the Coast Survey would become less time-consuming, he agreed to teach at Hopkins.[16] The trustees had

---

[13] JHR (1879), 19; TM, Feb. 3, 1879; Gilman to Morris, Feb. 4, 1879, second letter of date, quoted in Wenley, *Life of Morris*, 140; Morris to Gilman, Feb. 8, 1879, first letter of date.

[14] James to Gilman, Nov. 25, 1875; Frederic H. Young, "Charles Sanders Peirce, 1839–1914," in *Studies of Peirce*, ed. by Wiener and Young, 272.

[15] Peirce to Gilman, Jan. 13, 1878. The report has been twice published (Wiener and Young, eds., *Studies of Peirce*, 365–368; Philip P. Wiener, ed., *Values in a Universe of Chance: Selected Writings of Charles S. Peirce [1839–1914]* [Garden City, N.Y., 1958], 325–330).

[16] Gilman to Peirce, Jan. 23, 1878; Peirce to Gilman, March 12, 1878.

met earlier in the month, however, and decided that "in view of the financial condition of the country" they should not increase their expenditures. Peirce withdrew his premature acceptance gracefully, saying that he would be glad to come to Hopkins in the future.[17] A year later, the trustees did offer him a lectureship in logic at $1,500 with the understanding that he could continue his work with the Coast Survey.[18] He agreed to come if he were given sole charge of logic and if the trustees intended ultimately to have a professorship in logic. The board specifically declined to promise the establishment of such a post, but Peirce must have been too eager to start his teaching to insist on it.[19]

Peirce took up residence in Baltimore and taught logic for six months with four one-and-one-half-hour lectures a week. During his second year, he taught throughout the term.[20] He seemed to be fulfilling his prediction by giving something more than half-time service; he was, however, the only "lecturer" who failed to give public lecture series.

In December, 1880, Peirce informed Gilman that his Coast Survey responsibilities would require him to travel the next year and that his subordinate position at Hopkins did not justify further lessening of his government work. "Although there is no life which I could enjoy more than one which should attach me to the Johns Hopkins university," he wrote, "yet I fear that in the spring my connection with Baltimore must cease." He felt that his departure would mean the end of his study of logic and philosophy, though his interest in experimental psychology would continue. The proposed resignation evoked a resolution of regret and appreciation from the trustees. For his part, Peirce responded with a letter praising Hopkins as "this institution, so animate with youth and promise, [which] has been richly profitable to me," and commenting that he was leaving "upon a pure question of price for my services." The hint was not overlooked. The next term found

[17] Gilman to Peirce, March 20, 1878; Peirce to Gilman, March 27, 1878.
[18] ECM, May 26, 1879; Gilman to Peirce, May 30, 1879.
[19] TM, June 12, 1879. Fisch and Cope, "Peirce at Hopkins," in *Studies of Peirce,* ed. by Wiener and Young, 283, omit the fact that Peirce's "condition" had been specifically declined.
[20] JHR (1880), 2, 25, (1881), 61; Peirce to Gilman, Sept. 24, 1879, Aug. 19, [1880].

Peirce still at Johns Hopkins, with a three-year appointment at the same rank but with his salary increased to $2,500 a year.[21]

The 1881–1882 term also marked the appearance of a third lecturer in the department of philosophy, Granville Stanley Hall, who gave ten public lectures on psychology in January. Although Gilman was ill during the period of these lectures, Remsen reported that they had succeeded and that Hall's clearheadedness was impressive. For his part, Hall declared that he had never been "in a more stimulating academic atmosphere." He accepted an offer made in March to return to Hopkins for half of each of the next three years with the title "lecturer in psychology." [22]

It was the end of a long road for Hall. The Gilman Papers show scarcely any scholar more persistent in offering himself to the new university. He had written Gilman approximately every six months since a first letter in July, 1876. At that time, he wrote at the suggestion of Edward Everett Hale, telling Gilman that since his graduation from Williams in 1867 he had devoted himself exclusively to philosophy. He had spent a year at Union Theological Seminary, he said, and then gone to Germany for three years. For the four years past he had been teaching literature and philosophy at Antioch.[23] Gilman answered a request for an interview coldly, but a half-year later Hall, now an instructor in English at Harvard, reported that he was working with James in laboratory experiments in psychology and with Henry P. Bowditch on the nervous system. He said that he still longed to go to Johns Hopkins, not for the salary alone, but because he thought a new field would progress best at a new institution.[24] In the fall of 1877, he wrote again of his faith in the future of philosophy in American universities, observing that almost nothing was being done at Harvard. In 1878 Hall won a Ph.D. in psychology at Harvard and sailed for Germany. In February, 1879, James wrote Gilman that Hall was admirably prepared for the series of lectures Gilman had asked James

[21] Peirce to Gilman, Dec. 18, 1880, Feb. 9, 1881; TM, Feb. 7, 1881; T. R. Ball, note appended to F. M. Horn to "Secr'y of J.H.U.," July 25, 1885, GP.

[22] Remsen to Gilman, Jan. 19, 1882; Gilman to Hall, March 13, 1882; Hall to Gilman, March 18, 1882.

[23] Hall to Gilman, July 31, 1876; Henry D. Sheldon, "Granville Stanley Hall," DAB, VIII, 127–130.

[24] Gilman to Hall, Aug. 9, 1876; Hall to Gilman, Jan. 27, 1877.

193

to give, that he was almost unique in being an American psychologist with an adequate physiological background, that his work in Germany was broadening him, and that he was modest and unassuming. Hearing of James's recommendation, Hall returned to the charge, writing Gilman from Berlin.[25] No longer did he speak, as he had in 1876, of teaching philosophy safely with historical methods. His work, he reported, had been "entirely physiological for the last three years, with daily laboratory work, latterly with Wundt & Helmholtz—thus entirely in the same line as James—less specially perhaps with its [sic] eye, more, it may-be, with the ear, brain & muscles." Two more letters at six-month intervals indicated that Hall, failing to win the desired invitation, was seeking to remove all conceivable deterrents. He announced himself to be "as far as *possible* from materialism" and in the habit of churchgoing; with a little tact, his side of philosophy, the "logic of science and psychology," would offend no one's religious sentiments.[26]

In spite of Hall's best efforts, what probably turned the tide in his favor was the renewed recommendation of James, who in 1880 wrote Gilman that in the last two years Hall had surpassed him and that his great physical toughness enabled him to combine laboratory and literary work. Most to the point, perhaps, James pointed out that Hall's combined work in psychology and physiology would make him an excellent "connecting link between your medical and your philosophical departments." [27] A year and a half later Hall was giving his first lecture at Hopkins.

With the election of Hall and the re-election of Morris in March, 1882, to half-year lectureships for three years, the university had three leaders of American thought on its staff: Peirce, a founder of pragmatism with a strong bent toward mathematics and the natural sciences; Morris, a Hegelian idealist much interested in the philosophy of religion; and Hall, who kept his psychology empirical and eschewed speculation. Three more diverse philosophers could hardly have been found. Could they survive together in the same academic community? Besides their intellectual differences, they had sharply

[25] Hall to Gilman, [Oct. 7, 1877]; James to Gilman, Feb. 18, [1879]; Hall to Gilman, May 12, 1879.
[26] Hall to Gilman, June 27, 1879, Jan. 5, June 19, 1880.
[27] James to Gilman, July 18, 1880.

contrasting personalities. Worst of all, the authorities seemed dedicated to "the system of the one-man department." [28]

The temperament of Charles Peirce was the most disturbing factor in the situation. His work at the Harvard Observatory had involved him in a series of disputes, and President Eliot was determined that he should never join the regular staff of Harvard.[29] Before long Gilman began to understand some of Eliot's objections. It is not difficult to imagine the reaction of the Hopkins president to a letter from his new lecturer in logic wishing him merry Christmas and adding, "My physician in New York . . . informed me that he considered the state of my brain rather alarming. Not that he particularly feared regular insanity, but he did fear *something* of that sort." It was small consolation to learn that the lecturer did not think the matter important, but was only informing Gilman because he "might do some absurd thing." [30] Peirce's emotional instability led to a quarrelsomeness that marred his career at Johns Hopkins. His colleague Sylvester was equally erratic, and inevitably the two came into conflict. The fact that much of their controversy was carried into the pages of the *Circulars* could hardly have pleased Gilman or the trustees.[31] The peremptory note from Peirce asking Gilman to come to one of his lectures, saying, "I think you should do me the justice of learning what I am doing," must have taken the president aback. When he obeyed and found that Hall, then a visiting lecturer, was also present, he may have suspected that Peirce had sensed a competitor in this ever-obliging outsider.[32] Even with such a prologue, Gilman was probably not prepared for the recriminations that accompanied the departure of Peirce from Johns Hopkins.

In spite of the detailed researches of Professors Max H. Fisch and Jackson I. Cope, the cause for the trustees' decision not to reappoint Peirce after the 1883–1884 term must be declared unknown. In the fall of 1883, Gilman gave Peirce assurances that he could expect reappointment. As Gilman later described the development of events, several weeks after the beginning of the term "one of the Trustees

[28] Gilbert Chinard, "Johns Hopkins Twenty Years After," *JH Alumni Magazine,* XIX (1930–1931), 324, 328.

[29] William James, quoted in Fisch and Cope, "Peirce at Hopkins," in *Studies of Peirce,* ed. by Wiener and Young, 279–280.

[30] Peirce to Gilman, Dec. 25, 1879.   [31] JHC, I, 203, 242; II, 46, 86–88.

[32] Peirce to Gilman, Feb. 8, 1882; note appended thereto by Gilman.

made known to the Executive Committee & to me certain facts which had been brought to his knowledge quite derogatory to the standing of Mr. Peirce as a member of an academic staff." [33] In a resolution of January 26, 1884, the executive committee agreed to revise the plan of the philosophy department, declaring it "not desirable to continue the appointment of lecturers in philosophy and logic, on the present plan." [34] Peirce immediately saw the resolution as directed against him, since the appointments of Hall and Morris each had a year to run. He cited Gilman's assurances of October and the fact that he had leased a house for two years. Although he agreed that there were "defects" in the existing arrangements, he declared he could show that they were "not due to my fault or to that of Professors Morris and Hall." He asked to appear before the trustees:

I . . . desire to address you briefly upon the present state of philosophy, and to show you that the difficulty of finding a *modus vivendi* between different s[c]hools of thought, between philosophy, science, and religion, is now much less than it has been for a very long period; so that you have only to make the philosophical department really true to the actual condition of thought, and you will bring it into a state of warm sympathy and friendship with science on the one hand and with Christianity on the other.[35]

This may be considered Peirce's bid for future control of the department.

Such control was not forthcoming; in fact, the desired interview never occurred. The unhappy affair wore on. First Peirce asked to be released at once with pay; then he determined to stay till the end of the term. He sent an elaborate defense of his work, admitting his initial inexperience in teaching "several persons in a class," but citing his improvement and his success with advanced students. He begged the executive committee in the interests of fairness and for the sake of the university to reappoint him.[36] They refused. In informing Peirce of this, Gilman wrote him that he appreciated his "high intellectual powers"; however, he continued, "I am forced to believe

---

[33] Gilman to executive committee, Nov. 15, 1884. A letter, filed with other documents on Peirce's departure, from Simon Newcomb to Gilman, Dec. 22, 1883, says that Newcomb's "informant" would soon bring his charges to Gilman in person.

[34] ECM, Jan. 26, 1884. [35] Peirce to Gilman and trustees, Feb. 8, 1884.

[36] Gilman to Peirce, Feb. 18, 19, 1884; Peirce to Gilman, Feb. 19, March 7, 1884.

that you are better adapted to the work of an investigator, than you are to the guidance & instruction of young men in their university studies." The last phrase was changed, probably after a consultation with Brown, to read "than you are to that of a university professor." The episode led to a clarification of the tenure policies of the university, the trustees voting in June that appointments for a limited period implied no continuation beyond that specific period and that no one was authorized to imply otherwise.[37] It also gave Gilman ground for reflection, and in his articles on college controversy in the *Nation* that summer he observed that the college president was in "a place of danger," since "he cannot in every utterance make a distinction between his personal and his official opinions." Peirce reopened the matter in the fall, citing his financial losses and accusing Gilman of treachery. The executive committee exculpated Gilman, and the trustees voted the payment of $1,000, which Peirce had requested, in settlement of all claims.[38]

Somewhat in the manner of Ely, Peirce lost his rancor toward Gilman and the university in time. Ten years after his departure, he wrote Gilman expressing his sense of obligation: "For of all the impressions of my life, none stands out in finer & nobler relief than that of your conception of a university." He asked permission to dedicate a work to Gilman, and Gilman agreed with thanks. But though the bitterness died away, the loss to American philosophy was real. Professors Fisch and Cope have described the advantages if Peirce had remained at Hopkins:

There would have been at least one university in which philosophy was in living touch with science; in which it was a field of research, not of indoctrination or of "the strife of systems"; in which it was neither a conscious apologist nor a ventriloquist's dummy for the masters of business and property.[39]

But without knowing the full background of the decision against Peirce, the historian must stop short of condemning Gilman and the

[37] Gilman to Peirce, March 12, 1884 (draft); note by Gilman appended thereto; TM, June 2, 1884.
[38] *Nation*, XXXIX, 69; Peirce to George W. Brown, Oct. ?, Nov. 10, 1884, GP; statement of executive committee, Dec. 1, 1884, GP; TM, Dec. 1, 1884.
[39] Peirce to Gilman, Jan. 30, 1894; Gilman to Peirce, Feb. 6, 1894; Fisch and Cope, "Peirce at Hopkins," in *Studies of Peirce*, ed. by Wiener and Young, 286.

trustees. Some may assert that to be true to its ideal of a university Hopkins should have made room for a man so clearly destined to advance human knowledge, no matter what his personal failings or incapacities in the "guidance & instruction of young men." But this is to impute to these men a view of the university which they never held. Ironically, it is Peirce's famous definition of a university omitting any mention of instruction that is most often attributed to the leaders of Johns Hopkins. On the contrary, theirs was an eclectic view, and the increase of human knowledge was not their only consideration. The true cause for regret is that there was no Institute for Advanced Study in Peirce's day.[40]

The departure of George Sylvester Morris, though unaccompanied by the emotion of the Peirce case, has been described by his biographer as "a serious blunder in academic perspective, if nothing more," an error traceable to the exaggerated scientism of the period.[41] The decision against Morris certainly calls for some explanation, for he seemed fully to meet the religious criterion which the trustees had applied to Flint and Ward in 1881. But the need went beyond mere orthodoxy, as Peirce realized when he offered to develop at Hopkins an accommodation between science and Christianity.

As if sensing something hostile in the atmosphere, Morris accepted his first three-year appointment with the comment that there would be a need for him "to exhibit perspicaciously & to justify with cogent reasons what may be called the *universals* of philosophical theory." This interest in universals characterized a paper, "The Fundamental Conceptions of University and Philosophy," which he presented to the Metaphysical Club on December 12, 1882.[42] It can be read as Morris' bid for the professorship of philosophy which all three lecturers wanted. Beginning with the erroneous interpretation of *Universitas literarum et scientiarum* as meaning that "all 'letters and sciences' must be regarded as members of one organic whole, having . . . a common life and a common nature," [43] Morris presented

---

[40] Young, "Peirce, 1839–1914," in *Studies of Peirce,* ed. by Wiener and Young, 272, observes that such an institution would have been the "ideal connection" for Peirce.

[41] Wenley, *Life of Morris,* 147–155.

[42] G. S. Morris to Gilman, Jan. 28, 1879; JHC, II, 54.

[43] "A glance into any collection of medieval documents reveals the fact that the word 'university' means merely a number, a plurality, an aggregate of persons" (Rashdall, *Universities of Europe,* I, 5).

the position of philosophy in this organic whole as the dominant one, for philosophy was "peculiarly the 'science of wholes,' . . . the Science of Science itself." He cited the name Philosophical Faculty as further evidence of this pre-eminence and described certain special functions for philosophy in the university: "to act as a liberalizing agency, anticipating and so preventing the confessedly illiberal and narrowing tendencies of extreme specialism" and to serve the "public aims of the University" by producing "leaders capable of recognizing the true ideals and of intelligently directing the nation's energies to their accomplishment."

Morris' *Philosophy and Christianity,* lectures published in 1883, purported to show that "the fundamental ideal content of Christianity is 'philosophic'" and that "Christianity is 'absolute religion.'" The strong religious bent of his thinking again appeared in a paper of October, 1883, in which he told the Metaphysical Club that attempts to explain life as mere matter or mere force "must ever remain fruitless" and concluded that "the perfect life of man is to know God, as the living Truth, and, by doing his will, . . . to share in his life." [44]

If reflective Christianity, antimaterialism, and pastoral teaching meant so much to the trustees, why did Morris fail of promotion at Johns Hopkins, why was he allowed to depart to a professorship at the University of Michigan? Partly, it was that Gilman failed to appreciate a philosopher's duty to philosophize. When he reappointed Morris in 1882, he told him that the plan in philosophy was for Morris' work to be "based upon historical investigations" and Hall's upon "modern physiological researches." Of philosophical speculation he made no mention. But beyond Morris' leanings toward systematic philosophy, related personality traits also worked against him. Gilman frankly surveyed these qualities in a letter encouraging White to invite Morris to Cornell:

I like G. S. Morris personally very much. . . . He is a very safe man,—intelligent[,] catholic, well read, accessible, cooperative; but he is not quite forcible enough to hold his own in face of Sylvester, Pierce [*sic*], Gildersleeve & other men among us who are strong & pronounced. He retires into his shell.[45]

But Gilman's reactions to Morris' intellect and temperament tell only part of the story.

[44] JHC, III, 15, 12–13.
[45] Gilman to Morris, March 28, 1882; Gilman to A. D. White, Sept. 24, 1882.

The 1882–1883 term found Morris with a renewed appointment, working with great enthusiasm. He reported to Gilman that he had never been more confident of the university's future. He introduced a philosophical seminary, the first at Hopkins. But as he conferred optimistically with Gilman, the name of Stanley Hall seemed to dominate the conversation. He and Hall were thinking of founding a journal. He and Hall had pursued curiously similar paths in their training. He and Hall were in "good accord." Hall approved of his latest lecture on "Philosophy and Christianity." [46] Peirce's own vagaries had ended his Hopkins tenure. It was the long shadow of a promoter that barred the modest Morris from a full career there.

In a later description of the decision of 1884 to reorganize the philosophy department, Gilman said that the "infelicity" of the part-time lecturer system "was distinctly brought to the attention of the Trustees by one of the lecturers." Almost certainly, it was Hall who instigated the change and was responsible for the "elaborate statement in regard to instruction in Philosophy" which was presented to the executive committee before it reached its decision, for he was the lecturer most given to explaining his plans to trustees and to exhilarating the president by telling him how good his university was.[47] Hall had arrived to begin his half-year's work shortly before the trustees took up the matter. Not inconceivably, he may have brought an ultimatum with him, though Gilman's growing conviction that Peirce must go no doubt played a role in the timing. The unrenewability of the lectureships was announced to those involved in late January, 1884. In April the promotion of Hall to professor of psychology and pedagogics was announced.[48] But the delay seemed designed to spare the feelings of the other lecturers. Hall's future had probably been assured since January.

Morris, who was at Michigan for his half-year when Hall's promotion was announced, wrote Gilman that he considered it "a subject for congratulations on every ground." [49] His own appointment still had a year to run, and he returned for the first half of the 1884–1885 term. Although the resolution of January 26 had ended the lectureships,

---

[46] Gilman diary, "1882–1887 to California & Alaska," Jan. 31, [1883]; Morris to Gilman, March 12, 1883.

[47] ARJH (1884), 9; J. C. Thomas to Gilman, "Saturday"; Gilman diary, "1882–1887 to California & Alaska"; Hall to Gilman, [June, 1882 or 1883].

[48] JHC, III, 95.   [49] Morris to Gilman, May 15, 1884.

Morris may very well have hoped that like Hall he would win a full-time professorship. Hall's opinion, given many years later, that "the spirit of the university" led to the selection of his "experimental type" of philosophy rather than that of Morris,[50] presupposes that a mutually exclusive choice had to be made. This was not necessarily true. Although Gilman believed that each department needed only one full professor and seemed to regard psychology primarily as an approach to philosophy, he must have been aware of Morris' vigorous declarations that empirical psychology had no claim to be called philosophy.[51] Philosophy and psychology were listed as separate departments in the fall course announcements of 1884, and in the spring of 1885 the executive committee authorized Gilman to search for a professor of ethics.[52] By that time Morris had become full-time professor of philosophy at Michigan; nevertheless, he seems to have been at least tentatively considered. Whatever his chances, they received the *coup de grâce* from Hall, who wrote Gilman:

My own current & very deep conviction about Prof. Morris is that philosophically he represents just what ought not to be & never can be established & that he never can *touch* our best students. I have been outwardly in such friendly relations with him that I find it very hard to put myself down thus, but the more I *think* I see the [field?] of B[altimore], the more this feeling grows.[53]

Hall had won the three-way battle for control of the philosophy department, and he had no desire to relinquish part of the spoils.

The shift in control between Morris and Hall and the change in fields of effort had been symbolized by two successive meetings of the Metaphysical Club. At the meeting of January 17, 1884, Morris, still president, was in the chair and gave a review of William Torrey Harris' *Philosophy in Outline*, a work of Hegelian bent. At the next meeting, February 12, 1884, Hall presided, was elected president, and read a paper on "The Nisus Formitivus in Sane and Insane Minds." [54] Hall's

[50] Quoted in Wenley, *Life of Morris*, 153.

[51] Morton G. White, *The Origin of Dewey's Instrumentalism* (*Columbia Studies in Philosophy*, no. 4; New York, 1943), 15–16.

[52] JHC, IV, 6–7; ECM, May 23, 1885.

[53] Hall to Gilman, Aug. 18, [1885?].

[54] At the January meeting Peirce read the principal paper, "Design and Chance" (JHC, III, 70). Morris had succeeded Peirce as president on November 14, 1882 (JHC, II, 38).

later reference to the experimental method in psychology as one of "self-control and subordination" which "conservative administrative boards" preferred over "premature speculative views" sheds light on this transfer of power.[55] Although Hall represented the "self-control" of experimental science, he carefully maintained "subordination" to the Christian tradition. Morris was handicapped because—no matter how traditionally Christian he remained (and he showed tendencies toward far broader speculation)—to a university accused of ungodliness he could not bring "the healing word almost from the side of biology itself." [56] Also relevant to considerations of public opinion was the fact that Hall could assume a professorship of both psychology and pedagogy. Hall accepted the additional title grudgingly [57] and never taught the subject more than an hour a week, but a "Department of Psychology and Pedagogics" appeared unquestionably useful to the community.[58]

In the garb of Christianity, then, naturalistic psychology became the single representative of philosophy in the advanced work at Johns Hopkins.[59] If Morris or Peirce had won the professorship, the religious face shown to the public would have been the same. But with either of them it would have been less a disguise: with Morris, because his metaphysical strivings were deep and God-seeking; with Peirce, because he had the rare breadth of experience and intellectual power to make philosophy the bridge between science and religion.

Hall claimed in 1894 that he had founded the first laboratory in experimental psychology in the United States in 1881. Certainly

[55] The statement was made in 1891 (Fisch and Cope, "Peirce at Hopkins," in *Studies of Peirce*, ed. by Wiener and Young, 285).

[56] *Ibid.*   [57] Hall, *Life and Confessions*, 226.

[58] From the 1884–1885 term until his departure, Hall gave a course in pedagogics which met once a week. Although his preliminary announcement for the 1886–1887 term stated that "if found feasible" he would conduct "a practical seminary" in the subject the next year, all that eventuated was a series of excursions to local educational institutions (JHC, IV, 107; V, 136; VI, 114–115; VII, 6, 57). As if in apology for his scant offering in his second field, he issued the following statement: "Those who devote themselves to the work of education as a profession are strongly recommended to give their chief time and labor to grounding themselves in Psychology and Philosophy, which constitute the scientific basis of their profession. Pedagogy is a field of applied Psychology, and if the latter is known the application is not hard to make" (JHC, VI, 114).

[59] Hall's inaugural address, an elaborate defense of his field, was published in a journal of theological orientation ("The New Psychology," *Andover Review*, III [1885], 120–135, 239–248).

William James had had such a laboratory at Harvard in the 1870s: Hall himself had worked in it. Furthermore, Joseph Jastrow, who won the first Ph.D. in psychology from Hopkins in 1886, had begun his psychological experiments in his room under the direction of Peirce. James's biographer grants Hall the honor of the first formal "founding," but shows that he later claimed more than his due.[60] As to the date of the founding, it almost certainly was 1884 rather than 1881.[61]

Although psychology came to constitute nearly the total of advanced work offered in philosophy, Hall did not claim—as he said Wundt did—that there was nothing more to philosophy. He did feel, however, that it brought new methods in laboratory experimentation and in historical research to a field in which too many questions had been considered "accessible only to speculation." [62] Thus Hall was not unwilling to have Hopkins add a philosopher of different stripe (though not of so different a stripe as G. S. Morris). He dropped inviting hints to George Herbert Palmer of Harvard in 1886, but Palmer decided that he did not want to move to Baltimore in spite of "the many gains of a life there." [63] Nor would Hall object to John Dewey, but he would expect the younger man, he wrote Gilman, "to give himself up to teaching & let me examine his class in each subject though I am skeptical about the success of his work a little." [64] Neither of these promising philosophers was actually called. Either of them could have rebuilt a department of philosophy after Hall's departure in 1888 to the presidency of Clark shattered the domination of psychology and left an open field.

As for the program in psychology, it might have survived under the leadership of Henry Herbert Donaldson, a Hopkins Ph.D. in physiology, who was instructor in psychology in 1885–1886 and as-

[60] Ralph Barton Perry, *The Thought and Character of William James* (Boston, 1935), II, *Philosophy and Psychology*, 7–10, 22; Jastrow, quoted in Baltimore *Sun*, Oct. 24, 1926.

[61] French, *History of Johns Hopkins*, 140, gives 1884 as the date. Hall's autobiography does not date the opening of the laboratory (*Life and Confessions*, 227). The following sources support a claim for his having opened the laboratory in January, 1884, but not earlier: ARJH (1883), 35; ECM, March 8, 1883; JHC, II, 136, III, 85–86, 118.

[62] Hall, "New Psychology," *Andover Review*, III, 131, 125.

[63] Hall to Gilman, Aug. 18, [1885?]; George H. Palmer to Charles W. Eliot, May 19, 1886, Eliot Papers.

[64] Hall to Gilman, Jan. 6, 1887.

sociate in 1887–1888. Donaldson had made discoveries in temperature sensation which were among the first important fruits of the psychological laboratory.[65] Had he remained, the laboratory would have continued, though with an even stronger neurological emphasis; but Hall carried him off to Clark. In 1888–1889 there was no laboratory, the only teaching in psychology being instruction to undergraduates by two Ph.D.'s of 1888, Edmund Clark Sanford and William Henry Burnham, who remained for one year as instructors before they too answered the call to Clark. Their teaching, probably without pay, "consisted of frequent recitations with practical lectures" and lasted for approximately ten weeks.[66]

The needs of the undergraduates had formed a muted accompaniment to the turmoil in the philosophy department. Some may have profited from Royce's voluntary classes before 1878. From 1878 to 1880, Allan Marquand, another fellow, taught logic and ethics, and as fellow by courtesy he taught psychology during the 1880–1881 term. Benjamin E. Smith, who had been instructor at his alma mater, Amherst, came as assistant in philosophy for the 1881–1882 term, teaching what was called the "minor course." The appointment of a third part-time lecturer in the department in 1882 was probably what ended the need for his services. During the second half of the 1882–1883 term, John Dewey, having failed to win a fellowship but needing financial assistance, taught the history of philosophy for $150. For the next year, the undergraduate work was directed by Rendel Harris, whose major field was New Testament Greek, but whose background as a former fellow of Clare College, Cambridge, was probably thought to fit him for teaching the younger men.[67] Harris' control lasted only one year. Hall, after his appointment as professor in 1884, took charge of the course.[68]

Hall's way with the undergraduates did not fully satisfy the trustees; the executive committee in May, 1885, asked Gilman to re-examine the "ethical teaching of the University" and suggest a possible professor of ethics. Although Gilman apparently considered G. S. Morris for this chair, the trustees turned once again to Great Britain, feeling that the life in the English colleges offered a better

---

[65] JHC, IV, 76; V, 37.   [66] ARJH (1889), 60; JHC, VII, 104, VIII, 55.
[67] JHC, I, 159, II, 93; ECM, Feb. 3, 1883; ARJH (1884), 38.
[68] For the content of the course, see pp. 252–253 below.

background for undergraduate teaching than did German university training. By late fall they had found George Henry Emmott and appointed him associate professor of logic and ethics and lecturer on Roman law. Philosophical training seemed to be the least of their considerations. Emmott had taken a law degree in addition to his A.B. at Cambridge, and his first-class honors had been in law and history. His only teaching had been in Roman law and jurisprudence at Owens College, Manchester, and at Hopkins his teaching was to include Roman law and common law in alternate years. Emmott was a Quaker and Trustee Thomas' half-brother's wife's sister's husband.[69] Perhaps some watered-down nepotism contributed to his election. Arriving for his duties in the fall of 1886, Emmott took charge of logic and ethics in the required undergraduate "L.E.P." course, though Hall still taught the psychology. Emmott's undergraduate teaching in philosophy was pedestrian, and his only pretense at directing a graduate program was a fortnightly seminary in ethics for six students during the 1888–1889 term. He was remembered as "impregnated with English mannerisms and steeped in the British point of view" and "so naive that he became the target for much raillery and practical joking." [70] The undergraduate course was placed in more skillful hands with the appointment of Edward Herrick Griffin as professor of the history of philosophy in 1889.

The development of the philosophy department can win only a mixed historical verdict. It should be remembered, however, that in faculty building at Johns Hopkins carefully promulgated criteria, such as specialization and interest in investigation, brought results in new disciplines and university scholarship that transformed American educational life. But faculty expansion revealed a configuration forced by factors outside the control of Gilman and the trustees almost as much as by their conscious efforts. Among the less freely adopted policies extrinsic to intellectual considerations was the desire to avoid antagonizing the nonacademic community, especially religious powers. To this desire, in large part, can be traced the gingerly handling of the philosophy department; perhaps too it explains the incongruously

---

[69] ECM, May 23, Nov. 28, 1885; JHC, V, 33; ARJH (1888), 41; A. B. Thomas, *Baltimore Yearly Meeting*, 113.
[70] JHC, VI, 14; ARJH (1889), 60; Victor Rosewater, "Notes to Professor Woodburn's Article of January, 1934," *JH Alumni Magazine*, XXII (1933–1934), 294.

elaborate programs in New Testament Greek and Semitics. Similarly, the urgency of the trustees' wish to have a medical school ready with the new hospital led to premature curtailment of the plan for expansion of the philosophical faculty. Often the shibboleth "good work in a limited field" represented sadly understaffed one-professor departments and relegation to visiting lecturers of fields that deserved permanent appointments.

The reluctance of European scholars to move, though heightened by unimaginative tenure, retirement, and leave policies at Hopkins, was largely a circumstance which Gilman and the trustees could not control. They could scarcely provide by fiat social prestige for professors equal to that in Europe or replace the ties of a man's homeland. Certainly they made enough offers to European scholars—Klein, Von Holst, Flint, Sweet, Gosse. Haupt's acceptance was a rare exception; usually it was only when "the best available man" was an American with European training, as in the case of Welch, that the university could get an outstanding product of the world's leading universities. Furthermore, Hopkins faced the loyalty of the faculties at Harvard and Yale, thus failing to win such men as Farlow and Gibbs. (But James at one point could have been won from Harvard, G. S. Morris was lost to Michigan by default, and the all-out effort recommended to win Gibbs was not made.)

Such resistances were among those "Fates" which Brown saw thwarting the aspirations of Hopkins; so too were the economic forces that could satanically contract the university's income. If the authorities' dedication to thrift at times took a high intellectual toll, it must be remembered that only in part were these men masters of their course.

Often because of the "Fates," it was the young adjuncts of ability and promise who dominated the record of faculty growth. In the great majority of cases, heightened faculty stature and new course offerings trace to these young men of little status rather than to scholars imported at the highest rank or brought in for lecture series or half-year courses. Gilman had forecast such a process in his inaugural:

We shall hope to secure a strong staff of young men . . . selecting them on evidence of their ability; increasing constantly their emoluments, and promoting them because of their merit to successive posts. . . . This plan will give us an opportunity to introduce some of the features of the English fellowship and the German system of privat-docents.[71]

Such, with the notable exceptions of the professorial appointments of 1876, was the route by which the university found professors for most departments. Bright in English began as a graduate student; H. B. Adams in history and Bloomfield in Sanskrit as fellows; Williams in geology as fellow by courtesy; Ely in political economy as assistant; Elliott in Romance languages, Warren in Latin, and Wood in German as associates. Each of these men held the highest post in his department in 1889, and each was destined for a professorship in the trustees' good time (except Ely, who grew impatient). As to second men in departments, especially in sciences where initial professorial appointments were made—men like Craig in mathematics, Morse in chemistry, Brooks in biology, Clark in geology, Spieker in classics— they too rose gradually from humble academic status to professorships. Support for the thesis that the strength of the university lay in home-nurtured scholars appears in the record of failures among scholars brought in as professors or associate professors. Wright stayed only a year. Newcomb's chief interests lay outside Baltimore and outside mathematics. Hall (an ambiguous case, since he had risen from a part-time lectureship) allowed philosophy to languish and carried away the younger talent in psychology when he left. Gregory, initially appointed as associate professor, never took up residence; and Emmott, imported at that rank, could not discipline his classes. (The appointments of Haupt and Welch as professors were, of course, successes.)

Gilman did not give unqualified support to the grooming of the local fledgling for the local post of honor. In many instances he and the trustees struggled to win men of established reputation, only to find after many frustrations that the young man whom they had regarded as a stopgap had developed into a scholar who could represent his field with honor. Often Gilman appeared indifferent as to whether young men stayed—or even eager to push them from the nest. In 1879, on the eve of a drive for faculty expansion, he wrote to Brown: "I am more and more impressed with the value, to us, of men of acknowledged eminence. Our American colleges are full of good

[71] Gilman, "Hopkins Inaugural," 29.

men . . . ; but the number of those who rise above local distinction is small; the number of those who add anything to science is smaller still." Many of the young teachers at Hopkins would never have been advanced by Gilman had it not been for the difficulties of winning scholars from Europe or the older universities and the financial losses at the end of the 1880s. In letter after letter he wrote as he did to H. B. Adams in 1880: "If an older man . . . should consent to join us, it might delay your advancement,—or alter your work;—so I should not dare to dissuade you from listening to overtures." [72] Adams in his turn five years later could remind a junior colleague "how insecure a young man's tenure is here, how much Gilman believes in rotation." Professor Kemp Malone, in his removal of some of the romantic patina from the early Hopkins, has described the frequent practice:

Much of the early graduate work of the University was directed by young men of promise who could be got cheap and who were not given professorial rank—young men fresh from a German or a Hopkins doctorate, full of fire but with a professional equipment still meager and a professional reputation still to make. [73]

A comparable policy, which set one of the least admirable patterns of American higher education, was the use of graduate students as teachers at even lower salaries. This had occurred rather frequently in the first three years of the university, and occasionally thereafter. But toward the end of the 1880s, with a growing matriculate population and decreasing income, the university yielded repeatedly to this tempting expedient. The lowered value of the fellowships and their virtual limitation to one year increased the supply of graduate students obliged to sell their services. The *Annual Report* for 1889 listed fourteen graduate students who, without staff appointments, gave "more or less service" to the university. Seven of them taught classes. [74]

[72] Gilman to G. W. Brown, July 9, 1879; Gilman to Adams, April 29, 1880, in Holt, ed., *Historical Scholarship*, 39.

[73] Jameson diary, Jan. 24, 1885; Malone, "Gilman's Hopkins," *JH Alumni Magazine*, XIX, 305.

[74] Of the seven, three were fellows by courtesy and two were fellows. At least three candidates for the Ph.D. held regular appointments: Joseph S. Ames, assistant; J. Leverett Moore, instructor; and Albion W. Small, reader (ARJH [1889], 5–6; JHC, VIII, 1–7, 50–55).

Financial problems brought a new urgency to the expedient of utilizing young men at low salaries and rotating them rather than promoting them. Thus, the trustees in 1888 granted discretion to the executive committee to inform young faculty members "that it is the intention of the Trustees to regard such appointments as but temporary, and to open the positions as they become vacant from time to time to younger men, who in their turn will give place to others." Gilman's *Annual Report* of that year referred almost callously to "the usual changes among the staff of younger men engaged as assistants and instructors, most of whom hold their offices by annual appointment." [75]

But the impatience of some of the younger teachers had grown explosive. New information on the trustees' views and fear that the financial reverses might freeze them in the lower ranks brought revolt in the spring and summer of 1888. Awareness that Clark would soon open and that they might find alternative positions there may have made the rebels more self-assertive. With the departures of Hall and Jameson and the promotions of Councilman, Howell, Kimball, and Spieker to associate professor, certain assistants and associates felt that in this time of ferment they must speak up for their interests. The case of James Bright, who extracted a grudging promotion from assistant to associate, has already been traced. Henry Todd, associate in Romance languages, was not successful in his bid for promotion from a position which he felt compromised his increasing years and growing reputation. [76]

Probably most painful for Gilman was the protest of Fabian Franklin, one of the original graduate students and a participant in the mathematical advances of the Sylvester era. Wounded by his exclusion from the group promoted to associate professor, he sent Gilman his resignation for the end of the next year. Gilman answered that Franklin was valued, but that—as he had always tried to show him— he had little chance for a permanently attractive place at Hopkins. [77] Story's departure to Clark changed the situation. In 1889, Franklin became associate professor and in 1892 professor. In 1895 he left

[75] TM, Feb. 6, 1888; ARJH (1888), 51.
[76] Todd to Gilman, Aug. 7, 1888; Gilman to Todd, June 30, 1888 (draft).
[77] Franklin to Gilman, June 21, 1888; Gilman to Franklin, June 25, 1888.

teaching for newspaper editing. As Gilman's biographer, he was to demonstrate an admiration for the president undiminished by their disagreement of 1888.

Gilman's practice had its exploitive aspect. But many a young scholar was willing to take shelter at Johns Hopkins, even if underpaid and unpromoted. There he could wait till a position opened agreeable to the scholarly life that he had adopted in Germany or at Hopkins. Beginning in 1889, new universities and expanding old ones offered more and more of such opportunities. Part of the glory of Hopkins in the 1880s was this band of young men waiting for American higher education to catch up with their aspirations. They were young men of promise in a land of promise, and the spirit that they contributed at Johns Hopkins sprang from optimism and faith.

Part Three

❧

SHARING: IN SEARCH
OF COMMUNITY

: CHAPTER XII :

The Way of the Faculty

THE growth of the Johns Hopkins faculty from eighteen in 1876 to three times that number in 1889 entailed modifications of its role in governing the university. So too did the tendency toward greater faculty power which Gilman described in 1884 as a phenomenon of the times, and a laudable one.[1] But though faculty power may have increased at Hopkins vis-à-vis the trustees, it would be difficult to show any transfer of power from president to faculty. Nor was the power ever democratically distributed; meetings of the entire faculty during the 1870s and 1880s were rare and without authority.[2] When, during the expansion of the 1879–1880 term, the trustees turned their attention directly to the problem of faculty government, they agreed with Gilman that the traditional faculty meeting of American colleges was inappropriate to the needs of Hopkins. They favored instead a great deal of departmental independence and informal conferences among those involved in particular problems. The trustees' formal decision, however, followed German precedent and left "the chief responsibility of guiding the internal affairs of the University" in the hands of the president and professors, meeting under the name Academic Council.[3] The council's broad grant of authority included

[1] *Nation*, XXXIX, 50, 68.
[2] Lanman diary, March 8, 1879; Jameson diary, May 26, 1887.
[3] ARJH (1880), 26–27; TM, May 3, 1880; Friedrich Paulsen, *Die deutschen Universitäten und das Universitätsstudium* (Berlin, 1902), 94–95.

specifically the right to name fellows and in practice a veto over the appointment of associates. The professors had from the first year held what Gilman recalled as free and informal discussions from which a "sense of the meeting" usually emerged.[4] Their hierarchical status may have eased their counsels.

The inadequacies of an arrangement which left junior faculty members voiceless became gradually apparent. The trustees formally asked in 1881 for the opinions of all professors, lecturers, and associates on the needs of the university. But the younger men were not misled about their lack of power. Some of them at least regarded Gilman as responsible for the oligarchical nature of faculty government and expected help from the professors in opening the Academic Council to the whole faculty. According to one report, most of the associates were "dreadfully afraid" of Gilman and therefore were hesitant to demand greater participation in governing university affairs. The unrest among the younger faculty members probably hastened the creation by the Academic Council in May, 1882, of a lesser governing body, the Board of Collegiate Advisers, with one representative from each of the principal departments of undergraduate study. In October, 1883, those with the newly created rank of associate professor joined the professors on a new Board of University Studies, which had general charge of graduate instruction. The creation of the new rank thus not only kept ambitious faculty members from becoming professors, but diverted them from the Academic Council.[5]

Even with two additional organs of government, part of the faculty remained voiceless and unrepresented. This was made clear in the protests of Charles Peirce as his career at Hopkins was ending. Much of his lack of success he attributed to his exclusion "from all participation in or even knowledge of the conduct of instruction in general." [6]

The structure of government was not the only cause for faculty complaint. Short of what may legitimately be classed as violations of academic freedom, there existed many irritating pressures and controls. The early declarations of the trustees against sectarian tests

[4] TM, Dec. 6, 1880; Gilman, *Launching of a University*, 48. In 1891, the council proposed to the trustees the promotion of H. B. Adams to professor (TM, Jan. 5, 1891). I find no earlier example of such initiative.

[5] TM, April 26, 1881; Jameson diary, May 20, 1881; JHR (1889), 26.

[6] Peirce to Gilman, March 7, 1884.

in making appointments were not blanket exclusions of religious considerations, as was shown in the discussion of Von Holst on July 7, 1879. Gilman, who was absent from this trustee meeting, received the following report from Brown:

Mr. King inquired about the Professor's religious belief, but I was entirely unable to answer except that I felt confident that he was not a materialist nor a Roman Catholic. Johnson thought he had no special religious affiliations. Gwinn thought we might be fortunate if a German Professor had any belief at all.

In the earliest period of the university, then, the religious life of candidates for professorships was considered relevant, and not only in the philosophy department. No trustee chose to vote against Von Holst, unknown though his faith was, but two or three abstained.[7] From the fact that Johns Hopkins was nonsectarian it did not follow that the religious attitudes and practices of the faculty were not scrutinized. Inevitably, a teacher felt subtle pressures. But there is no evidence of any faculty member's being reprimanded or dismissed for religious nonconformity, and the faculty from the beginning included Jews.

In other matters, however, Gilman did not hesitate to inform his staff, especially the younger men, of their errors. As Cyrus Adler has written, "there was an outward decorum that had to be observed." Adler himself was called to Gilman's office and told that it was not the custom of Hopkins faculty members to smoke in public. In another case, the president sent a sharp note to an associate who had departed without permission before the conferring of degrees.[8] Time alone built up a crust of regulations, even though formal rules seem to have been easily forgotten at Hopkins.

The trustees' blanket regulation of June, 1878, directing all associates to give at least ten publicly announced lectures was in time forgotten, but pressures to lecture publicly remained. Gilman listed the series in various university publications and usually included the average attendance. This competitive publicity forced the teacher to defend his lectures if they proved "unpopular."[9] No rule was

[7] G. W. Brown to Gilman, July 12, 1879; Galloway Cheston to Gilman, July 8, 1879.
[8] Adler, *I Have Considered*, 65; Gilman to J. W. Bright, June 4, 1889.
[9] TM, June 3, 1878; Ely to Gilman, Aug. 2, 1882.

needed. Like church attendance, public lecturing was the way one played the game, the way one "sold" himself. The personality market is not an innovation of the twentieth century. Jameson's diary gives evidence of its early presence at Hopkins. In distress after receiving advice from H. B. Adams on winning reappointment, he wrote: "I declare, I wish I could be in a place where 'other considerations' didn't have quite so much weight. I don't enjoy diplomacy, and see its temptations to sacrifice of self-respect. At this univ., one must *please*. It is not enough to be a doctor philosophae, one must be magister artum." [10] A recognized scholar who arrived crowned with a professorship might let diplomacy go hang. But most of the younger men felt obliged to play at impression making.

This is not to characterize the university as a community of dissemblers and sycophants. Honesty and dedication enhanced many aspects of its life, notably the work of the faculty as investigators. There was Rowland, for instance, expressing in the same breath with which he announced his marriage the hope that it would add to his working power in his science. Morse, characterized as "the ideal, patient, cheerful, self-forgetful, painstaking investigator," would repeat to his students, "Time is the cheapest thing we have," and by his own refusal to publish or patent approximate results would sacrifice wealth and fame. And Jameson, though bemoaning the need for pretense, followed his view of duty in refusing opportunities for popular publication.[11]

Faculty members dedicated to investigation found the trustees generally loyal to their promise that Hopkins would nurture research as well as teaching. Especially was this principle preserved with the higher-ranking faculty. Although sabbaticals were nonexistent, the trustees often granted leaves that involved early departure or late return. But investigation too was stained with the worldly dye of publicity, and Gilman fostered the university's fame even as he fostered its members' scholarly development. Adler looked back on his feverish writing of papers for learned journals and societies as unwise, but something which seemed to be the duty of everyone at

[10] Jameson diary, Dec. 23, 1882.

[11] Rowland to Gilman, June 1, 1890; John M. Tyler, quoted in *Obituary Record of Graduates and Non-graduates of Amherst College for the Academic Year Ending June 20, 1921* (*Amherst College Bulletin*, X, no. 2; Amherst, Mass., 1921), 806; Jameson diary, April 4, 1883.

Hopkins.[12] How could it have seemed otherwise? Gilman included in the *Circulars* long bibliographies of "Recent Publications" by members of the university and its graduates.

But the dedication to research and publication (and publicity) was never allowed—at least in the rationale of the institution—to injure the teaching function. The policy was expressed indirectly by Brown when he urged Cooley to accept a professorship: "One of the features of this University is that the Professors are encouraged to pursue such original investigations in the line of their work *as may not only be of benefit to the students,* but which, when published, may be of permanent value." [13] This theory that investigation aided teaching was often repeated by Gilman, and he expressed its corollary in his Commemoration Day address of 1885: "The process of acquiring seems to be promoted by that of imparting." [14] The interrelationship was more moderately described by Gildersleeve: "True, an able explorer may be an indifferent teacher; a good teacher may not have the spirit of initiative which leads to successful investigation; but the two faculties, though not always in perfect balance, are seldom wholly divorced, and a university professor should possess both." [15] Much of the history of the Hopkins faculty represents the search for such a balance.

The advancement of knowledge always included in the Hopkins scheme the development of other knowers. Martin expressed the idea clearly in his inaugural: "We have to make provision for the advancement of knowledge, and for its diffusion; . . . while we must not suffer those engaged in research to be crowded out by beginners, neither must the beginners be overlooked in providing for those to whom they are one day to succeed." Peirce, before he came to the university, proposed that the advanced student should be made to regard himself as "an apprentice—a learner but yet a real worker," and his work should be subjected to serious criticism on its objective merits. Peirce's prescriptions applied specifically to physics, although their significance carries beyond it. The university's professor of physics, however, was probably the one who had least to do with

---

[12] Adler, *I Have Considered,* 70–71.

[13] Brown to Cooley, Nov. 17, 1880, GP. Italics added.

[14] JHC, IV, 47. For the same idea expressed by Rowland, see his *Physical Papers,* 606–607.

[15] Gildersleeve, *Essays and Studies,* 91.

students. One visitor found that Rowland did not know even approximately the number of students working in the Hopkins physics laboratories; and when asked what he would do with these students, he replied, without lifting his eyes from his photographic work, "Do with them? Do with them?—*I shall neglect them.*" [16]

Remsen, Rowland's best friend on the faculty, felt far more concern for students than did the physicist. His department consistently attained the largest enrollment among the sciences, and when overcrowding became a problem, he shared his private laboratory with students. The personal interest he took in the younger men extended to cheering them amid the harsh realities of academic job hunting.[17]

As a novice at college teaching, Jameson inscribed in his diary after his first day: "I am sure I shall like it, and I believe I shall succeed." Although he taught only a single two-hour introductory historical course throughout the year, he worked hard. After an eleven-hour day that provided only part of a single preparation, he declared, "Getting up a lecture of this sort is no child's play." By the opening of his second year, he had decided that his labor was in part ill-directed, and he determined "to do less hand-to-mouth cramming" for his own sake and give more thought to the students. He felt his responsibility to them, but at the same time found it hard to sacrifice the time which he would have preferred to use in making himself learned. "I never think enough of the things they don't know and I long have known, and give them more details than philosophy," he wrote. After two years on the faculty, a wave of disillusionment with the whole teaching process engulfed him, and he felt that the truth was dawning— teaching was drudgery:

You may think you are going to exert great influence over a considerable body of young men, wake them to enthusiasm, and greatly contribute to their political education. But the fact is, that you exercise no influence over them, they have no enthusiasm, and as to political education, that doesn't consist in retailing borrowed and unverified generalizations.[18]

The best palliation for this drudgery was the presence of good students. Jameson's more cheerful moments indicated this, as did the comment

[16] Martin, "Study of Biology," *Popular Science Monthly*, X, 300; Peirce to Gilman, Jan. 13, 1878; Mendenhall, "Rowland," in Rowland, *Physical Papers*, 16.
[17] Interview with Professor Whitehead; ARJH (1889), 38–39; William A. Noyes to Albert Shaw, June 7, 1882, Shaw Papers.
[18] Jameson diary, Sept. 28, Oct. 18, 1882, Sept. 26, Oct. 17, 1883, March 6, 1884.

of Minton Warren in 1887: "I have the best set of students this year that I ever had, and the more my students know, the more I feel that I ought to give them and hence I have to sit up late o'nights." [19]

Whether teachers were neglecting or mothering their students, disparaging or admiring them, an overarching importance attached to the method of teaching adopted. It was method which made the late-night drudgery a channel the next day leading students into the life of the mind. The university luxuriated in its variety of teaching methods. A formal statement announced instruction by "recitations, lectures, conferences, prolonged courses in laboratories, exercises in special libraries, personal counsel, study of nature out-of-doors." [20] But in spite of all the names attached, there seemed to be a unifying spirit—a spirit of work and freedom. The graduate student who remarked that at Hopkins the teachers "let the atmosphere work its proper course" [21] had felt this unity. The more lyrical evocations of the Hopkins spirit often ignored the element of work, but Gildersleeve, given to saying the hard things, did not. He told one graduating class that any education worthy of the name carried with it the tedium and pain of a surgical process. Gildersleeve did not, however, propose to imitate "the tutorial grind of England," and he called the German system of *Lernfreiheit* "a great thing." [22] The spirit of freedom appeared in the faculty's refusal to indoctrinate students with any particular system of belief. Ely wrote Gilman just before his teaching at Hopkins began that he would "not endeavor so much to teach or enforce any specific economic doctrines" as to explain the origin of the various schools, the sources of information, and the route to conducting one's own investigation.[23] Hall remembered that in philosophy he had tried to incline his students to a sympathetic view of each system in turn, his object being to avoid indoctrination and permit the student ultimately to choose his own position.[24] But though inculcation of any system of truths was rejected, the inculcation of respect for truth was an avowed purpose, and if one respected truth, he must work to find it. The problem of method, in fine, was one of uniting respect for truth (which required work) with respect for

[19] Warren to Lanman, March 6, 1887, Lanman Papers.
[20] JHC, IV, 108.
[21] Charles M. Andrews to his mother, Nov. 13, 1887, quoted in Eisenstadt, *Andrews,* 9.
[22] Gildersleeve, *Essays and Studies,* 511, 111.
[23] Ely to Gilman, Sept. 23, 1881.   [24] Hall, *Life and Confessions,* 234.

the individual as the perceiver and utilizer of truth (which required freedom). It was a problem of teaching the individual the splendor and difficulty of truth, of teaching him how to perceive and utilize it.

Some of the methods at Johns Hopkins trace directly to the American college. Conspicuous among these stood the staple of the old-time college, the recitation. Surprisingly, the languages rarely used the name or, it seems, the practice. The advanced standing demanded in languages allowed teachers to turn their attention to reading, composition, pronunciation, and conversation. In physics, biology, and philosophy, however, undergraduate courses were taught in part by recitation, though never more than in part. Midway in his teaching career at Hopkins, Jameson bemoaned his inability to inspire students and belittled his reliance on recitations. Yet two terms later, his course for first-year undergraduates, Herodotus and Thucydides in translation, consisted of "questioning upon assigned lessons, and of informal lectures." The recitation seems never to have appeared in graduate courses. Class reports, themes, and "essays upon assigned topics," already familiar in American colleges, appeared in philosophy, history, economics, and English.[25] The oft-derided demonstrations of the old-time science class were not spurned at Johns Hopkins, though they were carefully adapted to bring instruction rather than amazement.[26]

Other teaching techniques at Hopkins had not often appeared in the pre-Civil War college. There was, for example, guided student reading for credit, a program first used in classics. The same tendency appeared, less formalized, in history. When Albert Shaw arrived as a graduate student in 1882, he called on Austin Scott, who outlined a special course of reading for him apart from any class. The biology staff announced "advice on reading" in connection with the "close daily contact" by which they guided their graduate students.[27] The world beyond the classroom became a scene of instruction. Taking the student directly to the economic situation was the essence of what Ely called the "look and see" method. Similarly, Hall took his pedagogical class on "excursions" to Baltimore schools and his

[25] JHC, IV, 96–100, VI, 94, 97–98, 114; Jameson diary, Nov. 21, 1884; JHC, VI, 113, 114, 106.

[26] Martin, "Study of Biology," *Popular Science Monthly*, X, 305–306; interview with Judge Soper and Judge Moses.

[27] ARJH (1878), 24–25; Shaw diary, Jan. 10, 1882; JHC, II, 126.

psychology students to "cliniques" at mental asylums. Field trips to study the natural environment were familiar features of geology in the fall and spring, and in the summer students in morphology joined the Chesapeake Zoological Laboratory. Ely used the student lecture in a graduate course on money and banking, and H. B. Adams reported that the practice had "gradually grown up" in his courses, originating among undergraduates. He declared it to be quite unlike the burdensome reading of formal essays: only a few notes were used, and success turned on "kindling the interest" of one's classmates. This program, though independently developed, was not unique at Hopkins, nor did Adams claim that it was. He approvingly quoted a report by Moses Coit Tyler, professor of American history at Cornell: "My notion is that the lecturing must be reciprocal. As I lecture to [my students], so must they lecture to me." The most consistent use of student lectures came in the chemistry department, where advanced students gave lectures on assigned topics in the history of chemistry. The declared purpose was teacher training.[28]

Valuable as these miscellaneous teaching methods often were, the bulk of faculty effort involved lectures, laboratories, and seminars. The lecture, though distinctly secondary to recitation, had not been absent in the older colleges. It was unusual enough, however, that Hall could consider it a recommendation that he had taught his Antioch courses during the 1870s "almost entirely by lectures." American scholars recognized, partly through their experience in German universities, the ineffectiveness of dull or inert lecturing. H. C. Adams, writing back from Berlin to propose courses that he might give at Hopkins, stressed that he would not present lectures "written out and read." [29] Much use was made of the lecture in the natural sciences, though biology did not share the tendency of physics and chemistry to carry this technique into the training of advanced students. So important did this method seem to Remsen that he claimed his lectures to advanced students taught them both chemistry and the art of lecturing—and indeed his lectures were remembered as the best at

---

[28] Ely, *Ground under Our Feet*, 161; JHC, VI, 114, 96–98, 113; Herbert B. Adams, "Special Methods of Historical Study as Pursued at the Johns Hopkins University and Formerly at Smith College," in *Methods of Teaching History*, ed. by G. Stanley Hall (Boston, 1885), 141–142, 136; JHC, III, 103–104.

[29] Hall to Gilman, July 31, 1876; Gildersleeve, *Essays and Studies*, 109–111; H. C. Adams to Gilman, Jan. 7, 1878 [1879].

Hopkins. He used few notes, and many a beginner blessed him for his clarity.[30] At the other extreme, Rowland, though claiming that his interest in lecturing remained strong, made few changes in his original three-year cycle of lectures and often simply blew off a three-year accumulation of dust and carried his lecture into the class to read.[31]

A sense of the limitations of lecturing led often to its combination with some other method. H. B. Adams declared that lecturing to undergraduates without their doing research projects was deadening and turned "bright young pupils into note-taking machines." [32] To enliven his graduate lecture courses, he had another special technique, recalled by one of his students as follows:

> It was his habit to preface his graduate lectures with "prolegomena" on some current topic of public or academic interest. At such times he reported the progress of the men gone out, or described some new historical enterprise in which he was himself engaged. In this rôle he sparkled with freshness and the student frequently regretted the return to the regular schedule of the day.

What Adams "returned to" was branded by Woodrow Wilson as "a very meagre diet of ill-served lectures." Wilson felt that Adams and other teachers at Hopkins ignored the lessons of oratory. "Perfunctory lecturing is of no service to the world," he declared. "It's a nuisance." [33] But artistry as well as information marked the better lectures: one inspired scholar wrote home that Gildersleeve had "penetrated with a loving acuteness" the secret of the literature he was describing. Gildersleeve met his own criterion for the quickening lecture—the enhancing of the subject matter "by the living, plastic forces of personal research and personal communion with the

[30] JHC, II, 123; Allen, "Impressions of Remsen," *JH Alumni Magazine*, XVI, 217–218.

[31] Rowland to Gilman, March 12, 1884; Joseph S. Ames, "Henry Augustus Rowland," *JH Alumni Magazine*, IV (1915–1916), 97–98; Crum and Baker, "Picturesque Personalities," *ibid.*, XV, 151–152.

[32] JHC, VI, 112; Adams, "Special Methods," in *Methods of History*, ed. by Hall, 120.

[33] John Martin Vincent, "Herbert B. Adams," in *American Masters of Social Science: An Approach to the Study of the Social Sciences through a Neglected Field of Biography*, ed. by Howard W. Odum (New York, 1927), 126; Wilson to R. Heath Dabney, Feb. 17, 1884, and Wilson to Ellen Axson, Oct. 30, 1883, both quoted in Baker, *Wilson*, I, 179, 186–187.

sources." [34] The presence of the lecture system did little to individualize the university; in fact, a magazine article of 1879 categorized it along with recitations and theme writing as the more prosaic methods at Hopkins. Gilman observed in 1886 that lecture courses were "less frequent and less extended than in former times." The acclaim went to the laboratory and the seminar. Their pre-eminence was in keeping with the dictum of Charles Peirce: "This is the age of methods; and the university which is to be the exponent of the living condition of the human mind, must be the university of methods." [35]

Laboratory teaching had not gained universal respect in American higher education at the time that Hopkins opened; hence the faculty tried to strengthen it with standards and a philosophy. In an introduction to one of his textbooks, Remsen cautioned, "The instructor should be as watchful in the laboratory as in the recitation-room, and should be as exacting in regard to the experimental work as the teacher of languages is in regard to the words of a lesson." The laboratory course must prove itself worthy of a place in the curriculum, he contended. Properly directed, it yielded the boon of scientific habits of thought; but taught in a slovenly manner, it was "a poor substitute for a well-conducted course in mathematics or languages." [36]

Announcements of the first academic year had expressed the purposes of laboratory training for both beginning and advanced students. Knowledge of leading theories would not be enough, the biologists proclaimed; the beginning students would need the practical instruction of the laboratory to "gain an acquaintance with the methods and instruments employed in biological research." The role that the laboratory was to play for advanced students was described most clearly by the chemists:

[The] dissertation . . . shall be, not a mere compilation, such as could be worked up in a good library, but a discussion of some problem on the basis of experiments undertaken by the candidate for the purpose of solving the

[34] H. W. Smyth to his parents, Feb. 26, 1888, Smyth Papers; Gildersleeve, *Essays and Studies*, 75.

[35] Herrick, "Hopkins," *Scribner's Monthly*, XIX, 203; ARJH (1886), 12; JHC, II, 11.

[36] JHC, V, 43.

problem. The discipline attendant upon this work will lead him to see by what means the science has been built up, and his interest will be awakened in the work done in the chemical laboratories of the world.

For the transition of the student from beginning to advanced laboratory work, the biologists provided a solid steppingstone. Before undertaking original investigation, the student repeated some important research recently published, and verified or criticized it. Through such controls, the department protected itself from the "triflers" whom Martin described as having "a burning desire to undertake forthwith a complicated research . . . believing . . . that laboratories are stocked with automatic apparatus,—some sort of physiological sausage-machines, in which you put an animal at one end, turn the handle, and get out a valuable discovery at the other." [37] Students in the physics laboratory received little supervision from Rowland, who was far more interested in advancing physics than in training physicists. He would suggest to a student a problem that needed experimental investigation, leave him to work out his own method of attack and apparatus, and criticize the results "freely and frankly." [38] With the undergraduates Rowland had no connection.

It is revealing of the spell the laboratory cast at Hopkins that H. B. Adams called his historical seminars "laboratories where books are treated like mineralogical specimens." [39] Yet he had little reason to borrow glory, for the seminar (or seminary) had a novelty, influence, and identification with the name and nature of Johns Hopkins possessed by no other pedagogical device. Although the Hopkins scholars agreed that the seminar was a borrowing from the German universities, they were far from unanimous as to its precise nature. So much the style did it become that departments tended to attach the name "seminary" to some class simply to show that they were not lagging behind. No trace remains of seminars in pathology, chemistry, or geology during the 1880s, but this is true of no other department.

The key purpose of the German seminar, according to Friedrich Paulsen, was to teach not simply knowledge, but how to garner or

[37] JHU *Circulars*, no. 4 (August, 1876), 5–6, no. 8 (April, 1877), 87; JHC, II, 127, III, 87.

[38] Ames, "Rowland," *JH Alumni Magazine*, IV, 97–98.

[39] Herbert B. Adams, *Methods of Historical Study* (*JHU Studies in Historical and Political Science*, II, nos. 1–2; Baltimore, 1884), 103.

create knowledge. The student was to learn the methods of the master and thus become a master. Although the seminar in Germany was not limited to philological and other historical studies, it had originated in them; and their practices of interpretation and criticism of source documents, performed by the student in the presence of the teacher and other students, most clearly exemplified seminar usage. That practice varied considerably in Germany is, however, beyond dispute.[40]

In an article of 1905 on the historical seminary, George Burton Adams named "the training of the investigator" as its essential aim. By his criteria a true seminar would have to include (1) advanced students, (2) special problems, and (3) training in investigation (as opposed to citizenship or character, for instance). He thus doubted the appropriateness of the name "seminary" applied to classes of Charles Kendall Adams at the University of Michigan as early as 1871, but he declared the name properly denoted the work of Henry Adams at Harvard, 1874–1876, where it was not applied. Although he inveighed against the use of the name to describe such diverse practices as "genial comment on some standard historian by the instructor" or the reading of occasional papers by members of a club, G. B. Adams described a variety of techniques suitable for "true" historical seminaries. He presented these in a triad of developing complexity: (1) intensive analysis of a single document or body of documents, (2) "comparison and combination" in a series of studies based on a large but connected group of sources, and (3) essays written on assigned topics, more or less related, and subjected to seminary criticism only after completion.[41] These standards are valuable points of reference; nevertheless, examination of usage at Johns Hopkins shows that the seminary was far too protean for narrow definition.

The first formal seminar at Johns Hopkins, Gildersleeve's philological seminary, began its work on December 5, 1876. Its first secretary recalled that "Gildersleeve was clearly prepared to give us much leeway—no 'recitations' at all, but the elaboration of large tasks

---

[40] Paulsen, *Deutschen Universitäten*, 266–269; JHC, III, 2; Gildersleeve, *Essays and Studies*, 112.

[41] George Burton Adams, "Methods of Work in Historical Seminaries," *American Historical Review*, X (1905), 522, 520n, 528–529.

assigned in advance." With the Greek historians as the center of attention, the students prepared introductions, interpretations, and abstracts.[42] The basic work of the seminary had changed little a dozen years later, when the Attic orators were the central theme. As Gildersleeve described this work in the *Annual Report* of 1889, the seminary members "were required to present in turn exegetical and critical commentaries on select portions of the orators, and to make analyses of speeches and abstracts of rhetorical treatises." [43]

For Gildersleeve a principal purpose of the seminary was indeed "the training of the investigator," or, in his own words, "to guide individual research on all the lines of philological inquiry, grammatical, literary, historical and archaeological." But he held a second purpose to be equally important, "to train the future *teacher* in the exegesis and criticism of Greek authors." [44] This pedagogical role of the seminar was ignored by G. B. Adams; it had, however, a clear German precedent in the work of such men as Hermann Köchly, professor of Greek at Heidelberg, whose students in turn took the chair to try their abilities as instructors.[45] The opening words at Gildersleeve's first seminary meeting were, in fact, pedagogical advice. "Teaching," he said, "being an art, can only be learned by long experience." [46] So clear was this purpose in Gildersleeve's mind that during the first year he organized a separate "pedagogical seminary," centering on Thucydides, which held eight meetings. The practice-teaching aspect of this seminary is the more remarkable in that it is totally overlooked by those who criticize the early Johns Hopkins for ignoring its role as a trainer of future college teachers.[47] The nine students in this seminary the first year instructed undergraduates in the presence of Gildersleeve and C. D. Morris. This separate seminary was still in use in the third academic year.[48]

[42] Sihler, *From Maumee to Thames,* 102. Two bound volumes of Sihler's notes covering this seminary, the courses he taught himself, and his reading during 1876–1877 are in the classics library, JHU.

[43] P. 43.

[44] Gildersleeve, quoted in Herrick, "Hopkins," *Scribner's Monthly,* XIX, 203. Italics added.

[45] JHC, III, 2. Gildersleeve charged, however, that this second aim of the seminar—"power of presentation"—was "too much neglected in Germany" (*Essays and Studies,* 115).

[46] Quoted in Sihler, *From Maumee to Thames,* 103.

[47] E.g., Earnest, *Academic Procession,* 168.

[48] Lanman diary, Jan. 30, 1877, Nov. 7, 1878.

The name "pedagogical seminary" did not appear in later years, but the dual nature of Gildersleeve's seminar remained. It met twice a week. One of these meetings was for "criticism and interpretation of the authors in hand." Although the use of undergraduate guinea pigs did not continue, the presence as auditors of beginning graduate students provided a less-advanced group for instruction, and the preparation of "introductory lectures" was among the duties of seminar "members." The other weekly meeting was devoted to "auxiliary studies." This stressed the second seminar function, training investigators. Gildersleeve regularly announced in connection with the seminary "a series of conferences," which seem to have been lectures by him on a broader but related subject.[49]

The *Registers* of the first two years announced only the Greek seminary. However, Austin Scott's 1876–1877 course, "Sources of American History," was as deserving of the name, except that it was taught by an associate. Scott was in the midst of his researches for Bancroft's last volume and thus in an excellent position to show the nature of historical investigation. Books and manuscripts were brought from Bancroft's library to the seminar, and unsolved problems were considered, particularly the development of the Constitution. Bancroft wrote encouragement to those who undertook research papers, giving them the sense that they were helping in his work. Students found themselves freed from "the old passive methods of reliance upon standard authorities and text-books." [50] With such special procedures the special name could not long be withheld. The *Register* for the third academic year listed one of Scott's courses as the "Seminary of American History," and in private correspondence, Scott referred also to a course in English history which H. B. Adams taught in 1879–1880 as a "Seminary." [51]

It was, in fact, to be Adams who developed and publicized the historical seminar at Johns Hopkins. Like Gildersleeve, he saw that training of the professional investigator was a major function of the seminar. Again like Gildersleeve, he believed that the purpose did not end there. It was not pedagogical training, however, that Adams established as the second aim, but rather "the discovery of new truth in the training process." [52] This was a meaningful difference. The type of seminar that Adams founded is far better understood if "the

---

[49] JHC, VI, 101.　　[50] Adams, *Methods of Historical Study*, 98–99.
[51] JHR (1879), 20; Scott to Gilman, Dec. 12, 1879.　　[52] JHC, III, 2.

discovery of truth" is acknowledged as one of its goals. He sponsored no practice teaching. He did not labor with a small group of students to draw all possible meaning from a single unclear document. His program lay at the other end of the G. B. Adams triad: he sent students off to write essays that contributed new knowledge. These were brought into the seminar only in final form. Although as the years went by the essays were less and less related to a general topic and the field of "American Institutional and Economic History" proved remarkably elastic, Adams continued to declare that there was a "chosen field of seminary-work." [53]

During the 1882–1883 term, Jameson damned the seminary as "without character or unity": it was merely "a meeting for the reading of papers," and the papers were greeted with "too much mutual admiration and not enough savage criticism." What the seminar could be at its worst (admittedly to a jaundiced eye) appeared in Jameson's account of the meeting of January 27, 1882:

Oh, it was unspeakably stupid; Adams talked a while, introductorily; then [Lewis Webb] Wilhelm [a graduate student] read a compilation of the colonial school-acts of Maryland, a wretched piece of work; and Adams and [a local school official], a pretentious, half-educated Southern wiseacre, kept up a desultory talk on about every sort of institution, and kept us there till half-past ten.

Jameson forecast a transition to "a state of things wherein the seminary work consists, as in a German seminary, in practical exercises, giving practice in the use of sources by devoting attention to the most minute and thorough study of a very limited field each meeting." [54] But this transition never occurred; in fact, the seminar became more diffuse during the later 1880s. The inclusion of Ely's students and their works in political economy contributed to this. So too did Adams' use of the seminar (in time synonymous with the Historical and Political Science Association) as a public relations vehicle. Junior members of the department were admitted who were doing no original work, reviews of books and articles were read, and attendance averaged between thirty and forty. The frequent reading

[53] JHC, VI, 112.
[54] Jameson to Albert Shaw, Nov. 5, 1882, Shaw Papers; Jameson diary, Jan. 27, 1882; Jameson to Shaw, Feb. 27, [1883], Shaw Papers.

by faculty members of their own works was also a dubious seminar technique.[55]

The faculty always made clear that the German seminar had been modified, and there was no good reason to demand conformity to an ideal type. But the historical seminary at Johns Hopkins might far better have retained the name association or adopted the name that Ely later applied to it—"round table." Then separate seminars might have grown up under Adams, Jameson, and Ely, just as—once Sylvester was gone—the mathematical "seminary" took the name society, and Newcomb, Craig, and Story each founded a seminar. Adams himself in the 1883–1884 term directed a weekly "extra session" of the seminary, which studied the sources of colonial American history and pursued "certain lines of research suggested by the instructor." [56] But this program, with its greater similarity to the German seminar, was not repeated the next year. Some of Jameson's later courses had characteristics of a seminar, but in a department where something called *the seminary* existed, individual efforts in this direction were stifled.

G. S. Morris directed the first seminary in philosophy at Hopkins in the fall of 1882, with attention centered on Plato's *Theaetetus* and Aristotle's *De Anima*. Morris believed that the seminary showed promise and in the fall of 1883 led another on Spinoza's *Ethics*. His practice fitted Gildersleeve's theories of the pedagogical function: "the different members of the class by turns took the lead in the analytic exposition of the text and criticism of the argument." An example of the other side of the work, student investigations, was a paper by John Dewey on Empedocles, which, according to Morris, "embodied an ingenious attempt to find, in the fragments of doctrine attributed to the philosopher, justification for a spiritualistic interpretation of his maxim, 'Like is known by like.' " [57] In the 1884–1885 term there was no philosophy seminar, though during the second half-year, G. S. Hall, newly promoted to professor, held weekly "conferences" devoted to ethics and "scientific topics in psychology." But the laboratory lay closer to Hall's heart than the seminar. Not until the 1886–1887 term did he apply the name "seminary" to part of his teaching. A "Psycho-Physic Semi-

[55] JHC, VI, 110, 112.
[56] Ely, *Ground under Our Feet,* 193; ARJH (1884), 33.
[57] JHC, II, 136, III, 119; G. S. Morris to Gilman, March 12, 1883.

nary" dealt with "binocular vision and the bilateral function," and a "Historico-Ethical Seminary" consisted of the reading by members of essays on a wide variety of topics.[58] In 1887–1888 the Historico-Ethical did not meet, and the Psycho-Physic grew extremely diffuse: "essays were read and books and topics discussed systematically under Dr. Hall's direction." After Hall's departure, G. H. Emmott attempted to revive the philosophy seminar, now dubbed the Ethico-Historical Seminary; it met fortnightly, there was no organizing topic, and the name was at times given as "association." The project ended after a single year.[59]

If the history seminar evolved into something else and the philosophy seminar dissolved into nothing, it could still be said that seminars recognizable by German standards flourished at Johns Hopkins, for in some of the language departments this method was the capstone of all teaching. Although Minton Warren was not granted the privilege of conducting a seminar in Latin until his third year at Hopkins, 1881–1882, he then established one very much in the German pattern. He opened his seminar with a series of lectures on the specific topic or writer chosen. The members "in turn" analyzed part of the writings, and specially selected portions "were made the subject of critical interpretation." At the end of the seminary's second year, Warren modestly concluded: "It is believed that if nothing more, some insight into good methods was gained, and the power to apply them, which must be the chief object in all seminary training." [60]

One of the least consistent views of the seminary came, strangely enough, from the Hopkins professor who was also a professor in a German university. The teaching of Paul Haupt during his first year at Hopkins was described as being "after the seminary method," rather than by lectures, because it was "intended for beginners." [61] In a university where the seminar was looked on as the pinnacle of the educative process, a more incongruous statement is hard to imagine. Haupt gave a vast number of courses, and though the name "Shemitic Seminary" was occasionally used, it was never clear to which class it applied. The "Assyrian Seminary" of 1888–1889 was more clearly identifiable.

[58] ARJH (1885), 53–54; JHC, VI, 114.
[59] ARJH (1888), 88; (1889), 80; (1890), 57–58.
[60] ARJH (1882), 40; (1883), 28–29.   [61] JHC, III, 112; ARJH (1884), 27.

Haupt left no record of advanced students' performing either pedagogical or investigatory functions "in turn." The indications are that he himself did most of the talking.[62]

Not until the 1887–1888 term did Bloomfield announce a seminary. The loan of manuscripts by the British government in India seems to have been the stimulating factor. However, the most detailed instruction in using these manuscripts—"the elementary principles of text-criticism and emendation"—was given to four advanced students in work supplementary to the seminary, work which Bloomfield declared to be "somewhat in the manner of a privatissime at a German University." [63]

Although A. Marshall Elliott instituted seminary work as early as 1881, he did not declare the existence of "The Romance Seminary" until the 1884–1885 term.[64] Only his most advanced students attended the regular meetings of the seminar, which concentrated on intensive analysis of single documents, the students working from manuscript facsimiles. All graduate students in Romance language, however, attended fortnightly meetings at which original papers, journal reports, and professional correspondence were read. The advantage of this division is apparent. The work in the manuscripts was best followed by a smaller group with sound preparation. But the reading of an essay was equally effective in the larger group and could both instruct and inspire the novices.[65]

This pattern of the divided seminar appeared also in German and English. It is not clear, though it is extremely likely, that the fortnightly meetings of the two were combined. The separate seminars in these two languages seem at first to have lacked the practical training in investigation that Elliott provided through manuscript analysis. Wood's German seminar, not organized until 1885–1886, avowedly aimed at coverage of fields as broad as Low German; thus, training the student as investigator or teacher could be only an adventitious result. The work which Bright chose to call the English seminary, in 1886–1887, seemed equally to lack the advanced, specialized, practical nature of the ideal seminar. The work centered on the Romantic movement in

[62] JHC, VIII, 4; ARJH (1887), 12, (1889), 44–45.   [63] ARJH (1888), 57–58.
[64] ARJH (1882), 42; (1885), 51.
[65] JHC, VI, 108–109; ARJH (1889), 51–52.

English poetry, with students preparing in turn essays on various poets.[66]

In mathematics, specialized seminars came only after Sylvester's departure,[67] and it was not until 1888 that something called "The Physical Seminary" appeared. It was not Rowland, but Kimball, who planned and directed this course, in which all advanced physics graduates gathered for weekly reports on a broad variety of topics and discussions. The journal club with faculty-student reviews of current articles had long been a feature of the department's work, and it continued separate from the seminary.[68] The account of the year's work at the end of the 1887–1888 term included the first mention of biological seminaries—one in physiology and one in morphology. Their procedure was never detailed.[69]

The seminar, for all its prestige, represented so many different forms of class organization and of teaching method that generalization is difficult. Certainly its purpose became more complex than that assigned in 1881 by Gilman: "showing advanced students the processes by which independent researches are to be carried on." By 1886, Gilman himself presented a view far less precise; in fact, he seemed driven to the physical arrangement of the class as the one invariable factor: "seminaries, where the professor, by personal example and inspiration, guides the reading and study of a select class, seated around a reading-table, are becoming a significant feature in our work." [70] The seminar lay within wide extremes. It varied from Haupt's three members and two hearers to Adams' groups of over thirty. It might be led by a professor or an instructor. The students might present advanced researches or sophomoric reports or nothing. The professor might talk little or much. The material studied might be facsimile manuscript or textbook. In common was perhaps only this: the name "seminary" applied to graduate students alone. This was not true of either "lecture" or "laboratory." To the graduate students, therefore, the seminary appeared as a recognition of their advanced status. It was not merely another course. Here some change was to take place in *them*. At its best, the seminar did indeed transform them.

[66] ARJH (1886), 40, (1887), 16–18; JHC, VI, 105–106.
[67] ARJH (1885), 42.
[68] ARJH (1889), 35; JHC, VIII, 84–85; JHR (1889), 77.
[69] ARJH (1888), 25, (1890), 34–36; JHC, X, 16–17.
[70] ARJH (1881), 6; (1886), 12.

The Way of the Faculty

The contact of faculty member with student was recognized as the most important interpersonal relationship at Hopkins. But living with one's fellow teachers was another relationship that had great potentiality for good or ill. Sometimes contact among the faculty strengthened each participant, but there were unhappy occasions that threatened discord or open conflict. Although these conflicts never developed into the institution-wrecking feuds which Andrew D. White described as frequent at American colleges earlier in the century,[71] they nevertheless cost a price in emotional exhaustion and broken lines of communication. Gilman, after a year studded with controversy at his own institution, wrote two articles for the *Nation*, suggesting that though college conflicts took the form of personal quarrels they in fact sprang from poor definition of power; he suggested written constitutions as a possible solution.[72] Few of the disputes of record at Hopkins could have been prevented by a constitution, but the proposal showed that Gilman pondered the problem of intramural conflict. Gildersleeve could testify in 1900 that of such troubles Hopkins had had its share: "The universities and colleges that I know are full of rancour and jealousies and my close observation of the workings of the Johns Hopkins has revealed to me more of the [conflicting?] elements than might have been expected by those who were not so near to the machine." Still, Gildersleeve was willing to put the matter in perspective, and he agreed with Newcomb, who thought Gildersleeve's judgment too severe, that "institutions of learning are like all other human institutions in this regard, no better, no worse." [73]

Disaffections might be limited to grumblings in a diary over university expenditures on someone else's department or an outburst to a colleague over the more rapid promotion of one's junior in another discipline. Jealousies over students might come further into the open, as when Wood accused the history department of giving an easier Ph.D. in order to attract students.[74] Another sort of criticism which might be half-veiled, half-expressed, involved trespasses in course offerings. Hall felt opposition from two sides—Martin viewing his physiological experiments as an infringement and Gildersleeve questioning his right to teach Aristotle and Plato in translation. Gildersleeve's disappoint-

[71] White, *Autobiography*, I, 429–430.   [72] *Nation*, XXXIX, 49–50, 68–69.
[73] Gildersleeve to Newcomb, Feb. 13, 1900, Newcomb Papers.
[74] Jameson diary, April 16, Oct. 29, 1883; H. B. Adams to Gilman, July 7, 1885.

ment when Remsen was chosen acting president for the 1889–1890 term temporarily broke the cordial relationship between the two, though Remsen by December found his colleague largely reconciled.[75]

Criticisms bit hardest into faculty sensitivities when they were expressed at committee meetings. With departmental chauvinism at its height in the season of appointing fellows, Sylvester in 1883 felt himself threatened and isolated. He wrote Gilman:

The laboratory departments work as a unit together—the same is true of Latin and Greek: Mathematics has only a chance of receiving the full measure of consideration to which it is entitled when it receives assistance from your support. It is every where an unpopular department of science except to the initiated.

In this mood, he misinterpreted some comments by Rowland as an attack on his teaching, and he recalled with remorse, "I allowed myself to be transported into a vehemence of manner and I fear acerbity of expression." Rowland, the giver of offense in this case, was himself one of the readiest to feel offended. The trenchant wit of his colleague Gildersleeve particularly wounded him. After one committee episode, he wrote to Gilman that the classicist's remarks had always been "intensely disagreeable" to him and had often destroyed his interest in the meetings. In fact, he requested to be relieved of membership on "any board of studies"; he did not, he said, "care to be subjected to ridicule in the presence of those who are nominally my inferiors." [76] Rowland did not actually withdraw, but he lost little love on either Gildersleeve or his department. His boyhood aversion to Latin and Greek did not abate in this new community of scholars, and one of his disciples admitted that "he often failed to sympathize with ideals and purposes of those working in other departments of the institution, especially those engaged in linguistic investigations." Later in his life, at a Hopkins Phi Beta Kappa banquet, he made "a savage onslaught" against students of ancient languages.[77]

Although praise of interdepartmental co-operation was on many lips, interdepartmentalism sometimes brought charges of interference. Ely felt that Newcomb should stick to his specialty and not try to bring

[75] Hall, *Life and Confessions*, 232; Remsen to Gilman, Oct. 26, Dec. 17, 1889.

[76] Sylvester to Gilman, May 20, 23, 1883; Rowland to Gilman, March 12, 8, 1884.

[77] Mendenhall, "Rowland," in Rowland, *Physical Papers*, 11–12; Gilman, *Launching of a University*, 70; Ames, "Rowland," *JH Alumni Magazine*, IV, 99.

mathematical trappings into economics. Harris' public opposition to vivisection, regarded as interference with the biology department, led to his resignation.[78] When Remsen called for "official notice" of the unhealthful use of mercury in the physics laboratory and Gilman wrote of the matter to Rowland, the physicist protested violently.[79] The preservation of peace on such occasions shows why, after Gilman's death, Gildersleeve could attribute much of the effectiveness of even the greatest minds at Hopkins to the president's "infinite tact." [80]

In his farewell speech, Sylvester declared that the object of a university was "to bring men of different pursuits not only into contact, but into absolute intercommunication and contact and collision; and not only to intermingle, but collide studies about." [81] Some of the collisions, such as his public dispute with Peirce over priority in discovering a system of nonions,[82] proved painfully jarring, but contacts that aided and stimulated set the dominant tone of the institution. Specialization led the faculty toward a respect for each other's unique achievements. According to the view of Dean Griffin, presented in 1890, specialization also brought "a profounder realization of the unity of knowledge, leading us to understand that everything in some sort involves and leads to everything else." [83] Rowland could at once be pointed out as an exception here, and it may well be that the predominating spirit among the Hopkins faculty was liberal and inclusive despite rather than because of their specialization.

Attendance at each other's lectures gave visible evidence of this spirit. Sometimes a younger faculty member chose to profit from the learning of his senior. Minton Warren attended Gildersleeve's courses regularly from 1879 to 1881. But as often, a professor might go to a younger man's class in order to broaden himself; such was the motive of C. D. Morris in attending Bloomfield's Sanskrit courses.[84]

Faculty co-operation appeared in many ways. A physiologist might

---

[78] See pp. 179–186, 153–154, above.

[79] Remsen to [Gilman?], Feb. 8, 1884, GP; Rowland to Gilman, March 12, 1884.

[80] JHU *Circulars* (n.s. 1908, no. 10), 35.

[81] "Remarks at Farewell Reception," GP.

[82] JHC, I, 203, 242; II, 46, 86–88. A detailed account appears in Fisch and Cope, "Peirce at Hopkins," in *Studies of Peirce,* ed. by Wiener and Young, 294–302.

[83] JHC, IX, 40.

[84] Warren to Lanman, Feb. 9, 1881; C. D. Morris to Lanman, Feb. 29, 1884; both in Lanman Papers.

use in an experiment on taste a substance created by a chemist. A philologist might call an obscure German article to the attention of a colleague in another language. An associate in Sanskrit might give a guest lecture in a history class. Or a language teacher might help improve the diction of a colleague writing reviews for German periodicals.[85] By practice as well as proclamation the faculty proved its interdependence. But the proclaiming was frequent and notable. Martin, in his inaugural, cited the dependence of the biologist on the other natural sciences and declared, "However important we biologists may think ourselves, the fact remains that there are other studies to be provided for, and studies just as important as our own."[86] The necessary relationship among the disciplines was expressed even more sweepingly by Gildersleeve a decade later:

There is no form of art, no phase of philosophy, of ethics, no development of physical science, that is alien to the student of language, and the student of physical science in his turn needs the human interest of our study to save his life from an austere and merciless quest of fact and principle in a domain where man enters only as a factor like any other factor.[87]

Among the more remarkable demonstrations of this sense of community was the faculty's co-operative series of Saturday lectures on topics in education. Either Gilman or Hall could have originated the plan, which was first carried out in 1884 with seventeen lectures, the first and the last given by Gilman. The course encouraged graduate students (sixty-two of whom enrolled) to consider problems that they would face as college teachers. Beginning on February 16, it stirred up an interest which was heightened by Eliot's Commemoration Day address, "The Degree of Bachelor of Arts as an Evidence of a Liberal Education." The series continued for two more years.[88] Faculty members as well as graduate students attended these lectures, hearing their colleagues analyze their fields and describe their ideas of teaching. Another effort toward communication, this one without student par-

[85] JHC, VI, 54, III, 75; Lanman diary, Nov. 13, 1879; Jameson diary, April 2, 1884.
[86] Martin, "Study of Biology," *Popular Science Monthly*, X, 302, 304.
[87] JHC, V, 107.
[88] JHC, III, 32, 69, 49, V, 51; Jameson diary, Feb. 16, 1884; Henry Clarke Warren to Lanman, March 5, 1884, Lanman Papers. Somewhat similar series given largely by outsiders were offered in 1889 and 1891 (ARJH [1889], 59; JHC, X, 54, 71–72, 85).

ticipation, was recalled by Hall as "an informal faculty club which met evenings at different houses, at which each of us in turn . . . presented some topic in our own field." [89]

But when all the testimony on the sense of community among the faculty is in, it remains clear that as scholars they had a price in loneliness to pay. Harris wrote Gilman that he found it "extremely difficult" to get to know his fellow faculty members "so as to find out their circumstances, needs, & difficulties." Sylvester in his farewell address urged the establishment of "a place where the Professors can meet together and have a good time of it." He was shocked that faculty members had come and gone without meeting all their colleagues. The letters of Minton Warren showed that he wondered about his colleagues in the natural sciences, but knew little of them.[90] Gildersleeve's memorial address for Brooks revealed a similar gulf. Confessing his lack of intimacy with his late colleague, he lamented:

It is a sad fact that only a few in this body of seekers after truth ever come into close personal contact. In the rush of the life that we must lead if we are to be faithful, we only get glimpses of what is going forward in the minds and hearts of our colleagues. We are like trains moving on parallel tracks. We catch sight of some face, some form that appeals to us, and it is gone.[91]

The tragedy of man's institutional life has rarely been so clearly acknowledged. For most of those who taught at the Johns Hopkins University, however, there was the balm of knowing that they had been faithful.

[89] Hall, *Life and Confessions*, 241.
[90] J. R. Harris to Gilman, Dec. 25, 1883; Sylvester, "Remarks at Farewell Reception," GP; Minton Warren to Lanman, Jan. 18, 1887, Lanman Papers.
[91] JHU *Circulars* (n.s. 1909, no. 1), 4.

᛬ CHAPTER XIII ᛬

Matriculated Stepchildren

THE daring advances in graduate work of Johns Hopkins tend to blind observers to its innovations on the collegiate level. Its position as the first American institution to accommodate an undergraduate program to a major emphasis on graduate work cast Hopkins in the role of trail blazer. It may have been a reluctant pioneer in this case, but pioneer it was.

Although Gilman insisted that public opinion had not forced the collegiate section on the university and that it had been intended from the beginning,[1] the record is conclusive that community pressures had thwarted his early dream of a purely graduate university. The recurrent statement in early *Registers* that undergraduate instruction was designed "especially for young men from Baltimore and vicinity" (whereas the graduate work was always stressed as national in aim) recalls its original status as a sop to local sentiment. The university could truly announce, when pleading for support from other institutions, that it made "no effort to entice away the students" of good colleges.[2] The bursts of attention that the authorities from time to time turned on the college showed that it was not uppermost in their thoughts.

Gilman, for instance, pleaded in 1880 for some wealthy citizen to endow an undergraduate college in Baltimore. He linked the request

[1] Gilman, "The Group System of College Studies in the Johns Hopkins University," *Andover Review*, V (1886), 570.
[2] JHC, VIII, 14.

238

with one for a separately endowed woman's college, willing for both to be largely distinct from the university. In the spring of that year, the executive committee had voted, with a revealing choice of words, "that it is *expedient* to strengthen next year the collegiate work." [3] Few steps were taken. In 1882, Brown reported the continuation of the belief—unfounded he said—that Hopkins merely tolerated the undergraduates.[4]

Only after a major challenge did the university clearly affirm its interest in undergraduates. Early in 1883, Trustee John W. Garrett, as part of his effort to move the university to Clifton, implied that the stress on advanced work had prevented the university from doing anything for the young men of the region, whom Johns Hopkins had wanted to aid. This charge, spread on the front pages of local newspapers, threatened the good will that Gilman had nurtured so carefully. Fortunately, a special board of collegiate instructors had been studying the undergraduate problem since June, 1882. Its conclusions in April, 1883, furnished a strong rationale for undergraduate work at Hopkins, and Gilman guaranteed publicity. An entire issue of the *Circulars* was devoted to the college courses, and in a public answer to Garrett, Brown lauded the undergraduate department.[5] For Commemoration Day speaker that year the university chose the leading local attorney and literary figure, Severn Teackle Wallis, who stressed as one of the greatest advantages of the university to the city its "ample" collegiate training, as good, he said, as anything parents could obtain by sending their sons elsewhere. But public skepticism continued, and when Hopkins came into financial difficulties at the end of the decade, rumors spread that it would meet the problem by dropping its undergraduate department.[6] The rumors had a trace of a foundation,[7] but by that time the college was strong and healthy. It would not die without a struggle, and no one wanted it to die.

One historian, Professor Walter P. Metzger, has disparaged the inclusion of the college in the university as leaving the "parental assumptions of higher education" undispelled. Admitting some advantages

[3] ARJH (1880), 9; ECM, April 10, 1880. Italics added.
[4] Brown to Gilman, March 17, 1882.
[5] Garrett, *Address . . . of January, 1883;* ARJH (1883), 39–42; Baltimore *American,* May 22, 1883.
[6] JHC, II, 110–111; W. S. Marston to Gilman, Dec. 21, 1888.
[7] James Carey Thomas to Gilman, Oct. 11, 1888.

in the eclecticism of American universities (of which the inclusion of undergraduate study is a major element), he insists that it has blurred the public image of the university "as a center of independent thought, an agent of intellectual progress."[8] Yet the effect on intellectual achievement inside the university in the case of Johns Hopkins weighs in favor of the more inclusive policy. Early in the life of Hopkins, Gilman, still feeling his way toward a better definition of the university, listed in a personal notebook as one of the five "Special Features" of university work "Dependence on Collegiate Work."[9] At length he willingly gave institutional expression to this dependence in the structure of Johns Hopkins. Among other things, he saw that the college could serve as a feeder for the graduate department. Early *Registers* set forth the policy of the college "to encourage those who have taken their first degree in arts to prosecute advanced work for one or more years."[10] Of the 206 students earning A.B.'s from 1879 through 1889, 117 took at least one year's graduate work at Hopkins and 52 received Ph.D.'s there.[11] This contribution of the college to the graduate department became even more significant after Hopkins lost its unique position in advanced work. But the undergraduate section served through the quality of its preparation as well as through winning numbers of graduate students for Hopkins. By new practices and standards, which were spread through imitation and through student transfers, it led to more appropriately prepared graduate students throughout the nation. Less tangibly, the college served the university by what one newly arrived professor called keeping "the wholeness of life and knowledge . . . constantly in view."[12] In light of the narrowing specialization enforced by advanced study, this was no minor contribution.

Its coexistence with a graduate department transformed the college.

[8] Hofstadter and Metzger, *Development of Academic Freedom*, 378–383. Although the focus of this analysis is effect on academic freedom, its implications are much broader.

[9] Gilman notebook, "I. University [c1878]." Brackets in original title.

[10] For an analysis of the growth of this policy, see Irene M. Davis and Benjamin Ring, *The Hopkins Undergraduate in the Faculty of Philosophy: A Sample Survey of Catalogues of the Johns Hopkins University, 1876–1952* (Baltimore, 1956).

[11] Based on an analysis of the *Half-Century Directory*, 446–447, degrees *extra ordinem* not counted.

[12] John H. Wright, "The College in the University and Classical Philology in the College: An Address at the Opening of the Eleventh Academic Year," JHC, VI, 20.

Reciprocally, these new characteristics helped it to lay a better ground-work for advanced study. This concept of transformation appeared in-herently in Gilman's inaugural and explicitly elsewhere in Hopkins publications. Those who matriculated as candidates for the bachelor's degree the first year were officially described as having proved them-selves ready for "the *University* freedom of literary and scientific work." [13] The question of "freedom" still had some development to undergo in Gilman's mind, but he continued to picture the college vivified by the total university. The special issue of the *Circulars* in 1883 detailed this concept.

The undergraduates, the *Circulars* declared, benefited by their con-nection with graduate students from a variety of regions and back-grounds. Seeing an advanced student leave Hopkins "to assume a posi-tion of usefulness and honor" showed the younger student "what results follow devotion to study." The presence of renowned professors, even those under whom the student did not study, had a similar effect. The dean of the Harvard faculty had said that Harvard should build uni-versity work because it was the most effective way of insuring "the vigorous life of the *College*." This, the Hopkins authorities insisted, was precisely the result in Baltimore.[14] In the public dispute of 1883, Brown portrayed in a local newspaper these advantages: "The under-graduate and post-graduate departments do not clash, but, on the contrary, lend to each other mutual support. The college leads up to the university, while the university is not only fed by the college, but imparts to it a portion of its own enthusiasm and love of study." [15]

Its presence in a university primarily dedicated to advanced studies was only one of the unique aspects of the collegiate department at Hopkins. There was also, for example, the advanced standard for matriculation. Far from adopting a low standard out of deference to reportedly inferior Southern preparatory schools, the authorities adopted entrance requirements higher than those at either Yale or Harvard, in fact, including most of the freshman work at those in-stitutions. To matriculate at Johns Hopkins in 1876, a student must have learned solid geometry, plane trigonometry, and plane analytic geometry, none of which was necessary at Yale or Harvard, and one

[13] JHR (1877), 76. Italics added.   [14] JHC, II, 104.
[15] Baltimore *American*, May 22, 1883.

physical science, which was not necessary at Yale. Only in allowing the substitution of French *and* German for Greek and in including physical geography among the optional sciences (Harvard required it in addition to an optional science) did Hopkins demand less of matriculants than the two older colleges.[16]

These standards remained basically unchanged throughout the 1880s. As to age, there was soon no regulation at all. The special collegiate board set up in 1882 concluded that the university should encourage students to matriculate "about the age of sixteen," since they could then graduate young enough to pursue "non-professional university studies . . . among us, or elsewhere." [17] It was youth *and* quality that Hopkins hoped for. This ideal won for the university one of its most famous students, Charles Homer Haskins. When he applied at Harvard in 1886 at the age of fifteen, Haskins was refused. But Johns Hopkins admitted this unusual young man, who had attended Allegheny College for three years, granted him his A.B. one year later, and his Ph.D. in 1890.[18]

Gilman had not limited his hopes for gifted young men to the graduate division; he wanted them also among the matriculates. In trying to interest Baltimore boys in the university (which most of them would enter as undergraduates), he called for the "bright youths" and offered as models early-blooming Michael Faraday, Alexander Hamilton, and Karl Friedrich Gauss.[19] Hopkins initially offered five merit scholarships, but the high matriculation standards somewhat divorced it from the needs of young men of the area, and fewer than five were given in any year. In the wish to aid Southerners in search of education, a wish shared by founder, trustees, and president, there was also disappointment. Gilman and Gildersleeve visited Staunton, Richmond, and Raleigh in July, 1876, giving examinations and seeking to interest students, but very few applicants appeared. Of the twenty "Hopkins" scholarships the first year, fourteen went to residents of Maryland. But Hopkins did not lower its matriculation standards—it publicized them. Either five years' study at Baltimore City College or two at St. John's

[16] JHR (1877), 77–78; Yale College catalogue (1876–1877), 51–53; Harvard University catalogue (1876–1877), 41–43, 50–60.
[17] ARJH (1877), 28; (1883), 42.
[18] Joseph R. Strayer, "Charles Homer Haskins," DAB, XXII, 289.
[19] "Hopkins Inaugural," 38–39.

College was recommended.[20] Local preparatory schools began to adapt themselves, and a notable new one was set up by William Staples Marston, a Harvard graduate of 1874. The number of matriculates in residence rose steadily. It doubled the second year with 24. In the fall of 1880 there were 37; 1882, 49; 1884, 69; 1886, 108; and 1888, 129. But even the last figure was small compared with the 1,035 undergraduates at Harvard that year, the 688 at Yale, or even the 282 at Williams. Nor in comparison with the graduate students were the matriculates numerous, their number being only about one-third to one-half as large during the 1880s.[21]

Since medical schools of the time did not require a bachelor's degree for admission and Hopkins had elaborate facilities for premedical training which it did not want to waste, those desiring such a course were not obliged to matriculate, a special examination being set up for their admission. Room was made for other special students not candidates for a degree, and during the first five years the university usually had more special students than matriculates. The number of special students (many of them premedical) fluctuated, but never fell below thirty during the 1880s.[22]

Throughout that decade the university tried to ease the position of students not ready for its matriculation examinations. Undoubtedly this was stimulated by complaints such as that of the president of the District of Columbia school board that the gap between the District high school and Hopkins entrance requirements had obliged one aspirant to go to Princeton. From the first a student could gain tentative admission even if he did not pass all the examinations, but residence pending matriculation was limited to one year. The executive committee, after the negative publicity of the Garrett controversy, voted in April, 1884, that students should be admitted

upon such conditions as the particular acquirements of each candidate may make necessary; and to this end . . . that the duty of giving preliminary instruction in Mathematics be entrusted to Dr. Franklin, and that arrange-

[20] ARJH (1876), 32, (1877), 15–16, (1878), 25; Gilman to Rowland, June 29, 1876.

[21] Steiner, *Education in Maryland,* 160; Harvard University catalogue (1888–1889), 351; Yale University catalogue (1888–1889), 190; Williams College catalogue (1888–1889), 16.

[22] JHR (1880), 27; JHC, II, 96, 104; Steiner, *Education in Maryland,* 160.

ments should be made next year for preliminary instruction in classical and modern languages.

Here was the formalization of the "preliminary year," which was to become a fixed part of the Hopkins structure.[23] Although the use of this year became more and more common, until it was simply a quirk of the Hopkins system that one did not matriculate until the end of his first year, only in 1907 did Hopkins officially adopt the four-year undergraduate course.[24]

The reaction against the classical college with the single curriculum found expression at Hopkins not in the ever-expanding elective system that came to dominate at Harvard, but rather in the group system, which was a compromise. The newly organized Board of Collegiate Advisers, consisting of the president and representatives of eight departments, at the end of its first year's deliberations strongly supported the group system as allowing choice to the student without leaving him prey to "the infirmities of human nature." [25] This system was one of the leading features of Sheffield, and Gilman had introduced it at California. Characteristically, he found a European prototype for this program, calling it "quite in accord with the various plans of attaining academic honors in the English universities." [26] Although he intended to use the plan at Hopkins from the first, there was no need to elaborate it for twelve matriculates in the fall of 1876. Nevertheless, seven groups or "combinations" were announced during the first year: classical, premedical, mathematical, scientific, pretheological, prelaw, and literary (not rigidly classical). These suggested programs were not at first obligatory, and the subjects to be followed in each were outlined only in a general way.[27] The list remained the same the second and third years. Then for three years a "Preliminary to Business" group was listed. Its make-up was never defined, even in the vague terms of two

[23] William Birney to Gilman, April 3, 1882; JHR (1880), 26–27; ECM, April 5, 1884.

[24] Davis and Ring, *Hopkins Undergraduate*, 6; Edward H. Griffin, "The College in the University," *JH Alumni Magazine*, I (1912–1913), 192.

[25] ARJH (1883), 41.

[26] Gilman, "Group System," *Andover Review*, V, 571. The name "group system" originated at Bryn Mawr after the practice was adopted there ("Introductory Address of Daniel C. Gilman, President of the Johns Hopkins University, October 1, 1885," proofsheets, GP).

[27] JHR (1877), 70, 79–80. Unless otherwise cited, information in the following analysis comes from the applicable JHR.

majors and three (later four) minors applied to the other seven. The failure of the one group designed for the student "who does not propose to continue in an Academic or Professional course" indicated the decided bent of the Hopkins undergraduate work toward preparation for further study.

Seven proved to be the stable number of groups. After the 1882–1883 study of the Board of Collegiate Advisers, however, they were somewhat differently defined. Each group now involved a detailed curriculum, and the student must take every course listed in order to attain the A.B. The chemistry-biology group, excellent for the premedical student who chose to matriculate, was by far the most popular. Latin-Greek, physics-chemistry, and history-political science were also frequently chosen; but mathematics-physics, Latin-mathematics, and modern language lagged well behind, one year being chosen by only three matriculates each.[28] There was little significant choice once a student was in his group, which he could not change "without very special reasons" approved by the Board of Collegiate Advisers.[29] In the second year of the chemistry-biology sequence he might pursue either physiology or morphology (the plan for a third alternative, botany, remained unfulfilled during the 1880s). In modern language, he might stress either French or German, and at the end of the decade some flexibility was allowed in the language courses of the classical group. In any group, a student who early completed the French or German requirement could elect from a group of three subjects; otherwise, his optional courses consisted of whatever Hopkins Hall lectures he chose to follow. He was not forbidden to enroll in additional courses, but he faced a required schedule of fifteen hours a week for three years.

The rigid design of each group was not the only demonstration that "sufficient authority" was exerted "to prevent the student from shirking and from being listless and discursive." [30] He must also pursue a core of required subjects no matter what his group. The earliest reference to such requirements, in the second yearly *Register*, pledged only good intentions. After describing the possibilities of undergraduate speciali-

---

[28] JHC, VII, 13–14. Cf. French, *History of Johns Hopkins*, 68; Gilman, "Group System," *Andover Review*, V, 574.
[29] ARJH (1883), 41.
[30] Gilman, "Group System," *Andover Review*, V, 571.

zation, it added, "At the same time, no one will receive the Bachelor's degree, indicative of a liberal education, until he has become somewhat proficient in languages, in mathematics, and in one or more branches of natural science." The next year, French and German were specified as the languages, and it was noted that matriculates must attend certain of the courses of public lectures. The *Register* of 1880 reported the first attention to English composition: the student must provide proof of ability to write good English "by presenting for examination and criticism, during the period of his study, five papers suggested by the work he has here been engaged in." Vocal culture became a requirement at the same time.

As a part of the revolution of 1883 giving the new strict outlines to the seven groups, these vague requirements were replaced by a long and detailed core of obligatory subjects, which did not change during the eighties. Individual variations were not forgotten, however: by proving his proficiency the student could remove or abbreviate any of the requirements. Some of these were in keeping with the earlier tendencies. French and German and one natural science were still required (mathematics was dropped). The English requirements now included both composition and literature. The training in composition seems to have been provided on a highly individualistic, not to say casual, basis. The student submitted written essays "at appointed times" and received the instructor's suggestions, designed to teach expression in "clear, sound, manly English." Before receiving the A.B., the student must submit to the Board of Collegiate Advisers one or more original essays. Not until 1889 was a specific rhetoric course described. The English literature class surveyed the subject "from the earliest (Anglo-Saxon) period to the present time." It was scheduled with two other requirements—physical geography and ancient history —the three going under the short title "P.H.E." The physical geography was usually taught by some unwilling graduate student or assistant, such as Jameson.[31] Its inclusion reflected Gilman's background as a geography teacher, and at times he himself gave the opening lecture.[32] Also required was a full year's course in logic, ethics, and

[31] Donnan and Stock, eds., *Historian's World*, 31n87. Earlier, Samuel F. Clarke, one of the biologists, was paid $400 for his care of the osteological collections and $350 for teaching physical geography (ECM, June 14, 1879).
[32] JHC, VIII, 28.

psychology ("L.E.P."). A final block of required subjects was "Physical Culture, Vocal Culture, Drawing, and Theory of Accounts." The student "will pay attention to this group," the *Register* announced. Charles L. Woodworth, Jr., had begun teaching elocution in 1879, and a year later Hugh Newell became instructor in drawing.[33] Edward M. Hartwell, a Hopkins Ph.D. in physiology, taught physical culture from 1882 to 1890 and helped plan the university's gymnasium, which opened in 1883.[34] In these three subjects the student could make a standing appointment with the instructor, who was available during most of the day. Organized courses were the exception. Proofs of satisfactory achievement were certificates signed by the instructors. Although there is a hint of the arbitrary about some of these requirements, and available facilities and staff may have dictated too many of them, they thoroughly justified Gilman's claim of preventing the student "from having a narrow or one-sided development." [35]

The group system codified Gilman's belief in the equality of disciplines. He listed four ways in which the groups were equal—in length, in difficulty, in honor, and in the degree to which they led. The plan inherent in a published statement of February, 1877, would have required Greek for the A.B. and granted the B.S. or Ph.B. without it. But the ideal of equality of courses snuffed out the Greek requirement; Hopkins has never given the Ph.B. and did not give the B.S. during Gilman's administration.[36] Thus quietly was the Greek question, which later shook Harvard and Yale, early put to rest at Hopkins. The ancient history requirement and literature in translation could provide the classical element needed in a liberal education, Gilman felt. He repeatedly cited Sir William Hamilton's statement that requiring the classics of every student brought them into disrepute.[37] From the beginning it was possible for a Hopkins student to graduate without having studied Greek in college or preparatory school.

The disapproval of Eliot, who wrote Gilman that he regarded the

---

[33] Both supported themselves with other teaching in the city. In 1888, under financial pressure, the university ended the elocution program and cut Newell's salary and hours. Newell resigned the next year, but the work in drawing continued (Woodworth to Gilman, June 17, 1888; Gilman to Newell, June 15, 1888; Newell to Gilman, Aug. 26, 1889; JHC, IX, 14).

[34] JHC, III, 61–62.   [35] JHC, II, 95.

[36] Gilman, "Group System," *Andover Review,* V, 571; JHR (1877), 84; JHU *Circulars,* no. 10 (June, 1877), 129.

[37] Gilman to Seth Low, Nov. 6, 1891; Gilman, *University Problems,* 118–119.

group system as "the arbitrary device of a few minds," did not disturb the faith of the Hopkins president that he had found a good thing. Six months after receiving Eliot's objections, he published a strong defense of the system in the *Andover Review,* calling it the middle path between those who demanded one curriculum and those who demanded no curriculum.[38]

The group system was neither new nor unique. A contribution to American undergraduate education which traces more directly to Johns Hopkins is the adviser system.[39] Gilman credited C. D. Morris with this idea, saying that he had in mind the tutor system of the English colleges, but that the term "tutor" had been so robbed of meaning in American colleges that the name "adviser" was chosen instead. The plan appeared as early as 1877–1878. In the fall of 1878, a friend congratulated Gilman on the new plan, which she said overcame the chief objection to the elective system.[40]

Although in fact quite dissimilar from the essay-hearing English tutor, the adviser of this early period was far more than the faculty member who signed the students' new schedules. He brought into a university atmosphere some of the personal concern for students of the old-time college faculty. There were approximately thirty faculty members teaching forty-nine matriculates in 1882–1883, and enough of these were advisers to guarantee personal attention. An hour at which each faculty member could be consulted five days a week appeared in the *Circulars,* and it was the stated duty of every adviser "to establish relations of friendliness and confidence with the students assigned to his care." [41] Certainly there must have been variations in individual practice, but Gilman was not so distant from the workings of his institution that there can be any great inaccuracy in his description of the system:

The office is not that of an inspector, nor of a proctor, nor of a recipient of excuses, nor of a distant and unapproachable embodiment of the authority of the Faculty. It is the adviser's business to listen to difficulties which the

[38] Eliot to Gilman, Dec. 8, 1885; Gilman, "Group System," *Andover Review,* V, 571.

[39] Gilman described advisers as an "alternative" to the group system in preventing abuse of student course election (Gilman, "Present Aspects of College Training," *North American Review,* CXXXVI [1883], 537). To Gilman, then, Hopkins must have been doubly insured.

[40] Anna E. Ticknor to Gilman, Nov. 12, 1878; JHR (1878), 18, 21.

[41] JHC, II, 103–104, 20, 101.

student assigned to him may bring to his notice; to act as his representative if any collective action is necessary on the part of the board of instruction; to see that every part of his course of studies has received the proper attention.[42]

Gilman considered the wide imitation of the adviser system a gain for American colleges, but the favorable student-faculty ratio and the sense of innovation made it unusually effective in the opening years of Johns Hopkins.[43]

Innovation extended to examinations. Besides the tests given by the instructor, the university itself sponsored six-hour written examinations for each course at the end of the year. At first, both sets of grades were recorded; later an average was made up from the instructor's intermediate reports and the university's examination. For the latter, specialists were often brought in from outside. There was a general loathing of grades, despite the felt necessity for them. In 1889, an inquirer for an educational survey was told: "We should prefer not to use the marking system, but we do not think it possible to do away with it altogether at present. We have reduced it to its lowest limits. The objections to it are obvious. Working for marks is not an elevating occupation." [44]

Gilman in his inaugural rejected the "traditional four-year class system," saying that it was "a collegiate rather than a university method" and citing its absence from the University of Virginia and European universities as proving its relative unimportance. Harvard, Michigan, and Cornell were all playing it down, he said. Although he was later more willing to consider the appropriateness of collegiate methods in a complex university, Gilman would never admit that Hopkins had a class system. When work was truly fitted to the individual, the system was not necessary, he explained in 1876, proposing to "make attainments rather than time the condition of promotion." [45]

The promise of the inaugural was kept. Students who passed certain examinations at the time of their matriculation or even informal ones later could be excused from corresponding courses. They might graduate after only one year. Abraham Flexner, who graduated in two,

[42] Gilman, "Group System," *Andover Review*, V, 575.
[43] *Launching of a University*, 53.
[44] JHC, II, 101, 104; Ira Remsen, in Thomas R. Ball to W. R. Simms, Nov. 22, 1889, GP.
[45] "Hopkins Inaugural," 33–34.

enrolled in courses that met at identical hours, alternating his attendance. Gilman accepted this with equanimity. The matriculate received credit for private work, such as summer reading, if he passed an examination at the end of it. This practice was frequent in Greek and Latin.[46] In 1886, the university was considering an honors program, to "encourage special exertions and lead to superior attainments," but the plan remained undeveloped.

Absence of rules from the first characterized the undergraduate division, as it did the whole institution. "Example is more powerful than legislation in the training of young men," Gilman insisted.[47] As late as 1879, he could write to another university president that Hopkins had never made "a code of regulations" for undergraduates.[48] An early visiting lecturer remarked on "the absolute freedom from humbug" at Hopkins and "the entire subordination of the machinery to the work." Returning to his own institution, the University of Wisconsin, he reported that by comparison he was "very much struck with the amount of time we give to rolls, records, & all the other mere externals of the University." He attributed the happy condition at Hopkins in large part to the freedom made possible by the advanced requirements for matriculation.[49]

In a personal notebook Gilman once wrote an answer to the question "What constitutes a liberal education[?]" He listed first "Systematic & orderly training" and second "Encourag[emen]t to & guidance in independent thinking." [50] That is as near as he seems ever to have come to the essentials. As soon as he began writing for an official statement his lists grew, and so did the amount of qualification.

This developing qualification appeared in the *Annual Report* of 1882, where Gilman implied that the undergraduate division partook of the characteristics of a college more than of a university. He was thus moving away from his earliest position, which stressed the transformation of the undergraduate college when it existed within the university framework. Probably his most elaborate statement was one made in 1883:

---

[46] JHR (1878), 17; Flexner, *I Remember,* 60–61; ARJH (1878), 24–25, (1879), 54–55.

[47] Gilman, "Group System," *Andover Review,* V, 574, 576.

[48] Gilman to C. J. Stillé, Nov. 6, 1879.

[49] William F. Allen to Gilman, April 10, 1878.

[50] "Notes on Universities, Colleges, Teaching," GP.

Collegiate instruction . . . is largely devoted to the training of the intellectual powers and the formation of habits of attention, acquisition, memory, and judgment, while it stores the mind with the elements of knowledge. The lessons to be inculcated during a college course include obedience to recognized authority, the performance of appointed tasks, punctuality in meeting all engagements, and attention to physical development. . . . Such discipline implies but little freedom; but restraints, if wisely adjusted, are found to be as welcome to the scholar as they are to the athlete.

The phrase "implies but little freedom" is a far cry from the statement in the first *Register* that undergraduates were not admitted unless they proved themselves ready for "the University freedom of literary and scientific work." [51]

In part this distinction sprang from the growing importance which the trustees placed on the undergraduate program. Perhaps it was felt necessary to assure the citizens of Baltimore that their sons would be getting a solid and safe college course. But the strain of old-time college president in Gilman must not be overlooked. As he saw more and more beardless faces in the halls of his institution, he may well have felt responsibility to give these youngsters more than "freedom." Both the desire for parental approval and Gilman's own conservative qualities marked a statement in the *Circulars* booming the college in 1883. If parents who feared to send their sons to the city "would take the pains to inquire," it said, they could learn "that most of the temptations to which youth are exposed may be found in the neighborhood of country colleges as well as in large towns." Young men must of course always be on guard "against open as well as insidious allurements by which their physical, intellectual, and moral natures may be impaired for life." But Hopkins had raised bulwarks. The teachers were alert to their responsibilities. The students lived in private homes, not dormitories. The "attractive library" was open regularly until late in the evening. Gymnasiums near the university provided "physical culture and entertainment." There were many clubs, and often teachers were members. Nor should the fact that Hopkins was unsectarian be interpreted to mean it was irreligious. "All these circumstances," the statement concluded, "have been favorable . . . not only to the preservation of good order, but to the formation of good habits." [52]

[51] ARJH (1882), 5–7; JHC, II, 103; JHR (1877), 76.
[52] JHC, II, 105.

To the voluntary morning religious services, Gilman in 1883 added a special Friday assembly for undergraduates. Usually the content was an informal lecture by Gilman or some faculty member.[53] Some of Gilman's own homiletics rank beside any from the lips of a Mark Hopkins or an Eliphalet Nott. One counseled "Bodily Discipline." Another, "A Lesson on Truth," told of the ease with which one might slip into lies, citing habit as the great protector and St. Peter as the great example of recovery after repentance. "The Training of the Will" listed seven guides: training the attention, forecasting consequences, avoiding undue exertion or fatigue, avoiding "nervine stimulants," developing the habit of overcoming, "submission to wise authority," and the assimilation of the human will to the divine.[54] The course required of all matriculates in logic, ethics, and psychology included

such topics as mental and physical regimen and hygiene, methods and general ends of study, the needs and sanctions of positive personal convictions and purposes in the conduct of the understanding and of life, mental self-knowledge as opposed to self-consciousness, and the utilization of individual experience in self-education, social ethics, need of religious sentiments for the maturity and sanity of conscience, etc.

In addition, in the year 1883–1884 Stanley Hall presented to the matriculates twelve special lectures on mental hygiene.[55] Gilman was making no idle promise when he told parents that he would take good care of their boys.

The L.E.P. course was designated for the student's last year before graduation, a strong indication of its genesis in the president's course for seniors, the high point of the old-time college. Hall steeped this course in empiricism. Logic featured "practical drill," "occasional forensic exercises," and "copious examples from the field of scientific reasoning." Psychology was taught "with many important practical applications . . . to mental regimen and methods of work, but without much attention to those wider and more unsettled problems in the field which have no direct practical bearing." Similarly, in ethics, the "subtleties" were disparaged, while "the larger, clearer light of everyday experience" was called upon to develop principles of conduct.[56] After Emmott's arrival, Hall continued to teach the psychological

[54] GP.   [55] JHC, III, 118.   [53] JHC, III, 32.
[56] JHR (1886), 101–102, gives the most detailed description of the course.

portion of the course, but Emmott took charge of logic and ethics and presented them more prosaically. In logic he treated general theories of both induction and deduction and included numerous exercises. Ethics he taught "from the standpoint of the Christian Theory of Morals," and the first textbook that he used was Noah Porter's *Elements of Moral Science*. But the aim of the training in ethics was still declared to be "of a directly practical nature and to show the bearing of the problems discussed upon the actual conduct of human life and the formation of a manly character." [57]

The matriculates, never segregated in a college of arts and letters, remained part of the faculty of philosophy; however, each year the undergraduate experience at Hopkins seemed to differ less from that at the older colleges. This pulling into line paralleled the growing emphasis by the authorities on the collegiate section. A major landmark was the creation in June, 1882, of what later became the Board of Collegiate Advisers. During the term following its report of April, 1883, undergraduate activities greatly increased. The Friday assemblies for matriculates were introduced that year, and rooms were set aside for their study and conversation.[58] In early reports Gilman often cited the complete absence of disciplinary problems, but by 1886 so "normal" had the matriculates become that in the spring Gilman was forced to confer with the teachers on "Punctuality etc."; in 1889 a teacher of undergraduates asked for help in controlling disturbances in his classes, and by 1892 the classic prank—the explosion in the classroom —had occurred.[59] In 1889 the first yearbook was published, and the project became traditional. H. B. Adams later observed that class spirit had become especially noticeable after 1889. The interest in athletics during the 1888–1889 term was called "unusually great," and in 1891 the university alumni voted a grant of $50 to the "Athletic Association," representing a tendency hardly unique among American colleges.[60]

Undergraduate organizations had sprouted again and again, only to die young. The first of these, the "Demologian Literary Society," was

[57] JHC, VI, 115.   [58] ARJH (1883), 39; JHC, III, 32.
[59] JHC, I, 38; Gilman, untitled notes for address of Feb. 22, 1881, GP; Gilman diary "1886," May 5; Gilman to George H. Emmott, Jan. 9, 1889, Jan. 30, 1892.
[60] TM, Dec. 2, 1889; French, *History of Johns Hopkins*, 272–274; ARJH (1889), 63; JHC, X, 69.

founded on November 17, 1876, but its surviving minutes end a year later.[61] The students were kept busy enough and given enough intellectual stimulation that they did not feel the keen need to supplement the curriculum that had created such organizations in older colleges. The Matriculate Society founded in 1883 seems to have been part of the administration's drive to do right by the undergraduates. Its literary committee developed into a Literary Society, which gathered to hear essays, addresses, and debates, but was near dissolution when Woodrow Wilson transformed it in the fall of 1884.[62]

The topic of a debate sponsored by the Matriculate Society early in 1884, the value of secret societies, was not irrelevant. Fraternities, though inconspicuous, had been an element at Hopkins from almost the beginning. When urged to support the founding of a chapter of his own fraternity, Alpha Delta Phi, at Johns Hopkins in 1878, Gilman wrote that this was unadvisable because there were so many graduate students.[63] As a matter of fact, the presence of the graduate students was what brought the fraternity movement to Hopkins so early. During the first year, Walter Hines Page had led in petitioning Alpha Tau Omega for a chapter, but this plan fell through. The charter of the Beta Theta Pi chapter at Hopkins is dated 1877 and that of Phi Kappa Psi 1879, but there was no official encouragement of fraternities. It may well be that in a university lacking campus and dormitories but providing much intellectual stimulation the Greek-letter fraternity met the needs more truly than the old-style literary and debating society. Whether beneficial or not, the fraternity movement continued to grow. By 1889, Gilman cheerfully supported a chapter of his own fraternity.[64] Although there were only four fraternities at Hopkins by 1889, this familiar stone of the American college was firmly in place.

In spite of increasing conformity, there remained something special about working for an A.B. at Johns Hopkins. Underlying the changes

[61] Bound volume, "Demologian Literary Society: Johns Hopkins University: Minutes of the Society Nov. 17th, 1876–Dec. 15th, 1877," Lanier Room, JHU Library.

[62] JHC, III, 32, IV, 26; French, *History of Johns Hopkins*, 263–264. For the fate of the Literary Society, see pp. 277–278 below.

[63] Jameson diary, March 14, 20, 1884; Jameson to John Jameson, March 23, 1884, in Donnan and Stock, eds., *Historian's World*, 34; answer to E. L. Hutchinson to Gilman, April 10, 1878 (draft).

[64] French, *History of Johns Hopkins*, 280–281; Gilman to R. Sturgis, Feb. 5, 1889.

was a substratum of association with advanced workers which continued to foster maturity. As a graduate student, Jameson resented the presence of undergraduates in his courses and wrote in his diary, "I never saw such a silly, empty-headed set as the undergraduates here; unless the Amherst fellows are as bad." But a year later, having advanced to the faculty, he held a different view: "On the whole, I don't have much fault to find with my boys. They are gentlemanly, and most of them take hold well." [65] Even the worst undergraduate scandal revealed in the Gilman Papers is not altogether disparaging. The mother of one student reported that five Hopkins friends who had visited her son had talked of a shocking thing: "Many of them chew the leaves of cocaine in order to be able to sit up at night to study without being overpowered by the need of sleep. Then in the morning if they feel tired, they resort to the same stimulant." Gilman's consultation with Welch brought the assurance that chewing inert coca leaves was not the same as the "cocaine habit," but Thomas agreed with Gilman in favoring a lecture subtly referring to the danger.[66] Happy the college president whose greatest worry over his students is that they will abuse themselves with too much study! Two analysts of the Hopkins undergraduate throughout the history of the university have summarized his chief features thus: a scholarly bent and inclination toward later advanced study, freedom to advance at his own rate with a great deal of independent study, and direct personal stimulation by a faculty adviser and graduate students.[67] These were indeed his characteristics during the golden eighties.

Faculty attitude toward the early matriculates was mixed. C. D. Morris, until his death in 1886, delighted in the presence of the younger students. An undergraduate of the 1880s, Joseph S. Ames, later president of the university, testified that the most distinguished professors "always conducted college classes and took a deep interest in the undergraduates." Still, there were complaints. George Dobbin Penniman, A.B., 1884, observed that the undergraduates were "as welcome as red headed stepchildren" and that very little attention was paid to them. The faculty, as he recalled in later years, "were always think-

---

[65] Jameson diary, March 22, Oct. 21, 1881, Oct. 31, 1882.

[66] Elizabeth J. Warren to Gilman, Nov. 20, 1887; Gilman to Welch, Dec. 6, 1887; Thomas to Gilman, Dec. 7, 1887. The resulting lecture was probably Gilman's "The Training of the Will." See p. 252 above.

[67] Davis and Ring, *Hopkins Undergraduate,* 20.

ing of nothing but the glory that would come to the University through the training of the postgraduates." [68] There is an element of truth in this recollection, just as there is in that of Ames. By 1889, fifteen out of the fifty-five faculty members, including Newcomb, Rowland, Gildersleeve, and Haupt, had no direct connection with undergraduates.[69] On the other hand, Remsen long took pride in teaching beginning chemistry.

The search for a dean climaxed the university's drive toward collegiate orthodoxy. C. D. Morris, the one original professor designated "collegiate," had inconspicuously performed many deanlike functions. Probably the degree of his service in this area was not realized until after his death in 1886. It then became apparent that in searching for his successor the university must seek a man who would be both teacher and dean. Gilman early specified the need for an older man with "long continued familiarity with collegiate work." [70]

The perfect appointee, it seemed, was found in John Henry Wright, a son of missionaries, graduate of Dartmouth, for two years a student at Leipzig, and from 1878 associate professor of Greek at Dartmouth. Only in his age did he seem less than a substitute for Morris, since he was only thirty-four. Soon after Wright's appointment as "Dean of the College Board" and professor of classical philology, Gilman wrote of him that he was counted on "to give an impulse to our collegiate work," and indeed Gilman had elaborate plans for making the dean useful. The newcomer took charge of the morning chapel service and at the suggestion of the executive committee gave three public lectures in Hopkins Hall on "The Epochs of Greek Art." Perhaps so many duties were waiting that he was overburdened—by the middle of December he reported himself "dreadfully busy." [71]

[68] Ames, quoted in *ibid.*, 13; George S. Morris to Gilman, May 24, 1883; Simon Newcomb to Gilman, May 31, [?]; Penniman, "Hopkins Athletics," *JH Alumni Magazine*, XXVII, 102.

[69] The others were Story, Craig, Bolza, Wood, Elliott, Welch, Councilman, Williams, Clark, Donaldson, Mall (report by Thomas R. Ball, January, 1889, GP, basis for a public report by Gilman, Baltimore *Sun*, Jan. 17, 1889). Gildersleeve once horrified a citizen by saying that he was no longer interested in "remarkable boys," having served his time with them (Mrs. J. H. Fultz[?] to Gilman, May 15, 1879).

[70] Gilman to Lanman, April 9, 1886, Lanman Papers.

[71] Charles Burton Gulick, "John Henry Wright," DAB, XX, 556–557; Gilman to A. D. White, Aug. 30, 1886; Gilman diary "1886," Aug. 24, Oct. 7; ECM, Oct. 18, 1886; JHC, VI, 17–25, 35; Wright to Lanman, Dec. 15, 1886, Lanman Papers.

The fatal error had been in choosing a young man. Wright was neither unable nor unwilling to better his condition, and in January, totally to the surprise of Gilman, he announced his acceptance of a professorship of Greek at Harvard. Both the president and the executive committee displayed pique. Gilman wrote to Eliot that he did not blame him, but that Wright's usefulness in "planning for the improvement of our undergraduate work" was at an end. The trustees offered to let him leave the university as promptly as he wished. Gilman felt that after having called the Hopkins position precisely what he wanted, Wright had been precipitate in launching a correspondence about another position. "However," he concluded, "the matter is now closed & we have only to put off his old love & to presume, as the theologians say on 'the expulsive power of a new affection.'" [72]

The replacement was carefully and slowly sought. Not until the spring of 1889 was Edward Herrick Griffin appointed "Dean of the College Faculty" and professor of the history of philosophy. Gilman made it clear that his principal function would be as "a moral & intellectual force among the undergraduates," their "guide & friend," and entrusted him with the morning chapel service. Griffin was a graduate of Williams during the regime of Mark Hopkins and had been teaching there since 1872. The success of "the gentle dean," an ordained minister, was immediate and continuing; and by taking charge of ethics and psychology in the L.E.P. course, he greatly improved it. [73] Significantly, it was not the German-trained scholar, but Griffin, the Congregationalist minister with his training at Union Theological Seminary, who met the need of the university. In him it found its Mark Hopkins.

Upon the establishment of an undergraduate deanship, something of the unique freedom which had penetrated even to the lowliest candidate for matriculation, something of the sense of the experimental, departed. Toward the end of the 1889–1890 term, Remsen, then acting president, wrote to Gilman, announcing as precisely as anyone ever did that something had changed:

[72] Gilman to Charles W. Eliot, Jan. 14, 20, 1887, Eliot Papers; ECM, Jan. 15, 1887; TM, Feb. 7, 1887.

[73] Gilman statement of April, 1889, letter-press books, GP; Gilman to Griffin, May 9, 1889; French, *History of Johns Hopkins,* 354–355; W. Calvin Chesnut, *A Federal Judge Sums Up* ([Baltimore?], 1947), 9.

The student spirit has developed this year as never before—I mean especially the College spirit. . . . Nothing has happened in the way of disorder, or in any other way calling for unfavorable comment, unless one looks into the future, and, there, I confess, I see danger in the development of the *College*. Before we know it, we shall find our higher work suffering. I am not sure that it does not now to some extent. Certainly the moment the College gets considerably larger than the University, the effect will be felt.[74]

How exactly Remsen's forebodings were borne out is impossible to say. The university did change. But time had brought influences more powerful than the presence of the undergraduates to reshape it and remove its uniqueness. It is not hard, however, to imagine the reaction of the Ph.D. of 1884 when years later he received the following mimeographed information from a Hopkins undergraduate of the 1920s:

Now that the "Dorms" are well under way and Hopkins is fast becoming a real University with lots of pep, I'm sure you will want the NEWS-LETTER for the coming year. It will keep you in close touch with the progress of all Campus activities, our championship football team, as well as swimming, track, basketball, baseball and lacrosse.[75]

His heart must have felt a twinge, even as he smiled.

[74] Remsen to Gilman, April 3, 1890.
[75] Glover P. Fallon to "Dear Sir," [1922], mimeographed copy in Shaw Papers.

: CHAPTER XIV :

The Uninvited

GRANTING degrees on the basis of examination to nonresidents, as done by the University of London and by Syracuse University, was a question which long bemused Gilman and the trustees. In his inaugural Gilman had said that the university would not restrict its sphere to those enrolled, but would stand "ready to examine and confer degrees or other academic honors on those who are trained elsewhere." It was not a fleeting idea. The *Annual Report* of 1878 told of many inquiries regarding such a service, but said a decision had been postponed. That fall the executive committee, under the leadership of Gilman, recommended that the university accept applications for "examinations & certificates or diplomas" from nonresidents. But the matter hung fire. In 1882, Gilman wrote inquirers that he very much doubted "whether the effort will be made to mature a system of examinations for non-residents."[1]

Why was interest in this program at one time so high? The answer lies in the hopes of some of the board that it could solve one of the most explosive issues of the opening years, an issue that intimately involved members of trustees' families, brought the resignation of one trustee, and still remained unsettled. It was a dilemma indeed: what should be done with women applicants for the benefits of the university?

On the coeducational frontier, Johns Hopkins played the conservative.

[1] "Hopkins Inaugural," 34; ARJH (1878), 37–38; "Report from the Exec. Committee to the Board of Trustees, Dec. 2, 1878," JHUP; Gilman to L. L. McInnis, March 8, 1882.

The Johns Hopkins University

Vassar had opened in 1865, and Smith and Wellesley in 1875, all doing work very nearly on a level with the men's colleges, and in the Western state universities women were doing precisely the same work as men. The opening of advanced work to women graduates appeared to be the next step. Among the earliest to provide this answer was Boston University, which in 1877 became the first American institution to award the Ph.D. to a woman. Less daringly, Brown and Harvard gave examinations to women without granting them instruction or degrees, a policy which attracted the Baltimore officials.[2] Yet women could make a strong case for admission to Hopkins. Its offerings of advanced work were not available at any other institution in the country. Women graduates had already proved their seriousness of purpose. The absence of dormitories placed all students singly or in small groups in local homes, solving many supervisory problems. Such arguments, however, did not sway the powers at Hopkins. They looked abroad. Sometimes they thought of Germany where women, allowed to follow the work of some universities as auditors, could usually not take examinations and were not given degrees until late in the century. More frequently, they gave lip service to the English solution—co-ordinate colleges.

Gilman had taken a characteristic stance of compromise in his inaugural by recommending the latter course. He would not advocate coeducation, though it seemed to be succeeding at Cornell and the Western state universities, but neither did he want to bar women from the best possible educational opportunities. Sanguinely, he prophesied the endowment by some benefactor of

a "Girton College," which may avail itself of the advantages of the Peabody and Hopkins foundations, without obliging the pupils to give up the advantages of a home, or exposing them to the rougher influences which I am sorry to confess are still to be found in colleges and universities where young men resort.[3]

The trustees had talked the subject over among themselves, as their comments in the Eliot and Angell interviews proved. But they did not bring it up formally until November 18, 1876, when Thomas

[2] Walter Crosby Eells, "Earned Doctorates for Women in the Nineteenth Century," *AAUP Bulletin*, XLII (1956), 645; Thomas Woody, *A History of Women's Education in the United States* (New York and Lancaster, Pa., 1929), II, 264.

[3] "Hopkins Inaugural," 33.

called a special meeting of the board. He there presented his idea of "imparting, to a well guarded extent, the benefit of the teachings of the University to females, as well as to males, suitably prepared by age and acquirements to profit by such teachings." No doubt he had before him the images of his daughter Martha Carey Thomas, a senior at Cornell, and some of her bright young friends, including the daughters of King, Gwinn, and Garrett. The discussion was lively, with Johnson, the one trustee who had studied in Germany, leading the opposition against any participation by women. The final resolution committed the trustees to nothing; they left the matter up to Gilman "until instructed to the contrary." Thomas, Cheston, Brown, Dobbin, King, and Garrett backed the resolution; Johnson, White, and Gwinn opposed it. There the matter rested through the first academic year. No woman sought admission, and the university sought no women students.

The next year, however, the question came very much alive. Two women candidates, independently of each other, pressed for admission to the most distinctive sanctums of the university—the Greek seminary and the biological laboratory. Martha Carey Thomas was eager for learning and not unaware of the part that test cases play in gaining minority rights. Armed with her Cornell degree, she applied for admission and found Gilman "very polite." She was accepted as a candidate for a master's degree, "to have the direction of studies by the University Professors, and the final examination for degrees without class attendance in the University." These conditions excluded her from the Greek seminary, for which Gildersleeve's Hopkins Hall lectures were no substitute. Although he proved generous in advising her, she hesitated to encroach on his time. She struggled on without the stimulation of fellow students and passed her first-year examinations with commendation. But at the end of a summer's reflection, she sent an elaborate letter of withdrawal to the trustees, implying that they had placed her in an unsupportable position.[4] Miss Thomas' later career as dean and president of Bryn Mawr opened new opportunities for advanced study and recognition to women, but the doors of Johns Hopkins she had not opened.

The university, in an early effort to aid the lower schools, had

[4] TM, Nov. 5, 1877; Finch, *Carey Thomas,* 69–83; M. Carey Thomas to trustees, Oct. 7, 1878, copy in TM, Oct. 7, 1878.

offered a teacher's course in physiology with twenty Saturday sessions of lectures and laboratory work, led by Martin. Of the sixteen teachers enrolled in the course in the fall of 1877, eleven were women. One of these, Emily A. Nunn, who had studied at Cambridge University and was planning to teach at Wellesley, determined to pursue biology further than the limited Saturday course allowed. Through a misunderstanding by Martin of Gilman's wishes, she entered the regular biology laboratory. The trustees disallowed her request for such training on November 5. The next day, Gilman ordered her out of all but the teacher's course and wrote her defender, Henry F. Durant, founder of Wellesley: "I should be sorry to have this institution be discourteous to any one seeking knowledge but the Biological Laboratory where experiments in respect to animal life are in progress is not well adapted, in the opinion of some at least of our trustees, to the co-education of young women & young men." Miss Nunn, who was professor at Wellesley from 1878 to 1881, attended the 1879 summer session of the university's Chesapeake Zoological Laboratory. Although the program involved much rough outdoor life, her admission was a "deliberate selection," known to the trustees.[5]

These two episodes forced the board, with Johnson pressing hard for total exclusion, to adopt on November 5, 1877, a resolution that declared the board's willingness to confer with anyone planning a co-ordinate college and to allow the faculty to examine and certify women candidates for a degree. But though it empowered the executive committee to make exceptions for special lecture courses such as chemistry, the resolution concluded sternly: "For the present, the Board declines to receive young ladies as students in the usual classes, and as attendants upon lectures not specially excepted."

The "for the present" guaranteed reappearance of the problem. Early in 1880, a Miss Atkinson requested admission to the undergraduate classes of the university. Thomas felt that she should be admitted and the whole policy liberalized and clarified, but to Johnson this was the time to strengthen resistance. He wanted Miss Atkinson rejected and the mischievous phrase "for the present" removed. Calling a special meeting for March 8, he began something of a proxy fight.

[5] ARJH (1878), 33–34; Gilman to Emily A. Nunn, Nov. 5, 1877; Gilman to Durant, Nov. 6, 1877; JHC, III, 93; George W. Brown to Gilman, July 14, 1879.

Gilman told the trustees that other women awaited the outcome of Miss Atkinson's case, and Johnson warned that if she were admitted "we shall at once have the whole theory of coeducation fastened upon us." [6] The minutes show only that, as befitted the Quaker tradition of many of the trustees, they reached a sense of the meeting. Their two decisions were unanimous and without abstentions. Miss Atkinson's application they refused; but instead of Johnson's resolution to strike the phrase "for the present," they adopted a substitute reaffirming the earlier resolution and forbidding its reconsideration without three months' notice in writing. [7] But if the trustees thought that they had achieved peace in their time, they were mistaken.

In fact, they had themselves since 1878 been encouraging the presence in Hopkins classrooms of a living justification of the "theory of coeducation." A young woman of extraordinary intellect, Christine Ladd, had originally asked for admission in order to study under Sylvester. An 1869 graduate of Vassar, she had published several mathematical papers while teaching in secondary schools. Impressed by these papers, Sylvester urged Gilman to obtain her admission. On April 25, 1878, the executive committee agreed to permit Miss Ladd to attend the lectures of Sylvester, but no others. The resolution of November 5, 1877, allowed this, and the uniqueness of Sylvester's teaching probably made the committee think of the case as very special. As an additional bit of gallantry, they absolved the applicant from tuition. [8] After Miss Ladd had arrived and demonstrated her ability, her path was further smoothed. She attended other classes— those of Peirce and Story. In June, 1879, at the end of her first year's work, the trustees voted her the stipend of a fellow, but not the title. [9] This was continued for three years.

If ever a student was worth his stipend, Miss Ladd was. Her work under Peirce included the invention of a technique for reducing all syllogisms to one formula, called the antilogism, which still holds a

[6] James Carey Thomas to Gilman, Feb. 1, 1880; Reverdy Johnson, Jr., to John Work Garrett, three undated letters [Feb.–March, 1880], Garrett Papers; Garrett to Johnson, March 8, 1880, copy in Garrett Papers.

[7] TM, March 8, 1880.

[8] Robert S. Woodworth, "Christine Ladd-Franklin," DAB, X, 528–530; Sylvester to Gilman, April 6, 1878; Gilman to Ladd, April 26, 1878.

[9] JHC, I, 10, 12, 2.

significant place in logic.[10] Her later achievements in psychology—especially color vision theory—were also notable. But if fear of romance had made the trustees restrict the enrollment of women, they were proved correct. In 1882, after four years of diligent labor under Sylvester and Peirce, she and Fabian Franklin, then just promoted to associate in mathematics, were married. Although she had been admitted as "a candidate for a second degree," she knew from the beginning that the university was not likely to give her one. In 1926, as part of the fiftieth anniversary ceremonies, the university granted her the Ph.D., forty-four years late. Miss Ladd remained in the Hopkins community as a faculty wife for some years, and though refused a lectureship in 1893, she held such a post in logic and psychology from 1904 to 1909.[11] Inevitably she became a figure of legend, even while still living in Baltimore. One of her fellow students referred to her in an effusive article in a popular magazine as "logic incarné." [12] The contribution of the woman behind the legend proved that the pattern of Johns Hopkins could be exclusively masculine only at an intellectual sacrifice.

The encouragement of Miss Ladd cost the trustees dearly within their own ranks. Johnson, whose early labors inhered in the very foundations of the university, had expressed his dissatisfaction by withdrawing from the chairmanship of the executive committee at the beginning of 1879 (to be replaced by Brown) and from the committee a year later (to be replaced by Stewart). On the latter occasion, Gilman wrote him expressing concern. In answer Johnson informed him, or rather reinformed him, that his gradual dropping of responsibility was because of "certain leanings in the policy of the board" and fear that "the foreign element already within the walls" was "but an Entering-wedge for more of the same kind that is sure to seek an entrance." He had been forced to bear the brunt against the supporters of certain "innovations" and disliked the resulting unpleasantness.[13] Although the unanimity in the meeting of March 8,

[10] Christine Ladd, "On the Algebra of Logic," in Charles S. Peirce, ed., *Studies in Logic: By Members of the Johns Hopkins University* (Boston, 1883), 17–71.

[11] ECM, April 25, 1878; Finch, *Carey Thomas*, 79; Gilman to Ladd-Franklin, June 8, 1893.

[12] Charles W. de L. Nichols, "The Annals of a Remarkable Salon," *Home Journal*, Dec. 5, 1894.

[13] ECM, Feb. 6, 1879; TM, Jan. 21, 1880; Johnson to Gilman, Jan. 20, [1880].

1880, seemed to foretell a long truce, Johnson was not pacified. No shifts in policy occurred in the months following, but the irritating presence of Miss Ladd continued, and her stipend was renewed. During the summer Johnson reached a decision and submitted his resignation in a letter cordial but incontrovertible.[14]

Johnson had saved himself much painful argument, for his prediction that the question was still brewing proved correct. Gilman and the trustees were not allowed to rest easy: too many institutions had begun preparing women for the type of work done at Hopkins, and too many women were applying the democratic credo to themselves and universities. The authorities met each request as it came, sometimes adamant, sometimes compromising. They showed just enough attention to the merits of individual cases to keep the requests flowing in.[15]

The trustees did not remain without fresh insights during these years. King, chairman of the trustees who were planning Bryn Mawr, inspected the English women's colleges in 1881. Brown learned of the report of President Barnard of Columbia favoring coeducation and wrote Gilman that Hopkins had not heard the last of the question. He himself, he said, was prepared to accept new light, and he admitted, "In almost every respect there is no place so well adapted to try the experiment as the Johns Hopkins." [16]

But Brown was in advance of most of the trustees. There was no major reversal of policy. After the Methodist Episcopal Church opened the Woman's College of Baltimore (later Goucher) in 1888, with a curriculum closely patterned after that of Hopkins, there seemed to be a perfect answer to any woman asking admission to the undergraduate department.[17] In many ways, Hopkins now had its Girton. In graduate work there was no equally good answer. Still, there was at least a semblance of truth in saying that women could do as well elsewhere. Hopkins men co-operated wholeheartedly in the founding of Bryn Mawr; so many of them were among its first

[14] Johnson to Cheston, Sept. 13, 1880, copy in TM, Oct. 4, 1880; TM, Nov. 1, 1880.
[15] E.g., ECM, June 24, Dec. 27, 1886, Jan. 15, Dec. 21, 1887.
[16] King to Gilman, July 9, 1881; Brown to Gilman, July 15, 1881, July 17, [1881].
[17] John B. Van Meter, "The Woman's College of Baltimore (1885–1894)," in Steiner, *Education in Maryland*, 198–204; Anna Heubeck Knipp and Thaddeus P. Thomas, *The History of Goucher College* (Baltimore, 1938), 26, 420.

trustees and teachers that it was aptly labeled "the Miss Johns Hopkins." Bryn Mawr gave its first Ph.D. in 1888. Smith had given one to a woman in 1882, Pennsylvania in 1885, and Columbia in 1886.[18] But the very increase of alternatives for women applicants made the policy of refusing them appear more and more backward.

Masculine resistance began to weaken. In 1890, a woman gained admission to Craig's mathematical lectures, and in 1891 another entered the biological laboratory. Neither was enrolled as a student.[19] Nor was Florence Bascom, daughter of the former president of the University of Wisconsin, admitted as a student when she was allowed to follow the courses in geology, which were unobtainable anywhere else in the country.[20] But the board made a dramatic departure by awarding her the Ph.D. in 1893. After this exception, the university did not again give a Ph.D. to a woman until 1911.[21] The timing of the exception demands an explanation.

The early nineties was the period when most universities—notably Yale, Brown, Columbia, and Harvard—stopped dropping occasional crumbs and let women partake unhampered of graduate study. The University of Chicago welcomed women from its opening in 1892.[22] Clearly, the spirit of the times called for a revision at Hopkins such as the departure of 1893 seemed to represent.

But a problem closer home gives a plainer clue to the trustees' thinking. Precisely at the time when the hospital was opened and the long-heralded medical school was impatiently awaited by the public, the university found itself desperate for funds. In this dilemma, a group of influential and wealthy women offered what was, in spite of all the verbiage that surrounded it, a bribe. They proposed to raise an endowment in exchange for a guarantee that their sex

[18] Woodrow Wilson to Heath Dabney, Feb. 14, 1885, in *JH Alumni Magazine*, XXVIII (1939–1940), 80; Eells, "Earned Doctorates for Women," *AAUP Bulletin*, XLII, 647.

[19] Respectively, Miss Barnum and Miss Bickford (ECM, Dec. 15, 1890, Nov. 30, 1891).

[20] ECM, Feb. 19, April 13, 1891; Gilman to Mrs. Edward J. Rotter, June 6, 1893.

[21] Eells, "Earned Doctorates for Women," *AAUP Bulletin*, XLII, 650, errs in saying that Constance Pessels, who received the Ph.D. in English from Hopkins in 1894, was a woman. Information from the San Antonio high school where Pessels taught for many years establishes that he was a man (letter from Mrs. Dorothy Bundick, Sept. 8, 1958).

[22] Woody, *Women's Education*, II, 334–337.

would forever be admitted to the medical school with exactly the same entrance requirements as men. In October, 1890, the board accepted their gift of $100,000 and the special condition. In 1892, Mary Garrett assured the successful opening of the school by giving three times that much. She attached the condition not only of equality of the sexes, but also of very high standards in admissions policies.[23] It must have seemed ironical, to those trustees who chose to remember, that the initial reason for barring a woman had been the alleged inappropriateness for coeducation of what went on in the biological laboratory. One can surmise—certainly it is unprovable—that the trustees were put in a better frame of mind toward Miss Bascom during these years because, when the medical school hung in the balance, the scales were tipped by a woman's hand. Later at least one woman felt betrayed: Julia Rogers, an active figure in the Women's Fund drive, wrote Gilman in 1897 that she had torn up a will making Johns Hopkins her legatee because of the resurgent negative attitude toward her sex.[24]

Not until 1907, after a recommendation by the Academic Council, did the board establish the general policy of admitting women to graduate work; even then it gave a veto power to every faculty member in regard to his own courses. The historian of women's education in America has correctly named Johns Hopkins "the last of the great graduate institutions of the country to admit women." [25] Pioneer in so much, the university proved laggard here.

The story which recounts that Carey Thomas was informed she could hear Gildersleeve's teaching if she would sit behind a screen dividing her from the male students is almost surely apocryphal.[26] But its startling similarity to what happened to one Negro seeking higher education in the 1940s points to parallels in the struggle of these two minorities for equal educational privileges. Johns Hopkins came into existence in a period when women were demanding more and more the status of men; at the same moment Reconstruction was ending and the drive for Negro rights was grinding to a halt. Thus, while many women petitioned the trustees for access to the intellectual

---

[23] Chesney, *Johns Hopkins Hospital*, I, 193–221.

[24] Rogers to Gilman, March 6, 1897.

[25] French, *History of Johns Hopkins*, 75; Woody, *Women's Education*, II, 337.

[26] Finch, *Carey Thomas*, 71n.

offerings of Johns Hopkins, few Negroes had backgrounds that led them to expect such an opportunity. Nevertheless, the question of admitting Negroes arose.

In 1885, Moses S. Slaughter, a graduate student in Latin, entered a discussion of Johns Hopkins with a Negro who was interested in advanced study. The Negro maintained that his race was barred from the university. Slaughter denied this, but wrote to Gilman for reassurance. Gilman answered noncommittally, saying that all regulations on admission were published in the *Register.* He implied that Hopkins did not have the courses that the student wanted, and apparently the matter was dropped.[27]

A Hopkins Ph.D., writing in 1890, felt certain that Negroes would be admitted to the medical school when it opened.[28] His basis for this belief may have been the enrollment of Kelly Miller, a Negro, in the faculty of philosophy in 1887. Born in South Carolina during the war, Miller had received his bachelor's degree from Howard University in 1886. Under the influence of Newcomb, he entered Hopkins to study astronomy, mathematics, and physics. He stayed two years, but took no degree. As professor of mathematics at Howard after 1890 and later dean of the College of Arts and Science, he did important work in elevating standards there.[29]

Miller was not a conspicuous figure at Hopkins, and in 1923 a professor of the period erroneously recalled that no Negro was admitted during his day.[30] The local atmosphere must have been chilling. A young faculty member knew of no place in Baltimore where he could take as his luncheon guest a fellow Amherst alumnus, a Negro then teaching at Howard.[31] But when in the 1930s faculty members attacked a supposedly unexceptionable exclusion of Negroes, they found in the Gilman era the precedent they sought.[32]

[27] Slaughter to Gilman, June 5, 1885; Gilman to Slaughter, June 17, 1885 (draft). Since the Negro's name is not mentioned, it is impossible to be sure of the result.

[28] Jeffrey R. Brackett, *Notes on the Progress of the Colored People of Maryland since the War; A Supplement to The Negro in Maryland: A Study of the Institution of Slavery* (*JHU Studies in Historical and Political Science*, VIII, nos. 7–9; Baltimore, 1890), 65.

[29] E. Franklin Frazier, "Kelly Miller," DAB, XXII, 456–457.

[30] Hall, *Life and Confessions*, 246.

[31] Jameson diary, Feb. 8, 1885. The Negro friend was Wiley Lane.

[32] Broadus Mitchell, "Make Whom Free?" *JH Alumni Magazine*, XXVII (1938–1939), 1–3.

: CHAPTER XV :

The Student Adventure

ANY body of graduate students that included Woodrow Wilson, John Dewey, and Frederick Jackson Turner would merit historical attention, whether the institution harboring it were of special note in educational history or not. The context in which such men lived and thought even for so brief a time as a year (in the case of Turner) is worthy of study. It is highly probable, however, that gifted students like these arrive at a graduate school with the bent of their character and their avenues of intellectual interest largely determined. If the university provides such minds with encouragement and liberty to follow their own aspirations, it has filled an important need, and its defenders need claim no more for it.

Especially in the cases of Wilson and Turner, indications are strong that the teaching outside the home which influenced them most strongly took place at the collegiate level. Wilson's respect for President McCosh at Princeton bordered on adoration, and Turner was eminently the product of William F. Allen at Wisconsin. The case of Dewey is less clear. It was H. A. P. Torrey, his "excellent teacher" at the University of Vermont, who persuaded him to devote his life to philosophy, but the influence of G. S. Morris at Hopkins led Dewey into Hegelian idealism, which in spite of his later about-face left an indelible mark on his thought. Dewey himself remarked that regardless of his deviation from Morris' philosophic faith he would "be happy to believe that the influence of the spirit of his teaching has been an enduring influence." [1] Other students of noteworthy achievement showed a tendency to identify their intellectual awakening with college rather than postgraduate teachers. Jameson declared that it was while he was a freshman at Amherst that John W. Burgess' teaching made him resolve to devote his life to history, and his diary frequently holds up Professor Elihu Root of Amherst as his model of intellectual integrity. Shaw's continuing correspondence with Jesse Macy indicated that this teacher at Iowa College (Grinnell) had a strong shaping influence on his life.

Johns Hopkins did have a transforming impact on some of its students, though not on a Woodrow Wilson. To some who passed their days at Hopkins as inconspicuous undergraduates—men like Abraham Flexner and the astronomer James Edward Keeler, who arrived in 1878 as "a raw country boy from Florida"—the university was as much inspirational college as Amherst was for Jameson; and for the majority of graduate students, whose intellectual capacities promised usefulness but not greatness, Hopkins provided the influence that made them honest scholars and teachers. [2]

Quite aside from the formal intellectual offerings of the Hopkins faculty, the presence of students from all regions and many colleges stimulated those who enrolled there. Of the 923 students at Hopkins during its first decade, 45 per cent were from Maryland, but a great many of these were undergraduates. The four states ranking next after Maryland—New York, Massachusetts, Pennsylvania, and Ohio—accounted for 20 per cent. From the former Confederate states came 10 per cent; and from states west of the Mississippi, 6 per cent. The leaven of foreign students (over half of them from Canada, Germany, and Japan) made up 4 per cent of the total. [3] Students with degrees

[1] Baker, *Wilson*, I, 84; Fulmer Mood, "Turner's Formative Period," in *The Early Writings of Frederick Jackson Turner with a List of All His Works*, comp. by Everett E. Edwards (Madison, 1938), 9, 29; John Dewey, "From Absolutism to Experimentalism," in *Contemporary American Philosophy: Personal Statements*, ed. by George P. Adams and William Pepperell Montague (New York, 1930), II, 14, 18.

[2] Jameson, "A Possible Enrichment of the Teaching of History," *Amherst Graduates' Quarterly*, XVI (1926–1927), 69; Flexner, *I Remember, passim*; Gilman, *Launching of a University*, 18–19; Thomas R. Ball, "Memories," *JH Alumni Magazine*, XIV (1925–1926), 410.

[3] JHC, V, 79. Statistics given by H. B. Adams on the graduates in residence in 1888–1889 showed 98 from the South, 47 from the West, 26 from the Middle

from fifty-seven institutions had attended Hopkins by 1879, and in 1888–1889, graduates of ninety-six institutions were in residence.[4]

This breadth of origin was officially counted among the strengths of the institution. H. B. Adams, in a Commemoration Day address of 1889, claimed that Hopkins had realized George Washington's dream of a national university. In a plea for a lower tax burden on the university, Ely said of it, "It brings together American youth from every section and unites them in feelings of a common patriotism."[5] The students did indeed arrive with "local prejudices and sectional jealousies."[6] At times they verbally refought the Civil War.[7] Yet discussions of sectional problems between Northerner and Southerner at Hopkins were a part of the road to reunion. Wilson was especially adroit at "opening the eyes of northerners" during his student days, and after his return as a teacher he "emphasized the neglect of the sympathetic study of the South."[8] The bias against "Westernish" manners as being "a little too free and brusque," whether expressed by Walter B. Scaife of Pittsburgh or J. Franklin Jameson of Amherst, dwindled as one developed a friendship with Albert Shaw of Iowa or Charles Howard Shinn of California.[9] Jameson declared after two and a half years at Hopkins, "I have certainly done a great deal toward

---

States, and 18 from New England. He did not define his regions, but obviously included the many Marylanders as part of "the South." Had he set the Marylanders aside and combined the last two figures as representing "the East," he would have had less support for his contention that "this university is drawing college men from the same sources as those from which John[s] Hopkins drew his wealth, namely: from the South and West" (JHC, VIII, 42–43). Adams was, of course, trying to allay local complaints that the university was overrun with Northerners.

[4] ARJH (1879), 9; (1889), 28.   [5] JHC, VIII, 41–47; VII, 42–43.

[6] "By friendships and associations formed here in Baltimore these young men are learning to free themselves from local prejudices and sectional jealousies" (H. B. Adams, Commemoration Day address of 1889, in unidentified clipping, GP). I do not find this quotation in the address as it appears in JHC.

[7] "After lunch rummaged the Official Records (as far as I have them) with little result, in order to confute the opinion, which Bloomfield says is common in the South, that Massachusetts troops were the easiest to fight" (Jameson diary, April 15, 1884).

[8] Baker, *Wilson*, I, 190; Frederick Jackson Turner to Constance Lindsay Skinner, March 15, 1922, in Skinner, ed., "Turner's Autobiographic Letter," *Wisconsin Magazine of History*, XIX (1935–1936), 100.

[9] The quoted reference to this bias, which Scaife felt against Michigan residents and Jameson felt against Scaife, appears in Jameson to John Jameson, Oct. 15, 1882, quoted in Donnan and Stock, eds., *Historian's World*, 32n89.

outgrowing sectionalism since I came here." But he had no wish to lose his "hearty respect" for his native New England, and he challenged the opinion expressed in the *Nation* that student honesty on examinations was greater in the South than in the North.[10]

The variety of the graduate student body was more than regional. In age and experience it encompassed youths fresh from college and experienced teachers seeking another degree. John Ernest Matzke recalled of his arrival: "I was so immature that I scarcely knew what I wanted except this one thing: that I wanted to learn and knew I could work."[11] Albion Woodbury Small, on the other hand, left a professorship at Colby, spent one year at Hopkins earning a Ph.D., and returned to become president of the college. As to economic differences, the wealthy Allan Marquand lived at the St. James Hotel and gave money for an undergraduate scholarship, whereas John R. Commons attended on borrowed money which he was unable to repay for fourteen years.[12]

Visiting Boston in 1884, one Hopkins student wrote a friend: "This city offers so many advantages to make life full & happy, provided one has money; but with a small allowance I think Baltimore is to be preferred." Early and late, advocates of Johns Hopkins cited the economical living possible in the "overgrown town." In 1878 H. B. Adams compared expenses in Baltimore favorably with those in Germany:

It cost me $1,000 a year in Germany, and I didn't fare very well at that, although I tried all sorts of domestic economy, from the family of a pastor's widow to that of a Prussian baron. In Baltimore a student can live on the fat of the land for $500 a year. My actual living expenses, board, room, washing, etc., are $25 per month, and I board in a first-class place.

Eleven years later, he still preached the gospel that living in Baltimore was "vastly cheaper than at German universities."[13] Strict

[10] Jameson diary, Feb. 12, 1883; Jameson to editor, April 22, 1883, in *Nation*, XXXVI (April 26, 1883), 360.

[11] J. E. Matzke to A. M. Elliott, [1909–1910], quoted in Armstrong, "Elliott," *Elliott Monographs*, no. 15, p. 8.

[12] Sihler, *From Maumee to Thames*, 114; John R. Commons, *Myself* (New York, 1934), 41.

[13] W. B. Scaife to Albert Shaw, June 3, 1884; Alfred Emerson to Shaw, June 15, 1884; both in Shaw Papers; [Adams] to editor, May 14, 1878, *Amherst Student*, May 18, 1878; JHC, VIII, 47. For a similar description of the Baltimore price structure from the point of view of faculty life, see Ely, *Ground under Our Feet*, 174–175.

economy could bring discomforts, however. The motive announced for special furnishings in the biological library was that many students could "only afford to hire rather uncomfortable lodgings." One December, Jameson could count four successive days in which his room temperature did not rise to 60 degrees.[14]

But if the "room" had disadvantages, the "board" in Baltimore attained splendors undreamed of by cafeteria-fed students of a later day. At their best, boardinghouses could indeed preserve the advantages of "home life," which an official university statement attributed to them. None so surely deserves to be remembered as that of Mrs. DuBois Egerton, a woman who "laid no claim to literary attainments or social leadership," but who mothered students and bachelor teachers and provided them wholesome, delicious food for $5 a week. A few of her boarders had no connection with the university; thus, faculty, students, and townspeople met daily for good food and good talk, and participants often denoted the whole group as the "family." [15]

Like room and board, the tuition of $40 a half-year was low compared with that in universities farther north. A student who came without money enough and did not win one of the fellowships or scholarships could find other ways to keep financially above water. Early in 1878 the trustees set up a "Student Loan Fund," and in 1882 they approved a "scheme for enabling some students to earn a part of their tuition." A "press gang" among the students bolstered their incomes with newspaper work, and others lectured for pay in outlying towns. Admitting that many students worked for part of their support, Gilman concluded that they did so "usually at the expense of their orderly progress in intellectual pursuits." He felt that borrowing money was preferable.[16]

The necessities of shelter and food were not all that tied the Hopkins

---

[14] JHC, III, 85; Jameson diary, Dec. 10, 1880.

[15] ARJH (1882), 10; Nichols, "Remarkable Salon," *Home Journal,* Dec. 5, 1894; Lanman, "Living Reminiscences of Two or Three Generations Ago," printed copy of paper read before American Philosophical Society, April 24, 1937, Lanman Papers; Lanman diary, Oct. 15, 1876; Jameson to Shaw, Sept. 5, 1883, Shaw Papers; Albert S. Cook to Lanman, Oct. 17, 1880; Bloomfield to Lanman, Nov. 19, 1879; last two in Lanman Papers.

[16] JHC, II, 105; TM, Jan. 7, March 4, 1878; ECM, Dec. 2, 1882; Jameson diary, March 10, 1882; Ely, *Ground under Our Feet,* 109; Gilman to C. J. Goodwin, June 2, 1892. For further examples of student income making, see Howe, *Confessions,* 23.

students to Baltimore. They entered also into the religious life of the community. The father of Charles M. Andrews, though proud of Hopkins, where his son was pursuing graduate studies in history, wrote its president that he "could have wished for it a more decidedly *Christian* character." Charles had intimated to him that "the religious influences of his immediate associates have not been the most wholesome," and the father hoped that Gilman would give him counsel. Religious unorthodoxy indeed existed among the graduate students at Hopkins, but it rarely violated external conformity. In his first year at Hopkins, 1877–1878, Harvard graduate Irving Stringham announced, "Where there is no question of principle involved I avoid practices which offend the religious tastes of others." Albert Shaw referred to a minister whose sermon he had just heard as "an old-fashioned Presbyterian fogy who preaches too much systematic theology and too little practical gospel to suit me." Yet he went often to Wednesday-night prayer meetings and spoke to a church gathering on the work of home missions in the West.[17] John Dewey recalled that his personal religion did not constitute a leading philosophical problem for him during his Hopkins days because of "a feeling that any genuinely sound religious experience could and should adapt itself to whatever beliefs one found oneself intellectually entitled to hold." [18]

Dewey's feeling was very much in keeping with the general mood among Hopkins graduate students, whose religious lives proved profoundly adaptable. A student was no more likely to hear a sermon on "Eternal Punishment" by Mr. Jones or on "the insufficiency of the Confucian & Buddhist theologies" by Mr. Holmes in the morning than to hear James Freeman Clarke or Edward Everett Hale at the Unitarian church in the evening. On the next Sunday he might go to Quaker meeting to hear Trustee Thomas talk.[19] A Jewish student, with similar breadth, would go to more than one synagogue and occasionally to Protestant and Catholic churches.[20]

[17] W. W. Andrews to Gilman, April 15, 1889; W. I. Stringham to Charles Eliot Norton, March 29, 1878, C. E. Norton Papers (by permission of the Harvard College Library); Shaw diary, Jan. 18, 25, 29, Feb. 1, March 8, 1882.
[18] Dewey, "From Absolutism to Experimentalism," in *Contemporary American Philosophy,* ed. by Adams and Montague, II, 19.
[19] Lanman diary, Jan. 13, 1878, April 11, 1880, Jan. 26, 1879; Shaw diary, Feb. 5, March 26, 1882.
[20] Adler, *I Have Considered,* 54–55.

The Student Adventure

The social life of Baltimore in the 1870s and 1880s managed to retain both the romantic aura of the Lost Cause and the tangible benefits of having been geographically on the victorious side. It was the fate of university students, as well as faculty members, to be accepted wholeheartedly into this society, in fact to become rather the rage. Baltimoreans who felt themselves more "cultured" than their fellow townsmen were eager to form university associations. Students were encouraged to include not only the families of professors and trustees, but also other townspeople, in their rounds of calls, and young men gathered in the parlors of families with attractive daughters, since "dating" was unheard of. The girls showed great imagination in keeping Hopkins students about them, organizing clubs with little purpose other than party giving, such as a "Twenty Questions Club." [21]

Baltimore did not lack music and theater. The audiences at Peabody concerts and concert rehearsals included many Hopkins students. As to the opera, one did not hesitate to miss a lecture of John Fiske's in order to hear Etelka Gerster and Italo Campanini together, even if it were necessary to borrow money for the ticket.[22] A student at Hopkins could see the greatest actors of the day on tour—Edwin Booth in *Hamlet*, Joseph Jefferson in *Rip Van Winkle*, and Ernesto Rossi in *Edmund Kean*.[23] For less exalted entertainment, he could attend *Uncle Tom's Cabin*, the minstrels, "a 'Variety Show' of rather low tone," or a professional baseball game.[24] With its bright pretty girls and theatrical delights, Baltimore tempted one constantly to become less a student.

Besides the pleasures of the city, there was the comradeship of various clubs which were chiefly the creations of graduate students. Directly descended from the original *Kneipe* was the Johns Hopkins University Club of the 1880s, or so its membership and customs would indicate. Letters to Lanman after his departure for Harvard tell of

---

[21] Henry Holt, *Garrulities of an Octogenarian Editor: With Other Essays Somewhat Biographical and Autobiographical* (Boston and New York, 1923), 143; Penniman, "Hopkins Athletics," *JH Alumni Magazine*, XXVIII, 104; Shaw diary, Jan. 30, 1882; Lanman diary, March 18, 1880.

[22] Lanman diary, Feb. 17, March 3, 1877; Jameson diary, Jan. 20, 1881.

[23] Lanman diary, March 14, Dec. 25, 1877; Shaw diary, Jan. 6, 1882.

[24] Lanman diary, April 5, 1877, Jan. 16, Feb. 6, 1878; Woodrow Wilson to Ellen Axson, April 20, 1884, quoted in Baker, *Wilson*, I, 192.

the club's emergence in the fall of 1880. Cook wrote to Lanman that the new club was "designed to promote sociality, and all that." One member during the mid-eighties recalled that only fellows and faculty members were admitted, but in the beginning at least the only barrier was against undergraduates.[25] The group avoided organizational encumbrances: a steward, hired with the five-dollar annual dues, kept beer supplied and an open fire going in the rented room behind the Jordan Stabler grocery. A fellow wrote of his first visit to the club in December, 1881, that it was "stupid, all playing cards, smoking and drinking beer; . . . just the sort of thing that college fellows think is enjoyment." But enough Hopkins men valued "sociality, and all that" to keep the club going. A fellow who joined in 1884 or 1885 recalled more favorable aspects—chess, magazines, talk, and Saturday-night gatherings at which Professor Gildersleeve presided and English, Latin, and German songs were sung.[26]

The club behind Stabler's grocery did not end the metamorphosis of the *Kneipe* of 1876. It gave way in the fall of 1887 to an even more formal organization, the University Club, with Gildersleeve as president. The Stabler club was "dissolved in favor of" the University Club and its furniture sold at auction. The observation of Professor John C. French that the new club was "not in any sense a student organization" is clearly borne out by the contemporary comment of one of the readers: "The Cardinal, Mr. Bonaparte, Judge Brown, ('Bob' Garrett) and so on belong. I doubt much whether I shall make much use of [the club] this year, but at least it is pleasant to meet so many choice people." [27] From the beer drinkers of 1876 to the "choice people" of 1887 had been, surely, as remarkable an institutional development as any that H. B. Adams' students traced in the New England villages. Part of the informal social life shifted to the

[25] Minton Warren to Lanman, Nov. 28, 1880; Albert S. Cook to Lanman, Dec. 12, 1880, both in Lanman Papers; Adler, *I Have Considered*, 51. One historian of the university gives January 16, 1879, as the club's founding date (French, *History of Johns Hopkins*, 80). But Lanman, who attended this meeting in the rooms of Ernest and Christian Sihler, recorded in his diary only that it was "a reunion of the *Fellows*" at which he had "a jolly merry time" (Lanman diary, Jan. 16, 1879).

[26] French, *History of Johns Hopkins*, 80; Jameson diary, Dec. 3, 1881; Adler, *I Have Considered*, 51–52.

[27] Adler, *I Have Considered*, 60; French, *History of Johns Hopkins*, 80–81; H. W. Smyth to his mother, Nov. 8, 1887, Smyth Papers.

fraternities, which included many graduate students.[28] But the spirit of the earliest *Kneipe* could be revived whenever a small group of students decided on an evening of drinking and good talk.

In 1879 some undergraduates formed a glee club and elected Lanman president. A longer-lived glee club, predominated by graduate students, appeared in the fall of 1883 and included Woodrow Wilson among its original members. Its first concert, given in Hopkins Hall on February 14, 1884, attracted few members of the university, much to the satisfaction of Jameson who branded such activities by "young men who were old enough to know better" as "childish and undignified." However undignified, the singers tried to use their gifts for good works, performing on one occasion for the benefit of a suburban workingmen's library. The group survived the eighties, though it came close to being swallowed up by an even more undignified "banjo club," which also had graduate students as members.[29]

Had he never achieved fame, Woodrow Wilson would still merit a small place in any history of Johns Hopkins as founder of its most ambitious and original student organization, "The Students' 'House of Commons.'" It was on December 15, 1884, that Wilson transformed the moribund Literary Society, a branch of the Matriculate Society, by getting it to adopt a new constitution which he and others had drawn up.[30] A letter from an undergraduate to the *Nation* the next fall gave the credit for the new departure to "one of the Fellows in History," who had drafted the constitution on the model of one that had been used at another college.[31] Complete with speaker, prime minister, foreign secretary, and home secretary, the organization closely imitated the procedure of the British House of Commons; the ministry presented bills, the success of which determined its tenure

[28] William L. Devries to Gilman, May 18, 1890; Howe, *Confessions*, 30. See p. 254 above.

[29] Lanman diary, Oct. 6, 8, 11, 1879; J. F. Jameson to John Jameson, Feb. 17, 1884, in Donnan and Stock, eds., *Historian's World*, 33; Jameson diary, Feb. 11, 1884; Woodrow Wilson to Ellen Axson, April 27, 1884, quoted in Baker, *Wilson*, I, 191; JHC, VIII, 48; French, *History of Johns Hopkins*, 308–309; William L. Devries to Gilman, May 18, 1890.

[30] Diary of Henry R. Slack, quoted in French, *History of Johns Hopkins*, 265; "J.H.U., '83" to editor, Nov. 30, 1885, in *Nation*, XLI (Dec. 3, 1885), 464.

[31] This could be either the Liberal Debating Club of Princeton, which Wilson had organized in 1876–1877, or the Jefferson Society of the University of Virginia (French, *History of Johns Hopkins*, 265; Baker, *Wilson*, I, 94–95, 124).

of office. "The Opposition benches," wrote the correspondent to the *Nation*, "are, as a rule, almost as full as the ministerial seats, causing the rivalry to be very active and the interest unflagging." The group met every Monday evening, with twenty-five to thirty being considered a good attendance. By the fall of 1885, it had doubled its membership, apparently with more undergraduate members than graduate.

The faculty and president supported the venture and at times proposed subjects for debate—Ely even drafted a bill. Among the earliest bills debated were proposals for a Nicaraguan canal and admission of ex-Presidents to the Senate.[32] In the 1886–1887 term a bill to make voting compulsory lost and a resolution declaring the Knights of Labor unconstitutional and "not productive of good to the workingmen" passed; in 1887–1888 a prohibition of the leasing of convict labor lost and punishment for polygamy passed; in 1888–1889 regulation of transportation rates passed and prohibition of trusts lost.[33] The members of the House, despite the conservative tendency of their voting, were reformist enough to hope for the spread of their type of debating society; and Bryn Mawr, the Columbia law school, and Wesleyan imitated the Hopkins program. But letters to the *Nation* suggested that societies at Union and Cornell based on the Congressional pattern suited American colleges better.[34] Even with its expansionist zeal and national publicity, the Hopkins House of Commons suffered the same vicissitudes as its predecessors. In the fall of 1886 it could claim only undergraduate members, the quorum was cut to one-fourth, and at one meeting the ministry was censured for failure to provide bills. At the end of the decade the House languished. An address by Wilson in 1891 gave it a final burst of life, but it disappeared with the graduation of its leading members in 1892. A life of eight years was a long one as student organizations at Hopkins went, and this one had played a worthy role in keeping undergraduates and graduates in touch with each other and with social problems.[35]

[32] Langdon Williams to editor, Nov. 16, 1885, in *Nation*, XLI (Nov. 26, 1885), 445; quoted in JHC, V, 49.

[33] JHC, VI, 86; VII, 80; VIII, 105.

[34] Condé Hamlin to editor, *Nation*, XLI (Dec. 3, 1885), 464; F. to editor, *ibid.* (Dec. 17, 1885), 508; French, *History of Johns Hopkins*, 266; Baker, *Wilson*, I, 302–304.

[35] JHC, VI, 86, 127, X, 85; French, *History of Johns Hopkins*, 267.

The fall of 1884, when Wilson transformed the Literary Society, was a fruitful season for student organizations. An Art Circle appeared as an offshoot of the Archaeological Society, and two faculty members, Browne and Wood, guided a new Shakespeare Circle. More lasting than either of these was the Young Men's Christian Association, which a group of twenty-five organized on November 25. Although the connection with the national organization was broken from 1886 to 1889, the group continued active and growing. The breadth of its membership appeared in the officers elected in January, 1888: Marion D. Learned, a young faculty member, president; Frank W. Blackmar, a fellow, vice-president; and William L. Devries, an undergraduate, treasurer. The group met approximately twice a month and heard such speakers as Trustee Thomas on local mission work; Ely on Christian socialism; Toyokichi Iyenaga, a Japanese student, on the religion of his homeland; and the Rev. W. F. Slocum on education for Negroes in the South. But it did more than listen to lectures. It issued handbooks for new students and entered into the charity programs of the city, aiding such organizations as the South Baltimore Working-Men's Club and doing Sunday-school work in the state penitentiary and elsewhere.[36] Thus it probably brought its members closer to social realities than did the formalized reading and debating of bills in the House of Commons. The religious liberality which had long imbued student life at Hopkins characterized the YMCA. After a local merchant, Eugene C. Levering, gave $20,000 in 1889 to erect a building for the association, this liberality brought disagreement. Mr. Levering would not allow Roman Catholic or Unitarian periodicals in the reading room of the new building, whereas the association favored including them, observing that it had Roman Catholics as full members and Unitarians as associate members. Aside from this hindrance, Levering Hall was a blessing to the group, which by 1889 included 125 active members.[37] With the YMCA firmly established and Levering Hall as a monument to its work, Gilman could point to a tangible symbol of the religious spirit in the university, and he owed it to the zeal of a student organization and its recognition by a local citizen.

Stanley Hall reported the existence of a writer's club among the

[36] JHC, IV, 26; French, *History of Johns Hopkins*, 325; JHC, VII, 80, 90.
[37] Marion D. Learned to Gilman, May 4, 1890; JHC, VIII, 105.

students in May, 1888, but he decried the lack of faculty guidance for students with such interests.[38] Despite its failure to win a literary figure for the faculty, however, the university had tried to aid students with literary inclinations. To an anonymous gift for literary prizes in the spring of 1887 the trustees had added a year's free tuition. The two prizes, in a competition limited to graduate students, went to Richard E. Burton and James Cummings, both of the English department. Burton, who had read his "An Ode to the Johns Hopkins University" at the tenth anniversary observance, soon began publishing his poems in *Harper's* and the *Century*.[39]

The interest in newspaper work both as a part-time student occupation and as a future career made it inevitable that sooner or later a movement for a student newspaper would be launched. A graduate student, Erasmus Haworth, had failed in his efforts of 1882 to arouse interest in such an undertaking. Another graduate student, David Hull Holmes, made the first such formal request to the trustees in the spring of 1889. The next fall the board declared the project undesirable and forbade such a publication "by any person or persons connected with the university." [40] Although one sympathetic historian has attributed this suppression to fear that the small student body could not support the venture, a letter from Thomas to Gilman in 1890 proves otherwise. Thomas felt that the "Harvard boys" had disgraced themselves with their publication and that, despite the great pressure for a student newspaper at Hopkins, it could be "only a source of anxiety." It was eloquent of the changed nature of the university that when the trustees gave in at last, in 1897, and allowed the *News-Letter* to appear, it was controlled by undergraduates.[41]

The organizational tendencies which graduate students had carried with them to Johns Hopkins continued after they left the university. Former graduate students played the major roles in organizing the Alumni Association, and the fact that they had a loyalty to another alma mater seemed not in the least to dampen their ardor for

---

[38] Hall to Thomas Wentworth Higginson, May 12, 1888, Thomas Wentworth Higginson Papers, Houghton Library. By permission of the Harvard College Library.

[39] JHC, VI, 124; V, 100, 111–112; VII, 75.

[40] Jameson diary, March 6, 1882; ECM, May 31, 1889; TM, Oct. 7, 1889.

[41] French, *History of Johns Hopkins*, 275–276; Thomas to Gilman, June 4, 1890.

Johns Hopkins. The early presidents of the association were recipients of the Ph.D., the first three being Allan Marquand, Josiah Royce, and Woodrow Wilson. Those with Hopkins A.B.'s were also enthusiastic, and a member of this group was regularly elected secretary. The alumni's decision to organize came at a tenth anniversary luncheon in 1886. Jameson declared the organization to be "of course worked by wires from headquarters," but he felt that it might be useful. Certainly Gilman welcomed the group and the branch associations that appeared in Washington and New York by 1889. The prevalence of Ph.D.'s differentiated this organization little from other alumni groups. The principal function was a gathering on Commemoration Day for a luncheon and addresses, and one of the first projects was to present the university a bust of C. D. Morris. For a university that could already glimpse the shoals of poverty ahead, organized alumni were a reassurance, even if most of them did live on teachers' salaries.[42]

Although student organizational activities provided symbols of status and opportunities for conviviality, they often shared the serious intellectual purpose of the institution and provided channels for thoughtful intercourse. Discussions could easily take place around the clubroom fire behind the grocery. But students needed no clubs in order to talk. In their rooms, on their walks together, at the boarding-house dinner tables, almost everywhere, they indulged their desire to test and share their thinking. Politics was a favorite subject, never more so than in 1884 during the Blaine-Cleveland campaign. Student support was overwhelming for Cleveland, even among the many Republicans. The arts were not neglected: a student might exchange with two young faculty members ideas on Howells and James, and an evening's talk (over lowly oysters) might soar to "the relations of form to the idea." [43] Religion—the Salvation Army, Dwight L. Moody, materialism, immortality—could inspire hours of debate.[44] These

[42] JHC, V, 100, VI, 71, VII, 48; Jameson diary, Feb. 22, 1887; Gilman to Benjamin Tuska, Jan. 8, 1889. A detailed account appears in French, *History of Johns Hopkins*, 390–401.

[43] W. B. Scaife to Shaw, Dec. 1, 1884, Shaw Papers; Jameson diary, Dec. 3, 1884, March 2, 1883; H. W. Smyth to his parents, Feb. 26, 1888, Smyth Papers. The participants in the last case were a reader and an instructor, not graduate students.

[44] Jameson diary, Nov. 7, 11, 1880, Nov. 19, 1883.

shared explorations of ideas could often quicken the students more effectively than anything "taught" in the rooms of the university. But the harvest was not only one of intellect. Friendship flourished when it fed on honest and unrestrained talking together.

Sometimes this comradeship would include doing nonacademic reading in co-operation, for example, when two students read aloud together Owen Meredith's *Lucile* and poems and essays from the *Century*. More typically a student did his general reading alone, as in the case of Jameson, who reserved Friday mornings "for the Nation, the periodicals at the J.H.U., and the great writers" and read something not connected with his studies at the end of each day. The student seeking escape from the pressure of his intellectual chores might resort to novels: often the installments in the *Century* or *Atlantic* were irresistible. Jameson enjoyed *A Modern Instance, Daisy Miller,* and *Ecce Homo.*[45] Shaw found *Ben-Hur* disgusting, but fell under the spell of Mrs. Mulock-Craik and spent one day reading her *Young Mrs. Jardine* nearly through. The writer read by probably the greatest number of Hopkins students, however, was not a novelist; he was, appropriately, the early delineator of the American scholar —Ralph Waldo Emerson. Even in the private reading of the students, the university played its role, displaying in the "New Book Department" books received on consignment from publishers which students could examine and purchase.[46]

To speak only of social and religious life, of conversations held and novels read, is to stay on the periphery of graduate student life at Johns Hopkins. What brought these young men to one place and held them there was their common venture into the world of learning. The essential qualities that made them a community appeared in their studies, their relationships with the faculty, their shared scholarly dreams and ambitions. It was this fact of community that underlay the advice given by Jameson to Shaw on the question of his returning to Johns Hopkins in 1883. Jameson concluded that the university did not offer much in the way of instruction just then, but it might nevertheless be "a good place to work in." Shaw must

[45] Shaw diary, Jan. 14, 22, 29, 1882; Jameson diary, Oct. 11, March 22, Nov. 29, 1881, July 3, 1882, April 8, 22, 1883.

[46] Shaw diary, Feb. 12, 5, Jan. 29, 1882; Jameson diary, March 22, 1881; Lanman diary, Dec. 29, 1878; ARJH (1882), 57, (1883), 46; French, *History of Johns Hopkins,* 221.

have found it so, for his efforts resulted in his volume on Icaria, which James Bryce praised as giving "that truer & wider meaning to History which is to be preferred to the narrow Freemanic definition of History = past politics, Politics = present History." Looking back after his long career as editor of the *Review of Reviews*, Shaw observed, "In those early years we studied hard, had too little recreation, and offered no attractions for playboys." [47] There was recreation, of course, but hard work set the tone of the place. Martin traced a broken lock in the biology laboratory to two promising students who had insisted on working when the laboratory was closed; he asked Gilman to feign ignorance and take no action. Jameson was not atypical when he labored through the night on a political-economy paper for H. C. Adams, keeping himself awake with tea. Although the labor was not always directed toward the most elevated ideal of education, the student who engaged in cramming knew very well the limitations of that expedient.[48] Wilson in 1884 described the results of such forced ingestion:

The examination [in colonial history] took place on Saturday last, and a very fair, sensible examination it was. Adams gave out five topics and told us to choose, each man for himself, one from the number and spend the two hours in writing an informal essay upon it. That's the sort of examination I like. But it wasn't the sort I had expected; and I went in crammed with one or two hundred dates and one or two thousand minute particulars about the quarrels of nobody knows who with an obscure Governor, for nobody knows what. Just think of all that energy wasted! The only comfort is that this mass of information won't long burden me. I shall forget it with great ease.[49]

Worse than cramming was the unavoidable drudgery of copying. Cyrus Adler's transcribing of his dissertation of over six hundred pages in two weeks was herculean. Excepting the Sabbaths, his daily regimen allowed time for meals, an hour's walk, and two hours' sleep; the rest of each day he spent copying. Students paid a physical price for their intellectual excesses in headaches, strained eyes, and nervous

---

[47] Jameson to Shaw, Feb. 27, [1883], Shaw Papers; Albert Shaw, *Icaria: A Chapter in the History of Communism* (New York and London, 1884); Bryce to Shaw, Nov. 27, 1884, Shaw Papers; Shaw, "Recollections," GP.

[48] Martin to Gilman, Dec. 13, 1886; Jameson diary, Jan. 6, 7, Nov. 29, 1881.

[49] Woodrow Wilson to John Hanson Kennard, Jr., Nov. 18, 1884, in New York *Sun*, April 18, 1933.

dyspepsia.[50] But they found what Wilson called "a sort of grim satisfaction in tiring one's mind out" and loved the university even as it made them suffer.

What was the spur that drove these students? It was not far different, one may assume, from the ambition bred of an individualistic era or from the social mobility bred of an open society that drove millions of their fellow countrymen in careers outside academic halls. An internalized Calvinist heritage was plain in some efforts: "It's quite as necessary," wrote Wilson during his second year at Hopkins, "for the Christian to work as for him to be glad." [51] Sometimes the goad came as envy and frustration. After hearing a paper at the history seminary on "Von Holst's View of the Constitution of the United States," [52] Jameson went home to write in his diary, "Wilson showed the greatest logical skill and ability in the discussion of it, and I greatly envied him; when I got to my room, had a very discouraged feeling." [53] Inviting successful graduates back for lectures, a policy of some faculty members, stimulated the aspirations of those still laboring at Hopkins, and as early as 1887 students felt challenged by the achievements of former Hopkins students who were "spoken of as the lights of the past." [54] Although himself an intensely competitive person, H. B. Adams liked to stress the co-operative aspect of the work of his students:

A word is passed here, a hint is given there; a new fact or reference, casually discovered by one man, is communicated to another to whom it is of more special interest; a valuable book, found in some Baltimore library or antiquarian bookstore, is recommended, or purchased for a friend. . . .

[50] Adler, *I Have Considered,* 63–64; Lanman diary, Nov. 5, 1878; Wilson to Ellen Axson, Nov. 1, 1884, quoted in Baker, *Wilson,* I, 188.

[51] Wilson to Ellen Axson, Jan. 20, 1885, quoted in Baker, *Wilson,* I, 183.

[52] By Edward P. Allinson, a visiting Philadelphia lawyer (JHC, III, 70).

[53] Jameson diary, Jan. 18, 1884. His chagrin at Wilson's supposed superior abilities did not prevent him from calling Wilson's introduction to *Congressional Government* "about the ablest and maturest paper ever read" at the seminary, though a later portion of the work which Wilson read there "wasn't especially interesting" to Jameson (*ibid.,* May 9, Oct. 17, 1884). Wilson himself called the later chapter "the driest of the lot" (Wilson to Ellen Axson, Oct. 17, 1884, quoted in Baker, *Wilson,* I, 218). Another example of healthy envy because of Wilson's success (a favorable review of his *Congressional Government*) appears in Arthur Yager to Albert Shaw, Feb. 19, 1885, Shaw Papers.

[54] Vincent, "Adams," in *American Masters,* ed. by Odum, 125; Charles M. Andrews to his mother, Nov. 13, 1887, quoted in Eisenstadt, *Andrews,* 33.

It is interesting to observe this spirit of friendly reciprocity even among rivals for . . . fellowships and scholarships.

But the aftermath of the contest for stipends was not always friendly. Jameson wrote to Shaw in 1883: "The competition is going to be sharp, and I fear there will be, with our three prizes, n-3 'soreheads.'"[55]

Another force that made for hard-working students was the example of a hard-working faculty. Although the reappearance of one's successful predecessors might make the goal seem achievable, what made the goal seem glorious was the faculty at hand. Students knew that their professors were respected throughout the scholarly world and—more important—saw by what sheer hard work they accomplished their scholarship. The ratio of active faculty members to total enrollment—graduate, undergraduate, and special—was one to six in 1879–1880, one to seven in 1884–1885, and one to nine in 1888–1889. Thus, the student's opportunity for the "personal counsel and instruction" announced in 1878 declined somewhat during the years that followed.[56] But the most important relationships probably continued undiminished. Jameson observed that the major benefit from the faculty was not instruction, but stimulus and method, and Wilson reached the similar conclusion that professors gave bibliography and inspiration or suggestion, but not learning.[57] These contributions usually came best from example. This is not to say, of course, that an aloof example was all the student wanted or needed from the faculty. All but the most strongly motivated needed encouragement, and all but the most able needed guidance. John Ernest Matzke, writing to Marshall Elliott in after years, showed the confidence which the teacher had bestowed from the time of their first meeting: "I felt so small and ignorant that I did not know what to say. Yet before the interview was over I was at ease and confident that you would lead me. And you never failed me. I could always come to you and meet

[55] Adams, *Methods of Historical Study,* 108–109; Jameson to Shaw, Feb. 27, [1883], Shaw Papers.

[56] JHR (1878), 16. My count of faculty members, based on JHR, is more conservative than faculty totals found in official statements. I count 28, 41, and 45 "active" faculty members in each term respectively.

[57] Jameson to Shaw, Feb. 27, [1883], Shaw Papers; Wilson to R. Heath Dabney, Feb. 14, 1885, quoted in Baker, *Wilson,* I, 179.

the encouragement I needed." [58] As Gilman pointed out after his retirement, a student beginning his research activity must have guidance to prevent his investigations from being useless, repetitive, or "isolated and unrelated." [59] From such frustration, many Hopkins students were saved. They had instead the satisfaction of hearing their works hailed as worthy contributions to knowledge.

In some cases the students pressed for higher standards and longer schedules than the faculty planned. H. B. Adams infuriated Jameson in 1881 by making the comparative constitutional history course "broader and more general" and admitting "the element that knows not German." In 1884 Craig's seminar began to meet for an additional hour on Saturday—at the students' request. Student independence of immediate faculty supervision was perhaps never more clearly shown than in 1888–1889, when Minton Warren's illness forced him to take a year's absence. The advanced students simply transformed the seminary into "The Latin Society," elected as president John Leverett Moore, instructor in Latin and like themselves a candidate for the Ph.D., and continued to function with such bibliographical help and research suggestions as they could get by mail from Professor Emil Hübner of Berlin. [60]

The advantages of the university, though highly praised by many, showed their limitations to the students in actual residence, and Hopkins did not hold all who came there. Thorstein Veblen, after pursuing political economy for the first half of the 1881–1882 term (Ely's first), decided that he could work more profitably at Yale and departed. [61] Dissatisfied with many things at Hopkins in the 1880–1881 term, Jameson turned his attention to the new School of Political Science, which his former teacher at Amherst, John W. Burgess, had founded at Columbia. When he heard Burgess lecture in April, 1881, however, he decided that he could get as much himself from books and that the change would not be worth the expense. When he failed to get a fellowship in June, he told Gilman that he had decided to go to Harvard. Gilman said he thought this a good idea, but he saw to it that before the summer was over this promising student had a

---

[58] See note 11 above.   [59] Gilman, *Launching of a University*, 243.
[60] Jameson diary, Feb. 4, 1881; Craig to Gilman, Oct. 21, 1884; JHC, VIII, 52, 66–68.
[61] Jameson diary, Nov. 23, 1881, Feb. 4, 1882.

fellowship.[62] The official Hopkins policy did not necessarily oppose such transfers, and Gildersleeve expressed at the tenth anniversary celebration the wish

that the university departments in all American institutions of learning might be so organized that students could pass from one to the other in the prosecution of a line of study just as they do in Germany, much to the advantage of their breadth of vision, their freedom from local or personal influence.

But students dissatisfied with Hopkins or seeking "breadth of vision" found few alternatives for advanced study in the United States, especially alternatives with liberal scholarships and fellowships. After some initial disillusionment, Wilson declared Johns Hopkins "the best place in America to study." [63]

The dissatisfied student more often looked upon Europe as the proper destination if one shook the dust of Hopkins from his feet. Less than three months after his arrival at Hopkins, Jameson borrowed from H. C. Adams a prospectus of the Ecole Libre des Sciences Politiques in Paris. Examining it, he declared: "It is very attractive, giving me many things I need. I shall go there. My present plan for two years in Europe is a half year each at Berlin, Ghent or Heidelberg, Paris and London." In Jameson's case the plans for international study were never carried out. A student financially better able to please himself was Walter B. Scaife. In the 1883–1884 term, he became "fiercely dissatisfied" with H. B. Adams and had at least one "beastly row." Scaife's idea of escape was to "pull up stakes and go to Germany in June." Still at Hopkins the next year, he declared himself "often like a caged bird . . . pining for some solid food." In 1885 he did depart, and he became in 1887, according to Jameson, the first American to receive the Ph.D. at the University of Vienna. The professors of greatest reputation were not exempt from unrest among their students. Francis Albert Christie in 1885 felt that he was getting too little from Gildersleeve and "declared a project of going to Germany next summer for a year or two of study." [64]

[62] Jameson to John Jameson, Jan. 16, 1881, in Donnan and Stock, eds., *Historian's World,* 19; Jameson diary, Jan. 5, April 13, June 9, 1881.

[63] JHC, V, 105; Wilson to R. Heath Dabney, Feb. 17, 1884, quoted in Baker, *Wilson,* I, 173.

[64] Jameson diary, Dec. 1, 1880, Dec. 17, 1883, Jan. 3, 1884, Feb. 24, 1885; Scaife to Shaw, Dec. 1, 1884, Shaw Papers; Jameson to John Jameson, July 24, 1887, quoted in Donnan and Stock, eds., *Historian's World,* 32n89.

Although some claimed as the greatest achievement of Hopkins that it kept American youth at home for advanced study, its president and faculty encouraged students to go on for work in Europe. The leaders of Johns Hopkins looked on their institution as part of an international university community, and they were well aware of the rich offering of their brethren across the Atlantic. They wanted these fruits for their most promising students and at the same time hoped that exporting talent would gain prestige for Hopkins. In 1881 Craig wrote Gilman what he doubtless already knew: "The sending to Europe of such men as [Edwin H.] Hall and [Irving] Stringham does a very great deal in making the Johns Hopkins favorably known." The two had just won Hopkins Ph.D.'s. Hall, who was to return as assistant in physics, sent back at Gilman's request descriptions of his observations of European physics laboratories. He followed much of Rowland's itinerary of 1875 and worked in Helmholtz' laboratory in Berlin. Stringham sent back word of Klein's mathematical seminary at Leipzig. When John Dewey received his Ph.D. in 1884, Gilman called him to his office and after warning him not to remain so seclusive and bookish offered him a loan for study in Europe. In 1887 the university accepted the privilege of nominating one of its graduate students as "scholar" at the Ecole Libre des Sciences Politiques and granted him his Ph.D. at the end of his year there.[65] The attitude of the university was not misrepresented by H. B. Adams when he wrote in 1887, "Men who can afford to do so ought to combine the best that France, Germany, England and America have to teach in the line of methods and special literature . . . and to make the resultant culture connect with the academic, civic, economic or political needs of our own country."[66]

Relations with European universities and approval from European scholars were avidly sought by the faculty of Johns Hopkins, and encouraging European study by their students was part of this

[65] Craig to Gilman, [Oct., 1881]; Edwin H. Hall to Gilman, July 31, 1881; Stringham to Gilman, April 28, 1882; Jane M. Dewey, ed., "Biography of John Dewey," in *The Philosophy of John Dewey*, ed. by Paul Arthur Schilpp (2nd ed.; New York, 1951), 16; JHC, VI, 128. The student in the last case was Thomas Kimber Worthington.

[66] Introductory note to letter of T. K. Worthington to H. B. Adams, Dec. 1, 1887, in Andrew D. White, *European Schools of History and Politics* (*JHU Studies in Historical and Political Science*, V, no. 12; Baltimore, 1887), 57.

tendency. Nevertheless, the university felt itself in competition with its European counterparts, especially the German, and in the earliest years a youthful boasting occurred that verged on intellectual chauvinism. In his second year as fellow, H. B. Adams sent a letter to the student newspaper at Amherst boldly asserting that students who had been at Göttingen found the lecture and laboratory instruction they received at Hopkins just as good and that a former Hopkins fellow had reported from Leipzig that Hopkins methods in both Greek and Sanskrit were "more satisfactory to an *American student.*" In 1881 E. H. Hall wrote back from Berlin with similar pride: "The Phys[ics] Department of the J.H.U. need not feel ashamed of its Professors, its apparatus, or its corps of students, in comparison with any similar institution I have yet seen." Sometimes the status of Hopkins vis-à-vis German universities was described more analytically and calmly, as, for instance, in the comments of Gildersleeve while traveling in Europe in 1880. He wrote Gilman that he feared American students tended to adopt the least desirable qualities of German scholarship, such as cumbrousness of apparatus, thickness of material topped with thin conclusions, and mechanical application of routine methods of criticism. He himself had studied in Germany in an earlier period and felt that classical philology in America needed the sound basis of "the old ideal school." Philology, he maintained, could be kept scientific without sacrificing its connection with "our general life." His determination to link humanism and science implied that Hopkins might provide for the American student what would be missed in Germany, though he did not specifically say so.[67]

Within the family, Hopkins men might find fault with the German universities, but let them be attacked elsewhere in America and Hopkins would hurry to their defense as paragons of learning. Indeed, since Hopkins was so generally considered to be patterned on them, there was an element of self-justification in defending the German universities. In 1878 Royce answered strictures by President McCosh on German universities, which included accusations that they made supercilious scoffers of American students and alienated them from sober common sense. Royce replied that on the contrary much evidence indicated "calmness and freedom of discussion" and re-

[67] [Adams] to editor, May 14, 1878, *Amherst Student,* May 18, 1878; E. H. Hall to Gilman, July 31, 1881; Gildersleeve to Gilman, Aug. 8, 1880.

sistance to "hasty systematizing," especially in Germany's current Kant revival.[68] But though brash attack and brash defense, shallow objections and sober criticism were all adopted at times by Hopkins scholars speaking of European universities, the overriding attitude, which gained strength as the years passed, was a serene sense of fellowship and mutual reliance. This spirit nowhere emerges so clearly as in a letter which five former Hopkins students, on a sudden impulse, sent to Gilman in 1892:

When Hopkins men meet in foreign lands, they speak of their Alma Mater and themes they love. This has been our fate. Five of us have met by chance in this beautiful University town [Bonn], and while we admire this sister institution and her reputation we feel proud of our own school, worthy of such peers, and send to her through you our best wishes and greetings.[69]

What were the goals of the men who came to Johns Hopkins for advanced study? In spite of the changes in America since the 1850s, they were not very different from the goals of young Gilman and his generation. These students of the 1870s and 1880s wanted to do good, just as Gilman had then, and like him they could expand their concept of the good from the sacred to the secular. Most of them firmly believed that it must include serving God, improving their country, and relieving suffering and ignorance among their fellow men. They came to Johns Hopkins less in search of values than to prepare themselves to achieve a good that they already honored. Some, of course, showed the expectation of a student who entered in 1889 that the Ph.D. could "open doors to wealth and distinction." But the earlier one looks into the history of the university, the less often is this the case. H. C. Adams turned from preparing for the ministry to economic studies because he saw there a road to ethical reform, not because he hoped for fame or money.[70] Wilson, like H. C. Adams a minister's son, named as the ambition that lay behind his coming to Hopkins: "to become an invigorating and enlightening power in the world of political thought and a master in some of the

[68] Josiah Royce, "In the Footsteps of Kant," manuscript fragment, vol. LV, Royce Papers.

[69] John E. Matzke, Reid Hunt, Ross Manville Harrison, Emilio M. G. Pailato, and H. C. Jones to Gilman, June 30, 1892.

[70] Howe, *Confessions*, 20; Rosenberry, "H. C. Adams," in *Michigan and the Cleveland Era*, ed. by Babst and Vander Velde, 26; H. C. Adams to Gilman, Dec. 15, 1878.

less serious branches of literary art." Wilson decided at the beginning of his second year to follow a line of reading of his own choosing rather than to cram for the Ph.D., even though he knew that without it he would be less "marketable." [71]

The designation of the university as a "high normal school for special professional teachers" struck close to the mark. By 1886 half of all who had entered Johns Hopkins and were not still students were teachers. By 1891, 184 of the 212 who had won Hopkins Ph.D.'s were teaching, the great majority in colleges and universities.[72] Many preserved the marriage of pedagogy and original investigation which Hopkins fostered.[73] "To look through the list of first students at the Johns Hopkins University," wrote one scholar in the 1930s, "is to obtain a preview of the men who were to become the distinguished members of the faculties of American universities in the thirty or forty years that followed." [74] Although H. B. Adams could make this export of scholars and teachers sound like institutional imperialism, the individual life choices often represented a searching that had carried the student beyond himself. E. G. Sihler recaptured this attitude in his autobiography: "Not long before leaving Baltimore, I was sitting alone with President Gilman in his office. 'You are an enthusiastic scholar,' he said, 'but it means a poor life.' A chilling farewell, I dare say; but did anyone ever strive for true scholarship with an ultimate vision of Gold?" [75] Yet it was not chilling, after all. The sacrifice was not great for those who had caught the vision that let them gladly learn and gladly teach.

Altruism is not a measurable thing. A student who decided to give

[71] Wilson to Ellen Axson, Oct. 30, 1883, quoted in Baker, *Wilson*, I, 168; Wilson to Ellen Axson, Nov. 8, 1884, quoted in *ibid.*, 235–236. He did in fact receive the Ph.D. in 1886, a year after his departure.

[72] Hall, "New Psychology," *Andover Review*, III, 120; JHC, V, 79; ARJH (1891), 31.

[73] E.g., Herbert W. Conn to Albert Shaw, April 13, [1888 or 1890], Shaw Papers, telling of the possibilities of continued research and writing on the faculty of Wesleyan, which made a position there attractive to one who had become imbued "with the spirit of research which is so strong at Johns Hopkins." The position to which Shaw was being invited was the one held by Woodrow Wilson from 1888 to 1890.

[74] W. Carson Ryan, *Studies in Early Graduate Education: The Johns Hopkins, Clark University, the University of Chicago* (Carnegie Foundation for the Advancement of Teaching, Bul. no. 30; New York, 1939), 32.

[75] Sihler, *From Maumee to Thames*, 115.

up financial gain for the life of the scholar might have an inordinate yearning for fame, or for the status of a college professorship. Some students, of course, had largely materialistic aims. The alacrity with which Constantine Fahlberg turned the discovery of saccharin to his profit bespeaks a love of something other than abstract truth. A student who in 1883 spent much of one afternoon decrying "the absence of high aims, of most of the university men" devoted himself in later years to the insurance business,[76] and a student who took his Ph.D. under Remsen declined to go into teaching and instead set up a laboratory for Standard Oil, later becoming president of a leading oil company and a millionaire. But the fact that one had made a fortune did not necessarily mean that he had lost the vision of the early Hopkins. Gustav Bissing, A.B. 1882, Ph.D. 1885, attained wealth as a patent lawyer and canning industrialist. In accord with his wishes, his widow set up a fellowship program dedicated to keeping alive what he had remembered as the university's early spirit of enthusiastic pursuit of truth aside from any considerations of practicality or usefulness.[77]

The ideals that had gone into the making of the university and the ideals of young men that made them turn to it united to form a community spirit remarkable in its vitality and its standards of excellence. When students left—often unwillingly—to enter the wider community of the nation and the world, they carried with them a living heritage.

[76] Jameson diary, Nov. 19, 1883.   [77] Untitled JHU press release, AFJH.

: CHAPTER XVI :

A Community of Ideas

IF one had asked among the teachers and students of the early Johns Hopkins University what ideal they served, he would most often have been answered, "Truth" or "Truth for its own sake." Truth was the theme of most formal efforts to present the ideology of the university. A faculty pronouncement hailed the departing Sylvester for having brought "the example of reverent love of truth and of knowledge for its own sake," and Rowland spoke of the majesty of truth in such addresses as "A Plea for Pure Science." [1] Yet the workers at Johns Hopkins rarely obeyed their own injunction that one must serve truth without looking behind it for any other good. Remsen, writing in the opening year of the university, declared that from the dissemination of the "immortal truths" of science came an ennobling effect on the scientist and his pupils, an exercise of the intellect productive of great happiness. Rowland told a Commemoration Day audience in 1886 that physics must exist in the university for its own sake; however, he pointed out almost at once the great value of the kind of minds it made—minds careful and humbly aware of the possibility of error. Speaking on the same occasion, Gildersleeve offered an aesthetic value for truth, referring to "the visions of that cosmic beauty, which reveals itself when the infinitely little fills up the wavering outline and the features stand out pure and perfect against the sky of God's truth." Even the university's motto, "Veritas vos liberabit," justified truth through its results in human life.

[1] JHC, III, 31; Rowland, *Physical Papers*, 593–613.

This truth that must be served usually appeared in statements at Hopkins as absolute and universal. In their 1886 orations, both Rowland and Gildersleeve spoke of absolute truth, and Gildersleeve ended by quoting Plato: "Nothing imperfect is the measure of anything." [2] John Dewey was far from alone during his Hopkins days in craving some unifying view such as the Hegelian synthesis. [3] Royce could take for granted in 1877 "the ideal realm of Knowledge in which all is to be united in a grand Whole." [4] The arrival of Peirce, who had publicly described a pragmatic theory of meaning with stress on the conceivable practical bearings of any idea, may have influenced one author of a paper at the Metaphysical Club in his declaration that the mind reached its beliefs by steps "analogous to those in the reflex action of a brainless frog." But Peirce's theories did not dislodge the general view at Hopkins of a predetermined, ultimately attainable truth. Indeed, Peirce's description of truth as "a foreordained goal," the opinion "fated" to be ultimately agreed upon by all investigators, could be misinterpreted as preserving something like Royce's "grand Whole." [5]

The attitude of Hopkins men toward truth had, however, even before Peirce's arrival been "pragmatic" in that it was an attitude of extreme activism. Images of building and attacking were far more common than those of uncovering. As Royce expressed it, "to the enthusiastic truth-seeker an unsolved problem is an undeveloped life which he is commissioned to bring to perfection, a dark realm that is longing for light, a mass of gross matter which he must spiritualize." [6] Discussions of truth did not long remain abstract at Hopkins. The minds there quickly moved to ways of attaining truth, which meant in most cases, as it did to Peirce, the methods of empirical science. Martin in his inaugural pointed the way. He called for

a perseverance unabated by failure after failure, and a truthfulness incapable of the least perversion . . . in the description of an observation or of an

[2] Ira Remsen, "The Science *vs.* the Art of Chemistry," *Popular Science Monthly,* X (1876–1877), 691; JHC, V, 105–107.

[3] Dewey, "From Absolutism to Experimentalism," in *Contemporary American Philosophy,* ed. by Adams and Montague, II, 19.

[4] Josiah Royce, "The Spirit of Modern Philosophy," October, 1877, vol. LV, Royce Papers.

[5] JHC, I, 34. The definitions referred to appear in "How to Make Our Ideas Clear," *Popular Science Monthly,* XII (1877–1878), 286–302.

[6] See note 4 above.

experiment, or of the least reluctance to acknowledge an error once it is found to have been made . . . a constant searching and inquisition of the mind, with the perpetual endeavor to keep inferences from observation or experiment unbiased, so far as may be, by natural predilections or favorite theories.

Such an approach led Martin to a scorning, if not quite a denial, of any absolute. Physiologists, he claimed in 1884, had given up hunting essences and absolutes and had decided "that their business was to study the phenomena exhibited by living things, and leave the noumena, if there were such, to amuse metaphysicians."[7]

No talk of truth could go on long at Hopkins without becoming talk of science, and often science was defined more carefully than truth. Remsen called science "a collection of principles, well established, applying to a certain class of phenomena," and to Newcomb science meant "exact and systematized general knowledge." Gilman never reversed the definition that he had offered in his California inaugural: "Science is but accurate knowledge, systematically arranged and philosophically discussed." In 1885, he equated science and knowledge through the etymon *scientia*.[8] Yet the connotations of "science" at Johns Hopkins went far beyond these set definitions to include a much-admired way of living and thinking. So great was this admiration, in fact, that the name was used to appropriate prestige.[9] The historian who has observed that "working principles that seemed to be little more than common sense and common honesty" were "graced with the majestic garb of science"[10] could have been speaking directly of the early Johns Hopkins. There the representatives of every discipline at one time or another described their field as a "science."

In his first year as professor, Hall's principal course was "a general survey of the vast field of modern scientific psychology." In the boom for archaeology in 1884, its new critical spirit was praised as having raised it "to the rank of a science." The "scientific" ambitions of H. B. Adams are famous throughout the historical profession, but

---

[7] "Study of Biology," *Popular Science Monthly*, X, 301; JHC, III, 88.

[8] Remsen, "Science *vs.* Art of Chemistry," *Popular Science Monthly*, X, 694; Newcomb, "Aspects of the Economic Discussion," *Science*, VII (1886), 539; Gilman, *University Problems*, 169; JHC, IV, 43.

[9] Thomas Le Duc has pointed this out in his *Piety and Intellect at Amherst College, 1865–1912* (New York, 1946), 74.

[10] Stow Persons, *American Minds: A History of Ideas* (New York, 1958), 319.

his extravagances must be understood in the context of a university where a trustee wanted Von Holst as professor of history because he could demonstrate "a scientific method" and where the president could casually refer to the "historical laboratory." [11] Ely was more moderate than Adams, perhaps because he saw "science" used by men like Newcomb to defend laissez-faire policies. He pointed out in 1884 the inappropriateness of experimental techniques of the natural sciences in economics, and his prospectus for the American Economic Association in 1885 declared economics to be "still in the first stages of its scientific development." In his remarks at the first meeting he selected as aspects of science which should be imitated its attitude of inquiry and its attitude of modesty.[12] Gildersleeve, though urging classical philologists to avoid divorce from general culture, said that they must "do scientific work . . . in a scientific atmosphere." [13] His colleague Elliott, in an address of 1891, did more than adopt the name "science"; he analyzed the method of advanced study in language to demonstrate that it could be meaningfully so called, practicing as it did "an orderly progression from the known to the unknown, from the special to the general; a strict observation of the facts of living speech and then the induction is recorded regardless of traditional authority." [14] Even the personification of free imagination in the university, the poet Lanier, did not escape the scientism of the times. He called one of his lecture series, later a book, *The Science of English Verse*, and for his theories he relied heavily on the work of Helmholtz in sound. At the time of his death, Lanier seemed on the brink of creating a poetry

>Rooted in the soil of Science,
>Fruited in the air of Art.

[11] JHC, III, 117, IV, 17; G. W. Brown to Gilman, July 9, 1879; Gilman to H. B. Adams, July 15, 1883, in Holt, ed., *Historical Scholarship*, 69.

[12] *Past and Present of Political Economy*, 44–45; *Ground under Our Feet*, 136, 139.

[13] *Essays and Studies*, 76. Gildersleeve spoke more precisely of the "scientific" claims of his discipline at the end of the century: "In regard to the certainty and uncertainty of the results, in regard to the inexhaustibility and absolute trustworthiness of the material, there is no . . . thoroughgoing difference between [natural sciences and humanities]. . . . Neither physicist nor historian can rest satisfied with mere inductions, and both domains are open to the invasions of subjectivity. Law is for both often nothing more than a figure" (Miller, ed., *Selections from Brief Mention*, 48–49).

[14] JHC, X, 59.

His use of Darwinism in "The Cloud" showed how far he had moved toward such a synthesis.[15] In the department of philosophy, G. S. Morris, despite his strong metaphysical and religious interests, named one course "Ethics or the Science of Man" and referred in a letter to Gilman to his "chosen (& loved) life-work, as a student & teacher of Philosophic science." [16]

Almost drowned out by the paean to science and the scientific method were the murmurs from those who saw loyalties to evangelical religion and revelation threatened. The university had, of course, opened its doors amid something louder than murmurs against the secular implications of Huxley's address. But those who spoke with vehemence of the challenge to religion were in every case outside the university. Inside, the existence of any true conflict was regularly denied, and solution declared easy. There was no question in Remsen's mind that, as ideas about the physical universe grew, ideas of the Creator would become "larger, broader, grander," and men would "worship with a truer adoration, and a feeling of more perfect reverence." In his inaugural address Hall paid lip service to revelation as the one road to absolute truth and assured his audience that the insights of psychology would "effect a complete atonement between modern culture and religious sentiments and verities." [17]

Gilman's position comforted the religious public without hampering the work of the scientists in his university. According to him, science pointed "more and more steadily to the plan of a great designer." In a letter of 1882, he warned against "formulating an antagonism between Religion & Science which does not really exist." His admonition continued, "We who believe in Christianity & in Philosophy ought, I think, to be constantly on our guard that we do not throw obstacles in the way of the advancement of science,—for science is the unfolding of the Creator[']s Law & the laws of the Creator are the foundations of Religion." But Gilman was still the man who had said in California, "The institution that regards only the natural forces of this globe, without observing likewise the intellectual and spiritual forces, sees only half the world," and he could also admonish the scientists on occasion. He declined to become president of the corporation publishing *Science*

[15] Anderson, ed., *Lanier*, I, lxxii–lxxiv.
[16] JHC, III, 99; Morris to Gilman, May 24, 1883.
[17] Remsen, "Science *vs.* Art of Chemistry," *Popular Science Monthly*, X, 691–692; Hall, "New Psychology," *Andover Review*, III, 134.

"unless it were understood from the beginning that its pages were to be free from aspersions on Christianity." [18] But it is a fair conclusion that Gilman regarded science as faced with the greater threat, and in most cases it was the religionists on whom he urged restraint and understanding. Science and Christianity, he declared in a public statement of 1885, would lead to the same ethical standards: "As I believe that one truth is never in conflict with another truth, so I believe that the ethics of the New Testament will be accepted by the scientific as well as the religious faculties of man; to the former, as Law; to the latter, as Gospel." The question might appropriately have occurred to his audience, If science and its law can reach these ethical ends, why not let the Gospel go? By the time of Gilman's retirement, in his address at the twenty-fifth anniversary celebration, God had receded to the vagueness of an immanent divine power, to which the university as "a fearless and determined investigator of nature" gave "quiet, reverent, and unobtrusive recognition." [19]

Other minds in the university were less serene than Gilman's about the relationship of science and religion, though his view was doubtless the general one. To a group of graduate students it was a question for lively discussion whether or not science, and specifically Herbert Spencer, had found a new and nonreligious basis for ethics.[20] Among the trustees, Thomas seemed certain that science without Christianity was not enough. In his tenth anniversary address, he concluded: "In vain will science harness the powers of the universe unless they are yoked to the chariot of peace and good will. . . . The truth which sets free, is the truth which warms the heart and expands the sympathies, as well as enlightens the intellect, which is of Him who is the truth Himself." [21] Thus, at least one leader of the university did not forget the Christian source of the university's motto. Although Gildersleeve offered no Christian alternative to science, he took pains to avow the irrational sources of much that was good. He pointed out in 1878 that doubt of the total adequacy of science was springing up among the German scientists themselves and quoted Emil du Bois-Reymond, the Berlin physiologist, as saying, "Where physical science reigns ex-

[18] Gilman, *University Problems*, 96; Gilman to C.[?] F. Deems, Dec. 15, 1882; *University Problems*, 171; Gilman diary, "1882–1887 to California & Alaska," Dec. 9, 1882.

[19] JHC, IV, 49; *Launching of a University*, 133.

[20] Jameson diary, March 8, 1882.   [21] JHC, V, 111.

clusively, the intellect becomes poor in ideas, the fancy in images, the soul in sensibility, and the result is a narrow, hard and dry disposition." [22]

Was such a charge justified at Hopkins? It would seem to be so in the case of its scientist closest to genius, Rowland. His attack on the teaching of ancient languages at a Phi Beta Kappa banquet revealed a great blind spot, and other of his addresses showed that though "practicalism" was a bad word to him "imagination" was even more offensive. It was, he asserted, the loosened imagination of the ancients that had held them back from the insights of modern science. He linked the unscientific mind, whose faults must be corrected by education, with the mind "where everything has a personal aspect and we are guided by feelings rather than reason." This was the man, far more than its poets, humanists, or God seekers, who symbolized the university to both its members and the outside world.[23]

But though science tended to supplant religion as the center of loyalty for teachers and students at Johns Hopkins, the transition could be made without too great a wrench as long as science provided a universe of law. In fact, part of the appeal of science was that its investigations of a Newtonian universe promised more dependable law than could come from "untestable" revelation. The concept of moral law, long a fundamental of American thought, was carried along in the flood of natural law. Rowland, speaking as Newton's heir, added moral overtones to physical science and referred unquestioningly to "the great moral law of the universe." [24] Almost as quickly as they chose to honor themselves with the name "science," the various disciplines fearlessly attributed the quality of law to the truths they professed. In 1889 at the Boston Merchants Association, Ely compared the certainty of success for municipal ownership of natural monopolies with the certainty of the law of gravity. That such an assertion was an excess of the times is shown by his later judgment of this as "perhaps

[22] Quoted in *Essays and Studies,* 55–56.

[23] *Physical Papers,* 623; JHC, V, 104; interview with Judge Soper and Judge Moses; Ames, "Rowland," *JH Alumni Magazine,* IV, 99.

[24] *Physical Papers,* 636, 623–624. One had to look closely to see the antidemocratic overtones of this naturalism enshrined as universal law; but they were there, for instance, in the statement of Rowland: "It is a fact in nature, which no democracy can change, that men are *not* equal,—that some have brains, and some hands; and no idle talk about equality can ever subvert the order of the universe" (*ibid.,* 607).

the most absurd statement I have ever made." [25] Again Gilman took the lead. He assured the public that the motive for universities, besides making man better, was to discover "the laws which govern the world." [26]

Clearly, Ely and Gilman were at ease with the Newtonian world view, but could they absorb the impact of the Darwinian revolution with its organic universe of growth and transformation? Gilman had begun his adaptation long before coming to Hopkins, and he simply claimed evolutionary theory as further support for the belief in a universe of law, thus ignoring the views of Brooks and Peirce, who looked on evolution as anterior to natural laws.[27] In any case, Darwinian influences swept through the university, engulfing the obdurate as well as the willing, the obtuse as well as the comprehending.

The biologists tried to act as interpreters. Brooks gave a series of public lectures on Darwin in 1877 and in 1883 published *The Law of Heredity*, in which he attempted further development of Darwin's theories. Herbert W. Conn, who took his Ph.D. under Brooks and was assistant in 1883–1884, published shortly after leaving Hopkins *Evolution of To-day* (1886), a popularization of Darwinian theory. After Darwin's death in 1882, Martin lectured on his life and work before the Naturalists' Field Club.[28]

The scholars at Johns Hopkins had little time to spend on such precise descriptions of Darwin from their colleagues in biology. Yet his influence carried throughout the university; no department, no vocabulary, no body of thought escaped the mark of evolutionary theory. Very often it was Herbert Spencer whose ideas were cited, but the naturalistic bent of the university placed Darwin, as scientist, in a more fundamental position. Biologism pervaded the writings of the members of the university. G. H. Williams, associate professor of geology, whose discipline had established evolutionary doctrines before the biologists, nevertheless chose to consider the globe as "an organism" and spoke of the value of "the analogy to vital terms and processes" in his field. For such terms as embryology, histology, morphology, and physiology he found meaningful applications in geology.

[25] *Ground under Our Feet*, 255–256.   [26] *University Problems*, 48.

[27] JHC, III, 14; Richard Hofstadter, *Social Darwinism in American Thought* (rev. ed.; Boston, 1955), 127.

[28] Brooks, *The Law of Heredity: A Study of the Cause of Variation and the Origin of Living Organisms* (Baltimore, 1883); JHC, II, 38.

Sylvester could refer to the "natural selection" of an algebraical phenomenon. Gildersleeve presented language as "a true organism" which made itself felt "in every fibre of its structure." [29] Economists in their study of society, Ely insisted, must follow the example of the biologists by going back to the earliest periods, showing the development of "life-forms." A dissertation on New Haven was subtitled "A History of Municipal Evolution," and Wilson's *Congressional Government*, written while he was at Hopkins, attempted to present government not as a finished machine but as a living organism.[30] Turner recalled the influence during 1888–1889 of Wilson's conversations and lectures "expounding *politics* in a larger sense, discussing the evolution of institutions and constitutions as 'vehicles of life.'"[31] H. B. Adams' "germ theory" of history and Turner's environmental theory of frontier influence are usually presented as antithetical, but it reveals much of the climate of which these two were a part that both fitted human history into the developmental hypothesis of the evolutionists.

From time to time came warnings that analogy from the biological sciences might be carried too far. Some protested that the wave of evolutionary naturalism threatened to swallow up more meaningful concepts of man and society. Royce, for example, argued with Spencer in mind that any effort to set up a science of society with "the general Law of Evolution from Hom[ogeneous] to Heterog[eneous]" as a postulate omitted "the human element," used "false analogies," and was "opposed to experience." He urged that those seeking to form a sociology turn instead to "the consciousness of Individuals."[32] Four years later, John Dewey attacked Spencer's sensationalism in a paper read at the Metaphysical Club and declared that self-consciousness was "the true absolute, with reference to which knowledge is relative."[33] Ely chose to believe that "the beginning and end of all is man" and

[29] George H. Williams, "Some Modern Aspects of Geology," *Popular Science Monthly*, XXXV (1889), 640, 646–647; Baker, ed., *Collected Papers of Sylvester*, III, 609n; Gildersleeve, *Essays and Studies*, 107.

[30] Ely, "Ethics and Economics," *Science*, VII (1886), 530; JHC, VI, 25; Baker, *Wilson*, I, 211.

[31] Frederick J. Turner to William E. Dodd, Oct. 7, 1919, in Wendell H. Stephenson, ed., "The Influence of Woodrow Wilson on Frederick Jackson Turner," *Agricultural History*, XIX (1945), 252.

[32] "The Historical Method in Sociology:—Its Significance & Its Principles," 1878, vol. LV, Royce Papers.

[33] JHC, II, 54.

though he saw society involved in an evolutionary process insisted that "rational efforts at social reform" could help make it a peaceful evolution.[34]

Despite protests and qualifications, the general record at Johns Hopkins fits the national pattern of the era of John Fiske and Henry Ward Beecher, making way for the new truth and hailing its glory. Perhaps the easiest adjustment was that of Sylvester—simply to think of "the evolution of the human intellect" as proof of the beneficence of natural force operating in human life. Wilson believed in evolution, but saw no inconsistency with his orthodox Presbyterianism. James Hervey Hyslop, who took his Ph.D. in philosophy in 1887, explained to the readers of the *Andover Review* that evolution had "restored the old idea of perfection as an end which hedonistic motives must subserve" and that it had exalted "the social and altruistic principles of human nature." [35] This all-conquering movement of acceptance, explanation, and glorification Gilman joined; it was he, after all, who had invited Huxley to give the university's opening address. Gilman, who in his earlier years had often "sat silently listening to Dana and Guyot as they discussed the principles of development and evolution," had at the very opening of the university remarked that it would have to be "a growth,—a natural development,—and not a pre-ordained scheme." [36] In an article on the history of the university written in 1891, he boldly observed: "Germs that came from Harvard and Yale, from the University of Virginia and from Ithaca; germs, too, from Oxford and Cambridge, from Germany and France were here to be cultivated. . . . The fittest would survive." He delighted later in the decade in quoting "an orthodox theologian," who asserted that the doctrine of evolution confirmed the Christian faith. In 1904, declaring the triumph of the doctrine complete, Gilman still viewed it, as had its host of sympathizers in the early years of Johns Hopkins, as "an interpreter of the order of nature and of the progress of mankind." [37]

These words explain much of the ease and eagerness of acceptance of a theory that vitiated fervently held religious views. The theory came

[34] *Ground under Our Feet*, vii; JHC, VII, 28.

[35] Baker, ed., *Collected Papers of Sylvester*, III, 650; Wilson to Ellen Axson, June 26, 1884, quoted in Baker, *Wilson*, I, 210; JHC, VI, 57.

[36] Gilman, "Address at the Brooklyn Institute, 1896," James Dwight Dana Papers, Rare Book Room, Yale University Library; ARJH (1876), 13.

[37] "Hopkins," *Cosmopolitan*, XI, 463; *Launching of a University*, 230, 150.

veiled with two ideas which Americans already firmly believed on Newtonian grounds: a universe of law and a law of human progress. The injury which Darwinism would eventually work upon these ideas and the pessimism which it bore in its train were difficult to foresee amid the assurances that the good, the familiar, the encouraging were all enhanced by the new synthesis. In 1890, returning from a year's absence, Gilman listed among the habits "inculcated at Hopkins" "belief in the progress of science, literature, politics, religion." He saw "the law of progress" in the changing of Hopkins Hall into a chemistry lecture room. H. B. Adams in 1889 traced the history of the university as "a constant struggle with difficulties and a steady advance along the line." In the midst of overriding sentiment that change was "evolution" and must be for the better, "old-fashioned" became a leading pejorative.[38]

Remarkably enough, this view of progress as supported by evolution, indeed as a law of the universe, rarely presented progress as inevitable or divorced from human effort. To Rowland, there seemed no doubt that the Chinese had not experienced progress and that their lack of pure science largely explained its absence; to him, human beings who dedicated themselves to science were "the most important element in human progress." Brooks believed that man had partial "conscious control of his own destiny," though he must use his powers in harmony with the natural order. Ely claimed that there was a "path of safe progress," which man could discern and follow.[39] In an address of 1885, Gilman depicted the aims of historical inquiry as "to help on the progress of modern society by showing how the fetters which now bind us were forged, by what patient filing they must be severed," and to plan an ideal society. A month later Jameson echoed this as his own motive in historical writing: "helping on the race to its higher destiny." [40]

It was indeed a paradox, though one at least a century old, that progress, a law of the universe, did not come about in human life without human striving. But even greater is the paradox that those who stopped short of declaring progress inevitable displayed a fervid op-

---

[38] JHC, X, 2–3, VIII, 44; Shaw diary, Jan. 27, 29, 1882.
[39] Rowland, *Physical Papers*, 594, 609, 637; Brooks, *Law of Heredity*, 242; JHC, IV, 81.
[40] JHC, IV, 49; Jameson diary, March 26, 1885.

timism. It may be that the ultimate faith among Americans had not truly been in God before the challenge of naturalism and had not shifted to evolutionary process or any other law of the universe. The basis of the American world view and of American optimism would appear to have remained unchanged by the revisions of philosophers and scientists. The paradoxical optimism traces to a faith in man himself, in man as a free and efficacious agent. For this cheerful temper that appeared at Johns Hopkins the national experience and the national character seem to provide the most credible etiology. Such is the key suggested by an unusually revealing statement of Rowland's in 1883:

We know the speed with which we advance in this country: we see cities springing up in a night, and other wonders performed at an unprecedented rate. . . . Perhaps we have the feeling, common to all true Americans, that our country is going forward to a glorious future, when we shall lead the world in the strife for intellectual prizes as we now do in the strife for wealth.[41]

The world of the men at Johns Hopkins was still the radiant world of the Enlightenment.

But if progress came through human agency, after all, then the university had a duty to become an instrument of the better world; in other words, it must look to the utility of its undertakings. Through this process of thought, never clearly expressed, the institution where "truth for its own sake" was regularly declared to be the aim experienced an ever-growing sense of obligation to serve concrete social ends. The classics felt this influence least. In his Commemoration Day address of 1877, Gildersleeve drew back from requiring "useful" work, saying that " 'useful' . . . were better banished from the university vocabulary." [42] Other branches of knowledge, however, rarely appeared without a partial garb of utility. Often this usefulness was described as an inevitable by-product of serving truth for its own sake.[43] When the researches of Brooks on oyster reproduction proved to have valuable industrial applications, he declared, "Our own share in the work is . . . exactly what we should wish: the discovery of a new scientific truth, which has, in the hands of practical economists, contributed to the

---

[41] *Physical Papers*, 612.   [42] Baltimore *Evening Bulletin*, Feb. 23, 1877.
[43] Martin, "Study of Biology," *Popular Science Monthly*, X, 299; JHC, VII, 47.

welfare of mankind."[44] One could have one's pure science and eat oysters too. The moral law of the universe would, in fact, reward the pursuit of pure science with material applications. In later years Gilman found a quotation of Faraday which put the sentiment neatly: "There is nothing so prolific in utilities as abstractions."[45] But the aphorism, as Gilman used it, reduced abstractions to means and accepted the criterion of utility for intellectual endeavor.

The attitude described could transmute itself into a sense of obligation to aid the practical directly, even if such applications were "inevitable." An interesting shading off of belief appeared in a letter which the university's first Ph.D. in physics wrote shortly after taking his degree: "My wish is to be a *Physicist*—but it is necessary for me to be somewhat practical, both that I may earn my living & because I believe I may, in this way, *be of use*."[46] Utility never achieved among professors and students the glorification given it by Trustee Lewis N. Hopkins, who felt that great discoveries always came from those who were devoting themselves to practical applications;[47] but quite probably it was the pressure of a public including many with his views, heightened after Garrett's charges of uselessness, that led to Gilman's Commemoration Day speech of 1885, "The Benefits Which Society Derives from Universities." He took up the disciplines at Hopkins one by one, justifying each of them, proving each one "useful."[48] With such a statement in the record, the university could scarcely disclaim its professor of psychology, who wrote privately in 1888, "I feel that all learning & science however technical must not drift so far from the common consciousness of the race, that its utility cannot be explained in a way to be at heart *felt* by any intelligent & cultured man, no matter how non-expert."[49] When at the close of the decade the physics department began to include applied electricity and applied mechanics in its work, Gilman announced that the leaders of the department were "maintaining a helpful attitude toward the practical applications of

[44] JHC, III, 93. Gilman expressed the same attitude on this matter (JHC, III, 49).
[45] *University Problems,* 117.   [46] W. W. Jacques to Gilman, Aug. 11, 1879.
[47] Lewis N. Hopkins to John W. Garrett, June 22, 1883, GP. Yet G. H. Williams did give the practical work of miners credit for advancing geology ("Modern Aspects of Geology," *Popular Science Monthly,* XXXV, 640, 642).
[48] JHC, IV, 43–54; Gilman, *University Problems,* 45–76.
[49] G. S. Hall to T. W. Higginson, May 12, 1888, Higginson Papers. By permission of the Harvard College Library.

science." He hailed new discoveries in electricity and magnetism which enabled mankind "to make the forces of nature obedient slaves." Rowland and Martin also used the image of nature enslaved.[50] It looms as darkly in an institution declaring truth to be its own justification as did human slavery in a nation declaring man to be his own justification.

If knowledge of nature could lead to its manipulation for the use of man, what of knowledge of man and society? Why should it not also possess utility and lead to the improvement of man and society? The answer of the university was that it could and should. Lanier's image of the university's determination to continue striving

> Till man seem less a riddle unto man
> And fair Utopia less Utopian [51]

recalled the plea for human and civic betterment in Gilman's inaugural. During the 1880s, pronouncements became more specific. In his address on the utility of universities, Gilman described the world as "a great laboratory, in which human society is busily experimenting." [52] Should the experimentation remain haphazard? The obvious answer came a year later when Rowland declared that scientific minds were "destined to govern the world in the future and to solve problems pertaining to politics and humanity as well as to inanimate nature." A year after receiving his Ph.D., Albert Shaw sent back a letter listing proposed projects for the historical seminary. In referring to disputes over the value of the jury system, he called for "a scientific study of the facts," on which could be built "propositions looking towards an intelligent reform." [53] Shaw's attitude toward judicial reform precisely reflected the approach that his teacher Ely had fostered for economic reform. In many ways Ely's views and activities were more typical of the Hopkins of the 1890s than of the 1880s. During the earlier decade,

[50] ARJH (1888), 17–18; Rowland, *Physical Papers*, 621; H. Newell Martin, *Physiological Papers* (*Memoirs from the Biological Laboratory of the Johns Hopkins University*, III; Baltimore, 1895), 263.

[51] JHC, I, 38.

[52] JHC, IV, 44. Gilman urged upon social scientists "the careful ascertainment of facts by experiment and observation, and . . . reflection upon these facts, until laws were discovered from which, again, rules and *methods of management* might safely be deduced" (Gilman, "Opening Address at Saratoga, September 7, 1880," *Journal of Social Science*, XII [1880], xxiii; italics added).

[53] JHC, V, 105; Shaw to Ely, [1885], Shaw Papers.

it is true, there existed a moderate interest in local charities and correction and in economic and governmental reform;[54] but these interests expanded in the next decade until they set the dominant tone of the institution. By then the university was far more of the world of here and now and less of the world of "truth for its own sake." Frederic C. Howe, who entered as a graduate student in the fall of 1889, recalled a general desire to save democracy and change the world, a feeling that scholars were especially called to lead the people.[55] The seeds of such dedication were planted in the 1880s, but the full flower came later.

What delayed the flowering? One can hypothesize that the whole paradoxical structure of thought at the university had a tendency to bemuse. Science taught the truth. It revealed the laws of the universe. The greatest of these laws was evolution. Evolution meant progress. Whatever was, was heading in the right direction. In almost complete contradiction to this sequence was a view of man the free agent in a world of change, man the experimenter, the applier of knowledge, the utilitarian. It was, in brief, a conflict between "Conservative Darwinism" and "Reform Darwinism."[56] A remarkable revelation of this conflict appears in a letter which Charles Shinn wrote to Albert Shaw a few months after leaving Johns Hopkins in 1884, at a time when he was working on his *Land Laws of Mining Districts* for the *Studies*.[57] At the end of the letter, after recalling the warm spirit of comradeship at Johns Hopkins, he wrote: "I believe that one hundred young men who loved each other in the right spirit could revolutionise modern society." Then he changed "revolutionise" to "evolutionise," and added, "Let us leave the 'r' out."[58] During the 1880s, those at Johns Hopkins most concerned with society and its problems were hesitating amid an inconsistent structure of ideas. Should they add the letter "r" or leave

[54] Although not formally associated with the university, both a Civil Service Reform Association and the Charity Organization Society of Baltimore were organized at meetings in Hopkins Hall during the 1880–1881 term (ARJH [1881], 22).

[55] *Confessions*, 8.

[56] This is a somewhat broadened use of the terms of Eric F. Goldman, *Rendezvous with Destiny: A History of Modern American Reform* (New York, 1952), 93–97.

[57] *JHU Studies in Historical and Political Science*, II, no. 12 (Baltimore, 1884).

[58] Shinn to Shaw, Oct. 19, [1884], Shaw Papers.

it out and wait? Those concerned with nature faced a similar, though less hobbling, dilemma. Should they seek abstractions only, or was application also a duty?

The ideas at the university would undoubtedly change with time. The scholarly community that had nurtured them might, in the long view, be more important than they were. As long as it existed, criticism and change were possible and new structures of ideas could emerge. From within and without, this community was designated as the country's "first real university." [59] This claim is even less significant than most attempts to establish historical priority, for there was an inner unity to the university movement in America that paid no heed to institutional boundaries. What mattered was that Hopkins was a university, and as John Masefield has said, "There are few earthly things more beautiful." [60] The life and work at Hopkins concretized Royce's great lesson, "We are saved through the community." [61] A prescription such as Huxley's that a university ought to be a "factory of new knowledge" was never accepted at Johns Hopkins. Those who organized it, Gildersleeve reported, were "not content with the mere machinery of knowledge"; they believed rather "in the incalculable power of human sympathy and individual example." [62] It was as a community of thinking men that the leaders of Johns Hopkins saw its value. Thus, Thomas could cite with approval John Henry Newman's picture of savants in rival fields who learned "to respect, to consult, to aid each other. Thus is created a pure and clear atmosphere of thought, which the student also breathes."

Yet how truly did Johns Hopkins become a community with the interaction which that name implies? Undoubtedly, communication between Rowland and Gildersleeve, Martin and Harris, Newcomb and Ely stopped far short of Newman's ideal. The president once compared

[59] C. S. Peirce to Gilman, Jan. 13, 1878; A. D. Savage to Thomas Davidson, May 20, 1880, Davidson Papers; Melvil Dewey to Gilman, Dec. 15, 1888.

[60] Quoted in *The Johns Hopkins Magazine*, IV (1952–1953), 7.

[61] He specifically cited his seminary at Harvard as the "best concrete instance of the life of a community with which I have had the privilege to become well acquainted" ("Words of Professor Royce at the Walton Hotel at Philadelphia, December 29, 1915," in *Papers in Honor of Josiah Royce on His Sixtieth Birthday*, ed. by J. E. Creighton [n.p., n.d.], 283).

[62] Huxley to Ray Lankester, April 11, 1892, in Huxley, *Life of Huxley*, II, 328; *Johns Hopkins University, Baltimore: Visit of the Dean of Westminster, September 30th, 1878* ([Baltimore? 1878?]), copy in New York Public Library.

the members of the university to "a hive of bees, each storing up honey in a narrow cell unobserving and unobserved," and an assistant could write that most Hopkins men had "little real knowledge of what others are doing." [63] In his Phi Beta Kappa address at Harvard in 1886 Gilman cited the dangers of overspecialization, but they could be overcome, he felt, by a "sense of proportion." He did not claim that his institution had achieved such a balance; doubtless Hopkins fell short of his ideal as all human creations fall short of human ideals. But where was this sense of proportion more likely to arise than in a university? The isolated specialist, the man cut off from exchange of ideas, library resources, and standards for emulation was, as Professor Arthur Bestor has shown, the injured product of "the separatistic organization of the various branches of intellectual life" that preceded the assimilative new universities. The curse of isolation and narrowness could be avoided, especially if university leaders kept open a "broad range of vision," wrote Gildersleeve; but specialization there must be, for "enthusiasm dwells only in specialization." [64]

Enthusiasm there was. The mood of the first year proved to be more than the evanescent stimulation of novelty. C. D. Morris in 1880 cited the diligence, the "universal spirit of work" unmatched elsewhere, and declared that there was not a single idler. Enthusiasm nourished the will to work, and work kept enthusiasm fresh. Somehow, magically it would seem if one did not know of Gilman's efforts, the spirit of the new was retained, and in 1881 Peirce could refer to the university as "animate with youth and promise." Lanman wrote back from Harvard that he saw with new clarity the great Hopkins advantage of freedom from tradition and bad precedent. Harvard was also the vehicle of a comparison by H. B. Adams. After a visit there in 1880, he felt that he had examined "the bones of the Mammoth" and declared, "I believe there is more strength in growing ideas than in mere form and bigness, more hope for young life than for settled old age, which desires chiefly comfort and quiet." [65] The record of change at Harvard belies these disparaging opinions, but they reveal the feeling of youth

[63] JHC, V, 107; Gilman, untitled notes for address of Feb. 22, 1881, GP; Jameson to Shaw, Feb. 27, [1883], Shaw Papers.

[64] Gilman, *University Problems*, 104; Bestor, "Transformation of Scholarship," *Library Quarterly*, XXIII, 169; ARJH (1886), 28.

[65] JHC, I, 39–40; C. S. Peirce to Gilman, Feb. 9, 1881; Lanman to Gilman, Nov. 13, 1880; H. B. Adams to Gilman, May 19, 1880.

and the accompanying self-assurance at Johns Hopkins. From this forward-looking spirit emerged the image of the pioneer. Rowland spoke of pure science as "the pioneer who must not hover about cities and civilized countries, but must strike into unknown forests," and a student of history at work on his dissertation felt "the satisfaction of knowing that I am on pioneer ground." Only a few months after asserting that Hopkins urged too early specialization and writing, Jameson found himself caught in the spell and admitted, "This 'investigation' is a far more exciting occupation than the quiet reading on which I have spent the year hitherto." A Ph.D. in mathematics felt, after a two-year absence, that to return to Baltimore would mean being "furnished with wings in an atmosphere where I could fly." [66]

If enthusiasm and the spirit of work survived at Hopkins, what of freedom, which had also been boasted of on the first Commemoration Day? Was it a mere epiphenomenon, the gratuitous effect of newness, or had it too remained? The phrase "academic freedom" was little used in the 1870s and 1880s, and when it did appear, it usually referred to an aspect of the German universities, partly but not totally worthy of imitation.[67] A later day, when academic freedom is a more consciously embraced ideal, tends to exaggerate the liberality of past educational leaders and take out-of-context statements as the support of tradition. The goal that has not been achieved today had not been achieved in the 1870s and 1880s either. But a beginning was made.

Many contemporaries did, in fact, regard Johns Hopkins as the embodiment of German academic freedom in America. When Alexander Winchell lost his professorship at Vanderbilt in 1878 for his teaching of evolution, an outraged Andrew D. White wrote to Gilman comparing Winchell to Galileo; regarding Gilman as an ally in the struggle for the free pursuit of truth, he suggested that Winchell be employed at Johns Hopkins.[68] A Hopkins graduate teaching at the University of California wrote to Gilman after a removal there for insubordination, "Insubordination in a University instructor is a curious anomaly in the

[66] Rowland, *Physical Papers*, 608; E. R. L. Gould to Shaw, Aug. 15, 1882, Shaw Papers; Jameson diary, Oct. 8, 1881, March 1, 1882; W. I. Stringham to Gilman, April 28, 1882.

[67] Lanman to Gilman, May 22, 1880 (draft), Lanman Papers; Gildersleeve, *Essays and Studies*, 111. See Hofstadter and Metzger, *Development of Academic Freedom*, chap. viii.

[68] A. D. White to Gilman, July 24, 1878.

midst of *Lern- und Lehr-Freiheit"*; clearly he felt that he would have a sympathetic reader in Gilman.[69] One of the most notorious cases of the period, the dismissal of Professor James Woodrow from the Presbyterian Theological Seminary in Columbia, South Carolina, for his compromise with evolution, had echoes at Johns Hopkins: the professor's nephew, Woodrow Wilson, was a student there. Wilson directed his bitterness over his uncle's fate chiefly against hyperorthodox church leaders, but the atmosphere at Hopkins probably heightened his protest.[70] Each of the four major academic-freedom cases of the 1890s which Professor Metzger has chosen for detailed analysis [71] involved a former Hopkins scholar. Ely had been a faculty member, and Edward W. Bemis, John S. Bassett, and Edward A. Ross all held Hopkins Ph.D.'s. Although Professor Metzger has warned how easily these cases can be oversimplified, it may be hypothesized that part of each man's problem was a habit formed at Hopkins of expressing his ideas with impunity and that others bridled at the resulting intellectual impetuousness.[72] These men had, certainly, enjoyed comparatively great freedom at Hopkins and had heard many fine words about it, but even there bounds had existed that a scholar crossed at his peril.

Gilman's letter of 1875 to the trustees, calling for "intellectual freedom in the pursuit of truth and . . . the broadest charity toward those from whom we differ in opinion," was never published. When he referred to the letter in his inaugural, he cited a more negative passage stressing avoidance of "sectional, partizan, and provincial animosities." His essay for the trustees on the choosing of professors had even more directly precluded "uncalled-for expression of [religious and political] differences under circumstances which are likely to impair the usefulness of the University." [73] Gilman had seen in California and elsewhere the material damage that such partisanship could deal an institution; thus a practical motive may explain his standards. In fact, neutralism was far more prominent in his frame of values than academic freedom.

[69] W. I. Stringham to Gilman, [April, 1883].

[70] Hofstadter and Metzger, *Development of Academic Freedom,* 328–329; Baker, *Wilson,* I, 209–210.

[71] Hofstadter and Metzger, *Development of Academic Freedom,* 425–451.

[72] "Looking over old letters from Hopkins cronies just launched on their academic careers, I note something significant: *they are not afraid.* They show no concern as to how their utterances will strike powerful outsiders" (Edward A. Ross, *Seventy Years of It: An Autobiography* [New York and London, 1936], 51).

[73] "Hopkins Inaugural," 39–40. See also pp. 22–23, 40–41, above.

He did not show sectarian favoritism, but he was at great pains to find a "sound" professor of philosophy; he could note with pride that no teacher's political views had helped or hurt his career at Hopkins,[74] but the political parties of the day varied little in essentials.[75]

The ideal which Gilman sometimes called freedom thus resembled the ideal of avoidance of injurious internal and external disputes. The view of freedom as intrinsic to a university appeared only rarely and indirectly in his thinking, as in his inaugural: "If we would maintain a university, great freedom must be allowed to both teachers and scholars. This involves freedom of methods to be employed by the instructors on the one hand, and, on the other, freedom of courses to be selected by the students." [76] The inclusion of both teachers and students shows, no doubt, the influence of German ideals, but surely freedom of content was more significant in authentic *Lehrfreiheit* than freedom of method. Gilman stopped short of calling freedom an essential without which no institution could be a university, and in the next breath stated, "But this freedom is based on laws." Yet Johns Hopkins undeniably strengthened the developing concept of academic freedom in the United States. Whether Gilman said so or not, much freedom was implicit in the university ideal itself. Gildersleeve's elaboration of the university's motto in 1893 pointed to this implication: "If it is the truth that makes us free, it is freedom that opens the way to truth." [77]

The practice of the university should weigh as fully in any judgment as the statements of its ideals. The informing of Albert Cook in May, 1881, that he would not be re-employed lent an insecurity to the work of all junior faculty members,[78] but too little is known of the case for an accurate judgment of its relation to academic freedom.

An incident that does come under the rubric of violation of academic

---

[74] Gilman, *Launching of a University*, 134.

[75] Although Professor Metzger's evidence in the case of Cornell is more complete and convincing than in the case of Hopkins, there is much insight in his analysis of the weakness of these two new secular universities in matters of academic freedom: "More worldly than the New England colleges, they were less sure of themselves in the world; more openly committed to tolerance, they lacked a tradition of dissent; more secular in outlook and spirit, they were not chafed by the Puritan conscience that would brook no outer restraint" (Hofstadter and Metzger, *Development of Academic Freedom*, 339–340).

[76] "Hopkins Inaugural," 33.

[77] Quoted in French, *History of Johns Hopkins*, 274.

[78] See p. 166 above.

freedom, however, was the suppression of Clodd's *The Childhood of Religions* as a textbook in one of H. B. Adams' courses, after a complaint from the Episcopal bishop of Maryland.[79] A near repetition of the episode in 1889 showed the survival of the same fears and restraints. At that time a student wrote an account of Adams' course in church history for a local newspaper.[80] Apparently in good faith, the student declared that he was defending the university from "continually recurring charges of Agnosticism, and even atheism." Dr. Adams, he reported, said no word against any creed and praised the Bible, which he used "in no other way than as historic material from which to amass historic knowledge." The admirable professor often traced the miracles to natural causes and made historical comparisons of the Bible with other sources; in fact, he saw "no miraculous origin to anything" and looked on Paul as the founder of Christianity. He impressed on the class his view "that the true spirit of the religious is common to all creeds, and is seen working to the most advantage in our Christian and charity organizations, and the like." With pride, the student concluded, "The university will not admit of shackles to its right of free inquiry into historic causes and effects."

But the student's view of academic freedom did not find a totally harmonious response in the university's president. Gilman promptly sent the article to Adams and asked for the correct information so that he could speak with authority "if called upon." After peppering the margin with question marks, Adams returned the clipping, insisting that it was a crude misrepresentation of his teaching, though not maliciously intended.[81] Apparently, Gilman was not "called upon." It may be that he had been correct in his observation a year earlier that suspicions that Hopkins was adverse to Christian influences had "nearly if not quite disappeared from the minds of all well-informed persons." [82] The significant aspect of the affair for academic freedom was that it forced a teacher to bear in mind possible public reaction to his words in the classroom. The wound of 1876 was still sensitive thirteen years later.

The case of Rendel Harris and his public support of antivivisection

[79] See pp. 175–176 above.
[80] "About Church History," Baltimore *American*, June 30, 1889.
[81] Gilman to H. B. Adams, July 2, 1889; H. B. Adams to Gilman, July 4, 1889.
[82] JHC, VIII, 15.

posed a dilemma in which it seemed that someone's freedom must be curbed. Either Harris' right of public advocacy must yield, or Martin's right to pursue his scientific experiments. The decision went against Harris, and he resigned. Was there no other solution? One may wonder why Harris' "error" might not have been allowed where the "truth" was so free to combat it. A public antivivisectionist drive threatened, and the trustees may have feared any faculty aid to those forces; the medical future of the university seemed to deserve special protection. But as a matter of fact, Martin, whose work was under attack, offered a solution that was more in keeping with the university's ideals than was the stand of the authorities. He proposed that the leader of the antivivisectionists, a Mr. Bergh, be invited to give a lecture in Hopkins Hall explaining his views. He could be welcomed, Martin said, "as an opponent of cruelty to animals." It is unfortunate that no one had the courage and imagination to use such a procedure with Harris. If he had been allowed to present his views, Martin could have answered, and the work of the biological laboratory would surely have continued. The procedure would have been a tribute to the power of free expression and discussion. Instead, the tribute was paid to the sanctity of experimental science and to the security of the university from negative publicity. Most of those in the university, however, interpreted the episode as a victory over the forces of obscurantism.[83]

The phenomenon that was generally taken as proof positive that teachers at Johns Hopkins were free to teach and publish their conclusions, no matter what they were, was the continuation of Ely as a member of the faculty. Especially after the attacks of Newcomb and the *Nation* in 1886 there were grounds on which a timid president or narrow trustees could easily have "let him go." [84] Instead he was promoted. The attack and Ely's survival all occurred in broad daylight. His own allegations that he was conservative and the clerical pressures in his behalf were often overlooked or unknown. He seemed to most observers a likely candidate for academic martyrdom whom the university refused to martyr. As a student of the 1880s recalled, "freedom of teaching was vindicated in his person." [85] Some credit is here due

[83] Martin to Gilman, Feb. 8, 1884 [1885?]; Palmer, "The Old Johns Hopkins," *JH Alumni Magazine*, XI, 93. See also pp. 153–154 above.

[84] See pp. 179–186 above.

[85] James Albert Woodburn, "A Noteworthy University Seminary in History: Reminiscences and Personalities," *JH Alumni Magazine*, XXII (1933–1934), 116.

the president and trustees. Ely's career at Johns Hopkins was an episode from which beleaguered faculty members throughout the country could in later years extract an ideal of freedom and a hope for its fulfillment.

In the matter of academic freedom, as in so much else, Hopkins deserved the name of pioneer. But the territory waiting to be won in American higher education stretched far ahead. It would be conquered slowly, and it would not be conquered alone.

: CHAPTER XVII :

The Meaning of 1889

IF the Johns Hopkins University had ceased to exist in 1889, the world would have been poorer during every year that followed. Nevertheless, it had by 1889 already made contributions to American higher education that guaranteed it historical significance. The development of graduate education was the leading achievement, but not the only one. In high undergraduate standards, the adviser system, acceleration of the program for the bachelor's degree, viewing the professor as investigator, professional associationalism, scholarly publication, promoting varied teaching methods including laboratory and seminar, in all these the university had pioneered. It had harbored men destined to shape the thought and action of the nation and the world. Such was the record of the first thirteen years.

The year 1889 marks a turning point in the history of the university, or rather a congeries of turning points. Most apparent at the time was a financial crisis which threatened the survival of the institution and halted much of its development. The financial events which culminated in near tragedy in 1889 entwined the fates of the Garrett family, the B. & O. railroad, and the university. There had been forecasts of disaster in the 1870s. Even before the university opened, a break in the value of B. & O. stock, a cloud the size of a man's hand, aroused Gilman's fears. In 1878 the entire 8 per cent dividend on B. & O. common shares was given in stock rather than cash, and in 1879 the spring dividend was in stock. On March 4, 1878, the trustees voted not to spend more in 1878–1879 than in 1877–1878, departing from their original plan for gradual increase of expenditures and temporarily halting efforts to expand the faculty. Although the will of Johns Hopkins had recommended otherwise, the trustees sold all the dividend shares.[1] To John W. Garrett, president of the railroad and its largest private shareholder, this seemed a personal affront and a financial injury. He made a rare appearance at a trustees' meeting on October 6, 1879, and read a long defense of the B. & O. and its large surplus fund, citing the opinion of Johns Hopkins himself that stock dividends were wise. The recommendation of the will he called a "special and solemn request of Johns Hopkins" and pointed out that he himself had aided "in having these very instructions given to you in the interests of the University." He assailed Francis White, treasurer of the board, as "singularly ignorant" on the subject of B. & O. stock. After predicting that the university's income would double within five years, Garrett concluded dramatically with the announcement that the railroad would declare a cash dividend of 4 per cent the next day. The closing information must have heartened the trustees, but the insult to White and the domineering tone of the speech rankled.[2]

The cash dividend of 1879 marked the beginning of a brief prosperous era, but faculty expansion was restrained by caution. Garrett's estrangement from the board in 1883, centering on the failure to move to Clifton, did not lessen the prosperity, and his death in 1884 had no immediate effect on the value of B. & O. stock. His leadership had faltered toward the end of his life, and his son Robert, who succeeded him, was in ill-health and suffered a complete breakdown before his tenure ended. In 1886, the income dropped to 8 per cent, and H. B. Adams could refer to "growing economic embarrassment."[3] In 1887 the spring dividend of 4 per cent was paid, and then nothing. The years 1888, 1889, and 1890 passed without any dividend payment on the

[1] Gilman to C. W. Eliot, March 15, 1876; Gilman to C. S. Peirce, March 20, 1878; Gilman to A. D. White, March 31, 1878; TM, March 4, Oct. 7, 1878, March 3, May 5, 1879; untitled memorandum, Garrett Papers.

[2] "Remarks of Mr. John W. Garrett, Made before the Board of Trustees of the Johns Hopkins University, at Their Meeting on Monday, October 6th, 1879"; C. Morton Stewart to Garrett, Oct. 11, 1879; both in Garrett Papers.

[3] Edward Hungerford, *The Story of the Baltimore & Ohio Railroad, 1827–1927* (New York and London, 1928), II, 160, 162; Adams to Gilman and executive committee, May 29, 1886, in Holt, ed., *Historical Scholarship*, 87.

major holding of the university, which the founder had told it not to part with.

There was a ray of hope in 1887 that the university might be saved from the coming disaster. Robert Garrett, who had been elected to his father's seat on the university board on December 6, 1886, took an option in April, 1887, to purchase the entire university B. & O. holding of 15,000 shares at $175 per share. John K. Cowen, a director of the railroad, and Thomas M. King, second vice-president, insisted that the board invest the money from such a purchase in a group of stocks whose names they supplied. The finance committee of the trustees refused to be so manipulated, and the option was not taken up.[4]

Shortly before the initiation of this abortive plan, the Garretts had sought to remold the university into a technical institution, reviving many of the charges of failure to serve the founder's wishes and community interests. The detailed plan, included in a report of October 1, 1886, by W. T. Barnard, assistant to Robert Garrett, was published in 1887.[5] It was Mary Garrett who carried the proposals to Gilman, speaking in the name of her brother. At some of their conversations during February and March, 1887, Barnard was present. The proposal that emerged called for the university to set up a technical school; move to Clifton after a time, turning the Howard Street property over to the technical school; aid in reforming the public schools of Baltimore so that they would provide more industrial training; cut the expenses of its existing program if necessary; and admit women to all departments. The contribution of the Garretts would be to erect buildings at Clifton (across from Montebello, their country estate), to rent these buildings to the university, and to lend $35,000 a year, which need not be repaid if the value of the Clifton property did not rise that much each year. A remarkable mixture of motives and interests had inspired this proposal, including the "practicalist" leanings of certain Baltimore citizens and an element of the board, the B. & O.'s interest in industrializing Baltimore, the Garrett interest in land values in the Montebello-Clifton area, and Miss Garrett's feminist convictions. Accompanying the plan

[4] John K. Cowen to George W. Dobbin, June 17, 1887; report of the finance committee of the JHU trustees; both in TM, Oct. 3, 1887.

[5] W. T. Barnard, *Baltimore & Ohio Railroad Company, Office of the President: Service Report on Technical Education, with Special Reference to the Baltimore & Ohio Railroad Service* (Baltimore, 1887), esp. 77–87, 163–165. The trustees apparently received a copy in advance of publication (ECM, Oct. 28, 1886).

were hints that the public unpleasantness of 1883 might be repeated and that, if the trustees declined, Robert Garrett would seek other means to force the university out to Clifton. Throughout the negotiations, Gilman remained reserved and proper, saying always that he could not speak for the board. It is not difficult to imagine his fears, however. Robert Garrett himself at last appeared to present the proposal formally at a board meeting of March 7, 1887; at a special meeting on the last day of the month, which Garrett did not attend, the proposal was "respectfully declined" by a unanimous vote.[6] After the rapid decline of the fortunes of the B. & O. and the end of Garrett's presidency in October, 1887, nothing more was heard of the plan. The feminist aspect of the matter, however, was to bring the far more generous and acceptable gifts of Miss Garrett which allowed the opening of the medical school in 1893.

Despite the flurries of hope and fear stirred by the Garrett family, the university found itself almost without income when the November, 1887, dividend was omitted. The finance committee reported that competent observers believed no dividend was forthcoming in the next twelve months. They forecast a deficit of nearly $98,000 for the university during the current term. What saved the university for the moment was the special fund for buildings which the board had set up in 1884. Although the physics building, completed early in 1887, had lessened the fund, there was still enough to cover the 1887–1888 deficit.[7]

But in the fall of 1888, when B. & O. prospects looked even gloomier, Gilman asked the trustees to announce publicly the university's plight and appeal for further endowment and an emergency fund of $100,000. He reported "the most rigid economy"—leaving important positions unfilled, omitting library and laboratory appropriations, raising tuition, and cutting scholarship stipends. At Gilman's suggestion, a special committee on ways and means was organized, but the trustees hoped to delay a public cry of disaster.[8] In November, however, Dobbin was dropped from the board of directors of the B. & O., and the university, the largest private stockholder after the Garrett family, was left un-

[6] Series of memoranda in Gilman's hand, beginning "Feb. 6, 1887," GP; TM, Feb. 15, March 7, 31, 1887.

[7] TM, June 2, 1884, Dec. 5, 1887.

[8] Gilman to executive committee, copy in TM, Oct. 10, 1888; TM, Oct. 10, Nov. 5, 1888.

represented.[9] This heightened the alarm. The thought of selling the stock at whatever price could be gotten was entertained, but powerful English shipping interests warned that this would throw the B. & O. into the hands of the Richmond and West Point Terminal Company and ruin Baltimore. An offer from William Johnston of Liverpool to help with an emergency fund strengthened Gilman's plan. In December, William W. Spence, a Baltimore merchant not directly connected with the university, stepped forward to guide the fund raising.[10]

With the drive for the emergency fund, the value of Gilman's steady attention to relations with Baltimore became clear. The doubts of 1875 or even 1883 about the university were gone; the oversubscribing of the fund was announced in May, 1889, and the university escaped salary cuts. Gilman himself had given $5,000, and Mary Garrett had shown by an equal contribution that the university might still look with hope to representatives of her family.[11] Gilman returned alumni contributions with the comment that Baltimore businessmen should help first,[12] but it was a cause for encouragement that alumni might in the future be a source of financial aid.

It was not entirely his tendency toward euphemism that led Gilman to begin his *Annual Report* of 1889 with the words, "The year that is now closed has been one of the most interesting in the history of the University." [13] The university had done more than survive—it had seen the prospect of a new financial era, with sources other than the original Hopkins endowment. The alumni for the first time appeared as potential benefactors, the citizens of Baltimore had come forward with support for the emergency fund, and Gilman could report two other major gifts. Mr. and Mrs. Lawrence Turnbull had founded a Lectureship of Poetry with an income of $1,000 a year in memory of their son Percy. Eugene Levering had given $20,000 for the construction of a

[9] Baltimore *Sun*, Nov. 20, 1888; G. W. Dobbin to J. Pierpont Morgan, Sept. 25, 1887, copy in Dobbin-Brown Papers.

[10] Gilman diary, "1888–9 Opening Hospital," Nov. 19, Dec. 5, 8, 10, 1888.

[11] ARJH (1889), 4–5; TM, June 10, 1889; JHC, VIII, 110. A complete list of donors and amounts is in *Statement respecting the Johns Hopkins University of Baltimore Presented to the Public on the Twentieth Anniversary, 1896* ([Baltimore, 1896]), 22, copy in New York Public Library.

[12] Gilman to E. G. Richardson, March 12, 1889; Gilman to G. T. Kemp, March 12, 1889.

[13] ARJH (1889), 3.

building chiefly for the use of the YMCA.[14] Before the year 1889 ended, the university received two more gifts. John W. McCoy, who died on August 20, had made the university his residuary legatee. His interest in the university traced back to his election in 1884 as first president of the Baltimore branch of the Archaeological Institute of America. His home, which became the president's house, his library, and approximately a half-million dollars came to the university, without restriction.[15] In the fall, Mrs. Caroline Donovan, an eighty-six-year-old Baltimorean, influenced by Mayor Ferdinand C. Latrobe, gave $100,000 for endowment of a professorship, the type of gift that Gilman had long wished for.[16] Although he was overoptimistic in announcing, "The era of great gifts has begun," it was true that the university was at last reaping financial benefit from its good name. The bulk of the B. & O. stock was converted from common to preferred in 1890, thus cutting what had once been an income of $150,000 to $60,000.[17] Had aid not come from other sources, the university's plight would have approached disaster. Perhaps the long-range hope inspired by the appearance of Baltimore benefactors was even more important than the money given. As it was, the university had been saved from a major retreat and saved from despair, but any future advance would be slow and painful.

The year 1889 saw new emphasis on two developments that had been slowly growing inside the university. New demands and new benefits began to come from the collegiate and the medical programs, and these changes broke the focus of attention on graduate study that had made Hopkins unique.

No more after 1889 would the mistake be made that Hopkins admitted only graduate students. The appointment of Dean Griffin in the spring of that year symbolized the importance of the undergraduate work, as did the new high enrollment of 141 matriculates in the fall. There was a burst of undergraduate extracurricular activities, including athletics, and Remsen was torn between a desire to welcome the new "College spirit" and his fears that it was injuring the higher work.[18]

[14] JHC, VIII, 95; TM, April 1, May 6, 31, 1889.

[15] JHC, III, 138, VIII, 105; ECM, Sept. 23, 1889; French, *History of Johns Hopkins*, 380.

[16] TM, Nov. 8, 1889; Remsen to Gilman, Nov. 8, 1889; G. W. Brown to Gilman, Dec. 24, 1889.

[17] ARJH (1890), 16, 13; TM, June 2, Oct. 6, 1890.   [18] See pp. 257–258 above.

When the student body gathered outside Gilman's hotel on October 15, 1889, to give the "Johns Hopkins yell," he himself must have felt the change.[19]

The common error in the public mind after 1889 was to confuse the university with the hospital and the faculty of philosophy with the medical school or to forget that a nonmedical Johns Hopkins existed. On May 7, 1889, after a dozen years of frustration and delay,[20] the hospital was formally opened. The fulfillment of the other half of the Hopkins will was to prove the exciting story of the 1890s, especially after the medical school opened in 1893. A medical faculty had been declared in existence in 1886, and the work of the university had been weighted toward the biological sciences; the influence was not new, but it was distinctly increased in 1889. During the four years before the medical school opened, the trustees, Gilman, and their advisers Welch and Osler devoted many hours to its problems. In the matter of the school as well as the hospital, 1889 was a landmark year. In the midst of financial distress came the initial offer of funds from the source that was eventually to make the school possible. On January 1, 1889, Trustee Thomas and his daughter M. Carey Thomas, president of Bryn Mawr, called on Gilman to ask whether the university would accept a gift of $100,000 from various donors on condition that the medical school be open to women on the same terms as men. First named among the potential donors was Mary Garrett. Although Gilman remained noncommittal and urged delay until the completion of the emergency fund, he must have seen here the great opportunity for achieving another stage of the university's destiny, for making it a pioneer once again.[21]

Another turning point of 1889 involved Gilman himself. This man with so many irons in the fire all his life would not stay endlessly tending one of them. He had built his university by 1889. He knew that it was respected among the universities of Europe which had been its models, and though its omissions were many, he could look upon it and call it good. Having accomplished this much, he could listen to other challenges, which were bound to seek such a man. In

[19] Baltimore *Sun*, Oct. 16, 1889.

[20] Chesney, *Johns Hopkins Hospital*, I, *passim*.

[21] Gilman diary, "1888–9 Opening Hospital," Jan. 1, 1889. The pioneering years of the medical school are described in Chesney, *Johns Hopkins Hospital*, II, *1893–1905*.

1889 came the first outside call to remove him from intimate daily care of the university. On December 11, 1888, Francis T. King, chairman of the hospital board of trustees, told Gilman that ill-health would keep him from organizing the hospital and asked for help. The final agreement was that Gilman would temporarily become director of the hospital and take half his salary from hospital funds. He was officially named director on January 25, 1889. His leap into action was that of a peace-weary warrior welcoming the fray. At once he was making appointments, calling for reports, holding conferences, and sending telegrams, and the next day he set off for New York with Welch. He dispelled rumors that he had been permanently deflected from the university, but admitted himself "engrossed" by the hospital work.[22]

By March 8, he was beginning to "feel . . . the strain of double cares," and on April 1 he requested a long vacation. From October 16, 1889, to July 7, 1890, he was gone from Baltimore.[23] Remsen served as acting president, and Griffin, the new dean, took many responsibilities. With remarkable smoothness, the university kept on course during Gilman's absence. He had built well, and letter after letter reported the institution functioning without difficulty, "smoothly, without a jolt or a jostle to complain of." But there was a significant change in tone. Never in the early years would a trustee have written, as Brown did in December, 1889, "We shall hope and expect to take no steps backwards." [24] In the case of finances, the crisis proved that the university could survive by other means than its original endowment. In the case of leadership, Gilman's deflection by the hospital directorship and his year's absence proved that the university no longer depended on one man for survival.

When at the twenty-fifth anniversary celebration in 1902 Gilman read the list of candidates for honorary degrees,[25] he read the fate of his university during the preceding decade: Charles William Eliot of Harvard, Arthur Twining Hadley of Yale, Francis Landey Patton of Princeton, Nicholas Murray Butler of Columbia, James Burrill Angell of Michigan, Benjamin Ide Wheeler of California, Granville Stanley

[22] Gilman diary, "1888–9 Opening Hospital"; Franklin, *Life of Gilman*, 257–260; Gilman to C. W. Eliot, March 9, 1889, Eliot Papers.

[23] Gilman to J. T. Wightman, March 8, 1889; TM, April 1, 1889, Oct. 6, 1890.

[24] G. W. Dobbin to Gilman, Aug. 20, 1890; J. C. Thomas to Gilman, Dec. 19, 1889; G. W. Brown to Gilman, Dec. 24, 1889.

[25] *Hopkins Twenty-fifth Anniversary*, 97–103.

Hall of Clark, David Starr Jordan of Stanford, and William Rainey Harper of Chicago. Gilman's university was no longer unique. These men had created and expanded institutions that served many of the same ideals that Gilman had brought to Baltimore in 1875. They too had determined to make the "true university in America," and in 1902 no one would have thought of granting that title to Hopkins alone. Eliot, Hadley, Patton, and Butler stood at the helms of the oldest institutions in the country, scarcely recognizable now as the colonial colleges or the hidebound old-time colleges of the early nineteenth century that they had once been. In the 1890s many of their graduate programs had equaled or surpassed the work offered at Hopkins. Angell and Wheeler were two of the leaders who had tapped the resources of states to build complex universities that promoted many phases of education, including the most advanced. Hall, Jordan, and Harper represented the new universities of the last decade of the century that had replaced Hopkins as the youngest and destroyed its uniqueness as a university privately endowed from a single great fortune. They too were unhampered by political considerations and (despite Baptist origins in the case of Chicago) sectarian traditions in their imitation of the European universities. Hopkins had always been a member of the family of universities, but it had once been a member to whom others looked with admiration and envy, as an innovator to be followed. In 1902, Hopkins was still a worthy member of that family, but its special luster had faded.

The opening of Clark in 1889 as a university for graduates only, as what Hall called "the inevitable next step," [26] meant that the country now had such a university as Gilman pictured to E. L. Godkin in 1875, but failed to establish. The leaders at Hopkins gave constant aid to the early planners of Clark. Gilman was one of the first consulted by John D. Washburn, chief adviser of Jonas Clark, and two of the original trustees visited Hopkins in February, 1887. [27] The decimation of the Hopkins psychology department when Hall left to become Clark's first president forecast the transfer of men and ideas from Hopkins, now the older institution. Shortly after beginning his work, Hall expressed this debt: "At every step so far as I visit institutions I realize more &

[26] *Life and Confessions*, 247.
[27] Washburn to Gilman, Jan. 22, 1887; Washburn to C. W. Eliot, Jan. 24, 1887, Eliot Papers; George F. Hoar to Gilman, Feb. 13, 18, 1887.

more how great has been the change, always for the good, wrought by the institution you have shaped, & how far, if we succeed at Worcester our success will be based on & conditioned by the successes of Baltimore." [28] Clark University's brilliant promise was never realized, partly because of the disadvantage of having a living founder and partly because of president-faculty quarrels.[29] But at the moment of collapse at Clark, two other universities appeared that clearly ranked with Hopkins in promoting the most-advanced studies. On the West Coast, Leland Stanford Junior University began academic work in 1891 with more money than Hopkins and many of the same goals.[30] Opening in 1892, Chicago had in the gifts of John D. Rockefeller an endowment which soon dwarfed the Hopkins bequest and in its president, William Rainey Harper, a leader who lacked some of Gilman's virtues but surpassed him in executive power and energy.[31]

When Gilman returned from his year's absence and addressed the university on October 3, 1890,[32] he had begun to look on Hopkins with some historical perspective. The speech was mellow with the sense of good accomplished and crises survived. Gilman spoke of past achievements, the records of alumni. He stopped himself at one point, saying, "I have been talking as if the events of the last fourteen years made a chapter of ancient history." He cited the pleasures of advanced study, describing it without the hypercharged excitement of the opening years. Meeting Sylvester in England had recalled a bygone day, and the recent death of Brown gave a sense of the old order's changing.

The remodeling of Hopkins Hall as a chemistry classroom set Gilman reminiscing on the many lectures and ceremonies held there. He caught the spirit of the early courses given by visiting lecturers when he said that in Hopkins Hall learning had been made "a duty, a pleasure and even a fashion." He comforted the audience: the loss to sentiment would prove to be "in fact a gain for science."

It was fitting that after revisiting Europe, the source of ideas that

[28] G. S. Hall to Gilman, July 29, 1888.
[29] Ryan, *Early Graduate Education,* 57–59.
[30] Gilman was to a limited extent adviser here, too (Leland Stanford to Gilman, March 5, 1891 [telegram]; Jane Stanford to Gilman, Feb. 2, 1899).
[31] Gilman had also sought Rockefeller money for Hopkins, but without success (Augustus H. Strong to Gilman, Nov. 17, 1886, Dec. 15, 31, 1888; Strong to J. D. Rockefeller, Dec. 15, 1888, letter of introduction for Gilman, GP).
[32] JHC, X, 1–5.

had grown into the very frame of Johns Hopkins, Gilman should announce that Americans who thought they were making the greatest educational progress were wrong; he could point again to ferment across the Atlantic. It was fitting too that the leader of a university which had constantly relied for students, teachers, and ideas on the older colleges and universities of both Europe and America should refer to "the world of science and of letters" where Hopkins held "an honorable place."

For the citizens of Baltimore, the trustees, the faculty, the alumni, the graduate students, and the undergraduates, Gilman had warm and special words of thanks or encouragement. And those who could remember his inaugural must have felt the constancy of purpose when they heard him say, "Whatever gains we make in our material condition, whatever limitations are still obvious, let us never forget, my friends, that men and methods make universities, not halls, nor books, nor instruments, important as these are."

If the university's youth had ended, it was still true that the very nature of a university involves the constant renewal of youth through its students. If an era that many would look back upon as a golden age had ended, it was still true that something golden about knowledge and the love of knowledge would never tarnish. Youth and knowledge, imagination and learning would continue to work their wonderful chemistry upon each other. Life worth the living stretched ahead for the university.

APPENDIXES

BIBLIOGRAPHICAL NOTE

INDEX

: APPENDIX A :

Books Ordered by the

Trustees in 1874

THE following books are listed in "Accession Book: J.H.U.: 1–5000," Librarian's Office, Johns Hopkins University, and by French, *History of Johns Hopkins*, 24–25:

1. Matthew Arnold. *Higher Schools and Universities in Germany.* London, 1874.
2. E. H. Clarke. *Sex in Education.* Boston, 1874.
3. William Everett. *On the Cam.* Cambridge, Mass., 1867.
4. S. H. Taylor. *Classical Study.* Andover, Mass., 1870.
5. James Orton. *The Liberal Education of Women.* New York, 1873.
6. B. H. Hall. *A Collection of College Words and Customs.* Cambridge, Mass., 1856.
7. Walter Smith. *Art Education, Scholastic and Industrial.* Boston, 1873.
8. L. H. Bagg. *Four Years at Yale.* New Haven, 1871.
9. Horace Mann. *Lectures and Annual Reports on Education.* (*Life and Works of Horace Mann,* ed. Mary Mann, vol. II.) Boston, 1872.
10. J. H. Rigg. *National Education in Its Social Conditions and Aspects.* London, 1873.
11. Noah Porter. *The American Colleges and the American Public.* New Haven, 1870.
12. Josiah Quincy. *The History of Harvard University.* Cambridge, Mass., 1840.
13. C. A. Bristed. *Five Years in an English University.* New York, 1873.
14. E. L. Youmans. *The Culture Demanded by Modern Life.* New York, 1873.

329

15. B. G. Northrop. *Education Abroad.* New York, 1873.
16. Isaac Todhunter. *The Conflict of Studies.* London, 1873.
17. Herbert Spencer. *Education: Intellectual, Moral, and Physical.* New York, 1873.
18. W. B. Hazen. *The School and the Army in Germany and France.* New York, 1872.
19. L. B. Monroe. *Manual of Physical and Vocal Training.* Philadelphia, 1873.
20. Karl Rosenkranz. *Pedagogics as a System.* St. Louis, Mo., 1872.
21. S. D. Alexander. *Princeton College during the Eighteenth Century.* New York, 1872.
22. Calvin Durfee. *A History of Williams College.* Boston, 1860.

The following books were ordered by Reverdy Johnson, Jr., from Edward S. Allen, a London agent, in a letter of May 22, 1874, Johnson letter book. Those starred do not appear in the first accession book and were probably not received.

23. C. H. Cooper. *Memorials of Cambridge.* 3 vols. Cambridge, Eng., 1860–1866.
24. G. T. C. Bentley. *Schools for the People.* London, 1871.
25. D. W. Thompson. *Day Dreams of a Schoolmaster.* Edinburgh, 1864.
26. *The Public Schools.* Edinburgh, 1867.
27. Goldwin Smith. *The Reorganization of the University of Oxford.* London, 1868.
28. J. H. Newman. *The Office and Work of the Universities.* London, 1859.
*29. *Essays on Educational Reformers.* London, 1868.
*30. *Histoire de l'Education en France.* Paris, 1858.
31. George Dyer. *The Privileges of the University of Cambridge.* 2 vols. London, 1824.
32. Thomas Fuller. *The History of the University of Cambridge, and of Waltham Abbey.* London, 1840.
33. George Combe. *Lectures on Popular Education.* Edinburgh, 1848.
34. Andrew Amos. *Lectures on the Advantages of a Classical Education as Auxiliary to a Commercial Education.* London, 1846.
*35. J. C. Demogeot and H. Montucci. *De l'Enseignment Secondaire en Angleterre et en Ecosse.* Paris, 1868.
36. E. M. Goulburn. *The Book of Rugby School.* Rugby, 1856.
37. E. S. Creasy. *Some Account of the Foundation of Eton College and of the Past and Present Condition of the School.* London, 1848.
38. William Whewell. *On the Principles of English University Education.* London, 1838.
39. V. A. Huber. *The English Universities.* 3 vols. London, 1843.
40. *The University of Bonn: Its Rise, Progress, & Present State.* London, 1845.
41. W. B. S. Taylor. *History of the University of Dublin.* London, 1845.

*42. Charles Kingsley. *Alexandria and Her Schools*. Cambridge, Eng., 1854.

43. F. W. Farrar. *Essays on a Liberal Education*. London, 1867.

The following books are not in the list that Johnson sent to Allen, but since the first was accessioned on September 16, 1874, and the next two probably the same day, they appear to belong in this list.

44. Henry Barnard. *Pestalozzi and Pestalozzianism*. New York, 1862.

45. O. D. Tudor. *The Law of Charitable Trusts*. London, 1871.

46. Horace Mann. *Annual Reports on Education*. (*Life and Works of Horace Mann*, ed. Mary Mann, vol. III.) Boston, 1872.

: APPENDIX B :

Courses at the Johns Hopkins University, 1876-1877

THE following is taken verbatim from JHR (1877; identical with JHU *Circulars*, no. 7 [February, 1877]), 71–75. The second half-year courses only approximated those here listed. Parenthetical numbers represent the number of students.

ENUMERATION OF THE STUDIES OF THE CURRENT YEAR.

Some of the topics are treated continuously through the year,—and others are treated in special courses of lectures, longer or shorter in duration. Some voluntary classes formed by the Fellows are not included in this list.

Graphical Statics.
    Prof. Sylvester.
Modern Higher Algebra.
    Prof. Sylvester. Twice a week (last half-year). (9)
Spherical Harmonics.
    Prof. Sylvester. (Last half-year.)
Analytic Geometry.
    Dr. Story. 5 hours a week; through the year. (6)
Determinants and Theory of Equations.
    Dr. Story. 2 hours a week; through the year. (7)
Calculus.
    Mr. Craig. 5 hours a week; through the year. (5)
Theory of Definite Integrals.
    Mr. Craig. 3 hours a week. (First half-year.) (5)

Rational Mechanics.
     Mr. Craig. (Second half-year.)   (8)
History of Astronomy.
     Prof. Newcomb. 20 Lectures; beginning Nov. 3rd.
Methods and Results of Territorial Surveys.
     Prof. Hilgard. 20 Lectures; beginning April 9th.
Thermodynamics.
     Prof. Rowland. 15 Lectures (first half-year).   (7)
Electricity and Magnetism.
     Prof. Rowland. 20 Lectures (second half-year).
General Physics.
     Dr. Hastings. 4 hours a week; through the year.   (4)
Theory of Elasticity.
     Dr. Story. 20 Lectures.   (4)
General Chemistry.
     Prof. Remsen. 5 Lectures a week; through the year.   (35)
Technical Chemistry.
     Prof. Mallet. 20 Lectures; beginning May 10th.
Qualitative and Quantitative Analysis.
     Dr. Morse. 2 Lectures a week; through the year.
Animal Physiology.
     Prof. Martin. 2 Lectures a week; through the year.   (30)
On Theories in Biology.
     Dr. Brooks. 16 Lectures; beginning Jan. 4th.   (12)
Comparative Philology.
     Prof. Whitney. 20 Lectures; beginning March 6th.
Philological Seminary.
     Prof. Gildersleeve. Once a week (after Dec. 6).   (6)
Thucydides.
     Prof. Gildersleeve. Pedagogical Seminary; 8 meetings. (9)
Greek Lyric Poetry.
     Prof. Gildersleeve. 20 Lectures; beginning Oct. 4th.
Lectures on the Syntax of the Greek Verb.
     Prof. Gildersleeve. 1 Lecture a week (second half-year). (9)
Pindar.
     Prof. Gildersleeve. 2 Lectures a week; to begin in March.
Ajax.
     Prof. Morris. 5 hours a week (first half-year).   (3)
Aristotle's Ethics.
     Prof. Morris. 2 hours a week.   (4)
Thucydides, Bk. VII.
     Prof. Morris. 5 hours a week (second half-year).   (4)
Homer.
     Prof. Morris. 4 hours a week (second half-year).   (7)

Appendix B

Greek Composition.
    Prof. Morris. 1 hour a week; through the year. (7)
Xenophon's Memorabilia.
    Mr. Cross. 5 hours a week (first half-year). (7)
Xenophon's Anabasis.
    Prof. Morris. 5 hours a week (first half-year). (4)
Herodotus.
    Mr. Cross. 4 hours a week (second half-year). (6)
Plato's Apology.
    Mr. Cross. 5 hours a week (second half-year). (7)
Plautus.
    Prof. Morris. 4 hours a week. (6)
Tacitus.
    Prof. Morris. 5 hours a week (first half-year). (4)
Terence.
    Prof. Morris. 4 hours a week (second half-year). (6)
Horace.
    Mr. Cross. 5 hours a week; through the year. (14)
Latin Composition.
    Prof. Morris. 1 hour a week; through the year. (6)
Hermann and Dorothea.
    Mr. Brandt. 5 hours a week (first half-year). (12)
Nathan the Wise.
    Mr. Brandt. 4 hours a week (first half-year). (8)
Goethe's Prose.
    Mr. Brandt. 3 hours a week (first half-year). (8)
Chaucer.
    Prof. Child. 20 Lectures; beginning Jan. 31st.
Dante and the Literature of the Romance Languages
                 during the 13th and 14th Centuries.
    Prof. Lowell. 20 Lectures; beginning Jan. 31st.
Corneille.
    Prof. Rabillon. 2 hours a week. (4)
French Composition.
    Prof. Rabillon. 2 hours a week; through the year. (4)
French Literature of the 17th and 18th Centuries.
    Prof. Rabillon. 20 Lectures; beginning Oct. 5th.
Italian.
    Mr. Elliott. 3 hours a week. (3)
Sanskrit.
    Dr. Lanman. Hitopadeça.
        3 hours a week; through the year. (2)
    Dr. Lanman. Grammar and Nala. 2 hours a week. (5)
Persian: Grammar and Sâdi's Gulistan.
    Mr. Elliott.

Hebrew.

     Mr. Murray. 3 hours a week (second half-year).

Arabic.

     Mr. Murray. 2 hours a week (second half-year).

Sources of American History.

     Dr. Scott. 2 hours a week; through the year.   (6)

English History from the Accession of James I. to the death
               of Cromwell.

     Dr. Scott. 30 Lectures.   (34)

Law of Torts.

     Prof. Cooley. 26 Lectures; beginning May 7th.

Political Economy.

     Prof. Walker. 20 Lectures; beginning April 9th.

The Laboratories in Chemistry, Physics and Biology are constantly open through the academic year.

Bibliographical Note

THE following note includes only sources that were of major importance in providing information or shaping my thinking.

MANUSCRIPT COLLECTIONS AND UNPUBLISHED MINUTES
(arranged by location)

1. The Johns Hopkins University

The principal source for this study has been the Daniel Coit Gilman Papers in the Johns Hopkins University Library. The collection contains approximately thirteen thousand incoming letters, plus notebooks, diaries, clippings, and manuscript drafts of speeches and reports. Gilman once apologized for saving so much and advised others against it. After his retirement, when he tried to go through his correspondence and destroy inconsequential letters, he found the task too burdensome to carry far. The three-fifths of the material which is kept in the Lanier Room is catalogued. The rest, kept in the library stacks, is arranged alphabetically by author. The letter-press books containing Gilman's outgoing correspondence are especially full for 1876. Certain bound volumes concerning university history, such as the letter-press book of Reverdy Johnson, Jr., and a scrapbook of Thomas R. Ball, the registrar, are kept as part of the Gilman Papers.

The Johns Hopkins University Papers, in the Lanier Room, comprises a much smaller collection containing a wide range of material varying from data on the founder's childhood to documents dealing with the most recent history of the university. It appears to consist of material which has come to the university since about 1940 and which did not seem to belong directly with the Gilman Papers. However, several manuscripts by Gilman, especially outlines for proposed memoirs, are important for the period of this work.

The Alumni Records Office contains biographical data on alumni, professors, and trustees. Apparently, a portion of the early files of the President's Office was once transferred to the Alumni Records Office and has remained there. The files contain many surprising and valuable documents, such as the early transcript of the Angell interview of 1874.

The minutes of the Board of Trustees and of its executive committee are in the safe in the President's Office. The minutes of the trustees show little besides resolutions actually passed, though some letters and reports of committees are copied in full. These minutes are partially indexed. The minutes of the executive committee, which were recorded by Reverdy Johnson, Jr., in his own hand as long as he was chairman, give a better indication of how plans evolved and who originated them.

2. Division of Manuscripts, Library of Congress

The John Work Garrett Papers includes otherwise unobtainable information on the university, especially its financial and community relations problems.

The Simon Newcomb Papers is important for incoming letters from Hopkins officials and faculty members, but reveals little of Newcomb's career there.

The J. Franklin Jameson diary, part of the J. Franklin Jameson Papers, covers the entire period of his life at Hopkins, 1880–1888, and is remarkably full, though highly subjective. His criticisms of the Hopkins scene are an antidote for the promotional nature of many official accounts.

3. Maryland Historical Society

The Dobbin-Brown Papers contains mostly legal documents, but some of the letters to and from George Washington Dobbin deal directly with university matters. The collection does not include any of George William Brown's papers.

The biographical files of the society contain data on famous Marylanders, including early Hopkins figures.

4. Yale University Library

The papers of George Jarvis Brush, William Dwight Whitney, James Dwight Dana, and William Henry Brewer contain letters from Gilman and about him and his Baltimore experiment. They often indicate relationships between programs of Sheffield Scientific School and Hopkins.

The Thomas Davidson Papers reveals sympathetic relations with Hopkins.

5. Harvard University Archives, Widener Library

The Charles William Eliot Papers is not very inclusive for the 1870s and 1880s, but much of the interuniversity correspondence, valuable for this study, has survived.

The Charles Rockwell Lanman Papers is a rich collection. The diary, usually only a listing of events, solves certain mysteries from the opening year to 1880. After Lanman left Hopkins, he corresponded regularly with several of his former colleagues; thus, the collection is also valuable for the 1880s.

The Josiah Royce Papers includes few letters, but much of Royce's scholarly writing during his Hopkins years, 1876–1878.

The Benjamin Peirce Papers represents the relations of an elder statesman of academic life with the new foundation.

The Charles Sanders Peirce Papers contains little from his Hopkins years.

6. New York Public Library

The Albert Shaw Papers is the collection of an inveterate letter saver, active correspondent, and faithful Hopkins student and alumnus. The Shaw diary of 1882, a short-lived affair, reveals the impact of the university on a new arrival.

OFFICIAL PUBLICATIONS OF THE UNIVERSITY

University publications during the administration of Gilman were unusually detailed, regular, and accurate. The *Annual Reports* began in January, 1876, and were written almost completely by Gilman, though special reports by others were at times included. The *Annual Report* of 1878 was delayed from January to September so that the reports might follow the academic rather than the calendar year.

The *Circulars* has changed format drastically from time to time. From the summer of 1876 through the summer of 1877, it was in octavo form, varying greatly in length. Some issues dealt with isolated topics, such as the plan for premedical training; others included preliminary announcements in several fields. There was no *Circulars* during the 1877–1878 and 1878–1879 terms, but in December, 1879, a much expanded publication with the same title appeared in quarto form, containing detailed proceedings of the university societies, class lists, and even scholarly articles. In this form its was published approximately every other month until 1903, when it changed back to octavo form. By that time far less material was included.

The *Register*, which grew out of the original *Circulars*, was the catalogue of the university, containing regulations and lists of courses and personnel; at times it included course descriptions not given in the *Circulars*.

The *Johns Hopkins Alumni Magazine*, which began publication in 1912, contains valuable reminiscences and some surprisingly frank self-criticism.

The student yearbook was first published in 1889. For a few years the title varied, but it came to be called the *Hullabaloo*. In addition to pictures of the teachers of earlier years, it contains occasional articles by faculty members.

Four other official publications important for this work are *Johns Hopkins*

Bibliographical Note

University: Charter, Extracts of Will, Officers, and By-Laws (Baltimore, 1874), Addresses at the Inauguration of Daniel C. Gilman as President of the Johns Hopkins University, Baltimore, February 22, 1876 (Baltimore, 1876), Johns Hopkins University Celebration of the Twenty-fifth Anniversary of the Founding of the University and Inauguration of Ira Remsen, LL.D., as President of the University February Twenty-first and Twenty-second, 1902 (Baltimore, [1902]), and W. Norman Brown, comp., Johns Hopkins Half-Century Directory: A Catalogue of the Trustees, Faculty, Holders of Honorary Degrees, and Students, Graduates and Non-graduates, 1876–1926 (Baltimore, 1926).

AUTOBIOGRAPHIES, MEMOIRS, AND PUBLISHED CORRESPONDENCE

Autobiography of Andrew Dickson White, 2 vols. (New York, 1905), offers many insights into the development of American higher education and some specific observations of the Johns Hopkins University by a friend and adviser of the first president and trustees. The Yale which shaped White and Gilman and against which they revolted is described in Timothy Dwight, Memories of Yale Life and Men, 1845–1899 (New York, 1903).

Closest to an autobiography by a trustee is George William Brown, Baltimore and the Nineteenth of April, 1861: A Study of the War (JHU Studies in Historical and Political Science, extra vol. III; Baltimore, 1887); it is a self-revealing work. Among faculty autobiographies, Simon Newcomb, Reminiscences of an Astronomer (Boston, 1903), gives extremely sparse information. Granville Stanley Hall, Life and Confessions of a Psychologist (New York, 1923), passes many judgments on Hopkins men and practices, but the factual references are often wrong. Richard T. Ely's Ground under Our Feet (New York, 1938) was written with some consultation of documentary evidence and strives for objectivity about the author's career at Hopkins. Cyrus Adler, I Have Considered the Days (Philadelphia, 1941), reveals much of the spirit of both his student and faculty years at Hopkins.

Memoirs of former students tell more of the early Hopkins than do those of former teachers. Ernest G. Sihler, From Maumee to Thames and Tiber: The Life-Story of an American Classical Scholar (New York, 1930), includes much detail and shows use of documentary sources. I Remember: The Autobiography of Abraham Flexner (New York, 1940), though overadmiring in regard to Hopkins, has the great value of telling the undergraduate side of the story. The Hopkins years described in Frederic C. Howe, The Confessions of a Reformer (New York, 1925), and in Edward A. Ross, Seventy Years of It: An Autobiography (New York and London, 1936), fall just after the period of this study.

Two Hopkins history teachers have been well served in the matter of published correspondence. W. Stull Holt, ed., *Historical Scholarship in the United States, 1876–1901: As Revealed in the Correspondence of Herbert B. Adams* (*JHU Studies in Historical and Political Science*, LVI, no. 4; Baltimore, 1938), catches much of the spirit of the university as well as of the man and the profession. A monumental labor of love is Elizabeth Donnan and Leo F. Stock, eds., *An Historian's World: Selections from the Correspondence of John Franklin Jameson* (*Memoirs of the American Philosophical Society*, XLII; Philadelphia, 1956); probably no other work has ever brought the early Hopkins so fully alive, and its scholarship is meticulous. Charles R. Anderson, gen. ed., *The Centennial Edition of the Works of Sidney Lanier*, 10 vols. (Baltimore, 1945), reveals a side of Hopkins life and thought often forgotten. All three of these works have valuable introductions.

PUBLICATIONS OF PRESIDENT AND FACULTY

Two books by Gilman reveal his developing ideas on educational questions. *University Problems in the United States* (New York, 1898) contains his California and Hopkins inaugurals. The opening third of *The Launching of a University and Other Papers: A Sheaf of Remembrances* (New York, 1906) consists of reminiscences of his years at Hopkins. They are disappointingly sketchy. The last two-thirds includes addresses made during his later years.

Of interest beyond their authors' specialties are certain addresses and articles in the following collections: Basil Lanneau Gildersleeve, *Essays and Studies: Educational and Literary* (Baltimore, 1890); Charles William Emil Miller, ed., *Selections from the Brief Mention of Basil Lanneau Gildersleeve* (Baltimore, 1930); *The Physical Papers of Henry Augustus Rowland* (Baltimore, 1902); H. F. Baker, ed., *The Collected Mathematical Papers of James Joseph Sylvester*, 4 vols. (Cambridge, Eng., 1904–1912); and Henry Newell Martin, *Physiological Papers* (*Memoirs from the Biological Laboratory of the Johns Hopkins University*, III; Baltimore, 1895). Gilman seems to have drawn from each professor at least one considered statement of the meaning of scholarship and education.

Essays by Hall, Ely, H. B. Adams, and G. S. Morris make G. Stanley Hall, ed., *Methods of Teaching History* (Boston, 1885), a valuable source on a subject that past generations of college teachers have often left shrouded in secrecy. An expansion of one of these essays became Herbert B. Adams' *Methods of Historical Study* (*JHU Studies in Historical and Political Science*, II, nos. 1–2; Baltimore, 1884), which includes much detail on the Hopkins historical seminary. Significant as indications of the university's reaching out for social influence are two works of Richard T. Ely: *The Past and the*

Bibliographical Note

Present of Political Economy (*ibid.*, no. 3) and *Problems of To-Day: A Discussion of Protective Tariffs, Taxation, and Monopolies* (New York, 1888). A work whose theories were later discarded by its author, William Keith Brooks, *The Law of Heredity: A Study of the Cause of Variation and the Origin of Living Organisms* (Baltimore, 1883), is written in a personal and philosophic style that reveals much of the man and the times.

NEWSPAPERS AND MAGAZINES

The two most important Baltimore newspapers for the period of this study were the *Sun* and the *American;* however, the *Evening Standard* covered many university activities in detail. Articles on Hopkins often appeared in the New York press also.

Commentaries on Hopkins and articles by Hopkins faculty and students appeared probably with greatest regularity in the *Nation*. Gilman's business connection with *Science* guaranteed thorough coverage of Hopkins in its pages. Also looked upon as outlets for nonspecial articles were the *Andover Review, Century, Christian Union, Independent, North American Review, Overland Monthly* (which the influence of Charles H. Shinn made a market for faculty and student writings), *Princeton Review,* and *Popular Science Monthly*.

The periodicals established at Hopkins are described in Chapter VI above. In almost every case, their articles were highly technical.

BIOGRAPHIES

The only biography of the founder, Helen Hopkins Thom's *Johns Hopkins: A Silhouette* (Baltimore and London, 1929), is valuable for family tradition and personal reminiscence, but undependable in matters relating to the university.

In Fabian Franklin *et al., The Life of Daniel Coit Gilman* (New York, 1910), are included long quotations from letters and other documents, some of which are now lost. The fact that each section is written by someone near Gilman during the period covered gives this book considerable value as a primary source; at the same time, however, it prevents the unity and critical approach which a new Gilman biography could provide. Abraham Flexner's *Daniel Coit Gilman: Creator of the American Type of University* (New York, 1946) is a penetrating but brief biographical essay which fits Gilman's work at Hopkins into the context of his life.

Probably the best biographical treatment of any Hopkins faculty member is Max H. Fisch and Jackson I. Cope's "Peirce at the Johns Hopkins University," in *Studies in the Philosophy of Charles Sanders Peirce,* ed. by

Bibliographical Note

Philip P. Wiener and Frederic H. Young (Cambridge, Mass., 1952). Both the man and his institutional environment receive thorough and sympathetic analysis, and their interrelationship is brilliantly traced. Robert Mark Wenley, *The Life and Work of George Sylvester Morris: A Chapter in the History of American Thought in the Nineteenth Century* (New York, 1917), advances the thesis that an empirical temper at Hopkins destroyed what could have been a fruitful career for Morris there. A biography of a specialist which benefits from the skills of a historian and a medical scholar is Simon Flexner and James Thomas Flexner, *William Henry Welch and the Heroic Age of American Medicine* (New York, 1941). Frederick H. Getman's *The Life of Ira Remsen* (Easton, Pa., 1940) is uncritical and uninformative. The history of American history badly needs a study of Herbert Baxter Adams; until one appears, the sketches in *Herbert B. Adams: Tributes of Friends* (*JHU Studies in Historical and Political Science*, extra vol. XXIII; Baltimore, 1902) must serve. Abraham A. Neuman, *Cyrus Adler: A Biographical Sketch* (New York, 1942), written without use of Adler's memoirs, adds some information on his Hopkins years.

Biographies of Hopkins students which include much primary material are Burton J. Hendrick, *The Life and Letters of Walter H. Page*, 2 vols. (New York, 1922); Hendrick, *The Training of an American: The Earlier Life and Letters of Walter H. Page, 1855–1913* (Boston and New York, 1928); and Ray Stannard Baker, *Woodrow Wilson: Life and Letters*, 8 vols. (Garden City, N.Y., 1927–1939). A. S. Eisenstadt's *Charles McLean Andrews: A Study in American Historical Writing* (*Columbia Studies in the Social Sciences*, no. 588; New York, 1956) is a biography only in a limited sense; its intellectual focus brings out the most important aspects of Andrews' student years at Hopkins.

A life that touched Hopkins at many points is treated with thoroughness in Edith Finch, *Carey Thomas of Bryn Mawr* (New York and London, 1947). Of major importance to any historical study of American higher education during the past hundred years is Henry James, *Charles W. Eliot: President of Harvard University, 1869–1909* (Boston and New York, 1930).

HISTORIES OF HIGHER EDUCATION

Earlier studies of Johns Hopkins provided guidelines for this work. John C. French's *A History of the University Founded by Johns Hopkins* (Baltimore, 1946), written by the librarian emeritus, treats the university from its beginnings in the mind of Johns Hopkins through the Second World War. Much early material relevant to the faculty of philosophy is available in Alan M. Chesney, *The Johns Hopkins Hospital and the Johns Hopkins University School of Medicine: A Chronicle*, 2 vols., I, *Early Years, 1867–*

Bibliographical Note

1893, II, *1893–1905* (Baltimore, 1943–1958). Irene M. Davis and Benjamin Ring's *The Hopkins Undergraduate in the Faculty of Philosophy: A Sample Survey of Catalogues of the Johns Hopkins University, 1876–1952* (Baltimore, 1956) brings history meaningfully to bear on a contemporary institutional problem.

Three competent studies which have aided in placing Hopkins in context are W. Carson Ryan, *Studies in Early Graduate Education: The Johns Hopkins, Clark University, the University of Chicago* (Carnegie Foundation for the Advancement of Teaching, Bul. no. 30; New York, 1939); Bernard C. Steiner *et al.*, *History of Education in Maryland* (Bureau of Education, Circular of Information no. 2; Washington, 1894); and Russell H. Chittenden, *History of the Sheffield Scientific School of Yale University, 1846–1922*, 2 vols. (New Haven, 1928). Thomas Woody's *A History of Women's Education in the United States*, 2 vols. (New York and Lancaster, Pa., 1929), is massive but lacking in coherence and analysis.

Richard J. Storr, *The Beginnings of Graduate Education in America* (Chicago, 1953), provided essential pre-Civil War background for this study. Three histories that evoke the spirit of the old-time college played a role in the conception of this work not adequately represented by formal citations: George P. Schmidt, *The Old Time College President* (*Columbia University Studies in History, Economics, and Public Law*, no. 317; New York, 1930); Thomas Le Duc, *Piety and Intellect at Amherst College, 1865–1912* (New York, 1946); and Frederick Rudolph, *Mark Hopkins and the Log: Williams College, 1836–1872* (New Haven, 1956). Walter P. Rogers, *Andrew D. White and the Modern University* (Ithaca, 1942), analyzes many important post-Civil War problems and is by no means narrowly limited to Cornell.

That the group-attack plan of university history writing can bring results both detailed and unified has been proven by Merle Curti and Vernon Carstensen, *The University of Wisconsin: A History, 1848–1925*, 2 vols. (Madison, 1949), and by George Wilson Pierson, *Yale: College and University, 1871–1937*, 2 vols., I, *Yale College: An Educational History, 1871–1921*, II, *Yale: The University College, 1921–1937* (New Haven, 1952–1955). On Harvard history James's biography of Eliot proved more useful for this study than either Samuel Eliot Morison, ed., *The Development of Harvard University since the Inauguration of President Eliot, 1869–1929* (Cambridge, Mass., 1930), or Morison, *Three Centuries of Harvard, 1636–1936* (Cambridge, Mass., 1937). Paul H. Buck is at work on a history of the Eliot administration.

An adequate general history of higher education in America remains to be written. Ernest Earnest's *Academic Procession: An Informal History of the American College, 1636–1953* (Indianapolis and New York, 1953) is

343

anecdotal and frequently unreliable. John S. Brubacher and Willis Rudy's *Higher Education in Transition: An American History, 1636–1956* (New York, 1958) is a more sober attempt. George P. Schmidt, *The Liberal Arts College: A Chapter in American Cultural History* (New Brunswick, N.J., 1957), uses much of the recent monographic material, but makes no satisfactory synthesis. Richard Hofstadter and Walter P. Metzger's *The Development of Academic Freedom in the United States* (New York, 1955) treats its subject broadly and skillfully and is our closest approach so far to a history of American higher education.

Index

Index

Admissions policies (*cont.*)
10-11; in Gilman draft plan, 36-37;
at JHU, Harvard, Yale, 241-42;
women and, 259-67; at JHU medical
school, 267; Negroes and, 267-68
Advisers, 248-49
Agassiz, Alexander, 49
Agassiz, Louis, 38, 40, 49, 144
Albany, N.Y., 38
Allegheny College, 242
Allegheny Observatory, 107
Allen, W. F., 107, 250, 269
Alumni: lack of, and finances, 130; aid
athletics, 253; association formed,
280-81; inspire students, 284; careers
of, 291-92; offer aid, 320
American Academy of Arts and Sciences,
47
American Association of University Pro-
fessors, 128-29
American Chemical Journal, 75-76, 107
American Chemist, 75
American Economic Association, 181,
296
American Journal of Archaeology, 109
American Journal of Mathematics, 86;
origins, 74-75; JHU assumes owner-
ship, 107n; Newcomb edits, 137
American Journal of Philology, 108
American Journal of Psychology, 109-10
American Journal of Science, 73, 112;
rejects Rowland's article, 29-30; re-
fuses chemical reports, 75
American Oriental Society, 88
American School of Classical Studies,
151, 152
American Social Science Association,
55, 131
Ames, J. S., 139, 208n, 255
Amherst College, 48, 82, 142, 176, 204;
Gilman visits, 31; and JHU students
compared, 255
Andover Theological Seminary, 189
Andrews, C. M., 101, 219, 274
Angell, J. B., 98; advises trustees, 9-14;
recommends Gilman, 15; JHU honors,
323
Annual Report, 36, 51, 76, 110
Anti-intellectualism: Gilman attempts

to forestall, 67; *see also* Baltimore,
Grangers, Nonsectarianism, Prac-
ticalism, Provincialism, *and* Religion
Antioch College, 193, 221
Antivivisection, *see* Vivisection
Appleton, Charles, 36
Archaeology: society, 115; heyday of,
at JHU, 152; as science, 295; Ar-
chaeological Institute of America,
321
Architecture, 68; *see also* Buildings
Arnold, Matthew, 53, 164
Arnold, Thomas, 53
Arnolt, William Muss, 155
Art, *see* Drawing
Art Circle, 279
Assistant, 127
Assistant professor, 126-27
Associate, 126-27, 129
Associate professor, 127, 128
Associations, scholarly, 113-18
Assyriology, 159
Astronomy, 132-33, 137
Athletic Association, 253
Atlantic, 282
Ayres, P. W., 114

B. & O., *see* Baltimore and Ohio Railroad Company
B. Phil., 27
B.S., 247
Bache, Alexander, 38
Bacteriology, 148
Baird, S. F., 29
Baker, N. D., 70
Baldwin, J. M., 189n
Baltimore, 36, 67; Brown mayor of, 6;
impact of Civil War on, 22; Gilman
seeks support in, 25; special courses
for residents of, 28; inexpensiveness
of, 42; Gilman praises, 45; healthfulness investigated, 50; interest in JHU
lectures, 106; libraries of, 119; Welch
warned against, 147; as background
for Howells, 163; Gosse on, 164; Ely's
reform plans for, 178; public schools
visited, 220-21; school official at
seminar, 228; as source of undergraduates, 238; JHU benefits, 239;

346

Index

Browning, Robert, 164
Bruce, A. T., 121, 146n
Brush, G. J., 17, 40, 47, 56, 129
Bryan, J. P. K., 55n
Bryce, James, 33, 106n, 283
Bryn Mawr College, 261, 278; group system at, 244n; close ties with JHU, 265-66
Building(s): trustees advised on, 10; reserve fund for, 26; examples abroad, 33, 36; Gilman plays down, 67; discomforts of, 92-93; cost of, 130; savings for, 134; for physics, 137; for YMCA, 279
Burgess, J. W., 270, 286
Burnham, W. H., 204
Burton, R. E., 280
Business: Remsen objects to aid from, 140; Newcomb lectures on, 185; failure of course for, 244-45
Butler, N. M., 103, 323

California, University of, 36, 82, 166; and Gilman, 17, 18, 19; group system at, 244; academic freedom and, 310-11; shares JHU ideals, 324
Cambridge University, 107, 154, 164, 205, 262; Gilman's 1875 visit to, 32; JHU imitates *Reporter* of, 110; trustees visit, 171, 189
Campanini, Italo, 275
Canada: Osler's training in, 148; students from, 270
Candidates for matriculation, 243-44
Cayley, Arthur, 34, 107, 133, 136
Century, 280, 282
Ceremonies, at JHU, 97-98
Certificate of Proficiency in Applied Electricity, 140
Channing, Edward, 117
Chapel: for undergraduates, 69, 252; nonreligious, 253
Charity Organization Society of Baltimore, 307n
Chemistry: original staff, 47-48; public lectures on, 73; development of, at JHU, 140-42; student lectures in, 221; laboratory method and, 223-24; no seminar in, 224

Chesapeake Zoological Laboratory, 98, 144, 262
Cheston, Galloway, 4n, 5n, 22, 105, 133
Chicago, University of, 138, 145, 148, 157; Von Holst at, 171; seeks H. B. Adams, 174; coeducational, 266; founded with JHU ideals, 324-25; *see also* Harper, W. R.
Child, F. J.: Goodwin consults, 49; sought by JHU, 53; lectures at JHU, 73, 106; Gilman's ideal, 163
Chinese (language), 56
Christie, F. A., 287
Circulars: described, 110-11; dispute in, 195; faculty bibliographies in, 217; issue on college courses, 239
Civil Service Reform Association, 307n
Civil War, 7, 22, 271
Clark, J. B., 82-83
Clark, W. B., 138, 142, 207
Clark University, 145, 148; Hall's journal and, 110; interests Warren, 156, Bloomfield, 157; psychologists depart for, 203-4; impact on young scholars, 209; founded with JHU ideals, 324-25
Clarke, J. F., 274
Clarke, S. F., 80n, 82, 83, 246n
Class system, 249, 253
Clerk Maxwell, James, *see* Maxwell, James Clerk
Cleveland, Grover, 281
Clifton, 3, 5, 145; buildings planned at, 66; plans to move to, 239, 318; *see also* Howard Street site
Clodd, Edward, 175-76
Clough, Anne Jemima, 32
Coast Survey: employs former fellows, 83; Peirce employed by, 191
Coeducation, 36; at Cornell, 7; trustees advised on, 11; at JHU, 259-68; Mary Garrett urges, 318; medical school and, 322
Cohnheim, Julius, 147
Colby College, 272
College of Physicians and Surgeons, 47
Collegiate education, 36; Gilman hopes JHU can avoid, 23; frustrates German-trained teachers, 60; C. D.

Index

Dobbin, G. W. (*cont.*)
dent of trustees, 105; dropped from
B. & O. board, 319
Donaldson, H. H., 129, 145, 203-4
Donovan, Caroline, 321
Drawing: faculty expansion and, 132;
required, 247
Dresden, 32
Dropsie College, 160
Duncan, Louis, 139-40
Durant, H. F., 262

Ecole Libre des Sciences Politiques,
287, 288
Economics, *see* Political economy
Edinburgh, University of, 188
Education, *see* Pedagogy
Egerton, Mrs. DuBois, 273
Elective system, 7-8, 12-13; *see also*
Curriculum *and* Group system
Electrical engineering, 139-40
Eliot, C. W., 19n, 40, 45, 98; reforms
Harvard, 7-8; advises trustees, 9-14;
recommends Gilman, 15; Gilman
confers with, in 1875, 31; Wolcott
Gibbs and, 45; advises on salary, 47;
Greek and, 50; holds his faculty, 52;
influence on JHU and Gilman, 76-
78; on administrators, 102; on pub-
licizing lectures, 106; dislike of C. S.
Peirce, 195; on A.B., 236; on group
system, 247-48; JHU honors, 323; *see
also* Harvard University
Eliot, W. G., 25
Elliott, A. M., 207; chosen associate, 53;
founds journal, 109; career at JHU,
160-61; leads seminar, 231; guides
Matzke, 285; on science, 296
Elliott, J. P., 104-5
Ely, R. T., 207; on religious press, 72;
career at JHU, 177-86; *Past and
Present of Political Economy*, 179-80;
Labor Movement, 181; on indoctrination, 219; teaching methods, 220-21;
seminar and, 228-29; on sectionalism,
271; House of Commons and, 278; on
Christian Socialism, 279; on limits of
science, 296; on natural law, 299-300;
uses biological terms, 301; on human

efficacy, 301, 303; close to JHU of
1890s, 306; academic freedom and,
311, 314-15
Emergency fund, 319-20
Emeritus status, 136
Emerson, Alfred, 152
Emerson, R. W., 51, 282
Emmott, G. H., 207; career at JHU, 205;
seminar and, 230; L.E.P. course and,
252-53
Endowment: by Turnbulls, 107, 320;
of Bruce fellowship, 121; by Baxley,
146; Gilman pleads for, 238-39; of
woman's college hoped for, 260; for
medical school, 266-67; sought during crisis, 319; by Levering, 320-21;
by C. Donovan, 321; by McCoy, 321
Engineering, 56, 68, 139-40
England, *see* Great Britain
English (department of): first search
for staff, 53; faculty expansion and,
132-34; development of, at JHU, 162-
68; student essays in, 220; seminar
in, 231-32; undergraduate courses in,
246
Enlightenment, 304
Epigraphy, 156
Ethics: faculty expansion and, 132; Ely
stresses, 182; G. S. Morris lectures on,
190; professorship planned in, 201;
trustees interested in, 204; Emmott
appointed in, 205
Europe (academic life of): observed
by Brown, 6; model for Jefferson, 7;
as standard for JHU, 14; Gilman's
experience of, 16; Rowland allowed
year in, 31; Gilman visits, in 1875,
31-37; hospitality to JHU representatives, 33; Gilman gains ideas from,
in 1875, 35-37; Sylvester as representative of, 57; JHU periodicals and,
73-76; summer visits to, 98; pensions
and, 130; standards for teaching profession and, 131; considered source
of teachers, 132-33; as source of
medical scholars, 146-48; Welch
spends year in, 147; as source of
philosopher, 188-89; difficult to win
scholars from, 206; class system and,

Index

Index

Gore, J. W., 83

Gosse, E. W., 164

Göttingen, University of, 47, 48, 50, 81, 158, 162; compared with JHU, 289

Goucher College, 265

Gould, Jay, 182

Government, U.S.: nearness to JHU stressed, 45; Gilman wins co-operation of, 99; Rowland and, 138; effect on salaries, 142; aids Brooks's program, 144; solicited by Haupt, 159

Graduate students: fields of first, 90; Gilman's encouragement of, 100; as teachers, 208; relation to seminars, 232; attend pedagogy lectures, 236; import fraternity system, 254; life of, 269-92; goals of, 290-92; discuss Spencer, 298; *see also* Graduate study

Graduate study: trustees not encouraged to establish, 13-14; Gilman's, 16; expansion urged at Yale, 18; Gilman plans university for, 21-22, 65-66; controversy over Gilman's stress on, 23-25; provided in 1875 plan, 28; as Gildersleeve's field at JHU, 51; JHU example of, affects Harvard, 77; fellowships and, 79-80; clarified at JHU, 90; college work at JHU and, 240-41

Grangers, 19, 23

Great Britain (academic life of): trustees interested in reforms of, 9; women's colleges in, praised by Eliot, 11; fellowships and, 11, 79, 206-7; topics discussed in, 36; faculty policies in, 40; as source of biologist, 48; C. D. Morris brings influence of, 61-62; H. B. Adams seeks link with, 108; journal links JHU with, 110; Bolza's studies in, 138; interest in JHU medical school, 146; Ely attacks political economy of, 178, 180; as source of undergraduate teachers, 204-5; "tutorial grind" in, 219; honors degree in, 244; tutorships in, 248; coeducation and, 260, 265

Greek: first staff, 49-51; C. D. Morris to teach, 52; Page as student in, 84-

85; reader in, 128; development of, at JHU, 151-52; as requirement for A.B., 247; methods at JHU and Leipzig, 289

Greek, New Testament, 152-55

Gregory, C. R., 154-55, 207

Griffin, E. H.: and L.E.P. course, 205; on specialization, 235; chosen dean, 257; appointment of, reveals change, 321

Grinnell College, 82

Group system: at Cornell and Michigan, 13; for JHU undergraduates, 244-48

Guilford College, 5

Guyot, A. H., 302

Gwinn, C. J. M., 5, 131, 215

Gymnasium, 247

Hadley, A. T., 323

Hadley, James, 86

Hale, E. E., 18, 193, 274

Hall, C. C., 131

Hall, E. H., 139, 288-89

Hall, G. S., 207; founds journal, 109-10; impact on Metaphysical Club, 115; Ward on, 189n; seeks JHU post, 193-94; philosophical position, 194; C. S. Peirce and, 195; promoted, 200; on G. S. Morris, 201; on "safety" of psychology, 201-2; teaches philosophy to undergraduates, 204; on indoctrination, 219; "excursions," 220-21; pride in lectures, 221; seminars and, 229-30; criticized, 233; pedagogy lectures and, 236; on faculty club, 236-37; undergraduates and, 252; science and, 295; on revelation, 297; practicalism and, 305; founding of Clark and, 324-25

Hall, L. B., 83

Halsted, G. B., 83

Hamilton, Alexander, 242

Hamilton, William, 247

Hamilton College, 53, 162

Harper, W. R., 141, 324-25

Harper's, 280

Harris, J. R., 116; career at JHU, 152-

Index

Huxley, Thomas (*cont.*)
33; address of 1875 and reaction, 69-70; on premedical study, 144; later effects of address by, 188-89; sees university as factory, 308

Hyslop, J. H., 302

Iles, M. W., 83

Immortality, students discuss, 281

Inaugural, Gilman's, at JHU: inspires Gildersleeve, 51; stresses gradualness, 63; veils research aim, 64-65; shows financial limits, 67; on relations with other institutions, 76; discusses freedom, 91

Independent, 54-55

Indians, papers on, 117-18

Individualism: Ely on, 181; JHU spirit and, 219-20; sociology and, 301

Institute for Advanced Study, 198

Instructor, rank of, 127

Interdepartmentalism: as interference, 234-35; *see also* Community, sense of

International relations of JHU: to be example, 68; Rowland and, 138; British government aids Sanskritists, 231; foreign students, 270

Interuniversity relations: between Harvard and JHU, 76-78; interlibrary loans, 120; student migration recommended, 287

Investigation, *see* Research

Iowa College (Grinnell), 82

Italian, Elliott teaches, 160

Iyenaga, Toyokichi, 279

Jacques, W. W.: describes JHU duties, 81; later career, 83-84; friendship with Page, 84-85; practicalism and, 305

James, Henry, 281-82

James, William: recommends C. S. Peirce, 54; seeks JHU post, 187-88; Hall and, 193-94; psychological laboratory, 202-3

Jameson, J. F.: on college presidents, 98; on Gilman's speeches, 102; on Gilman's *Monroe,* 103; on Mrs. Gilman, 104; on publication, 112, 216;

salary, 129; admires Cook, 166; on H. B. Adams, 174-75, 286; career at JHU, 176-77; on "diplomacy," 216; as teacher, 218; recitations and, 220; on seminar, 228; teaches geography, 246; on undergraduates, 255; influenced by Amherst, 270; sectionalism and, 271-72; lodgings, 273; derides glee club, 277; on Alumni Association, 281; nonacademic reading, 282; on JHU atmosphere, 282; on Wilson, 284; on role of faculty, 285; on student competition, 285; on human efficacy, 303; on research, 310

Japan, students from, 270, 279

Jastrow, Joseph, 203

Jefferson, Joseph, 275

Jefferson, Thomas, *see* Virginia, University of

Jena, University of, 166

Jevons, W. S., 54, 179, 180

Jewish Theological Seminary, 160

Jews: at JHU, 215; and student religious life, 274

Johns Hopkins Hospital, the: less freedom allowed trustees of, 4; planned opening of, affects JHU, 146; Osler's post in, 149; opens, 322; Gilman as director of, 323

Johns Hopkins News-Letter, 280

Johns Hopkins Press, the, 109, 112; *see also* Publication Agency

Johns Hopkins University, the: founded, 3-4; Brown forecasts character of, 6; trustees' ambitions for, 7; first location of, 26; "plan of procedure" for, 26-28; praised in British Parliament, 33; Gilman's draft plan for, 36-37; European ideas for, 37; compared with classical college, 62; absence of rules at, 63; early principles of, 63-68; relations with Harvard, 76-78; makes fellows faculty members, 83; early spirit of, 90-93; as "normal school," 136, 291; Lanier's ode to, 165; H. C. Adams' preference for, 177; Ely's connection with, stressed, 182-83; C. S. Peirce praises, 192; G. S. Hall praises, 193; identified with

Index

Index

Index

Music (*cont.*)
hopes for chair of, 164; students hear, 275
Muss Arnolt, William, *see* Arnolt, W. M.
Mythology, Lanier provides, 165-66

Nation, 282; publicizes plan for JHU, 22; opposes Ely, 179-84; publicizes House of Commons, 277-78
National Academy of Sciences, 113
National character, displayed at JHU, 304
National stature, ideal of, for JHU: not predicted by early advisers, 13; Johnson warns on, 23; compromise on, 27-28; importance of fellowships for, 81-82; Sylvester on, 136; H. B. Adams and, 271
National surveys, *see* Surveys, national, *and specific surveys*
Nationalism, Lanman's, 87
Natural law, as idea at JHU, 299-300
Naturalists' Field Club, 114-15
Nautical Almanac, 136
Naval Observatory, 136
Negroes: admissions policy regarding, 267-68; speech on, 279
New Book Department, 282
"New education": Eliot advocate of, 7-8, 12; *see also* Curriculum
New Testament Greek, 152-55
New York *Evening Post,* 179
New York *Observer,* 70-71, 188
New York University (University of the City of New York), 52, 54, 83
Newcomb, Simon, 74, 207; considered for JHU post, 42; as nonresident lecturer, 73; aids Craig, 86; career at JHU, 136-37; seminar, 138; solicited by Haupt, 159; interest in economics, 179; criticisms of Ely, 179-86; *Principles of Political Economy,* 181-82; on faculty controversy, 233; teaches only graduates, 256; aids Miller, 268; on science, 295
Newell, Hugh, 247
Newman, J. H., 79, 308
Newspaper, student, 280
Newspapers, *see* Press

Newtonianism, *see* Natural law
Nicolassen, G. F., 152
Nineteenth Century, 190
Nonresident lecturers, *see* Lecturer, nonresident
Nonsectarianism: at Cornell, 7; trustees assured on, 10; at California, 17, 19; declared policy at JHU, 21; desired by trustees, 22, 27; press favors for JHU, 25; lack of, in England deplored, 36; and philosophy staff, 54; Gilman and, 68, 72; not irreligion at JHU, 251; at other universities, 324
North Carolina, University of, 83
Norton, C. E., 77
Norwich Free Academy, 86
Notes from the Chemical Laboratory, 75-76
Notes Supplementary to the Studies, 109
Nott, Eliphalet, 252
Nunn, E. A., 262

Observatory, at JHU, 137
Old-time college president, 54
Optimism, at JHU, 303-4
Organizations, student: at JHU, 253-54; among graduates, 275-80
Osler, William, 148-49
Owens College, Manchester, 205; example for JHU, 32, 54
Oxford University, 52, 107; Gilman's 1875 visit to, 32; Sylvester moves to, 136
Oyster industry, Brooks aids, 144

P.H.E., course at JHU, 246
Page, W. H., 84-85, 93, 254
Paleography, 153, 156
Paleontology, 142
Palmer, G. H., 203
Paret, William, 175
Pasteur, Louis, 154n
Pathology: and faculty expansion, 134; development of, at JHU, 146-49; no seminar in, 224
Pattison, Mark, 36n, 79
Patton, F. L., 323

Index

Index

Rowland, H. A. (*cont.*)
views, 29-30; early significance, 29-31, 59; hired at JHU, 30; accompanies Gilman to Europe, 31; praised in Dublin, 32; achievements of, 1875–1876, 45-47; exemplifies JHU aims, 65; maps solar spectrum, 111; on publication, 113; on Maxwell, 114; receives honorary Ph.D., 124; personality of, 138; Peirce's view of, 139; marriage, 216; as teacher, 218; as lecturer, 222; laboratory method and, 224; faculty disagreements and, 234-35; as specialist, 235; teaches only graduates, 256; on truth, 293-94; on ancient languages, 299; on imagination, 299; on moral law, 299; human efficacy and, 303; national character and, 304; sees scientists governing world, 306; on pure science, 310

Royal Military Academy, Woolwich, 34

Royce, Josiah, 81; travels with Gilman, 35; as fellow, 83, 89; studies Sanskrit, 88; on early spirit, 92; on Spinoza, 116; first Ph.D., 122; course on Schopenhauer, 187; Gilman on, 190; heads alumni, 281; defends German scholarship, 289; on "ideal realm," 294; attacks Spencer, 301; on community, 308

Rutgers University, 6, 171

S.D., at Harvard, 8, 122

Sabbaticals, 129, 156

Saccharin, discovered at JHU, 141

St. Andrews, University of, 32

St. John's College (Annapolis), 6; as preparation for JHU, 242-43

Salary, 46, 48, 52-53, 56, 90, 137, 139, 142, 156-57, 163, 170-71, 190, 246n; increases at Harvard, 8; of JHU president, 21; early plans regarding, 27; Rowland's, 30; Henry cites importance of, 40; Sylvester's requests on, 42-43; Remsen protests, 47-48; JHU affects, elsewhere, 77; general policies, 129-30; Gilman stresses, 131; no increases in 1884, 134n; dispute over Martin's, 143; compared with student fee system, 147; Haupt's complaints on, 158; Bright's request on, 168; H. B. Adams' requests on, 173; Ely's, increased, 178; requested by James, 188; Peirce obtains increase in, 191-92

Salvation Army, 281

Sanford, E. C., 204

Sanskrit, 160; postponed, 56; Lanman's first classes in, 88; faculty expansion and, 133; development of, at JHU, 156-57; seminar in, 231; methods in, at JHU and Leipzig, 289

Savage, A. D., 83, 120

Scaife, W. B., 112, 271, 287

Schaff, Philip, 53

Schimper, A. F. W., 146n

Scholarship, *see* Research

Scholarships: in founder's will, 3; trustees advised on, 11; at California, 19; provision for, 28, 121-22; for undergraduates, 242

Science: conflict with religion, 68-69; economics as, 180-82, 184n; psychology as, 187; Peirce on, 196; philosophy as, 199; role of, at JHU, 294-308; definitions of, 295; Rowland sees, as pioneer, 310; *see also* Laboratory *entries and* Sciences, natural

Science, Ely-Newcomb debate in, 182

Sciences, natural: university neglect of, 36; buildings for, 134; development of, at JHU, 138-49; Gilman disavows stress on, 150; demonstration method and, 220

Scientific Association: founded, 114-16; Newcomb uses, 180

Scientific Lazzaroni, 38

Scientific schools, *see specific institutions*

Scotland, Gilman's 1875 visit to, 32-33

Scott, Austin: chosen associate, 56; hopes for periodical, 108n; career at JHU, 171-72; as teacher, 220; leads seminar, 227

Sectionalism: JHU said to be free from, 21; trustees want to avoid, 22, 27; press warns JHU against, 25; Gildersleeve's choice of fellows and, 84; shown by Page, 84; undergraduates and, 241; student origins and, 270-72

Sedgwick, W. T., 145

Index

Index